THE GERMAN BOURGEOISIE

THE GERMAN BOURGEOISIE

Essays on the social history of the
German middle class from the late
eighteenth to the early twentieth century

Edited by
David Blackbourn and
Richard J. Evans

London and New York

First published in hardback 1991
First published in paperback 1993
by Routledge
11 New Fetter Lane, London EC4P 4EE

Simultaneously published in the USA and Canada
by Routledge
29 West 35th Street, New York, NY 10001

This collection © 1991, 1993 Routledge;
individual chapters © 1991, 1993 contributors
Phototypeset in 10/12pt Palatino by Intype, London
Printed in Great Britain by
T J Press (Padstow) Ltd, Padstow, Cornwall

British Library Cataloguing in Publication Data
The German bourgeoisie : essays on the social history of the
German middle class from the late eighteenth to the early
twentieth century.
1. Germany. Social structure, history
I. Blackbourn, David   II. Evans, Richard J.
305.0943

Library of Congress Cataloging in Publication Data
The German bourgeoisie : essays on the social history of the German
middle class from the late eighteenth to the early twentieth century
/ edited by David Blackbourn and Richard J. Evans.
p. cm.
1. Middle classes—Germany—History—19th century. 2. Middle
classes—Germany—History—20th century. I. Blackbourn, David.
II. Evans, Richard J.
HT690.G3G45   1991
305.5′5′0943–dc20   90–35016

ISBN 0–415–09358–9

To the students of Birkbeck College

Contents

CONTENTS

Tables

Contributors

Celia Applegate was born in New York State in 1959 and studied at Bryn Mawr College, Pennsylvania, graduating in 1981, and Stanford University, California, where she received her Ph.D. in 1987. She has taught at Smith College, Massachusetts, and is currently Assistant Professor of History at the University of Rochester, in New York State. Her study of German localism, *A Nation of Provincials: The German Idea of Heimat*, will shortly be published by the University of California Press. She is now pursuing the theme of German identity through an examination of the role of music in German national life.

Dolores L. Augustine was born in 1955 in Washington, DC and studied at Georgetown University, graduating with a BSc. in Foreign Service, before going on to take an MA and DPhil. in History at the Free University of Berlin. From 1989 to 1990 she taught European history at Sweet Briar College, Virginia and she is now Assistant Professor of History at St John's University, New York. Her publications include 'Very Wealthy Businessmen in Imperial Germany', *Journal of Social History*, 22 (1988) 299–32, 'The Banker in German Society' in Youssef Cassis (ed.), *Finance and Financiers in European History, 1880–1960* (London: Cambridge University Press, 1991), 161–85; and 'The Business Elites of Hamburg and Berlin', *Central European History*, 24 (1991), 132–46. Her book, *Wealth, Big Business and High Society in pre-1914 Germany*, a revised version of her dissertation, will appear in 1993 with Berg Publishers.

David Blackbourn was born in Spilsby, Lincolnshire, in 1949 and studied History at the University of Cambridge. He was a

Research Fellow of Jesus College, Cambridge, from 1973 to 1976, and taught at the University of London from 1976 to 1992, first at Queen Mary College, then at Birkbeck College. He has been a Research Fellow of the Alexander von Humboldt Foundation and the Institute for European History in Mainz, and in 1989–90 was Visiting Kratter Professor at Stanford University, California. His publications include *Class, Religion and Local Politics in Wilhelmine Germany* (1980), *The Peculiarities of German History: Bourgeois Society and Politics in Nineteenth-Century Germany* (with Geoff Eley, 1984), *Populists and Patricians* (1987) and *Marpingen: Apparitions of the Virgin Mary in Bismarckian Germany* (1993).

Thomas Childers was born outside Chattanooga, Tennessee, in 1946. He was educated at the Universities of Tennessee and Harvard, receiving his doctorate in history in 1976. He is the author of *The Nazi Voter: The Social Foundations of Fascism in Germany 1919–1933*, Chapel Hill and London, 1983, and editor of two additional collections on National Socialism: *The Formation of the Nazi Constituency 1919–1933*, London, 1986, and, with Jane Caplan, *Revaluating the Third Reich*, New York, 1990. He is Professor of History at the University of Pennsylvania in Philadelphia.

Geoff Eley was born in Burton-on-Trent, Staffordshire, in 1949, and studied Modern History at the Universities of Oxford and Sussex. He has been a Research Fellow at the University of Swansea and Lecturer in History at the University of Keele, and from 1975 to 1980 was Fellow of Emmanuel College, Cambridge. Since 1980 he has taught at the University of Michigan, Ann Arbor, where he is currently Professor of History. His publications include *Reshaping the German Right: Radical Nationalism and Political Change after Bismarck* (1980), *The Peculiarities of German History: Bourgeois Society and Politics in Nineteenth-Century Germany* (with David Blackbourn, 1984), and *From Unification to Nazism* (1985). He is currently completing a study of nationalism in the modern world.

Richard J. Evans was born in Woodford, Essex, in 1947 and studied Modern History at the University of Oxford. From 1972 to 1976 he taught at the University of Stirling, subsequently moving to the University of East Anglia, Norwich, where he was Professor of European History from 1983 to 1989. He has been a Research Fellow of the Alexander von Humboldt Foundation at the Free University of Berlin, and in 1980 was Visiting Associate Professor of European History at Columbia University, New York. He is currently Professor of History at Birkbeck College, University of London. His book *Death in Hamburg: Society and Politics in the Cholera Years 1830–1910* (1987) won the Wolfson Literary Award for History 1988 and the William H. Welch Medal of the American Association for the History of Medicine 1989. His most recent book, *Proletarians and Politics*, appeared in 1990. He is now completing a history of capital punishment in Germany since 1750.

Ute Frevert was born in West Germany in 1954 and studied History and Social Science at the Universities of Münster and Bielefeld and at the London School of Economics. Her publications include *Women in German History: from Bourgeois Emancipation to Sexual Liberation* (1989) and *Krankheit als politisches Problem* (1984), a study of the politics of health and medicine in nineteenth-century Prussia. She has also edited a collection of essays on gender and the German bourgeoisie, *Bürgerinnen und Bürger*, which appeared in 1988. She taught at the University of Bielefeld from 1983 to 1988, was a Fellow of the Institute for Advanced Study (*Wissenschaftskolleg*) in Berlin in 1989–90 and then Professor of History at the Free University of Berlin. Her history of duelling in modern Germany was published in 1991. Since 1992 she has been Professor of History at the University of Konstanz.

Dick Geary was born in Leicester in 1945 and studied History at the University of Cambridge, where he was a Research Fellow at Emmanuel College. From 1973 to 1989 he taught at the University of Lancaster, and from 1984 to 1986 was Research Fellow of the Alexander von Humboldt Foundation at the Ruhr University, Bochum. He is currently Professor of Modern History at the University of Nottingham. His publications include *European Labour Protest 1848–1939* (1981) and *Karl Kautsky* (1987), and he is the editor of *The German Unemployed* (1987, with Richard J. Evans), *Labour and Socialist Movements in Europe before 1914* (1989) and *European Labour Politics from 1900 to the Depression* (1991). He is currently engaged in research on unemployment in Germany between the wars.

Michael John was born in Altrincham, Cheshire, in 1957, and studied Modern History at the University of Oxford. In 1982–3 he was Research Fellow of Nuffield College, Oxford, and from 1983 to 1985 Fellow of Jesus College, Cambridge. He is currently Fellow and Tutor in Modern History at Magdalen College, Oxford. His publications include *Politics and the Law in Late Nineteenth-Century Germany: The Origins of the Civil Code* (1989), and articles on nineteenth-century German liberalism, nationalism, and law. He is at present completing a history of liberalism in the province of Hanover between 1866 and 1914, and preparing a study of the German legal profession in the nineteenth century.

Karin Kaudelka-Hanisch was born in Isingdorf (Arrode) in 1956 and studied History and German at the University of Bielefeld, graduating in 1981. In 1982–3 she completed a teacher training course in Gelsenkirchen. Since then she has been preparing a dissertation on the social history of Prussian 'Commercial Councillors' (*Kommerzienräte*) at Bielefeld University. In 1988 she took up a post as social historian with the permanent exhibition on labour protection (*Deutsche Arbeitsschutzausstellung*) in Dortmund.

Paul Weindling was born in London in 1953 and studied Modern History at the University of Oxford. After taking an MSc. in the History of Science at University College London, he went on to complete a doctorate on Darwinism in Imperial Germany. Since 1978 he has been on the staff of the Wellcome Unit for the History of Medicine at the University of Oxford, where he is currently Senior Research Officer. He has edited *The Social History of Occupational Health* (London, 1985) and is the author of *Health, Race and German Politics between National Unification and Nazism* (Cambridge, 1989) and *Darwinism and Social Darwinism in Imperial Germany* (Stuttgart, 1991). He is currently researching on the international politics of infectious diseases, health and welfare between the First and Second World Wars.

Preface

This book brings together eleven essays on the German bourgeoisie, a subject that until recently has been little studied by social historians. Part of the reason for this neglect lies in the fact that research, for a variety of reasons, has tended to concentrate on numerically much larger social groups at the lower end of German society, such as the peasantry or the working class. Problems of definition may also have been a deterrent. 'Bourgeoisie', after all, is a French word, the precise equivalent neither of the English 'middle classes' nor of the German *Bürgertum*. But too much heavy weather has been made of the problem of definition in the literature. It was Marx who did most to popularize the term 'bourgeoisie' by taking it from the French to use for a social class which he believed was present, actually or potentially, in every European country. One does not have to accept everything that he wrote about the subject to conclude that it is both useful and legitimate to regard such groups as bankers, merchants, industrialists, higher civil servants, doctors, lawyers, professors, and other professionals as constituting a social stratum bound by common values, a shared culture and a degree of prosperity founded directly or indirectly on property and earned income, which marked it off both from the titled aristocracy above and the humble and impecunious lower middle class (or petty bourgeoisie) and proletariat below. Questions of definition remain, of course, and many of them are taken up in the following essays. But it should be clear enough that we are dealing here with the group whose alleged collective sins of omission over the course of modern German history, from 1848 to 1933, have been an additional reason why historians have treated them for so long as an absence rather than a presence on the historical stage.

PREFACE

The centrality of the German bourgeoisie to the debate over the German *Sonderweg* – Germany's supposed 'special path' to modernity by way of industrializing without destroying the social and political hegemony of the aristocracy, of modernizing economically while remaining entrapped in a pre-industrial nexus of authoritarian social structures, values, and political attitudes – has led in the second half of the 1980s to a revival of interest in the history of this social stratum, and research has been gathering pace rapidly. Much of this has been inspired by a large-scale project funded by the *Deutsche Forschungsgemeinschaft* at the University of Bielefeld under the leadership of Jürgen Kocka, and no publication in this area can begin without paying tribute to the way in which he and his colleagues have transformed our knowledge of many aspects of the history of the German bourgeoisie. There is no doubt either that the project has helped raise the *Sonderweg* debate to a new level of subtlety and sophistication. The present volume is in the fortunate position of being able to benefit from this advance in the discussion. It also seeks to make its own contribution. It includes essays by David Blackbourn and Geoff Eley, whose book *The Peculiarities of German History*, originally published in German in 1980, may be said to have reopened the debate. In chapter 1, David Blackbourn sets the scene by providing an account of the development of the German bourgeoisie from the eighteenth century to the twentieth, which is also at the same time a survey of the research that has been carried out in this field. Both Blackbourn and Eley (in chapter 10) address the question of bourgeois politics and the nature of German liberalism, and ask whether the conventional equation of liberal politics with the bourgeoisie is really helpful. As Eley argues, there has been too great a tendency in the literature to treat an idealized version of British liberalism as the norm from which the German deviated, while a broader European comparison would seem to indicate that it was in fact the British case that was exceptional.

The book then goes on to look in rather more detail at some of the major groupings within the German bourgeoisie: in particular, the moneyed or propertied bourgeoisie (the *Wirtschafts-* or *Besitzbürgertum*) (chapters 2, 3, 4, and 5) and the educated or professional bourgeoisie (the *Bildungsbürgertum*) (chapters 6 and 7), before considering some of the values which cut across these internal divisions yet remained at the same time distinctively bourgeois: localism (chapter 8) and honour (chapter 9). But besides presenting the results of current research in these areas, the contributions also address a number of the central issues in the debate. Many of them deal at varying length with the assumption, still widespread in the literature, that the German bourgeoisie was 'feudalized', seduced away from its historical commitment to liberalism and democracy by the lure of titles and honours (chapters 2, 3, 4, 5, and 9). Others address the related question of bourgeois values and suggest that rather than constituting a mere imitation of aristocratic behaviour patterns, attitudes such as hostility to trade unions on the part of employers, or sensitivity to insults to one's honour, or a habit of building grand houses in the country or the suburbs, had their own peculiarly bourgeois rationale (chapters 2, 5, and 9). Like all social classes, the bourgeoisie was structured among other things by gender, and while it has not been possible in the current state of research to include a contribution on bourgeois women as such, chapters 2, 3, and 4 deal with the role of marriage and the family, while chapter 9 examines the place of notions of masculinity in the formation of bourgeois attitudes and behaviour patterns. Chapters 6, 7 and 10 raise the vital question of how far the German bourgeoisie was comparable with its counterparts elsewhere, particularly in view of the prominent role which the state took – in contrast to the situation in Britain, for example – in the training and thus the control of major bourgeois professions such as medicine and the law. Finally, chapter 11 rounds off the book by surveying recent research on the extent to which the German bourgeoisie can be held responsible for the electoral success of the Nazi Party at the end of the Weimar Republic.

The contributions thus seek not only to provide an introduction to recent and current British, German, and American research on the German bourgeoisie, but also to illustrate by example how the subject can be approached from a variety of different angles using a range of different methods and sources. Chapters 2 and 3 demonstrate the importance of prosopography – of a quantitative collective biography – in an area where, in contrast to the situation facing those who write the history of the lower classes, a good deal is known about a large number of individuals. Chapter 4 explores some of the uses of another kind of source virtually unique to the upper and upper middle classes, the family genealogy. Chapters 5, 6, and 7 turn to the world of work, where the material gathered in the archives of business enterprises, law firms, and medical practices can usefully be brought together with the documentation left by the regulating activities of the state. Chapter 8 examines the history of voluntary associations, with their wealth of public and private documentation, not so much in search of their political impact, as in an attempt to explore the hidden assumptions and values which informed them. Chapter 9, which brings together judicial records with the public debate about duelling and the personal accounts of participants, also suggests how taking these sources together can reveal the value-system which underpinned the continued recourse to the 'field of honour' by middle-class German men well into the twentieth century. Finally, chapter 11 surveys recent work on electoral statistics, much of which has been based on sophisticated methods of quantitative analysis.

The origins of this volume go back, with varying degrees of directness, to the sixth, eighth, and tenth meetings of the Research Seminar Group on German Social History, held at the University of East Anglia, Norwich, in 1982, 1985, and 1986 respectively on the subjects of the bourgeoisie, medicine, and elites. Although the great majority of chapters in the book were specially written, and do not have their origin in papers presented to these conferences, most of the authors took part in one or more of these meetings and, in a more general sense, the overall direction and thrust of the book have been strongly influenced by the discussions that took place. This is the seventh publication to appear in the series based on the Seminar Group's meetings, and, like its predecessors – *The German Family* (ed. Richard J. Evans and W. R. Lee, 1981), *The German Working Class* (ed. Richard J. Evans, 1982), 'Religion and society in Germany' (*European Studies Review*, 13:3, 1982, special issue), *The German Peasantry* (ed. Richard J. Evans and W. R. Lee, 1986), *The German Unemployed* (ed. Richard J. Evans and Dick Geary, 1987) and *The German Underworld* (ed. Richard J. Evans, 1988) – it seeks to present new research, mainly by young British, German, and American historians, to bring recent work in an important area of German social history to the attention of English-speaking students, and to contribute to the continuing debate on the topic with which it deals. All the essays appear here in English for the first time: a shortened version of chapter 10 has been published previously in German, and a German version of chapter 9 has also appeared recently.

Altogether the Research Seminar Group met ten times over a

period of eight years. Its last meeting took place in 1986, and this is therefore the final publication to which it has given rise. Thanks are due to the University of East Anglia for providing support facilities and for financing the last five meetings in the series, and to all the participants for providing the stimulus for keeping it going so long, and for helping by their contributions to the discussion to shape many of the ideas which have gone into the making of this book. We are also grateful to the Alexander von Humboldt Foundation for its continuing support over the years, and in particular for providing the time in which much of the preparation for this book could be undertaken. Marie Mactavish has earned our thanks by typing some of the contributions. Finally, we owe a wider debt of gratitude to the students of Birkbeck College, University of London, which now provides both of us with a congenial and stimulating academic home.

David Blackbourn
Richard J. Evans
London and Stanford
November 1989

Abbreviations

AEG	Allgemeine Elektrizitäts-Gesellschaft
AG	Aktiengesellschaft
BASF	Badische Anilin- und Sodafabrik
DDP	Deutsche Demokratische Partei
DNVP	Deutschnationale Volkspartei
DVP	Deutsche Volkspartei
GDR	German Democratic Republic
GHH	Gutehoffnungshütte
GStA	Geheimes Staatsarchiv
HAPAG	Hamburg-Amerika Paketfahrt-Aktiengesellschaft
HStA	Hauptstaatsarchiv
KPD	Kommunistische Partei Deutschlands
LHA	Landeshauptarchiv
NSDAP	Nationalsozialistische Deutsche Arbeiterpartei
SA	Sturmabteilung
SBRT	Stenographische Berichte über die Verhandlungen des Deutschen Reichstags
SPD	Sozialdemokratische Partei Deutschlands
StA	Staatsarchiv
ZStA	Zentrales Staatsarchiv

1

The German bourgeoisie: an introduction

David Blackbourn

I

The German bourgeoisie has not been very well treated by historians. This has been partly a question of simple neglect. The *Bürgertum* has been eclipsed by groups such as the landowning Junkers and their allies when it comes to studies of the German ruling class or 'power elite'. At the same time, social historians have usually been more inclined to devote attention to the peasantry and working class than to members of the business and professional middle classes. A primary focus on the lives and experiences of the lower classes has also been characteristic of the mounting volume of work in recent years on the 'history of everyday life' (*Alltagsgeschichte*). Where attention has been paid to the bourgeoisie and its role in modern German history, there has often been slighting treatment in a second sense. It is the failures and sins of omission of the bourgeoisie that have so often attracted attention. It has been variously depicted as a supine class, genuflecting to the authoritarian state, aping the social values and manners of the aristocracy, lacking in civic spirit and political engagement. Much of the celebrated *Sonderweg* thesis, concerning the alleged long-term misdevelopment of German society and politics and its contribution to the eventual success of National Socialism, has rested heavily on a series of propositions about bourgeois weakness, timidity, and abdication of political responsibility.[1]

In the last decade there have been many signs that a richer and more differentiated picture of the German bourgeoisie is starting to emerge. There has been an increasing number of detailed investigations of particular occupational groups, whether businessmen, professionals, or academics.[2] There have also been studies that

1

cast new light on the material position, the social networks, and the political activities of local bourgeois elites.[3] New work in fields such as the family and the history of illness and medicine has similarly helped to give us a greater appreciation of bourgeois Germany.[4] Works dealing with nineteenth-century Germany now refer to a 'bourgeois world' or a 'bourgeois epoch' with a naturalness that would have been unthinkable twenty years ago.[5] There has been, finally, a new interest in sustained comparative investigation of the German bourgeoisie with its counterparts in a variety of other countries.[6] This welcome development promises more fruitful results than the tendency, widespread for so long, to judge the German bourgeoisie against an idealized Anglo-Saxon yardstick – and find it wanting. The present introduction looks at some of these valuable new departures, as well as the more important established literature on the subject. It attempts to place the chapters that follow in a larger context, by providing a general account of the development of the German bourgeoisie from the end of the eighteenth century to the 1930s. It examines the changing size and boundaries of the bourgeoisie, and its economic and social importance. There is discussion of internal divisions, but also of the forces and values that united the bourgeoisie, not least in relation to other classes. Consideration is given, finally, to the controversial issue of bourgeois politics, the varied forms it assumed, and the alleged shortcomings it displayed.

II

At the end of the eighteenth century two principal bourgeois groupings were identified by contemporaries. The first were the *Stadtbürger*, members of the urban middle class who enjoyed citizenship rights and associated privileges, and who corresponded broadly to the sense conveyed by the antiquated English expression 'burghers'.[7] This was a group that included merchants and businessmen, but also independent master craftsmen. The second group was what the historian Friedrich Meinecke in a classic account dubbed the *Weltbürgertum*, or cosmopolitan bourgeoisie.[8] Defined above all by education, it was these officials and academics who provided a large part of the membership of the burgeoning (although still socially restrictive) reading clubs and lodges in the late eighteenth and early nineteenth century. It was in this milieu that the Enlightenment had its principal supporters in the last

years of the Holy Roman Empire, among this group of the educated also that the idea of the German nation took shape as a
cultural aspiration at a time when 'Germany' remained politically
fragmented and divided economically into countless local and
regional markets.[9] Members of the first middle-class group
remained largely limited in their geographical and social horizons,
and it was burghers of this sort who acquired the label *Spiesser*, or
philistines, from aristocratic or more cosmopolitan contemporaries.[10] The exception was perhaps to be found in important commercial cities like Cologne and Hamburg, where wealthy and self-
confident merchants with national and even international connections set the tone. It was also in cities of this sort that businessmen
– especially merchants – mingled with academics and officials in
the new associations of the period.[11] Mostly, however, membership
of the latter was dominated by those whose occupations were
defined by education or state service, rather than relationship to
production or the market.

These early patterns left their traces on the subsequent development of the German bourgeoisie. We see this in the persistent
localist orientation of the middle classes, discussed in Celia Applegate's contribution to this collection, and in the divisions that
continued to exist between the 'makers' and the 'thinkers'. It is
sometimes also claimed – although this is more hazardous territory
– that portents of a future German bourgeois weakness were apparent in these years, namely its fateful other-worldliness.[12] The
German bourgeoisie at the end of the eighteenth century was, we
are told, overshadowed by its English counterpart when it came
to manufacturing and business, while at the same time it made
far fewer political demands than its French equivalent. The result,
in the seductive words of one historian, is that England had an
industrial revolution, France a political revolution – and Germany
a reading revolution.[13] There is a good deal here with which one
might quarrel, not least the assumptions that are made about the
pattern of historical development in contemporary England and
France. It is also perfectly possible to see the 'reading revolution'
in Germany as a factor of enormous importance with positive
implications for the future role of the bourgeoisie. It was, after all,
a symbol of the way in which one particular part of the bourgeoisie
was growing in size and self-consciousness through the incipient
process of state-building. Education and cultivation were also to
form a central part of bourgeois claims to social leadership.

It is nevertheless undeniable that the bourgeois presence in the patchwork of German states that existed at the turn of the eighteenth and nineteenth centuries was less than imposing. Weak and fragmented, like 'Germany' itself, the various bourgeois groupings were frequently tied to the small German courts either as suppliers or as employees, the so-called 'servants of princes' (*Fürstendiener*); and they were overshadowed by an aristocracy that enjoyed legal privileges in the corporate or estates-based society (*ständische Gesellschaft*), and viewed the modest middle classes with disdain. Yet the signs of change were already there. The impact of the French occupation of Germany not only brought about the dissolution of the Holy Roman Empire in 1803 and ended the chronic fragmentation of the German states-system.[14] It was also accompanied by a wave of administrative reforms which found their counterpart in the indigenous reform movement associated with figures such as Heinrich Friedrich Karl vom Stein, Karl August von Hardenberg, and Wilhelm Karl von Humboldt in Prussia. The abolition or weakening of the corporate powers wielded by the church, aristocracy, and guilds belonged to a powerful movement of institutional change and modern state-building which had major importance for the place of the bourgeoisie in German society.[15]

One of the most important developments here was legal equality, which removed many – although not all – bourgeois handicaps. The law was to remain central to bourgeois aspirations throughout the nineteenth century, whether in the form of the defence of formal equality, the importance attached to legal property rights, or calls for the legal accountability of state bureaucracies. At the same time, legal studies formed a central part of the training of bureaucrats to man the growing machinery of state.[16] This process of state-building provided a general boost to members of the educated bourgeoisie, who went in growing numbers to reformed classical grammar schools (*Gymnasien*) and the new universities that were founded in Prussia and elsewhere at the beginning of the nineteenth century.[17] This group became a crucial element in the emergence of powerful state bureaucracies recruited on merit rather than birth. For the rest of the nineteenth century, and into the twentieth, a vital element in the growth of the bourgeoisie was the growth in the numbers (and the prestige) of state officials: local, regional, and provincial administrators, judges and other

4

legal officials, professors and school teachers, forestry officials, doctors in state employment.[18]

These groups partly moved into the gap left by the decline of the corporate state, in a development that had its counterpart elsewhere in Europe. Officials also increased in numbers as the state increased its areas of competence, and the growth of the interventionist, regulatory, and social state at end of the nineteenth century produced a further leap in numbers.[19] It has sometimes been argued that this stratum was exceptionally large, even hypertrophied in Germany, and this in turn has been seen as a sign of the way in which the dynamism in German society was injected 'from above', by the state and its officials, rather than by a 'proper' bourgeoisie.[20] Several points are worth making here. First, the personnel of the growing German bureaucracies were – outside aristocratic bastions such as the Prussian field administration – largely bourgeois by social origin, and they certainly worked in ways that strengthened the underpinning values of bourgeois society.[21] No less important, the growth of educated bourgeois officials in Germany, and their relative weight *vis-à-vis* businessmen, formed part of a Continental pattern that was very different from the one to be found in Anglo-Saxon countries where the state was weaker. Nevertheless, it is probably true to say that the importance and prestige of state officials within the German bourgeoisie was striking even by Continental standards. This spilled over into the way in which the educated middle classes more generally thought about themselves. Take, for instance, the growing ranks of the professions. It is true that the Anglo-Saxon term 'free professions' can be misleading when applied to almost anywhere in Continental Europe. There was nothing uniquely German about the fact that there the state had a much greater role in the training, recruitment patterns, and regulation of professions such as law and medicine than it did in, say, Britain. But it is also true that even in France and Italy the state did not enjoy the monopoly over the training of lawyers that existed in Germany.[22] As Michael John points out in his contribution (chapter 6), all German lawyers were in one sense state officials until the 1870s, and any desires they had for emancipation from the tutelage of the state and a greater degree of self-regulation were offset by the value they placed on the enjoyment of an official's status. In the case of doctors, too, the borderline between free professional and official was often difficult to draw.

5

At the same time, the enormous growth in the bourgeois professions that was such an important – and long-neglected – feature of nineteenth-century Germany also had features that would have been recognizable anywhere in the advanced capitalist parts of the world. Like their counterparts in other countries, German doctors, lawyers, architects, and engineers placed great emphasis on the specialized knowledge and qualifications that signalled their expertise; they developed their own codes of ethics and professional bodies, and fought hard to outlaw those who challenged their monopoly service – 'quacks' and herbal healers in the case of doctors, *Winkeladvokaten* in the case of lawyers.[23] The rhetorical importance that German professional men attached to their disinterested service for the public good was common currency among professionals elsewhere. In Germany, however, perhaps even more than in other Continental countries, the parallels with the claims of the administrative bureaucracy to represent a 'general interest' were especially close. It is the difficulty of making a clear separation between officials (who included clergymen, schoolteachers, and academics) and members of the 'free' professions that explains why in Germany a single term came to describe both: the *Bildungsbürgertum*, or educated middle class.

In the first half of the nineteenth century the *Bildungsbürgertum* was the most important constituent part of the German bourgeoisie. With the transformation of the predominantly agricultural and craft-based economy into an industrial and mercantile giant, however, there emerged a powerful manufacturing and commercial bourgeoisie in Germany. Of course, we should not exaggerate the scale of this. On the eve of the First World War over a third of those gainfully employed in Germany were engaged in agriculture, while the persistence of a small business sector was striking – although not as striking as it was in France. In the middle of the 1870s, after the first great industrial spurt, almost two-thirds of those engaged in manufacturing production were employed in concerns with five employees or fewer; one in five was still employed in the putting-out system.[24] The speed of industrialization was nevertheless impressive, with a take-off in coal, iron, steel, and engineering and the rapid development of the textile sector in the 1850s and 1860s, followed by the 'second industrial revolution' from around the 1890s, in which branches such as chemicals, optics, electrics and – eventually – automobiles were prominent. As the German economy became increasingly sophisticated in the decades before the First World War there was also a very rapid growth in the tertiary sector, in businesses such as banking, shipping, and insurance, as well as large-scale retailing.[25]

The result was the emergence of a diverse and powerful economic bourgeoisie. It included the clans of textile entrepreneurs in Westphalia, the Upper Rhine and Central Germany, great iron and steel magnates such as Stumm on the Saar and Krupp in the Ruhr, as well as prominent pioneers of the second industrial revolution such as Emil Rathenau, of the electrical company AEG, and the Württemberg entrepreneur Robert Bosch. But the dynamism of economic development created new opportunities for investment and profit in every area of life. Men made their fortunes from the putting-out system (especially in the clothing and furniture businesses), from the property and construction booms in the latter half of the nineteenth century, from department stores – even from the sugar industry, one of the most capital-intensive in Germany. As Dolores Augustine shows (chapter 2), German industrialization threw up a business elite of the very wealthy, as it did in England and France.[26] But perhaps the most important point about the economic bourgeoisie as a whole in Germany, compared with those countries, was the relative speed of its emergence as a social and economic force, which was linked to the explosive character of German industrialization. This, in turn, probably increased the homogeneity of the German economic bourgeoisie by minimizing the divisions between old-established and newcomer firms.[27] It almost certainly helps to explain the resourcefulness and lack of sentimentality with which German businesses organized themselves, particularly under the impact of the recession in the 1870s, in matters such as price-fixing and cartels, and in forming interest organizations on a branch and sectional basis.[28]

III

The groups we have been considering made up the German propertied and educated bourgeoisie (*Besitz- und Bildungsbürgertum*). Whether or not we include those whose claim to inclusion is less clear-cut – members of marginal professions such as pharmacists or veterinary surgeons, or the managerial and technical staff who grew in importance in German companies from the end of the nineteenth century – it is plain that the German bourgeoisie was marked by many internal divisions. Some of these divisions might be described as sectional: between heavy industry on the one hand, and export-orientated industry, commerce, and banking on the other,[29] or between different professional groups within the educated middle classes. But there were also underlying (although not absolute) differences between the two wings of the *Besitz- und Bildungsbürgertum* in their relationship to the market, the degree of economic security they enjoyed, and in the divergent patterns of education and recruitment to their respective occupations.[30] While the difference should not be overdrawn, there is also evidence that the propertied and the educated preferred intermarriage with their own kind. Karin Kaudelka-Hanisch (chapter 3) points to the way in which leading businessmen used marriage strategies to forge links with other businesses, while abundant evidence exists on the formation of heavily interrelated clans or dynasties among the educated (and especially academic) middle classes. Nevertheless, as Richard Evans shows in his contribution to this volume (chapter 4) intermarriage between different sectors of the bourgeoisie was far from unknown in some parts of Germany, and may well have increased over time. And there were many other ties of sociability which helped bind the different parts of the bourgeoisie together in various ways.[31]

One of the areas in which differences within the bourgeoisie have been diagnosed is in attitudes to the world, where the allegedly materialist values of the propertied contrasted with the 'inward', reflective stance of the *Bildungsbürger*. This subject has had important literary treatment in works such as Thomas Mann's *Buddenbrooks*.[32] Another way of putting this is to see a division between 'optimism' and 'pessimism', the former associated with the propertied middle class and the latter with the *Bildungsbürgertum*, one extolling material and mechanical achievements from the railway to the Zeppelin, the other more inclined to cultural despair and Mandarin disenchantment with everything 'modern'.[33] But, however it is formulated, this is a problematic distinction that is difficult to sustain empirically. It is true that there were leading industrialists, like the Westphalian Friedrich Harkort, who gave an exceptionally robust welcome to the new mechanical civilization; but in the middle decades of the nineteenth century, at least, it was members of the *Bildungsbürgertum* who were more likely to extol innovations such as the railway as symbols of progress (as their bourgeois counterparts did elsewhere); the manufacturers were too busy manufacturing to have the time for such things.[34] Ludwig Beutin was probably right, in fact, when he argued that in these years a belief in material and moral progress was one of the things that actually united the propertied and educated middle classes.[35] But within the middle classes as a whole there was always a degree of ambivalence about some aspects of material advancement, for most of the things which the bourgeoisie liked to think of as monuments to its own energy and culture had another, darker side to them. We see this clearly in attitudes towards the growing towns and cities, where pride in material and cultural achievements was offset by fears about hygiene, crime, and class conflict.[36]

It is in fact here, in the realm of cultural and social identity in the broadest sense, that the *Besitz- und Bildungsbürgertum* was probably most united. This bourgeois identity included a widely shared belief in hard work, competition, achievement (*Leistung*), and the rewards and recognition that should flow from these; in rationality and the rule of law, in the taming of nature, and in the importance of living life by rules. Correct table manners, sartorial codes, the emphasis placed on cleanliness and hygiene, and the importance attached to timetables (whether in the school or on the railway) all provide instances of the way in which these bourgeois values operated at the level of everyday life.[37] To this roster of beliefs (they were, of course, perceived as virtues) one should certainly add a powerful shared idea of 'independence', which rested on economic security, the possession of sufficient time and money to plan ahead, and certain minimum standards of education and literacy. A general respect for literary, artistic, and musical culture – for the *idea* of it, at any rate – was also a common denominator, although it was probably stronger among the educated than the propertied middle class. The connoisseurs and patrons of the arts described by Dolores Augustine in her essay were very much a minority among businessmen. At the same time, the suspicion of Bohemians and the avant-garde that was almost universal in the propertied middle class was also widely shared by their university-educated counterparts in public service and the professions.

The great exception to this impressive cultural unity was caused by the religious division of the German bourgeoisie. It is often argued, for example, that a commitment to secularization and secular culture was a unifying belief among the middle classes. And so it was, for the most part – among the Protestant majority (and among middle-class Jews). But this did not hold true of the self-consciously Catholic middle class. It was small in proportion to the overall Catholic share of the population, but its separate cultural life was one measure of the larger denominational divide in German society. For middle-class Catholics not only formed their own musical and literary societies; they tended to read different authors, to prefer different historians, even to travel (that great badge of bourgeois status) to different places. The denominational divide had effects in virtually every sphere of life, and assumed great importance when it came to an issue such as education.[38]

Even this division in the ranks of the bourgeoisie was not absolute. The denominational rift was probably widest during the middle decades of the nineteenth century, culminating in the mutual bitterness of the church-state dispute of the 1870s known as the *Kulturkampf*.[39] In subsequent decades, as middle-class Catholics placed themselves in the forefront of Catholic efforts to break out of their 'ghetto', and the proportion of Catholics in business, the professions, and official posts rose, the gap that separated Catholic lawyers and merchants from their non-Catholic counterparts grew narrower.[40] And important as fundamental disagreements about education and secularization were, they were offset by a much greater degree of consensus over everyday concerns of the kind discussed above, whether the belief in the rule of law and the sanctity of property, or the imperatives of hard work, respectability, and correct manners.

One of the institutions over which no basic disagreement existed between the Protestant and Catholic middle classes, which indeed epitomized many shared bourgeois values, was the family. The bourgeois family rested, in the first place, on the separation of the workplace from the home, and on the possession of sufficient material resources for servants to be employed to run the household. The family thus became a sphere of private, domestic compensation for the hard-working and 'public' male, while his wife devoted herself to the cultivation of domesticity and the passing on of correct cultural values and norms to the next generation. The family was the institution which displayed the wealth and cultural capital of the bourgeois, provided the means through which dynastic ambitions were realized, and offered to the male a haven from the rigours of business or professional life.[41] The subordinate place of women (and children) within the bourgeois family was therefore built in to its structure and functioning, even

10

if we should not neglect the fact that the material and cultural resources of women from bourgeois backgrounds were important in enabling them to take the first steps towards their own public emancipation towards the end of the nineteenth century.[42]

The bourgeois family was also one of the key institutions that provided a model through which the German bourgeoisie was able to generalize its outlook and values within the larger society. We should not be tempted to exaggerate this. The great majority of lower-class families lacked the material resources and security, the domestic servants, and the presence of a non-working mother which were characteristic of the bourgeois family. It was precisely those features which provided the basis for cultural activities, reflection, and extended play with children in the bourgeois family, and their absence set real limits on the extent to which it could serve as a model to imitate, even for those who wished to. Among the peasantry, outworkers, and the more insecure and unskilled parts of the working class there was little imitation of bourgeois family norms, certainly before the First World War. The major impact was on the pattern of family life among the lower middle class and skilled working class, although even here we should beware of attributing to them any wholesale 'embourgeoisement'.[43]

At same time, the German bourgeoisie offered its own institutions and values as a larger model in other ways. Through the works celebrations and outings referred to by Karin Kaudelka-Hanisch, by presenting the factory as a 'family', and by emphasizing the need for hard work, self-improvement, and respectability, the economic bourgeoisie presented its own businesses as models. In the educated middle class, public officials claimed to represent a general social interest. They presentt 1 the values that were embodied, for example, in schools or in hygiene regulations, as a means by which the allegedly short-sighted, selfish, or sectional attitudes of lower social classes could be countered, and those classes themselves 'civilized'. Similar views can be found among the increasingly self-confident bourgeois professionals of nineteenth-century Germany, most obviously perhaps among the doctors.[44]

One of the most important institutions through which bourgeois views of the world were expressed and propagated was the voluntary association, or *Verein*. The number of voluntary associations grew rapidly in Germany from the end of the nineteenth century, prompting contemporaries to talk of the 'mania' for associations.[45] They were 'bourgeois' in a two-fold sense: first, because they were a product of the (formally) more open, bourgeois society that developed in place of the semi-absolutist, status-bound society of the eighteenth century; and second, because – as many empirical studies have shown – *Vereine* were in practice dominated by members of the middle class, even when their overall membership was more socially inclusive. Associations were institutions where the bourgeoisie met, in order to organize everything from the disbursement of philanthropy and the fostering of culture to the prevention of cruelty to animals. Where lower social classes were members of associations, such institutions gave the bourgeoisie an opportunity to lay claim to natural social leadership.[46] A classic example was the effort made in the 1850s and 1860s to organize workers' education associations (*Arbeiterbildungsvereine*).[47] At the same time, many of the associations formed by local bourgeois notables – associations with titles such as the Monday Club or the Museum Society, or simply named after a well-established inn – were intended to be exclusive places, where the local businessmen, officials, and professional men met to talk among 'their own kind'.[48] Celia Applegate's essay shows how the *Heimat* movement in the Palatinate generated both more and less exclusive associations. The associations she discusses were of course, by definition, preoccupied with local concerns; but this local orientation was true of associations more generally, and it indicates where the real centre of gravity of the German middle class was located. For if the upper reaches of the economic bourgeoisie had international ties, especially those involved in banking and shipping, most middle-class Germans exerted power and influence in their own town, locality, or region. Here they were very influential indeed.

We have so far been considering the social and cultural unity of the German bourgeoisie as an internal matter, by looking at the values, structures, and institutions that held it together. But there is something else which united the bourgeoisie. That was its sense of itself *vis-à-vis* other classes. In the later eighteenth century and the first half of the nineteenth, bourgeois identity was most likely to define itself against the aristocracy, with its positions of influence within the corporate state, its legal privileges and the lofty disdain which some of its members showed for values such as hard work and achievement.[49] This hardly amounted to an anti-aristocratic front. But there was a sharp edge of dislike and contempt in some of the more self-consciously bourgeois figures in the first half of the nineteenth century. Friedrich Harkort believed that the railway engine would be the hearse that conveyed the nobility to the graveyard; popular bourgeois novelists such as Spielhagen and Gutzkow had gloating references in their novels to outmoded aristocrats wearing out their horses in the vain attempt to outrace the iron steed, and of aristocratic ladies having to come to terms with the tribulations of the public railway carriage.[50] Even the plain living and unpretentious domestic interiors of the middle class in the Biedermeier period in the first half of the nineteenth century were worn almost as a badge of virtue and contrasted with aristocratic extravagance.

Anti-aristocratic sentiment certainly did not disappear after the middle of the century as one defining characteristic of bourgeois identity. Over large swathes of Imperial Germany, members of the middle classes whose self-image was that of industrious and respectable men were happy to believe themselves superior to the Prussian Junkers. But there were, on the other hand, clear signs that after mid-century, and certainly from the 1870s, bourgeois antagonism towards the aristocracy was becoming more muted. The language recorded in contemporary political encyclopaedias and dictionaries shows that *Bürger* and *bürgerlich* were no longer defined so often *vis-à-vis* the old social elite.[51] Heavy industrialists and landowners made common cause against the consumer in their support for the protective tariffs that were reintroduced in 1878–9, in the so-called 'marriage of iron and rye'.[52] Conspicuous consumption and luxury, scorned in the Biedermeier years, became evident in wealthier bourgeois households. Some of the most successful and wealthiest bourgeois acquired the prefix 'von' in front of their names or purchased country estates.

It was customary until a few years ago to refer to these phenomena as a form of 'feudalization' of the German bourgeoisie, as indications that an important part of the bourgeoisie had given up its own values and begun to ape those of the aristocracy.[53] Such arguments are nowadays advanced with a good deal more caution. Even where such an intermingling of grand bourgeoisie and aristocracy took place, it is not clear that it entailed the casting-off of bourgeois identity. There is, moreover, a growing body of evidence that undermines basic assumptions of the feudalization thesis. In her contribution to this volume, Dolores Augustine demonstrates that the very wealthiest businessmen of Wilhelmine Germany had broken off from the middle classes, but without assimilating to the aristocracy. Karin Kaudelka-Hanisch shows (chapter 3) how the receipt of the title Commercial Councillor by prominent businessmen had nothing to do with angling after pseudo-aristocratic status, but was rather sought after because it signified the seal of approval of the state on their business activities and their place in the bourgeois social order. In neither case was there any significant degree of intermarriage, or even social contact, with the aristocracy. Ute Frevert (chapter 9) provides a much-needed corrective on another issue often taken as symptomatic of bourgeois feudalization: duelling. She shows that those German bourgeois who engaged in duels were not simply imitating aristocratic norms; the meaning of the duel for middle-class Germans was shaped by the place it occupied within a specifically bourgeois code of honour.

We should therefore be extremely cautious in talking about the feudalization of the German bourgeoisie. Yet however we judge the way in which relations developed between bourgeoisie and longer-established elite groups, there was a clear tendency for the bourgeoisie to separate itself off increasingly from lower social classes. This is perhaps least true of the peasantry, with which it had enjoyed little contact anyway. The contempt for (and occasional fear of) the 'uncivilized' and 'dependent' peasant which marked bourgeois attitudes earlier in the nineteenth century, tended to give way after mid-century to a more idealized view of the peasantry, made up of yodelling rustics and cherry-picking maids who appeared in the pages of bourgeois 'family journals' like *Die Gartenlaube*. A partial appropriation of a prettified version of the rural way of life by local bourgeois notables later in the century was part of this modification.[54] But the social contacts remained minimal, and with the exception of some politically progressive circles the underlying bourgeois attitude towards the peasantry remained contemptuous.[55]

A more obvious separation of the bourgeoisie from the classes below it can be seen in the case of the petty bourgeoisie. Here, once again, language mirrored social change. The *Stadtbürger*, or burghers, of the late eighteenth and early nineteenth century had included master craftsmen as well as merchants, small businessmen as well as large. Similarly, the term *Mittelstand*, or middle estate, had embraced members of the petty bourgeoisie like craftsmen and shopkeepers in addition to more substantial manufacturers. The changing meaning of the term, as *Mittelstand* came to be limited in its application to the petty bourgeoisie alone, was a sign of the actual separating out of the classes.[56] But two important qualifications should be entered here. The first is that the more substantial and secure petty-bourgeois households became a classic case of bourgeois social influence – the master craftsman or draper aspiring to the piano in the drawing room, played upon occasionally by a non-working daughter. This relationship found a parallel in the milieu of clubs and local associations: if bourgeois notables – middling and senior officials, grammar-school teachers, doctors, lawyers, or merchants – took leading roles, it was commonly the case that a publican, pharmacist, or reputable tradesman would fill the post of secretary.[57] Something of this pattern also holds true for parts (by no means all) of the growing white-collar lower middle class of private sector office workers (*Angestellte*) and minor state employees. A clear social gulf separated them from the established bourgeoisie, yet the attraction of a bourgeois style of life for some white-collar workers was evident, even if the limitation of family size pioneered in these new lower-middle-class strata in order to better their condition represented an abnegation of the family dynasticism displayed by the *Bürgertum* proper, and described in Richard Evans' contribution.[58]

It is over the questions of the family and social mobility that the other qualification should be made to the general argument about the separation between the bourgeoisie and the lower middle class, both old and new. For if it is true, on the one hand, that the opportunities for small businessmen to enter the ranks of the economic bourgeoisie were diminishing in the course of the nineteenth century, there was a partly compensatory pattern at work when it came to the access of the sons of the old and new lower middle class to the educated middle class. For striking numbers of craftsmen, small tradesmen, and shopkeepers saw their male offspring advance via classical grammar school and university education into the ranks of officialdom or the free professions. Characteristically, this occurred over two generations, as the first generation moved up into lower official posts or the minor professions, and was able to 'place' its children into the bourgeoisie proper. For all the powerful dynamics of so-called self-recruitment among the educated middle class, the statistics on the social origin of entrants into these occupations leave no doubt that they also sustained themselves by regularly replenishing their ranks with the sons of the lower middle class. Evidence suggests close parallels here with France, and probably also with other parts of Continental Europe.[59]

It was against the urban lower class, however, that the German bourgeoisie defined itself most clearly. During the early decades of the nineteenth century and in the revolutionary upheavals of 1848–9, this embraced a variety of groups: journeymen and impoverished small masters, day labourers, and the 'mob'. When bourgeois philanthropic associations concerned themselves in the 1840s with what they called the 'proletariat', and expressed fear of the threat it posed to the social order, it was to such groups that the term was applied.[60] The heady economic boom of the 1850s and 1860s then witnessed the emergence of an industrial working class, a process of class formation that took on increasingly clear contours in later decades under the impact of economic concentration, together with altered residential patterns and new recreational forms in the growing towns.[61] This urban working class, in both its 'respectable' and 'unrespectable' manifestations, provided a negative reference point for members of the propertied and educated middle classes in a number of important respects.

For the economic bourgeoisie, the advent of a class-conscious proletariat was perceived as a challenge to the rights of capital. The response varied. In industries such as printing and the skilled building trades, and in smaller concerns in many branches, there was often acceptance of trade unions and the arbitration of disputes; in heavy industrial branches – iron, steel, engineering – reactions were much more uncompromising, and the employers' repertoire included the repressive stick of bans on non-company unions, blacklisting, and intimidation, as well as the paternalist carrot of company housing and welfare schemes. This heavy-handed response on the part of industrial barons like Stumm and Krupp, the desire to be *Herr im Hause* or 'lord of the manor' in their own mines and factories, has often been seen as further evidence of a feudal mentality. The existence of 'pre-industrial' values among entrepreneurs in this group cannot be dismissed out of hand. But as Dick Geary shows (chapter 5), and as other historians have recently suggested, the responses in question had obvious roots in the strategic power such employers wielded in the labour market and their capacity to develop 'modern' means of control over the workforce.[62]

Open class conflict of this sort had an impact beyond the group of industrialists directly concerned. A bourgeois ideal of mid-century had been the growth of class harmony on the basis of the bourgeois virtues of hard work, independence, and respectability. The initiatives that came from the politically liberal segment of the bourgeoisie, its dominant orientation in the middle third of the century, to encourage workers' co-operatives and educational associations, were an expression of such hopes. The working-class rejection of bourgeois tutelage, already evident by the 1860s, and the sharpening of class antagonism that became apparent, undermined bourgeois faith in social harmony.[63] These developments did not end bourgeois rhetoric about the worker advancing himself materially and socially through merit and industry; nor did they stop references to the need for co-operation between the classes. But within the different sections of the bourgeoisie the formation of the working class and the evidence of class conflict produced a variety of negative reactions that included regret, disenchantment, and fear.

The working-class challenge constituted the most obvious sign, although by no means the only one, that the bourgeois ideal of a harmonious society of citizens was being called into question. And just as this challenge took political form, in the spectacular growth of the Social Democratic Party from the end of the nineteenth century, so it left its mark on the politics of the bourgeoisie. This has generally been considered by historians under two main heads. The first is the much-debated question of bourgeois liberalism and its weakness; the second is the no less controversial issue of the unhealthy attitudes supposedly harboured by the German bourgeoisie towards the powerful state and the strong leader. The two are naturally interrelated, but it may be helpful to examine them in turn.

IV

Liberalism is associated historically with the bourgeoisie, and in modern German history both are associated with political failure. Before we turn to the question of failure, it is worth considering for a moment the coupling together of 'bourgeois' and 'liberalism'. Should they be so inextricably linked?[64] In at least two important respects the answer might seem to be no. If we look at the political affiliations of members of the German bourgeoisie, it is clear that liberalism never enjoyed anything like monopoly support. Even at the liberal high-point of the 1860s and 1870s, many bourgeois

Germans counted themselves as conservatives (the Free Conservative Party enjoyed particularly strong support among large industrialists), while a talented array of Catholic lawyers, officials, academics, and publicists helped to found and sustain the Catholic Centre Party. The political splintering of the German bourgeoisie was to become even more evident in later decades. Secondly, German liberalism was a political movement that aimed to appeal across class lines. It looked for support from the peasant, the craftsman, and the worker, as well as the official and businessman; and its political and electoral support remained characteristically broad-based in social terms, in bad times as well as good. That was, indeed, one of the problems of liberalism in the period after the unification era: the lack of identification with one particular constituency or interest was transformed, under changed political conditions, from a strength into a weakness.[65]

There can be no simple equation between a social class and a political movement, a point that Geoff Eley makes forcefully (in chapter 10). There is nevertheless good reason to talk of German bourgeois liberalism. In the decades before the 1848 revolutions most politically engaged members of the German bourgeoisie would have considered themselves broadly liberal, and liberalism was still more dominant as a bourgeois creed (for the Protestant and Jewish bourgeoisie, at least) in the third quarter of the nineteenth century. In the political vicissitudes of later years, it was generally to the middle strata of Imperial Germany that the various liberal parties looked with most confidence for support. Conversely, it was legal and administrative officials, members of the professions and (to a lesser degree) businessmen who provided the liberal political movement with the great bulk of its parliamentarians, local leaders, and intellectuals.[66]

The affinities between the bourgeoisie and liberalism amounted, however, to more than a matter of personnel. To a striking degree, the bourgeois values described earlier were also liberal values. This is true of the emphasis placed on education, merit and hard work, the belief in culture, science and progress, the importance attached to 'independence' and 'character'. In these and numerous other particulars, German liberals mouthed general bourgeois preoccupations. As Dieter Langewiesche has recently put it, it seems right to assume 'a close link between liberal views of the world and bourgeois norms of conduct. Liberalism and "bourgeois society" appear to have formed a symbiosis.'[67]

As Langewiesche also notes, these liberal – and bourgeois – views of the world had a formative effect on German society and politics even though liberalism itself never achieved political power. That is one of the points argued by Geoff Eley in his essay, where he urges that we look at what bourgeois and liberal aspirations in Germany actually were, rather than what they 'ought' to have been. It was once commonplace to recount the history of liberalism as one of pusillanimity and even betrayal. The events of 1848 became a 'missed opportunity', the circumstances of unification a 'capitulation' to Bismarck and the Prussian army.[68] Few historians would now present such a bald view. The constraints under which liberals operated are recognized even by those inclined to criticize their actions. It is also generally agreed that bourgeois liberalism was actually at its peak in the third quarter of the nineteenth century. More a movement than a narrow party-political affiliation, liberalism in these years enjoyed a dominant position within the still relatively narrow political nation – among the urban notables, or *Honoratioren*, among the propertied and educated generally (including officials), in the press.

Liberalism also achieved a good deal of what it sought politically. It welcomed the creation of a German nation-state, a development that – initially, at least – was anathema to conservatives, whether in the Prussian heartlands of the east or in southern states such as Bavaria. In this period, liberalism and nationalism ran together. A unified nation would, it was believed, produce a much-desired uniformity and predictability in matters that affected trade and professional life, while advancing the cause of progress.[69] For the nation-state was seen as a powerful, progressive foe of entrenched states-rights, local particularisms and – not least – clerical influence. That is why both National Liberals and Progressives were such wholehearted supporters of repressive Bismarckian measures against the Catholic Church in the 1870s. They could see few better liberal causes than a crusade against the clerical pretensions and 'backwardness' of an allegedly anti-national Church.[70]

The fact that unification was achieved under the auspices of the Prussian army did not automatically lead to liberal hand-wringing. Prussia was not associated only with the barracks and the spiked helmet: it was broadly identified with the cause of modernity in fields ranging from education and communications to the scientific management of forests. Liberals concerned about the authoritarian and 'Borussian' features of the Prussian state also had hopes of taming them within the new structure of the nation-state. And there were indeed many respects in which the new German nation-state embodied and secured the legal and constitutional safeguards liberals held dear – the freedoms of association, assembly, speech and petition, the legal accountability of the bureaucracy, the creation of a national parliament whose elected members had specific powers to check the actions of the executive. Much of what we might be tempted to label as a liberal failure to achieve parliamentary government was actually a modestly satisfied acceptance of constitutionalism as such. The tradition of German 'dualism', which emphasized the separate tasks of government and parliament, provides part of the explanation for this.[71] It is also true that even during its most militantly oppositional phases, German liberalism tended to couch its demands in legal rather than political terms. Liberals in 1848 were centrally concerned with the problem of arbitrary government; Bismarck's liberal opponents in the Prussian constitutional conflict of the 1860s called for the legal rather than political accountability of ministers; and the liberal Reichstag majority of the 1870s was preoccupied with consolidating the rule of law in the new Germany.[72] This was, indeed, one area in which genuine liberal achievements proved largely resistant to challenges in the Imperial period. In the heady days of the 1860s and 1870s, when the Progressive Party, the National Liberal Party, and other liberal groupings dominated German elections and parliamentary chambers, there seemed reason to believe that these advances had laid the foundations for truly constitutional and (eventually) parliamentary government in Germany.

That was not the way events unfolded. The national political structure that arose out of the liberal era of the 1860s and 1870s was neither autocratic nor unchanging, but its shortcomings are plain enough. Imperial Germany did not become a limited parliamentary monarchy. The structure created by Bismarck left the Kaiser, not the elected parliament or *Reichstag*, responsible for the choice of chancellor and state secretaries. Indeed, the latter were constitutionally debarred from being members of parliament, thus excluding active party leaders from consideration. The Kaiser's government was not responsible to parliament, and the negative blocking powers the Reichstag did possess, especially in financial matters, were weakened in the years after unification when it came to the crucial matter of the army budget. Moreover, the political institutions of the new nation continued to be closely interwoven at every level with those of Prussia, the dominant state within the federal German Empire. And in Prussia, whatever its other virtues in liberal eyes, constitutionalism was more a sham than it was in the Empire as a whole.[73]

It would be wrong to pass over the real failures and weaknesses of bourgeois liberalism. For the unification era of the 1860s and 1870s did present liberal opportunities, yet fifty years later Germany still lacked anything resembling parliamentary government and liberalism itself was a much weakened force. This is partly a chicken-and-egg question: liberal political leverage was always limited, and liberal failure was often an effect as well as a cause of the power wielded by the monarchical executive and the interests that supported it (which included the landowning nobility and the army). But we should also note the importance of internal liberal weaknesses. One of these was the sheer modesty of its demands, a point made by Hermann Baumgarten in a celebrated article written in 1866. In his *German Liberalism: A Self-Critique*, Baumgarten linked this failing to the lack of instinct for political power on the part of the class with which liberalism was most closely identified: the bourgeoisie.[74] There was a kernel of truth in this.[75] On the other hand, an important liberal weakness in subsequent decades was precisely the loosening of its political support among the German bourgeoisie. This was partly the result of a drift towards conservatism that matched the growing social conservatism of the bourgeoisie, although this was probably less pronounced, certainly in party-political terms, than it was in some other parts of Europe (or in England). Urban conservatism remained relatively weak in Germany into the twentieth century.[76] More important was the defection of bourgeois Catholics, driven into support for the Catholic Centre Party by the liberal aggression and disdain towards the Church and its defenders that came to a head in the *Kulturkampf*. This also had its counterparts elsewhere in Europe – in Austria, Belgium and Switzerland, for example – but its impact was especially severe in Germany.[77] Finally, and perhaps most paradoxically, the bourgeois attachment to liberalism was weakened by the ways in which nationalist sentiment developed. The National Liberal Party had expressed the liberal-nationalist bourgeois attitudes that were dominant at the time of its foundation in 1866. By the end of the century it had become stuck in the ideological grooves of the unification era, and found itself outflanked by radical-nationalist organizations such as the Pan-German and Navy Leagues. These exerted a powerful attraction on the educated middle class, and especially on a younger generation that took unification for granted and wanted to move on to newer challenges. The rabid nationalism of the Pan-Germans showed the inroads which anti-semitism and 'Social Darwinism' had made in some bourgeois circles. The growth of radical nationalism also demonstrated how the liberal bourgeois consensus of the 1860s had fractured.[78]

But bourgeois liberalism had a further problem that came to assume even greater importance: its increasingly uncertain popular support. Liberals had always been uneasy at the prospect of the 'masses' playing a political role. Their alarm in 1848 was matched by the vehemence with which they warned in the 1860s against the dangers of stirring the 'passions' of the lower orders through electoral enfranchisement.[79] Bismarck's introduction of universal manhood suffrage for elections to the Reichstag therefore posed a potential threat to liberals – as it was intended to.[80] The low electoral turn-outs in the first decade or so after 1871 disguised the severity of the threat. By the 1890s, however, liberalism found itself facing major difficulties. The increasingly class-based nature of politics eroded liberal support not only among the working class, but among peasants and the petty bourgeoisie.[81] Both ideologically and organizationally, bourgeois liberalism was poorly equipped for an age of pressure groups and vulgar mass politics. The bourgeois-liberal ideal of a society of independent men was undermined by socio-economic developments, while the aloof, rather patrician organization and style of liberal 'notable politics' was exposed on the electoral battlefield.[82]

We should not underestimate the political resources of German liberalism at the beginning of the twentieth century, or write off its political future. There were clear signs of liberal organizational and intellectual renewal in the years before the First World War, especially in the reunited parties of left liberalism and on the emergent Young Liberal wing of the National Liberal Party.[83] Liberalism also continued to have a powerful presence in municipal government.[84] But the restricted franchises that help to explain this municipal power-base also pointed to the dilemma of bourgeois liberalism. Just as liberals in 1848 had been fearful of enlisting popular backing behind their cause, so their successors in the early twentieth century saw democracy as a potentially dangerous weapon. In this period liberals supported suffrage restrictions in Saxony and Hamburg, while continuing to vote against reform of the undemocratic Prussian three-class franchise.[85] Dissatisfied though they were with aspects of the Imperial German state and constitution, liberals shied away from the implications of invoking popular support to apply pressure for reform. They were torn, in James Sheehan's phrase, 'between state and people'.[86]

In this respect, as in others, an examination of bourgeois liberalism raises issues that are important in considering the relationship of the German bourgeoisie to the state more generally. It is a subject that has frequently exercised historians. The abject quiescence of German doctors, university professors, and officials in the face of the Nazi state, indeed the willingness with which some of them implemented repressive and barbarous policies,[87] has provided an understandable starting point for many commentators. Explanations have been sought in longer-term mentalities, and found in the fateful absence of civic spirit shown by the German bourgeoisie, in its lack of political maturity or engagement. This has been expressed as the weak German tradition of the *Bürger* as citizen or *citoyen*, as opposed to the *Bürger* as bourgeois (in the German language, unlike English or French, the same word does service for both concepts).[88] It is perhaps more familiar to Anglo-Saxon readers as the idea of the 'Unpolitical German', a figure praised by Thomas Mann in a work of 1918 and excoriated by postwar historians writing in the shadow of the 'Third Reich'.[89]

Such arguments are plausibly attractive; but do they stand up to scrutiny? The tendency has been to give an unduly attenuated picture of bourgeois 'initiative' in Germany, perhaps because this attribute is implicitly equated with a particular kind of Anglo-Saxon dissent. There was in fact a powerful concept of citizenship and of active participation in civic life among the bourgeoisie. It found expression most obviously in the *Verein*, the direct equivalent of the Anglo-Saxon voluntary association. By the end of the nineteenth century, moreover, many aspects of German public and political life were shaped in accordance with bourgeois tenets. Formal equality before the law, the independence of the judiciary, vigorously fought and largely unmanipulated elections, a free press that was far from uncritical of the established order – these were not negligible, and none had been granted without a struggle by German rulers.[90] They do not suggest quite the supine indifference of the bourgeoisie that is sometimes suggested, or allow an obvious leap to the apparent bourgeois capitulation in the face of Nazi blandishments.

However lengthy the list of caveats, however, there were unmistakable signs of a gelded civic activism in the German bourgeoisie. This was most obvious in the extraordinary prestige enjoyed by the state and the respect accorded to officials. That is one of the threads running through the contributions to the present collection of essays. In the liberal middle decades of the nineteenth century this prestige and respect were strongly bound up with the idea of the benign state as the harbinger of progress 'from above'. This attitude continued to be widespread into the twentieth century, in the era of the interventionist 'social state'. It was joined by a more conservative bourgeois attachment to the powerful state as the guarantor of social order and stability, as it became clear that these would not result automatically from the operation of free market competition.[91] In a parallel trend, the bourgeois emphasis on the rule of law took on the increasingly conservative colouring of an attachment to law and order.[92]

Bourgeois deference to authority took other forms, especially from around the 1860s onwards. One was the particular respect accorded to the army, for all the minority tradition that pointed the other way. This manifested itself in the institution of the reserve officer corps, and found vivid expression in the way a middle-aged and respected civilian would step off the pavement in order not to impede a young lieutenant.[93] It is also worth noting that equality before the law stopped at the barrack gates. The anti-militarist barbs of the satirists, and the fact that military misbehaviour at Zabern in 1913 caused general outrage, place all of this in perspective; but they do not alter the reality of the everyday respect generally accorded to the army by bourgeois Germans.[94]

Alongside this went a persistent strain of hankering after a 'strong man' in political life. This was particularly associated, of course, with the figure of Bismarck. In his celebrated inaugural address at Freiburg in 1894, Max Weber criticized sections of the German bourgeoisie for their hopes of a 'New Caesar' to fill the gap left by the departure from office of the Iron Chancellor.[95] The Bismarck hagiography of the 1890s and the Bismarck monuments that sprang up after his death in 1898 illustrate what Weber was talking about; so does the transference of the sentiment on to the figure of Kaiser Wilhelm II, to the extent that younger members of the bourgeoisie sought to imitate the Kaiser's moustache and his rasping voice, or *Kaiserstimme*.[96] Nearly thirty years earlier, Weber's mentor Hermann Baumgarten linked his critique of liberalism to the apolitical leanings of the German bourgeoisie. The bourgeois would, argued Baumgarten, 'invariably be a major factor in the life of the state, his insight, his activity, his resources w[ould] always be given primary consideration by the state'. But, he continued, 'the middle class is little suited for real political action'; the bourgeois was 'made for work, not for governing, and the essential task of the statesman is to govern'.[97]

In the end there remains some point in using the category of the 'Unpolitical German' when talking of the German bourgeoisie, although the term as usually understood focuses too narrowly on certain aspects of the unworldiness or *Innerlichkeit* of elements within the educated middle class. The tendency to cultivate its own garden – to retreat into the world of business, profession or scholarship, into the satisfactions of family life or local networks, where bourgeoisie identity was anchored – was widespread. This was accompanied by a persistent longing for a form of social and political harmony, in which the claims of state and officialdom to represent a general interest in society were widely accepted, while conflictual party politics was viewed as divisive, and by some even as un-German. In the last decades before the First World War, attitudes of this kind were found perhaps at their most rabid in the educated bourgeois ranks of the radical nationalists, but in more moderate form they were extremely common. Recent work has shown just how pervasively this mentality informed the bourgeois 'apolitical politics' of what might be called 'middle Germany', the small to medium-sized non-industrial towns which still had an enormous demographic and social importance in Germany on the eve of war.[98]

V

A composite picture of the German bourgeoisie in 1914 would have to include at least the following features. Politically it was disunited and removed from decision-making, but it had many reasons for satisfaction. It was a growing and generally buoyant class, increasingly wealthy, and aware of what it believed was due to its achievements – its contribution to Germany's rapid economic advance, to the renown of German scholarship and culture, to the virtues of a bureaucracy generally regarded as uncorrupt and efficient.[99] A small minority of industrial magnates and the extremely wealthy may have acquired titles, bought country estates, or even intermarried with the aristocracy. The vast majority of industrialists, merchants, officials, and professional men, however, did not take their cue from a 'feudal' elite. They did, on the other hand, subscribe to the importance of a strong state, with which they broadly identified. They were also, for the most part, supporters of an active German search for a place in the sun through a vigorous foreign policy.

Even before 1914 there were some shadows in this bourgeois high summer. Germany's bombastic imperialism was rightly seen by the more perceptive to have generated noise in greater quantities than success. At home, economic growth was heady but uneven, and it also aroused fears about the supposedly debilitating effects of 'mass culture'.[100] There was concern at the growth of the labour movement, while the predominantly Protestant bourgeoisie was united in its loathing of the political influence – both real and imagined – wielded by the Catholic Centre Party.[101] At the same time, there were intimations of a challenge to the domestic basis of bourgeois social life in the greater difficulty of acquiring servants and the advent of the New Woman.

But it was war, revolution, and the tribulations of the 1920s that turned the world of the bourgeoisie on its head. German wars of the nineteenth century had brought victories; defeat in 1918 was traumatic. Members of the middle classes – especially the educated middle classes – had dominated organizations such as the National Association and the Pan-German League, and there was a more general and close bourgeois identification with the national cause. The effects of defeat – the losses of territory and restrictions on the size of the German army, the 'war guilt clause' of the 1919 Versailles settlement, the imposition of reparations payments – were perceived as humiliations. The fact that defeat issued in revolution and rule by 'People's Deputies' removed the Hohenzollern dynasty and presented the spectacle of radical soldiers forcibly removing officers' epaulettes, simultaneously destroyed a number of the most central bourgeois assumptions about the world in which they lived. These dramatic reversals helped to fuel the 'stab in the back legend' that emerged, portraying German defeat as the product of malcontents and socialists on the home front.[102]

Few would dispute that the German revolution was, by any standard, incomplete. Elements of a political and social system that was more reassuring from the bourgeois perspective began to emerge soon after November 1918, and from 1923 at the latest it is possible to speak of a stabilization. This formed part of what Charles Maier has called the 'recasting' of bourgeois Europe.[103] But numerous grievances and fears remained. Many of these concerned material circumstances and sense of status. The long inflation of 1914–23, it is true, benefited the owners of factory plant and other fixed property, especially those who were indebted.[104] But it wiped out many bourgeois savings, and severely damaged those who drew rents or dividends; it also destroyed the certainty on which so much bourgeois calculation rested. The ability to place one's children in appropriate occupations was a case in point. The spectre of family members becoming 'de-classed' haunted the post-war educated middle classes. It was reinforced by graduate unemployment and 'overcrowding' in the civil service and professions that was more severe in the 1920s than the periodic over-supply of students in earlier periods.[105] For the male, Protestant bourgeois, the supposed influx of 'outsider' groups – women, Catholics, Socialists, Jews – into scarce positions compounded the offence. There was similar bourgeois resentment over the shortage of domestic servants, the narrowing differentials between middle-class and manual earnings, and the welfare provisions of Weimar Germany.[106] In the case of businessmen, large and small, the latter concerns took especially sharp form. While many of the initial gains made by labour in the wake of the revolution, such as the eight-hour day, were soon eroded, Dick Geary shows in his essay that employers continued to resent many features of the Weimar status quo. These included its tax, welfare, and arbitration systems. Businessmen also shared with other members of the middle classes a more general belief that workers occupied an overmighty position in the 1920s.

Grievances of this kind were closely linked to the perceived failures of the political system. The Republic was associated with divisive party politics, parliamentary horse-trading and weakness, and important sections of the bourgeoisie explicitly rejected the conflict and messiness with which parliamentary democracy was identified. This was true of pressure groups that placed their own sectional interests above the compromises necessary for coalition government, of the many middle-class para-military organizations, of those who supported the more authoritarian political system advocated by the League for the Renewal of the Constitution, and of conservative organizations and intellectuals like those grouped around *Die Tat* who called for wholesale spiritual and national regeneration.[107] In numerous bourgeois local associations of the period we find a less explicit but powerfully pervasive belief that neither national humiliation, nor the class conflict and cultural crisis associated with the 'mass age', could be remedied within the prevailing political structure. The familiar longing for a form of politics that was essentially apolitical or 'above politics' grew stronger as the actual fragmentation of bourgeois parliamentary and extra-parliamentary politics proceeded.[108]

The Depression of the early 1930s crystallized bourgeois disenchantment with the Weimar Republic. It produced a squeeze on profits and a crisis of confidence among important sectors of industry, created unemployment among groups such as architects, engineers, and doctors, and alarmed the middle classes as a whole with the sight of workers on the streets and the spectre of Communist revolution. The failure of Weimar parliamentary democracy, already seriously undermined, to cope with the crisis, hardened the bourgeois' contempt for it and accelerated their desertion. Yet the attempts by the old elite to apply conventional authoritarian solutions also failed and discredited those who undertook them.[109]

This raises the crucial question: how far did the German bourgeoisie lend active or tacit support to the Nazi Party, which held out the promise of combining authoritarianism with a plebiscitarian mass base in the electorate? One aspect of this question has been perennially controversial. It concerns the relationship between German big business and Hitler in the last years of the Republic.[110] There is little doubt that major German capitalists did not play the role of Nazi paymasters, preferring to finance other bourgeois parties less given to hair-raising rhetoric. Nor did large industrialists generally enthuse about Hitler (as many small businessmen did). At the same time, big business faced a crisis in the early 1930s, as the Depression threatened profits, put the tax and welfare system under chronic pressure, and undermined the conservative political parties that favoured their interests. In these circumstances, elements within German capitalism, unsympathetic to what Weimar stood for and hemmed in like other elite groups by the electoral gains of both Communists and Nazis, favoured a nationalist–authoritarian solution to the crisis that undermined democracy and eventually helped to give Hitler his opportunity. The sectional divisions within German industry, and the correlation between these and the political positions taken up by different branches and interests, remain the subjects of sometimes heated argument. This is especially true of the role played by heavy industry. But, as Dick Geary argues in his essay, the importance of the part played by big business in the overall downfall of the Weimar Republic was considerable.

Recent research has also suggested a larger bourgeois contribution to Nazi success than used to be believed. As Thomas Childers notes in the final chapter of this book, a remarkable consensus existed for decades concerning the social composition of the Nazi electorate and party membership. This emphasized the centrality of the lower middle class of independent craftsmen, shopkeepers, peasants, and minor officials. These 'little men', it was argued, felt themselves trapped between big business and organized labour, and were drawn to Nazism out of fear and resentment. The importance of the lower middle class to the mass base of Nazism is undeniable. But new research on the Nazi electorate, including that of Richard Hamilton, Jürgen Falter, and Thomas Childers, has enlarged the picture. One result has been to focus greater attention on the role played by the more substantial middle class.[111] Michael Kater's detailed study of party membership has revised our views in a similar direction, especially in showing how there was a middle-class influx into the NSDAP during the early 1930s.[112]

These recent works have shown the volume of bourgeois support for National Socialism; they and others have also demonstrated the channels through which this support spread. The Nazis were beneficiaries of the 'apolitical politics' of local associational life. They addressed the everyday concerns that were common currency among the members of bourgeois clubs – resentment about loss of status or the role of the Social Democrats in municipal government, antagonism towards the Jews or avant-garde culture, anxiety about the economic future or law and order. At a time of political crisis, the Nazis offered action.[113] Some of the party's adherents were rowdy and violent, it was true; but even the violence had a vicarious attraction, given that its selective targets were generally approved.[114] The Nazis offered a potent cocktail of nationalism, anti-socialism, and dynamism. In a period when the chronic fragmentation of bourgeois politics seemed to be a luxury, they held out the prospect of a powerful and unified movement.

Fear obviously played a role here. There are some parallels between the bourgeois stampede into the Nazi camp during the early 1930s and the 'social panic' by which the contemporary sociologist Theodor Geiger explained lower-middle-class susceptibility to Hitler.[115] But we should not exaggerate the political inertness or unworldiness of the bourgeoisie. For the ambitious but frustrated architect, engineer, or medical health officer, the Nazis seemed to offer positive opportunities. Nor should we assume that it was necessarily status anxiety among the more marginal bourgeoisie that induced Nazi leanings: it was often the most established, the 'notables', who set the tone in a locality by joining the party.[116] Similarly, we should not lay undue emphasis on the purely irrational lure of the parades and banners: these succeeded because the Nazis worked with the grain of bourgeois political sentiment. However volatile Nazi support was in the early 1930s, among the bourgeoisie it rested on a large measure of consensus.

That is important for what happened in the years 1933–45. Those identified with the 'restoration' of West Germany after 1945 depicted the Third Reich as a revolutionary and nihilistic episode, and included the bourgeoisie among the victims.[117] To question that view is not to deny the barbarism of the Nazi regime, its destructive, and ultimately self-destructive instability, or the opposition it encountered from parts of the bourgeoisie. But we should also recognize the active support the Third Reich received from many middle-class Germans, and the lack of moral resistance which allowed even larger numbers to give it their tacit support. Historians such as Martin Broszat and Hans Mommsen have shown that the inbuilt destructiveness of the Hitler state was by no means incompatible with – indeed required – the normal functioning of industry, bureaucracy, and professions under the most appallingly abnormal conditions.[118]

NOTES

1 David Blackbourn and Geoff Eley, *The Peculiarities of German History: Bourgeois Society and Politics in Nineteenth-Century Germany* (Oxford, 1984). For discussion of the argument advanced there, see also Richard J. Evans, *Rethinking German History* (London, 1987), ch. 3; Robert G. Moeller, 'The Kaiserreich recast? Continuity and change in modern German historiography', *Journal of Social History*, 17 (1985),

655–83; Jürgen Kocka, 'Der "deutsche Sonderweg" in der Diskussion', *German Studies Review*, 5 (1982), 365–79; and 'German history before Hitler. The debate about the German "Sonderweg"'', *Journal of Contemporary History*, 23 (1988), 3–16.

2 For businessmen, see Jürgen Kocka, *Unternehmer in der deutschen Industrialisierung* (Göttingen, 1975); Toni Pierenkemper, *Die westfälischen Schwerindustriellen 1852–1913* (Göttingen, 1979); Jeffry Diefendorf, *Businessmen and Politics in the Rhineland, 1789–1834* (Princeton, 1980). See also the older works by Friedrich Zunkel, *Der rheinisch-westfälische Unternehmer 1834–1879* (Cologne, 1962), and Hartmut Kaelble, *Berliner Unternehmer während der frühen Industrialisierung* (Berlin, 1972), and the further references in the contributions to the present volume by Dolores Augustine, Karin Kaudelka-Hanisch, and Dick Geary. On the professions, see Klaus Vondung (ed.), *Das wilhelminische Bildungsbürgertum* (Göttingen, 1976); Werner Conze and Jürgen Kocka (eds), *Bildungsbürgertum im 19. Jahrhundert, Teil I: Bildungsbürgertum und Professionalisierung in internationalen Vergleichen* (Stuttgart, 1985); Hannes Siegrist (ed.), *Bürgerliche Berufe. Zur Sozialgeschichte der freien und akademischen Berufe im internationalen Vergleich* (Göttingen, 1988); Geoffrey Cocks and Konrad H. Jarausch (eds), *German Professions, 1800–1950* (New York, 1988); Konrad H. Jarausch, *The Unfree Professions: German Lawyers, Teachers and Engineers between Democracy and National Socialism* (Oxford, 1989); Fritz Ringer, *The Decline of the German Mandarins 1890–1933* (Cambridge, Mass., 1969); F. Ostler, *Die deutschen Rechtsanwälte 1871–1971* (Essen, 1971); Claudia Huerkamp, *Der Aufstieg der deutschen Ärzte im 19. Jahrhundert* (Göttingen, 1985); Michael Kater, 'Professionalization and socialization of physicians in Wilhelmine and Weimar Germany', *Journal of Contemporary History*, 20 (1985), 677–701; C.M. Gispen, 'Selbstverständnis und Professionalisierung deutscher Ingenieure', *Technikgeschichte*, 50 (1983), 34–61.

3 See Gert Zang, *Provinzialisierung einer Region. Zur Entstehung der bürgerlichen Gesellschaft in der Provinz* (Frankfurt-on-Main, 1978); Rudy Koshar, *Social Life, Local Politics and Nazism: Bourgeois Marburg, 1880 to 1935* (Chapel Hill, 1986); Richard J. Evans, *Death in Hamburg. Society and Politics in the Cholera Years* (Oxford, 1987).

4 On the family, see Heidi Rosenbaum, *Formen der Familie* (Frankfurt-on-Main, 1982); Peter Gay, *The Tender Passion* '(New York, 1986); Reinhard Sieder, *Sozialgeschichte der Familie* (Frankfurt-on-Main, 1987); Karin Hausen, *Frauen suchen ihre Geschichte* (Munich, 1983); Ute Frevert (ed.), *Bürgerinnen und Bürger. Geschlechterverhältnisse im 19. Jahrhundert* (Göttingen, 1988); Dirk Blasius, *Ehescheidung in Deutschland 1794–1945* (Göttingen, 1987). On illness and medicine, see Klaus Dorner, *Bürger und Irre. Zur Sozialgeschichte und Wissenschaftssoziologie der Psychiatrie* (Frankfurt-on-Main, 1969); Ute Frevert, *Krankheit als politisches Problem* (Göttingen, 1984); Gerd Göckenjan, *Kurieren und Staat machen. Gesundheit und Medizin in der bürgerlichen Welt* (Frankfurt-on-Main, 1985); Evans, *Death in Hamburg.*

5 See, for example, Thomas Nipperdey, *Deutsche Geschichte 1800–1866.*

Bürgerwelt und starker Staat (Munich, 1983); cf. the introductory remarks to Siegrist (ed.), *Bürgerliche Berufe*, 42.

6 See Conze and Kocka (eds), *Bildungsbürgertum*; Siegrist (ed.), *Bürgerliche Berufe*; Frevert (ed.), *Bürgerinnen*; Jürgen Kocka (ed.), *Bürger und Bürgerlichkeit im 19. Jahrhundert* (Göttingen, 1987); and, especially, Jürgen Kocka (ed.), *Bürgertum im 19. Jahrhundert. Deutschland im europäischen Vergleich*, 3 vols (Munich, 1988). Four of these five volumes (the Conze and Kocka collection is the exception) derive from a major research project on the European bourgeoisie, led by Jürgen Kocka at the Centre for Interdisciplinary Research (ZiF), University of Bielefeld. For an account of the project see *Jahrbuch der historischen Forschung in der Bundesrepublik Deutschland. Berichtungsjahr 1986* (Munich, 1987). 36–40.

7 Manfred Riedel, 'Bürger, Staatsbürger, Bürgertum', in Otto Brunner *et al.* (eds), *Geschichtliche Grundbegriffe*, 1 (Stuttgart, 1972), 672–725, remains the best introduction to the history of the concept of *Bürgertum*. See also Mack Walker, *German Home Towns* (Ithaca, New York, 1971).

8 Meinecke's *Weltbürgertum und Nationalstaat* first appeared in Germany in 1907. An English translation, *Cosmopolitanism and the National State*, was published by Princeton University Press in 1970.

9 Hans Gerth, *Bürgerliche Intelligenz um 1800* (Göttingen, 1976); Rudolf Vierhaus (ed.), *Deutsche patriotische und gemeinnützige Gesellschaften* (Munich, 1980); Otto Dann (ed.), *Lesegesellschaften und bürgerliche Emanzipation* (Munich, 1981); Franklin Kopitzsch, *Grundzüge einer Geschichte der Aufklärung in Norddeutschland* (Hamburg, 1984); Richard van Dülmen, *Die Gesellschaft der Aufklärer. Zur bürgerlichen Emanzipation und aufklärerischen Kultur in Deutschland* (Frankfurt-on-Main, 1986).

10 Cf. the excellent compilation edited by Gerd Stein, *Philister – Kleinbürger – Spiesser* (Frankfurt-on-Main, 1985).

11 For studies of the urban elite in the late eighteenth and nineteenth centuries, see note 9 above. See also Rainer Koch, *Grundlagen bürgerlicher Herrschaft. Verfassungs- und sozialgeschichtliche Studien zur bürgerlichen Gesellschaft in Frankfurt am Main (1612–1866)* (Wiesbaden, 1983); Evans, *Death in Hamburg*; Lothar Gall, 'Die Stadt der bürgerlichen Gesellschaft – das Beispiel Mannheim', in *Forschungen zur Stadtgeschichte. Drei Vorträge* (Opladen, 1986); Jürgen Reulecke, 'Städtisches Bürgertum in der deutschen Frühindustrialisierung', in M. Glettler *et al.* (eds), *Zentrale Städte und ihr Umland* (St Katharinen, 1985), 296–311.

12 See Helmuth Plessner, *Die verspätete Nation* (Stuttgart, 1959), and Hans Kohn, *The Mind of Germany* (London, 1961) – both works that refer in subtitles to the problematic bourgeois mentality; Dolf Sternberger, *Ich wünschte ein Bürger zu sein* (Frankfurt-on-Main, 1967). Judicious observations on this problem can be found in Rudolf Vierhaus, 'Der Aufstieg des Bürgertums vom späten 18. Jahrhundert bis 1848/49', in Kocka (ed.), *Bürger und Bürgerlichkeit*, 67–8; and in Ute Frevert, ' "Tatenarm und Gedankenvoll"? Bürgertum in Deutschland

1807–1820', in Helmut Berding *et al.*, (eds), *Deutschland und Frankreich im Zeitalter der Revolution* (Frankfurt-on-Main, 1989).

13 Rolf Engelsing, *Zur Sozialgeschichte deutscher Mittel- und Unterschichten* (Göttingen, 1973), and in more developed form in Engelsing, *Der Bürger als Leser* (Stuttgart, 1974), esp. 256–67. More generally, for the cultural history of the German bourgeoisie in this period, see the works cited in note 9; also Rudolf Vierhaus (ed.), *Bürger und Bürgerlichkeit im Zeitalter der Aufklärung* (Heidelberg, 1981); W. Ruppert, *Bürgerlicher Wandel. Studien zur Herausbildung einer nationalen deutschen Kultur im 18. Jahrhundert* (Frankfurt-on-Main, 1981).

14 See Berding (ed.), *Deutschland und Frankreich*; T.C.W. Blanning, *The French Revolution in Germany* (Cambridge, 1983).

15 See, generally, Hans-Ulrich Wehler, *Deutsche Gesellschaftsgeschichte*, 1 (Munich, 1987), 347ff.; Nipperdey, *Deutsche Geschichte*, 11ff. On the reform era and state-building, see Reinhard Koselleck, *Preussen zwischen Reform und Revolution* (Stuttgart, 1967); Barbara Vogel (ed.), *Preussische Reformen 1807–1820* (Königstein, 1980); Helmut Berding and Hans-Peter Ullmann (eds), *Deutschland zwischen Revolution und Restauration* (Düsseldorf, 1981).

16 On the rule of law and legal accountability, see Michael John, 'The Peculiarities of the German State: Bourgeois Law and Society in the Imperial Era,' *Past and Present*, 119 (1988), 105–31; and Kocka (ed.), *Bürgertum*, 1; 340–405 (the contributions by Dieter Grimm and Regina Ogorek). On the importance of legal studies in the training of officials, see W. Bleek, *Von der Kameralausbildung zum Juristenprivileg. Studium, Prüfung und Ausbildung der höheren Beamten des allgemeinen Verwaltungsdienstes in Deutschland im 18 u. 19 Jahrhundert* (Berlin, 1972).

17 See, most recently, Charles McClelland, *State, Society, and University in Germany 1700–1914* (Cambridge, 1980); Konrad H. Jarausch, *Students, Society and Politics in Imperial Germany* (Princeton, 1982), as well as the works in note 2 that deal with the educated middle class.

18 For a variety of perspectives on the character of the Prussian bureaucracy, see Hans Rosenberg, *Bureaucracy, Aristocracy and Autocracy: The Prussian Experience, 1660–1815* (Cambridge, Mass., 1958); Koselleck, *Zwischen Reform und Revolution*; John R. Gillis, *The Prussian Bureaucracy in Crisis 1840–1860* (Stanford, 1971); D. Wegemann, *Die leitenden staatlichen Verwaltungsbeamten der Provinz Westfalen 1815–1918* (Münster, 1969), T. Süle, *Preussische Bürokratietradition. Zur Entwicklung von Verwaltung und Beamtenschaft in Deutschland 1871–1918* (Göttingen, 1988).

19 A good introduction to the growth of the interventionist state is provided by Heinrich August Winkler (ed.), *Organisierter Kapitalismus* (Göttingen, 1974).

20 The literature on this 'revolution from above' is very large. The argument can be found both in works that address the alleged long-term misdevelopment of Germany, such as Ralf Dahrendorf, *Society and Democracy in Germany* (London, 1968), and classic works on Germany's state-led economic development, such as Gustav Stolper, *The German Economy, 1870–1940* (London, 1940). The importance of state bureaucracy in Germany is discussed in a comparative context and

with great sensitivity by Jürgen Kocka, in Kocka (ed.), *Bürgertum* 1: 70–5.

21 See Blackbourn and Eley, *Peculiarities*, 241–50.

22 Siegrist (ed.), *Bürgerliche Berufe*, 30.

23 Manfred Späth, 'Der Ingenieur als Bürger. Frankreich, Deutschland und Russland im Vergleich', in Siegrist (ed.), *Bürgerliche Berufe*, 84–105; Peter Lundgreen, 'Wissen und Bürgertum. Skizze eines historischen Vergleichs zwischen Preussen/Deutschland, Frankreich, England und den USA, 18.–20. Jahrhundert', ibid., 106–26; Huerkamp, *Aufstieg*; Hannes Siegrist, 'Die Rechtsanwälte und das Bürgertum in Deutschland, die Schweiz und Italien im 19. Jahrhundert', in Kocka (ed.), *Bürgertum*, 2: 92–123.

24 Wolfram Fischer, 'Die Rolle des Kleingewerbes im wirtschaftlichen Wachstumsprozess in Deutschland 1850–1914', in F. Lütge (ed.), *Wirtschaftliche und soziale Probleme der gewerblichen Entwicklung im 15.–16. und 19. Jahrhundert* (Stuttgart, 1968), 136; F.-W. Henning, 'Industrialisierung und dörfliche Einkommensmöglichkeiten', in H. Kellenbenz (ed.), *Agrarisches Nebengewerbe und Formen der Reagrarisierung im Spätmittelalter und 19./20. Jahrhundert* (Stuttgart, 1975), 159.

25 Useful introductions to the pattern of German industrialization are: Knut Borchardt, 'Germany 1700–1917', in Carlo M.Cipolla (ed.), *The Fontana Economic History of Europe, 4/1: The Emergence of Industrial Societies* (Glasgow, 1973), 76–160; Martin Kitchen, *The Political Economy of Germany 1815–1914* (London, 1978); Helmut Böhme, *An Introduction to the Social and Economic History of Germany* (London, 1978).

26 W.D. Rubinstein, *Men of Property. The Very Wealthy in Britain since the Industrial Revolution* (London, 1981); Adeline Daumard, *La Bourgeoisie parisienne de 1815 à 1848* (Paris, 1963), and *Les Bourgeois et la bourgeoisie en France depuis 1815* (Paris, 1987); Youssef Cassis, 'Wirtschaftselite und Bürgertum. England, Frankreich und Deutschland um 1900', in Kocka (ed.), *Bürgertum*, 2: 9–34.

27 Jürgen Kocka, 'Bürgertum und bürgerliche Gesellschaft im 19. Jahrhundert. Europäische Entwicklungen und deutsche Eigenarten', in Kocka (ed.), *Bürgertum*, 1, 11–78, here 58–9; Patrick Fridenson, 'Herrschaft im Wirtschaftsunternehmen. Deutschland und Frankreich 1880–1914', in Kocka (ed.), *Bürgertum*, 2: 65–9.

28 The importance of the 1870s as a watershed is brought out in the pioneering work of Hans Rosenberg, *Grosse Depression und Bismarckzeit* (Berlin, 1967). On cartels, see F. Blaich, *Kartell- und Monopolpolitik im Kaiserlichen Deutschland* (Düsseldorf, 1973). On interest groups, see Hartmut Kaelble, *Industrielle Interessenpolitik in der Wilhelminischen Gesellschaft* (Berlin, 1967); Wolfram Fischer, 'Staatsverwaltung und Interessenverbände im Deutschen Reich 1871–1914', in Fischer, *Wirtschaft und Gesellschaft im Zeitalter der Industrialisierung* (Göttingen, 1972), 194–213; H.J. Varain (ed.), *Die Interessenverbände in Deutschland* (Cologne, 1973).

29 On the different sectional groupings within industry, see Kaelble, *Industrielle Interessenpolitik*; Siegfried Mielke, *Der Hansa-Bund für Gewerbe, Handel und Industrie 1909–1914* (Göttingen, 1976); Hans-Peter

Ullmann, *Der Bund der Industriellen* (Göttingen, 1976); Dirk Stegmann, *Die Erben Bismarcks. Parteien und Verbände in der Spätphase des Wilhelminischen Deutschlands* (Cologne, 1970).

30 However, these differences were relative rather than absolute. Siegrist (*Bürgerliche Berufe*, 25–7, 32) notes the professionals' preoccupation with the supply of and demand for their services in the market. See also Claudia Huerkamp and Reinhard Spree, 'Arbeitsmarktstrategien der deutschen Ärzteschaft im späten 19. und frühen 20. Jahrhundert. Zur Entwicklung des Marktes für professionelle ärztliche Dienstleistungen', in Toni Pierenkemper and Richard Tilly (eds), *Historische Arbeitsmarktforschung* (Göttingen, 1982), 77–116. The differences in education and training were perhaps more clear-cut. A good regional study of the completely different educational paths followed by future businessmen and by those who went on to the university and then into government service or the professions is Rainer S. Elkar, *Junges Deutschland in polemischem Zeitalter. Das schleswig-holsteinische Bildungsbürgertum in der ersten Hälfte des 19. Jahrhunderts* (Düsseldof, 1979). See also Evans, *Death in Hamburg*, 4, 18–20, 37, 103–4, 560.

31 On business marriages see, in addition to Chapters 3 and 4 in this volume, H. Henning, 'Soziale Verflechtungen der Unternehmer in Westfalen 1860–1914', *Zeitschrift für Unternehmensgeschichte*, 23 (1978), 1–30. A compelling picture of educated middle-class clans emerges from the discussion of the Baumgartens, Mommsens, and Webers in Wolfgang. J. Mommsen, *Max Weber and German Politics 1890–1920* (Chicago, 1984).

32 See also Mann's classic celebration of 'inwardness', *Reflections of a Nonpolitical Man* (New York, 1983), originally published in 1918 as *Betrachtungen eines Unpolitischen*; Fritz Stern, 'The political consequences of the unpolitical German', in Stern, *The Failure of Illiberalism* (New York, 1972), 3–25.

33 Fritz Stern, *The Politics of Cultural Despair* (Berkeley and Los Angeles, 1961); Ringer, *Mandarins*; Klaus Bergmann, *Agrarromantik und Grossstadtfeindschaft* (Meisenheim, 1970).

34 See, for example, Wolfgang Schivelbusch, *The Railway Journey* (Oxford, 1980); also, more generally, Blackbourn and Eley, *Peculiarities*, 185–8; James J. Sheehan, *German Liberalism in the Nineteenth Century* (Chicago, 1978), 28.

35 Ludwig Beutin, 'Das Bürgertum als Gesellschaftsstand im 19. Jahrhundert', *Gesammelte Schriften zur Wirschafts- und Sozialgeschichte*, ed. Hermann Kellenbenz (Cologne and Graz, 1963), 292–4.

36 Bergmann, *Agrarromantik*; Evans, *Death in Hamburg* 78–108, 346–72; Evans, *Rethinking*, ch. 8; Blackbourn and Eley, *Peculiarities*, 215–16; Andrew Lees, *Cities Perceived* (New York, 1985).

37 Kocka, 'Bürgertum', in Kocka, *Bürgertum*, 1:27–33; Wolfgang Kaschuba, 'Deutsche Bürgerlichkeit nach 1800. Kultur als symbolische Praxis', in ibid., 3:9–44; Kocka (ed.), *Bürger und Bürgerlichkeit*, 21–63, 121–48 (contributions by Kocka, Bausinger, and Nipperdey); Evans, *Death in Hamburg*, 351–3.

38 This is one of the subjects most neglected in the three volumes of

35

Kocka (ed.), *Bürgertum* (although see Gabriel Motzkin, 'Säkulari-sierung, Bürgertum and Intellektuelle in Frankreich und Deutschland während des 19. Jahrhunderts', 3:141–71). The neglect, however, reflects the general paucity of research. Jonathan Sperber's excellent *Popular Catholicism in Nineteenth-Century Germany* (Princeton, 1984), has some valuable points, although the bourgeoisie is not central to his concerns, and I have tried to talk about the Catholic bourgeoisie in *Populists and Patricians: Essays in Modern German History* (London, 1987), chs 7 and 9. In the absence of a work on Germany which places the faith of the Catholic bourgeoisie in its full social context – as Bonnie Smith very successfully does in *Ladies of the Leisure Class. The Bourgeoisies of Northern France in the Nineteenth Century* (Princeton, 1981) – the best way into that world is probably via a sensitive biography such as Winfried Becker, *Georg von Hertling 1843–1919, 1, Jugend und Selbstfindung zwischen Romantik und Kulturkampf* (Mainz, 1981).

39 On the *Kulturkampf*, see Sperber, *Popular Catholicism*, ch. 5; Black-bourn, *Populists and Patricians*, ch. 7; and *Central European History* 19: 1 (March, 1986), a special issue on the *Kulturkampf*.

40 David Blackbourn, *Class, Religion and Local Politics in Wilhelmine Germany* (London and New Haven, 1980), esp. ch. 1; Wilfried Loth, *Katholiken im Kaiserreich* (Düsseldorf, 1984).

41 See Karin Hausen, ' "eine Ulme für das schwanke Efeu". Ehepaare im Bildungsbürgertum. Ideale und Wirklichkeit im späten 18. und 19. Jahrhundert', in Frevert (ed.), *Bürgerinnen*, pp. 85–117; Rosen-baum, *Formen der Familie*; Sieder, *Sozialgeschichte der Familie*; Michael Mitterauer and Reinhard Sieder, *From Patriarchy to Partnership* (Cambridge, 1985); Ute Gerhard, *Verhältnisse und Verhinderungen. Frauenarbeit. Familie und Rechte der Frauen im 19. Jahrhundert* (Frankfurt-on-Main, 1978).

42 See Frevert (ed.), *Bürgerinnen*; Frevert, *Frauen-Geschichte*; Kocka, 'Bürg-ertum', in Kocka (ed.), *Bürgertum*, 1:44–6. On the movement for women's emancipation, see Richard J. Evans, *The Feminist Movement in Germany 1894–1933* (London, 1976). See also Chapter 4.

43 This is one of the central arguments in Rosenbaum, *Formen der Fami-lie*. On the limits of embourgeoisement, see Hermann Bausinger, 'Verbürgerlichung – Folgen eines Interpretaments', in Günter Wiegelmann (ed.), *Kultureller Wandel im 19. Jahrhundert* (Göttingen, 1973), 24–49; Wiegelmann, 'Bürgerlichkeit und Kultur', in Kocka (ed.), *Bürger und Bürgerlichkeit*, 121–41. On the ambivalent feelings of the pretty bourgeoisie towards the bourgeois family model, see Black-bourn, *Populists and Patricians*. ch. 5.

44 On doctors, see Paul Weindling's essay in this volume; Ute Frevert, ' "Fürsorgliche Belagerung". Hygienebewegung und Arbeiterfrauen im 19. und 20. Jahrhundert', *Geschichte und Gesellschaft*, 11 (1980), 420–46; Frevert, 'Professional medicine and the working classes in Imperial Germany', *Journal of Contemporary History*, 20 (1985), 637–58; Evans, *Death in Hamburg*, 467–8, 517–22. For a French-German comparison, see Allan Mitchell, 'Bürgerlicher Liberalismus und Volks-

gesundheit im deutsch-französischen Vergleich 1870–1914', in Kocka
(ed.), *Bürgertum* 3: 395–417.

45 Thomas Nipperdey, 'Verein als soziale Struktur in Deutschland im
späten 18. und frühen 19. Jahrhundert', in Nipperdey, *Gesellschaft,
Kultur, Theorie* (Göttingen, 1976), 174–205, here 175. Rudolf Braun
talks similarly of a 'hypertrophic growth' of voluntary associations:
Braun, 'Probleme des sozio-kulturellen Wandels im 19, Jahrhundert',
in Wiegelmann (ed.), *Kultureller Wandel*, 17.

46 In addition to the works cited in note 45, see Otto Dann (ed.),
Vereinswesen und bürgerliche Gesellschaft in Deutschland (Munich, 1984),
especially the contribution by Klaus Tenfelde; Wolfgang Kaschuba
and Carola Lipp, 'Zur Organisation des bürgerlichen Optimismus',
Sozialwissenschaftliche Information für Unterricht und Studium, 8 (1979),
74–82; Herbert Freudenthal, *Vereine in Hamburg* (Hamburg, 1958);
Heinz Schmitt, *Das Vereinsleben der Stadt Weinheim an der Bergstrasse*
(Weinheim, 1963); Blackbourn and Eley, *Peculiarities*, 195–8, 224–7.

47 Toni Offermann, *Arbeiterbewegung und liberales Bürgertum in Deutschland
1850–1863* (Bonn, 1979); Wolfgang Schmierer, *Von der Arbeiterbildung
zur Arbeiterpolitik* (Hanover, 1970); Christiane Eisenberg, 'Arbeiter,
Bürger und der "bürgerliche Verein" 1820–1870. Deutschland und
England im Vergleich', in Kocka (ed.), *Bürgertum*, vol. 2, esp. 202–8.

48 Nipperdey, 'Verein als soziale Struktur', 186–7. Zang (ed.),
Provinzialisierung, contains excellent detail on the Konstanz Monday
Club, while a description of the Stuttgart Museum Club can be
found in W. Pöls (ed.), *Deutsche Sozialgeschichte*, 1, *1815–1870* (Munich,
1972), 94–5.

49 See Kocka, 'Bürgertum', in Kocka (ed.), *Bürgertum*, 1: 20–6, and the
detailed references given there, especially on the social connotations
of the words *Bürger* and *Bürgertum* to be found in contemporary
political encyclopaedias and dictionaries.

50 See Ernest K. Bramsted, *Aristocracy and the Middle Classes in Germany*
(Chicago, 1964), chs 1–5; Sheehan, *German Liberalism*, p. 28; Blackbourn and Eley, *Peculiarities*, 185–9.

51 See Kocka, 'Bürgertum', in Kocka (ed.), *Bürgertum*, 1: 20–4, and the
detailed references there.

52 See Rosenberg, *Grosse Depression*, esp. chs 4–5; Helmut Böhme, *Deuts-
chlands Weg zur Grossmacht. Studien zum Verhältnis von Wirtschaft und
Staat während der Reichsgründungszeit 1848–1881* (Cologne, 1966), 530–86;
Michael Stürmer, *Regierung und Reichstag im Bismarckstaat 1871–1880*
(Düsseldorf, 1974), 278–88.

53 On the 'feudalization' thesis, see Hans Rosenberg, 'Die Pseudodemokratisierung der Rittergutsbesitzerklasse', orginally published in 1958
and reprinted in Rosenberg, *Machteliten und Wirtschaftskonjunktur* (Göttingen, 1978), 83–101; Zunkel, *Der rheinisch-westfälische Unternehmer*;
Hans-Ulrich Wehler, *The German Empire 1871–1918* (Leamington Spa,
1985), 125–7; Kocka, 'Bürgertum', in Kocka (ed.), *Bürgertum*, 1: 65–9;
Blackbourn and Eley, *Peculiarities*, esp. 106ff, 221ff; Hartmut Kaelble,
'Wie feudal waren die deutschen Unternehmer im Kaiserreich?' in
Richard Tilly (ed.), *Beiträge zur quantitativen vergleichenden*

Unternehmensgeschichte (Stuttgart, 1985), 148–71. Contemporaries such as Max Weber have often been cited in support of the 'feudalization' thesis, but it is worth noting that Weber's own arguments were neither unambiguous, nor focused exclusively on Germany. See, for example, Weber, 'Capitalism and rural society in Germany', in Hans Gerth and C. Wright Mills (eds), *From Max Weber. Essays in Translation* (London, 1974), 383.

54 Bausinger, 'Verbürgerlichung', 34–9. Bramsted, *Aristocracy and Middle Classes*. 200ff, is good on the *Gartenlaube*; so is Hermann Glaser, *The Cultural Roots of National Socialism* (London, 1978), 82–5. See also Wolfgang Jacobeit, 'Dorf und dörfliche Bevölkerung Deutschlands im bürgerlichen 19. Jahrhundert; in Kocka (ed.), *Bürgertum*, 2: 315–39. The appropriation by the English bourgeoisie of an idealized version of the countryside and rural life is a central argument in Raymond Williams, *The Country and the City* (London, 1973) and Martin Wiener, *English Culture and the Decline of the Industrial Spirit 1850–1980* (Cambridge, 1981).

55 While some celebrated the idealized, conservative peasantry portrayed in so-called 'Heimat' literature, the genre provoked the underlying contempt of others. For the historian Heinrich von Treitschke, 'Heimat' literature portrayed an endless succession of peasant 'louts and boors': P. Mettenleiter, *Destruktion der Heimatdichtung* (Tübingen, 1974), 325. See David Blackbourn, 'Peasants and politics in Germany, 1871–1914', *European History Quarterly*, 14 (1984), 47–75.

56 See Heinrich August Winkler, *Mittelstand, Demokratie und Nationalsozialismus* (Cologne, 1972), ch. 1; David Blackbourn, 'The *Mittelstand* in German society and politics, 1871–1914', *Social History*, 4 (1977), 409–33; Annette Leppert-Fögen, *Die deklassierte Klasse* (Frankfurt-on-Main, 1974).

57 Examples and references in Blackbourn, *Populists and Patricians*, ch. 5.

58 Reinhard Spree, 'Angestellte als Modernisierungsagenten. Indikatoren und Thesen zum reproduktiven Verhalten von Angestellten im späten 19. und frühen 20. Jahrhundert', in Jürgen Kocka (ed.), *Angestellte im europäischen Vergleich* (Göttingen, 1981), 279–308. See also the classic by Siegfried Kracauer, *Die Angestellten*, first published in 1930, and Jürgen Kocka, *Angestellte in der deutschen Geschichte 1850–1980* (Göttingen, 1981).

59 See Blackbourn, *Populists and Patricians*, ch. 5; Konrad H. Jarausch, 'The social transformation of the university: the case of Prussia, 1865–1914', *Journal of Social History*, 12 (1979), 609–36; Jarausch, *Students, Society, and Politics in Imperial Germany*, esp. 114–32; Kocka (ed.), *Angestellte im europäischen Vergleich*; Heinz-Gerhard Haupt, 'Kleine und grosse Bürger in Deutschland und Frankreich am Ende des 19. Jahrhunderts', in Kocka (ed.), *Bürgertum*, 2: 262–8.

60 Werner Conze, 'Vom "Pöbel" zum "Proletariat". Sozialgeschichtliche Voraussetzungen für den Sozialismus in Deutschland', in Hans-Ulrich Wehler (ed.), *Moderne deutsche Sozialgeschichte* (Cologne and Berlin, 1966), 111–36.

61 See Hartmut Zwahr, *Zur Konstituierung des Proletariats als Klasse.*

Strukturuntersuchung über das Leipziger Proletariat während der industriellen Revolution (Berlin, 1978); Jürgen Kocka, *Lohnarbeit und Klassenbildung. Arbeiter und Arbeiterbewegung in Deutschland 1800–1875* (Berlin, 1983). The growing divisions between bourgeoisie and working class, in areas of life ranging from religion to housing, as well as at the point of production, are emphasized by many contributors to Jürgen Kocka and Elisabeth Müller-Luckner (eds), *Arbeiter und Bürger im 19. Jahrhundert. Varianten ihres Verhältnisses im europäischen Vergleich* (Munich, 1986).

62 See Geoff Eley, 'Capitalism and the Wilhelmine state: industrial growth and political backwardness in recent German historiography, 1890–1918', *Historical Journal*, 21 (1978), 737–50; David Crew, *Town in the Ruhr. A Social History of Bochum 1860–1914* (New York, 1979).

63 Sheehan, *German Liberalism*, 79–107; Dieter Langewiesche, *Liberalismus in Deutschland* (Frankfurt-on-Main, 1988), 111ff; Offermann, *Arbeiterbewegung und liberales Bürgertum*; Lothar Gall, 'Liberalismus und "Bürgerliche Gesellschaft": zu Charakter und Entwicklung der liberalen Bewegung in Deutschland', *Historische Zeitschrift*, 220 (1975), 324–56.

64 This is one of the questions posed in Blackbourn and Eley, *Peculiarities*. It has recently been directly addressed in James J. Sheehan, 'Wie bürgerlich war der deutsche Liberalismus?', in Dieter Langewiesche (ed.), *Liberalismus im 19. Jahrhundert* (Göttingen, 1988), 28–44. Langewiesche himself has also written extensively and illuminatingly on German liberalism. See *Liberalismus in Deutschland*, and 'Liberalismus und Bürgertum in Europa', in Kocka (ed.), *Bürgertum*, 3: 360–94.

65 See Sheehan, *German Liberalism*, chs 11, 16.

66 This is essentially common ground among historians of liberalism. In addition to the works already cited, see Theodor Schieder, 'Die Krise des bürgerlichen Liberalismus', in Schieder, *Staat und Gesellschaft im Wandel unserer Zeit* (Munich, 1974), 58–88: Heinrich August Winkler, *Preussischer Liberalismus und der Nationalstaat* (Tübingen, 1964); Lothar Gall, *Der Liberalismus als regierende Partei* (Wiesbaden, 1968); James C. Hunt, *The People's Party in Württemberg and Southern Germany 1890–1914* (Stuttgart, 1975); Dan White, *The Splintered Party. National Liberalism in Hessen and the Reich, 1867–1918* (Cambridge, Mass. 1976).

67 Langewiesche, in Langewiesche (ed.), *Liberalismus im 19. Jahrhundert*, 13.

68 See, for example, Friedrich Sell, *Die Tragödie des deutschen Liberalismus* (Stuttgart, 1953), with its echoes in works such as Hans Kohn's *The Mind of Germany*.

69 Sheehan, *German Liberalism*, 121ff. See also Theodor S. Hamerow, *The Social Foundations of German Unification 1858–1871*, 2 vols (Princeton, 1969, 1972).

70 See Adolf Birke, 'Zur Entwicklung des bürgerlichen Kulturkampfverständnisses in Preussen-Deutschland', in D. Kürze (ed.), *Aus Theorie und Praxis der Geschichtswissenschaft* (Berlin, 1972), 257–79; Sperber, *Popular Catholicism*, ch. 5; Blackbourn, *Populists and Patricians*, ch. 7; Margaret L. Anderson, 'The Kulturkampf and the course of German

history', *Central European History*, 19 (1986), 82–115; Anderson, *Windthorst*, chs 6–7.

71 Leonard Krieger, *The German Idea of Freedom* (Boston, 1957) remains an outstanding account of dualism, as well as illuminating liberal goals and values more generally.

72 On the centrality of this aspect of liberal thinking, see Sheehan, *German Liberalism*, 115–16; Michael Gugel, *Industrieller Aufstieg und bürgerliche Herrschaft* (Cologne, 1975), 81–91. Michael John, *Politics and the Law in Late Nineteenth-Century Germany: the Origins of the Civil Code* (Oxford, 1989), also brings out how closely liberal aspirations in these years were linked to the cause of national legal codification.

73 The issue of 'sham constitutionalism' is addressed in Wehler, *German Empire*, 52ff. There is a good summary of constitutional arrangements in Gordon Craig, *Germany 1866–1945* (Oxford, 1978), 38–55.

74 Hermann Baumgarten, 'Der deutsche Liberalismus: Eine Selbstkritik', *Preussische Jahrbücher*, 18: 5 and 6 (1866), 455–517, 575–628.

75 It is also true, however, that bourgeois liberal politicians in Germany had prudential reasons to avoid being identified as the wielders of political power. The French July Monarchy, for example, which came to be seen as a 'bourgeois monarchy', was often cited by German liberals as something to be avoided. See Gugel, *Industrieller Aufstieg*, 207–11.

76 In 1912, the Conservative Party's share of the vote in towns of over 10,000 was a mere 3 per cent. See James N. Retallack, *Notables of the Right. The Conservative Party and Political Mobilization in Germany 1876–1918* (London, 1988), 183.

77 See the works cited in note 70. The European context of the *Kulturkampf* is discussed in Winfried Becker, 'Der Kulturkampf als europäisches und als deutsches Phänomen', *Historisches Jahrbuch*, 101 (1981), 422–46.

78 See Geoff Eley, *Reshaping the German Right. Radical Nationalism and Political Change after Bismarck* (London, 1980); Roger Chickering, *We Men Who Feel Most German. A Cultural Study of the Pan-German League, 1886–1914* (London, 1984). As Dieter Langewiesche has recently noted, one paradox of the liberals' position in Germany is that their political fortunes suffered from the fact that the German nation–state rapidly achieved a major degree of legitimacy (although not necessarily enthusiastic support) in the eyes of Germans as a whole. This deprived liberals of the opportunity to identify themselves exclusively with the national cause. In Italy and Hungary, where the circumstances were different, liberal party-political dominance persisted for much longer. See Langewiesche, 'Deutscher Liberalismus im europäischen Vergleich', in Langewiesche (ed.), *Liberalismus im 19. Jahrhundert*, 15–16.

79 David Hansemann, a noted 1848 liberal, described popular sovereignty as a 'pernicious theory'. See Diefendorf, *Businessmen and Politics*, 344. Examples of liberal hostility to universal manhood suffrage in the 1860s, and references, in Blackbourn and Eley, *Peculiarities*, 256–9.

80 There is a very large literature on Bismarck as a 'Bonapartist', using

universal manhood suffrage as an anti-liberal weapon. See Wehler, *German Empire*, 55–62; Wolfgang Sauer, 'Das Problem des deutschen Nationalstaats', in Wehler (ed.), *Moderne deutsche Sozialgeschichte*, 407–36; Stürmer, *Regierung und Reichstag* (subtitled 'Cäsarismus oder Parlamentarismus'). Sceptics include Lothar Gall, 'Bismarck und der Bonapartismus', *Historische Zeitschrift*, 223 (1976), 618–37, and Allan Mitchell, 'Bonapartism as a model of Bismarckian politics', *Journal of Modern History*, 49 (1977), 181–209. This issue of the *Journal* also includes comments by O. Pflanze, C. Fohlen, and M. Stürmer. See also Otto Pflanze, 'Bismarcks Herrschaftstechnik als Problem der gegenwärtigen Historiographie', *Historische Zeitschrift*, 234 (1982), 562–99.

81 Langewiesche, *Liberalismus in Deutschland*, 128ff; Sheehan, *German Liberalism*, 159–77, 239–57. On the challenge of the SPD, see W. L. Guttsman, *The German Social Democratic Party 1875–1933* (London, 1981). On the problems posed by the peasantry and petty bourgeoisie, see Blackbourn, *Populists and Patricians*, esp. chs 5, 6 and 10; White, *Splintered Party*; Shulamit Volkov, *The Rise of Popular Antimodernism in Germany: the Urban Master Artisans, 1873–1896* (Princeton, 1978), esp. ch. 6.

82 The problem of 'notable politics' is a commonplace of virtually all the works on liberalism in this period. The impact of growing mass political participation has been fruitfully examined in Stanley Suval, *Electoral Politics in Wilhelmine Germany* (Chapel Hill, 1985).

83 Beverly Heckart, *From Bassermann to Bebel. The Grand Bloc's Quest for Reform in the Kaiserreich* (New Haven, 1974); Peter Gilg, *Die Erneuerung des demokratischen Denkens im Wilhelminischen Deutschland* (Wiesbaden, 1965). There is an enormous literature on the social liberalism associated with Friedrich Naumann and the National-Social Association of 1896. A good introduction to this, and to the intellectual revival of the 'new liberalism', remains James J. Sheehan, *The Career of Lujo Brentano: A Study of Liberalism and Social Reform in Imperial Germany* (Chicago, 1966).

84 See James J. Sheehan, 'Liberalism and the city in nineteenth-century Germany', *Past and Present*, 51 (1971), 116–37.

85 See Walter Gagel, *Die Wahlrechtsfrage in der Geschichte der deutschen liberalen Parteien 1848–1918* (Düsseldorf, 1958); Heckart, *From Bassermann to Bebel*, 55–6, 154–60.

86 The theme of a liberal movement caught between *Volk* and *Staat* runs through Sheehan, *German Liberalism*.

87 See Michael Kater, 'Medizin und Mediziner im Dritten Reich. Eine Bestandsaufnahme', *Historische Zeitschrift*, 244 (1987), 299–352; Ernst Klee, *Was sie taten – was sie wurden. Ärzte, Juristen und andere Beteiligte am Kranken- oder Judenmord* (Frankfurt-on-Main, 1986); Konrad H. Jarausch, 'The perils of professionalism. Lawyers, teachers and engineers in Nazi Germany', *German Studies Review*, 9 (1986), 107–37; Hans Mommsen, *Beamtentum im Dritten Reich* (Stuttgart, 1966); Hans-Günther Assel, *Die Perversion der politischen Pädagogik im Nationalsozialismus* (Munich, 1969); Michael H. Kater, 'Die nationalsozialistische

Machtergreifung an den deutschen Hochschulen: Zum politischen Verhalten akademischer Lehrer bis 1939', in Hans Jochen Vogel *et al.* (eds), *Die Freiheit des Anderen: Festschrift für Martin Hirsch* (Baden-Baden, 1981), 49–75.

88 See especially Kocka, 'Bürgertum', in Kocka (ed.), *Bürgertum*, 1: 33–9.

89 See the references in note 32.

90 More detailed arguments on these points, and references, can be found in Blackbourn and Eley, *Peculiarities*. See also Kocka, 'Bürgertum', in Kocka (ed.), *Bürgertum*, 1: 51.

91 The cyclical downturns in the economy that occurred in 1857, in the Great Depression period 1873–96, in 1901–2, and in 1907–9, together with the economic and social disturbances they threatened to set off, had an important role in prompting industrial interests to seek accommodation with the state. For discussion of the forms this took, see Winkler (ed.), *Organisierter Kapitalismus*, and Eley, 'Capitalism and the Wilhelmine state'.

92 See Gugel, *Industrieller Aufstieg*, 89–91, 190–95.

93 The phenomenon of 'social militarism' in Imperial Germany has been widely discussed. See, for example, Eckart Kehr, 'Zur Genesis des Kgl. Preuss. Reserveoffiziers', in Kehr, *Der Primat der Innenpolitik*, Hans-Ulrich Wehler (ed.) (Berlin, 1965), 53–63; Martin Kitchen, *The German Officer Corps 1890–1914* (Oxford, 1968); H. John, *Das Reserveoffizierkorps im deutschen Kaiserreich 1890–1914* (Frankfurt-on-Main, 1981).

94 On the brazen misconduct of the Prussian army in the Alsatian town of Zabern, see David Schoenbaum, *Zabern 1913. Consensus Politics in Imperial Germany* (London, 1982).

95 See Max Weber, 'Economic policy and the national interest in Imperial Germany', in Walter G. Runciman (ed.), *Max Weber: Selections in Translation* (London, 1978), 264–8; also Weber, 'Parliament and government in a reconstructed Germany', in Günther Roth and Carl Wittich (eds), *Economy and Society* (New York, 1968), appendix, 1385–92 ('Bismarck's Legacy').

96 One historian has described the Bismarck cult as a 'substitute religion'. See Michael Stürmer, *Das ruhelose Reich. Deutschland 1866–1918* (Berlin, 1983), 248. The uses to which the cult was put by the Pan-German League are examined in Chickering, *We Men* (Ernst Hasse, the early leader of the League, collected Bismarck portraits: p. 101, note 156). Perhaps the most frequently cited case of the propensity to imitate the Kaiser is fictional: Diederich Hessling, the central character of Heinrich Mann's contemporary satire, *Man of Straw (Der Untertan* in the German original).

97 Cited in Beutin, 'Das Bürgertum', 297–8.

98 See, especially, Rudy Koshar, *Social Life*, chs 1–3; also chapter 8 by Celia Applegate in the present volume.

99 For a less wholesome side of the Prussian field administration, see Peter-Christian Witt, 'Der preussische Landrat als Steuerbeamter 1891–1918. Bermerkungen zur politischen und sozialen Funktion des deutschen Beamtentums', in Imanuel Geiss and Bernd-Jürgen Wendt

(eds), *Deutschland in der Weltpolitik des 19. und 20. Jahrhunderts* (Düsseldorf, 1973), 205–19.

100 Hans Mommsen gives an outstanding account of the way in which bourgeois movements such as the *Wandervögel* and the *Dürerbund* voiced this perceived threat to 'national cultural values'. See Mommsen, 'Die Auflösung des Bürgertums seit dem späten 19. Jahrhundert', in Kocka (ed.), *Bürger und Bürgerlichkeit*, 288–315, here esp. 198–99.

101 Historians have long – and rightly – emphasized bourgeois alarm about the labour movement. Anti-Catholic sentiment has recently received the attention it deserves. The venomous anti-Catholicism and violent hostility to the Centre Party among radical nationalists has been brought out by Eley, *Reshaping*, and Chickering, *We Men*. The broader contours of bourgeois anti-Catholicism are discussed in Blackbourn, *Populists and Patricians*, chs 7, 9.

102 Works on the experience of war and revolution tend to concentrate, understandably, on the urban working class, the petty bourgeoisie, the peasantry, and rural labourers, rather than on the middle classes. That is true of Jürgen Kocka's *Facing Total War. German Society 1914–1918* (Leamington Spa, 1984), although it remains an indispensable work. A valuable work that covers the bourgeoisie and the revolution is a collection of essays on Bavaria: Karl Bosl (ed.), *Bayern im Umbruch* (Munich, 1969). On the stab-in-the-back legend, see Anneliese Thimme, *Flucht in den Mythos. Die Deutschnationale Volkspartei und die Niederlage von 1918* (Göttingen, 1969).

103 Charles S. Maier, *Recasting Bourgeois Europe. Stabilization in France, Germany, and Italy in the Decade after World War 1* (Princeton, 1975).

104 The most detailed modern study on the economics of the inflation is Carl-Ludwig Holtfrerich, *Die deutsche Inflation 1914–1923. Ursachen und Folgen in internationaler Perspektive* (Berlin and New York, 1980). See also Gerald D. Feldman *et al.* (eds), *Die deutsche Inflation. Eine Zwischenbilanz/The German Inflation Reconsidered: A Preliminary Balance* (Berlin and New York. 1982). A good case study is Andreas Kunz, *Civil Servants and the Politics of Inflation in Germany, 1914–1924* (Berlin, 1986).

105 See Michael H. Kater, 'The work student: a socio-economic phenomenon of early Weimar Germany', *Journal of Contemporary History* 10 (1975), 71–94; Konrad H. Jarausch, 'The crisis of German professions 1918–1933', *Journal of Contemporary History* 20 (1985), 379–98; Ringer, *Decline of the German Mandarins*, 63–4; Mommsen, *Beamtentum*, 197.

106 These grievances emerge from studies of individual occupational groups, such as those cited in the previous note. They can also be seen vividly in works that concentrate on particular localities. See, for example, Koshar, *Social Life*, ch. 4; and William S. Allen's classic, *The Nazi Seizure of Power. The Experience of a Single German Town 1930–1935* (Chicago, 1965), pt 1.

107 Representative of the enormous literature on these subjects are: Larry E. Jones, *German Liberalism and the Dissolution of the Weimar Party System 1918–1933* (Chapel Hill, 1988); and more briefly, Jones ' "The Dying Middle". Weimar Germany and the fragmentation of bourgeois poli-

DAVID BLACKBOURN

tics', *Central European History*, 5 (1972), 23–54; James M. Diehl, *Paramilitary Politics in Weimar Germany* (Bloomington, 1977); Hermann Lebovics, *Social Conservatism and the Middle Classes in Germany 1914–1933* (Princeton, 1969); Walter Struve, *Elites Against Democracy. Leadership Ideals in Bourgeois Political Thought in Germany 1890–1933* (Princeton, 1973); Klaus Fritzsche, *Politische Romantik und Gegenrevolution. Fluchtwege in der Krise der bürgerlichen Gesellschaft: Das Beispiel des Tat-Kreises* (Frankfurt-on-Main, 1976). An excellent overview of many of these developments can be found in Hans Mommsen, 'Die Auflösung des Bürgertums'.

108 On the fragmentation, see Jones, ' "The Dying Middle" '; James C. Hunt, 'The bourgeois middle in German politics, 1871–1933', *Central European History*, 11 (1978), 83–106. On the apolitical politics of local associations, Koshar, *Social Life;* and for parallel attitudes within the Protestant Church, J.R.C. Wright, *"Above parties": the political attitudes of the German Protestant Church leadership 1918–1933* (Oxford, 1974).

109 See Peter Wulf, 'Die Mittelschichten in der Krise der Weimarer Republik 1930–1933', in Karl Holl (ed.), *Wirtschaftskrise und liberale Demokratie* (Göttingen, 1978), 89–102; Jones, *German Liberalism and the Dissolution of the Weimar Party System*, 406ff.

110 See Bernd Weisbrod, *Schwerindustrie in der Weimarer Republik. Interessenpolitik zwischen Stabilisierung und Krise* (Wuppertal, 1978); Reinhard Neebe, *Grossindustrie, Staat und NSDAP 1930–1933* (Göttingen, 1981); Henry A. Turner, *German Big Business and the Rise of Hitler* (Oxford, 1985); David Abraham, *The Collapse of the Weimar Republic: Political Economy and Crisis* (New York, 1987, rev. ed).

111 Richard Hamilton, *Who Voted for Hitler?* (Princeton, 1982); Jürgen Falter, 'Wer verhalf der NSDAP zum Sieg?', *Aus Politik und Zeitgeschichte*, B 28–29 (14 July 1979), 3–21: Thomas Childers, *The Nazi Voter. The Social Foundations of Fascism in Germany, 1919–1933* (Chapel Hill, 1983).

112 Michael H. Kater, *The Nazi Party: A Social Profile of Members and Leaders 1919–1945* (Cambridge, Mass., 1985).

113 In addition to the works cited in the previous two notes, see Jones, ' "The Dying Middle" ', 45–54; Allen, *Nazi Seizure of Power*, pt 1; Koshar, *Social Life*, chs 5–6. See also many of the contributions to two valuable collections of essays: Peter D. Stachura (ed.), *The Nazi Machtergreifung* (London, 1983); Thomas Childers (ed.), *The Formation of the Nazi Constituency, 1919–1933* (Totowa, NJ, 1986).

114 See, for example, Richard Bessel, *Political Violence and the Rise of Nazism: The Stormtroopers in Eastern Germany 1925–34* (London and New Haven, 1984).

115 Theodor Geiger, *Die soziale Schichtung des deutschen Volkes* (Stuttgart, 1932). Geiger's book is one of the earliest and most subtle accounts of the reasons that drew the lower middle class towards Nazism, but it also deals with the established middle classes.

116 In addition to the works cited in note 113, see the excellent local study by Zdenek Zofka, *Die Ausbreitung des Nationalsozialismus auf dem Lande* (Munich, 1979). The work of Michael Kater and others has

44

also helped to revise an earlier view that over-emphasized the role of 'marginal' or 'uprooted' figures among Nazi leaders. Alongside the failed pig-farmer Walter Darré and the failed vacuum-cleaner sales-man Adolf Eichmann we have to set the senior civil servant Wilhelm Frick and the IG Farben chemist Robert Ley. See Kater, *Nazi Party*, 194–5.

117 Perhaps the best guide to the vast literature on interpretations of the Third Reich is Pierre Ayçoberry, *The Nazi Question. An Essay on the Interpretations of National Socialism (1922–1975)* (New York, 1981).

118 Martin Broszat, *The Hitler State* (London, 1981); Mommsen, *Beam-tentum*.

2

Arriving in the upper class: the wealthy business elite of Wilhelmine Germany

Dolores L. Augustine

I

The chauvinist spirit and bombastic, pretentious style associated with the reign of Kaiser Wilhelm II (1888–1918) also found its expression in changes in the mentality of the wealthy business elite. The Wilhelmine upper bourgeoisie may have claimed thrift as a middle-class value, but it lived in ever-growing luxury. After moving from a house by the factory to a mansion in an exclusive residential suburb, purchasing landed estates, and mixing with the nobility at grand festivities, the wealthy businessman had in large part lost contact with his middle-class roots. This reorientation has been seen by many as symptomatic of the decline of the German bourgeoisie. According to this school of thought, the German *Bürgertum* – unlike its British and French counterparts – capitulated in the late nineteenth century to the aristocracy both politically (as exemplified by the coalition of rye and iron) and socially. It thus became 'feudalized'.[1] The German bourgeoisie – along with other segments of German society – failed to play its historic role. And this, so the theory goes, set Germany off on a fateful path of development (the *Sonderweg*) that ended with National Socialism.

But it is not difficult to demonstrate that the feudalization thesis represents a major distortion of the social history of the German bourgeoisie. It fails to recognize the self-confidence and social autonomy of the wealthy business elite, a group that had turned Germany into a world-class economic power and reaped the very great benefits of these successes. This chapter is intended as a contribution to a more general re-evaluation of the ascent of this elite into the upper class in late nineteenth and early twentieth century Germany, focusing on key aspects of the material and social life of its members. The findings presented are part of a larger prosopographic study, comprising a comprehensive quantitative study on the 502 wealthiest businessmen[2] listed in Rudolf Martin's *Yearbook of Millionaires*[3] and an analysis of 200 autobiographies, biographies, public and private papers of a more broadly defined group of Wilhelmine millionaires in business. In addition to trying to determine the extent of feudalization according to widely used indicators of feudalization, we must take a critical look at these indicators and the feudalization model itself. As both David Blackbourn and Hartmut Kaelble have pointed out, the adoption on the part of the bourgeoisie of patterns of behaviour normally associated with the nobility does not necessarily mean a loss of sense of identity; it may instead reflect the tendency of new elites to legitimize their position by incorporating elements of social behaviour used by established elites into their own behaviour. Both argue that the growing social distance between the *haute bourgeoisie* and the middle class is not necessarily the same thing as feudalization, but may instead have led to social isolation. Kaelble also makes the point that many phenomena usually interpreted as forms of imitation of the aristocratic model are in actual fact indicative of a new loyalty to the state, a state which did not solely represent the interests of the pre-industrial elite, but also those of the capitalist bourgeoisie.[4] A social history of the Wilhelmine business elite clearly cannot be reduced to a discussion of the feudalization thesis. Other areas of interest include the relationship of this elite to other sectors of the middle class and bourgeois upper class,[5] social isolation, social barriers, and mechanisms of social distinction.

The approach taken in this chapter to the material life of the Wilhelmine *haute bourgeoisie* is in part inspired by Thorstein Veblen's work on elite behaviour, and in particular his *Theory of the Leisure Class*, first published in 1899. This was not only an exposé of social climbing in *fin-de-siècle* America, but also a work of considerable sociological merit. 'In order to gain and hold the esteem of men,' he wrote, 'it is not sufficient to possess wealth or power. The wealth or power must be put in evidence, for esteem is awarded only on evidence.' The main ways of demonstrating wealth are conspicuous leisure and conspicuous consumption. Entertaining is an important form in which the upper class puts its consumption level on display. It is natural for the standards of taste of a social group whose wealth and power are growing to rise commensurately:

> a fresh advance in conspicuous expenditure is relatively easy; indeed, it takes place almost as a matter of course. In the rare cases where it occurs, a failure to increase one's visible consumption when the means for an increase are at hand is felt in popular apprehension to call for explanation, and unworthy motives of miserliness are imputed to those who fall short in this respect . . . The motive is emulation – the stimulus of an invidious comparison which prompts us to outdo those with whom we are in the habit of classing ourselves. Substantially the same proposition is expressed in the commonplace that each class envies and emulates the class next above it in the social scale, while it rarely compares itself with those below or with those who are considerably in advance.[6]

Part of the Wilhelmine business elite had risen nearly to the level of the wealthiest and most powerful segment of the aristocracy, and was therefore in Veblen's terms logically inclined to compete in terms of standards of living and taste with this group. Another tendency can be observed, however. The rising European bourgeoisie, confronted with a society not organized according to the principle of achievement, but rather according to the principle of birthright, developed a code of values in opposition to those of the nobility. In mid-nineteenth century Germany, these bourgeois values included rationality, punctuality, cleanliness, honesty, and thrift (much complicated by the fact that parts of the nobility – making a virtue out of a necessity – also propagated an ideology of anti-materialism). The very rapid rise of the bourgeoisie in Germany did not extinguish this sense of being different from the pre-industrial elite. Thus, there was a tension between the old bourgeois values and the new tendency to 'emulate the class next above it in the social scale', the aristocracy, or to be more exact, the wealthiest segment of the aristocracy.

The following discussion of values and lifestyle will focus first on changing residential patterns and social segregation, the exodus to the suburbs and beyond, the prevalence of the second home, and the significance of the purchase of castles, manors, and landed estates. Attention then shifts (pp. 56–73) to social life in two major centres of business wealth – Berlin and Rhineland-Westphalia.

The important areas here are the patterns of social networking and friendship, the extent of social obligations and frequency of social events, the relative importance of family versus social life, the level of expenditures for entertainment and conspicuous consumption, and the way this class presented itself to society.

II

The Wilhelmine era marks a period of major change in the residential patterns of the business elite. For much of the nineteenth century, a businessman's living quarters and his offices or factories were often located in close proximity to one another or even in the same building, thus allowing the constant supervision of employees. With the growing bureaucratization of business enterprises and the resulting weakening of patriarchal structures, management took over the function of direct supervision, thus allowing the owner of the company or head of the corporation to live elsewhere. Secondly, the increasing level of noise, filth, and stench that accompanied the growth of plant capacity made life next to the factories unbearable. General levels of pollution were also rising in the inner cities.[7] A third factor involved was the difference in outlook between the generation of the company founders and the generations of the sons and grandsons. The generation that built up the company was in many cases not used to middle-class comfort, and, after the years of struggle, could view with pride the smoke billowing out of the smoke-stacks. The next generations had a greater sense of economic security, and were not content to make do. This transition could take place within one generation, as in the case of the heavy industrialist August Thyssen, a banker's son who built up an industrial empire and moved to the country in 1903.[8] Accounts of moving to the outskirts of town are legion in autobiographies and biographies of members of the economic elite, peaking around the turn of the century.[9] This trend was channelled in some cities by property developers, who opened up suburban 'colonies', where the wealthy bought tracts of land and built, at first, summer homes. With the extension of train and tram lines out into the suburbs, the wealthy began to build imposing homes they could live in all year round.

Berlin had the largest suburbs of any city on the Continent. The wealthy business elite of Berlin was heavily concentrated in Grunewald.[10] City life none the less did not lose its appeal for this class everywhere. By contrast, Hamburg's wealthy apparently did not move to suburbs in nearly such great numbers. The great patrician families of Hamburg lived mainly in the fairly centrally located districts of Harvestehude and Rotherbaum. Originally living in the old part of the city, where narrow town houses were crowded along unhealthy canals, the wealthy citizens of Hamburg adopted the custom of spending the summer in a country home in the first half of the nineteenth century. Many turn-of-the-century businessmen had country homes near Hamburg. In Essen, wealthy businessmen lived mainly in the city. Exclusive residential areas were also to be found in the centres of Cologne and Frankfurt. In Berlin, the 'Tiergarten' became a virtual bankers' quarter. Bankers apparently needed to be able to get to their offices more quickly than other businessmen. A few bankers (in Berlin, Carl Fürstenberg and Hermann Rosenberg, in Munich Wilhelm von Finck) still lived in their own banks – an old bankers' custom.[11] In Berlin, it was not uncommon for a multimillionaire to live in an apartment. Of fifty-three very wealthy Berlin businessmen, twenty-five leased apartments. Obviously these were magnificent dwellings, consisting on the whole of 10 to 15 rooms and costing 5,000 to 15,000 Marks in rent per year. Several also had summer villas in the suburbs.[12] Nevertheless, it is interesting that a group that could have lived in a mansion in the suburbs would have chosen to live in an apartment because of the central location. Carl Fürstenberg moved during the course of his life a number of times back and forth between central Berlin and Grunewald, torn between the two alternatives. Urban living meant a short trip to work and an intensive social life. The city was not lacking in fashionable, elegant residential areas. A particular prestige was undoubtedly attached to buying the palatial home of one of the many aristocrats whose turning financial fortunes had forced them to leave the city. On the other hand, the suburbs offered quiet, clear air and pleasant scenery. At first, the summer home in Grunewald was an attractive solution for many, especially since it was important not to miss out on social events during the (winter) 'season'. Gradually, however, Grunewald became the place to live year-round, as ever more millionaires moved there, thus increasing the prestige of Grunewald and making it possible to conduct an active social life there.[13]

The growth of exclusive residential areas led to a high degree of social segregation. This was part of a more general process going on in German cities, involving the lower middle and working classes as well. Grunewald was dominated by wealthy businessmen, with a sprinkling of prominent intellectuals, artists, and the like. The Tiergarten district in Berlin and Harvestehude in Hamburg were largely upper-class areas. Some members of the lower middle class lived in Harvestehude as well, though only the very wealthy lived directly on the Alster lake. In the Cologne suburb of Marienburg – founded by a developer – businessmen constituted about a third of the mansion owners, with retired persons and other upper-middle-class professions making up most of the rest. The residential patterns of the wealthiest segment of the Wilhelmine business elite show it becoming part of the bourgeois upper class. Largely absent from these exclusive neighbourhoods was the aristocracy.[14]

Many very wealthy businessmen of the Wilhelmine era had summer homes out of reach of the cities they worked in. Bavaria was particularly popular. A few had houses in Italy (for example, banker Georg von Siemens, merchant Eduard Arnhold, and prominent metal industrialist Wilhelm Merton). These were secluded vacation spots intended above all for the family's enjoyment. Such an expenditure reveals a profound shift in the value system of this class. Increasingly, capitalists enjoyed what they viewed as the fruits of their labour without negating the work ethic. It is typical that the businessman brought work along on his holiday, had his business correspondence sent to him, answered letters, and that he had to cut his holiday short to take care of matters that came up unexpectedly.[15]

Much has been written about the luxurious homes of German businessmen in this period. The tendency on the part of historians has been to overestimate the significance of aristocratization. Art historians and architects on the other hand argue that the wealthy bourgeoisie instrumentalized the castle and historicism (the architectural use of historic styles, as in neo-Classical, neo-Baroque, and neo-Gothic architecture) for its own purposes. The bourgeois castle, whether a modern imitation or – more rarely – an authentic medieval or Baroque structure, represented an attempt to outdo the aristocracy according to the latter's standards. The wealthy, responding to the 'stimulus of invidious comparison', incorporated into their mansions other elements of aristocratic architecture and lifestyle as well: the sheer size, the impressive façade and often monumental style, the park, luxurious furnishings, a large staff of servants.[16] These 'aristocratic' forms, aimed at upper-class peers, had a certain legitimizing effect. In addition, the fortress-like appearance of these mansions, the turrets and parapets, were part of an almost crude demonstration of power.[17] The Renaissance villa also had a major impact on Wilhelmine architecture. The villa in neo-Classical or neo-Baroque style contributed to the businessman's image as a cultivated person. Historicism was also an 'architecture of domination'. Renaissance copies of ancient villas advertised that their owners felt as mighty as the ruling class of ancient Rome and Greece; Wilhelmine copies of Renaissance villas had a similar function.[18]

Some historians have failed to realize that German businessmen borrowed style to achieve their own goals. This is particularly true of work on the best-known – but none the less untypical – businessman's mansion in Germany, the Villa Hügel. Knut Borchardt sees the Krupps' move from a house near their factories in Essen to the Villa Hügel in 1873 as part of a conscious or subconscious attempt to bolster their power by creating a mystique such as that of the princely courts of the eighteenth century. This thesis seems somewhat far-fetched in the light of the above discussion on the separation of the work-place and place of residence in the economic elite. In the same volume of essays, devoted entirely to the Villa Hügel, Michael Stürmer suggests parallels to princely residences as far as size and grandeur are concerned. The Krupp mansion contained as many guest rooms and suites as the castles of the great Junker families. It filled the visitor with the same feeling of awe as a visit to a princely court a century earlier, he observes.[19] But Stürmer seems to forget that the Krupps, as arms manufacturers, were very dependent on state contracts, and thus had to present themselves to the old guard (ministers and high officials, generals, and foreign diplomats, and the Kaiser in particular) as social equals. In addition, the very unusual amount of entertaining in the Krupp household called for a house of unusual dimensions.

The social function of the businessman's villa was obvious to contemporary observers. The architect Hermann Muthesius wrote in 1910 that while the English country house was an outwardly unpretentious house built to meet the needs of the inhabitants, the exterior of the German villa was ostentatious, intended to impress the passer-by.[20] The homes of most members of the wealthy business elite were built on an entirely different scale from that of the

Villa Hügel. Businessmen were none the less generally willing to invest large sums of money in housing. While the value of the home of the Cologne businessman Gustav von Mallinckrodt was estimated at a fairly modest 222,000 Marks in 1901, Gustav Adt invested over 1 million Marks in the renovation of a castle in 1911–13. The heavy industrialist August Thyssen offered 300,000 Marks for the castle 'Schloss Landsberg' and 80,000 Marks for the land around it; it is unclear what he actually paid. According to his granddaughter, Emil Rathenau, the founder of the major electrical company AEG, refused for more than a year to move into his new house, completed in 1912, because he was angry at himself for having spent so much money on it.[21] An *haut-bourgeois* standard had established itself in this class. Some wealthy businessmen stressed the importance of thrift and simplicity in their lives, yet these values had no visible impact on houses. One is hard pressed to come up with an example of a small, middle-class house owned by a very wealthy entrepreneur of the Wilhelmine period.[22]

Thyssen, a man dedicated to his firm to the exclusion of all else, fought the aristocratic tendencies of his children with great tenacity, from his son's membership in the aristocratic Union Club to his children's efforts to persuade him to establish an entail and ask to be granted the title of 'Baron'. None the less, he bought the old, but fairly small castle Schloss Landsberg in 1903, renovated it and resided there. Otherwise rather unprepossessing, he apparently deemed the purchase of a castle necessary to underline his social status. In private very careful with money, he 'knew how to put his wealth on public display like a prince', according to banker Hjalmar Schacht, and used his castle as a backdrop for elegant parties. Though Thyssen was a man almost fanatically dedicated to the business world, he could not ignore the importance of certain status symbols.[23]

In the mansions of wealthy businessmen, rooms for guests were seldom more numerous than rooms for private use. Nevertheless, these homes often contained large reception halls, dining rooms, and ballrooms. Many businessmen could receive 100 or more guests at a time, for example the Berlin bankers Hermann Wallich and Carl Fürstenberg, Berlin department store owner Oskar Tietz, the Frankfurt chemical industrialist Carl von Weinberg, and the Hamburg bankers Albert Warburg and Max von Schinckel.[24] Especially in the suburbs, a style of architecture came into fashion around 1905 that stressed the private sphere. These mansions, modelled on English country houses, faced the garden, instead of the street (as was the case with the 'villa'), and the rooms were very individualized, not interconnected like those of the villa, and were thus not well suited for entertaining. Whereas the villa had an imposing façade, the 'country home' did not. Though most wealthy businessmen still lived in villas, it is still interesting to observe this trend towards a more private lifestyle.[25]

Thus, lifestyle in the business elite cannot be reduced to a façade intended for the outside world. The mansion was also a home intended for private use – and this is especially true of English-style country houses built in the suburbs. Going far beyond the middle-class ideal of a home of one's own, wealthy men's villas and summer houses were the ultimate luxury in this class. The prevalence of the summer residence was part of an elite lifestyle virtually unknown even in large parts of the German upper middle class. This elite lifestyle meant that they were cut off from the life of the masses in a way their middle-class forebears were not. Richard J. Evans writes for example of the custom of spending the summer in the country: 'Virtually all the nuisances which afflicted Hamburg, from rotten food and sour milk, smoke and dust, animal smells and ordure, vermin, parasites, and rats, were at their most unbearable in the summer months. The wealthiest taxpayers did little to improve the city's environment until they were forced to, because they could always escape from it when it became unbearable.'[26]

The purchase of landed estates, including East Elbian *Rittergüter*, by wealthy commoners had become widespread in the late nineteenth century. Almost a quarter of the 502 wealthiest businessmen in the *Yearbook of Millionaires* who were not of old aristocratic lineage were big landowners. None the less, only about 6 per cent of the sons of these businessmen became fulltime landowners,[27] which means that these families were not being assimilated into the landowning class at any appreciable rate. Only a very few families retired in the Wilhelmine era from business life to move to the country to take up the life of a great estate owner. Most landowners of the business elite had a pragmatic attitude, seeing their estates primarily as vacation spots, status symbols, or investment objects. Many bourgeois landowners employed the same rational techniques used in their businesses in the running of their farms. The Munich banker Wilhelm von Finck, who lived in his bank in Munich, conducting business eleven hours a day and only visiting his farm on Sundays, took pleasure in buying run-down farms and turning them into profitable enterprises. This did not lead the family out of the business world. His son August, who ran the family bank and owned large tracts of land in Bavaria, was conjectured at the time of his death in 1980 to be the wealthiest man in the Federal Republic. One branch of the Siemens family had been landowners for generations. Both Wilhelm von Siemens, who ran the Siemens Corporation and Georg von Siemens, a director of the Deutsche Bank, owned estates. Georg von Siemens was very much interested in increasing farm production on his *Rittergut*, which he had inherited from his father. There are exceptions. The Jewish merchant Eduard Arnhold's attachment to his land reveals a mystical, romantic ideology that is perhaps indicative of a deeper inability to accept his own social and ethnic identity. The Leipzig publisher Alfred Ackermann adopted some feudal attitudes, trying to maintain a patriarchal relationship with the farm hands on his estate 'Gundorf'.[28] But these were far from normal cases.

Berlin bank directors often spent the summer in the country, and often invited guests. Hildegard Wallich has the following to say about the motives of her in-laws, retired bank director Hermann Wallich and his wife, in purchasing a *Rittergut*:

> He [Hermann Wallich] would have preferred to take account of practical considerations and wanted an estate that would bring in profits. But Mum [Mrs Wallich] wanted it to be as close to Berlin as possible so that guests would not have to spend the night . . . The house should also be comfortable and 'fit for a lord', with a lovely park, as was befitting of a bank director.

In the end, they settled on a beautiful *Rittergut* with poor soil. It was run by an overseer.[29] The manors owned by the banker Paul von Schwabach and the heavy industrialist Fritz von Friedländer-Fuld provided an appropriate setting for the entertainment of an exclusive group of friends. Arthur von Gwinner, a director of the Deutsche Bank, writes of the decision to buy land: 'Finally we grew weary of holiday trips and stays in overfilled inns, and longed for land of our own.' They found an estate: 'It was our beloved Krumbke, which came to occupy a place in all our hearts, whose magnificent park and lovely woods persuaded us to take it.'[30] According to police reports, Arthur Gilka, partner in the Gilka distillery in Berlin, purchased his *Rittergut* as an investment and for his own enjoyment.[31] In sum, true feudalization, in the sense of moving to a *Rittergut* and retiring from business, was rare. Secondary aristocratization, that is, the adoption of feudal values (mystical attachment to the soil and the adoption of a feudal attitude towards farm employees, perhaps love of farming as well) were not widespread in this class either. Landownership was above all an important way of documenting wealth and social status in a country in which industrial wealth was generally not very old. In addition, the motives of personal enjoyment and rational invest-ment played a role.

III

To understand the social world of wealthy Wilhelmine business-men, it is important to ask who they associated with, how they conducted their social lives, and how they presented themselves to the world. Here, two regions – Berlin and the Western Prussian provinces of the Rhineland and Westphalia – will serve as contrast-ing examples. Entrepeneurs from these two major economic centres each made up roughly a quarter of the 502 wealthiest businessmen in the *Yearbook of Millionaires*.[32] The feudalization thesis rests in large part on evidence from Berlin and Rhineland-Westphalia, making these two regions especially interesting for our purposes.[33] The two groups represent very different sections of the wealthy business elite. Whereas Jews predominated among business millionaires in Berlin,[34] their numbers were hardly significant in the Rhine Province and Westphalia, where Protestants constituted 68 per cent of the wealthiest businessmen, and Catholics 22 per cent.[35] Almost half of the wealthiest Berlin businessmen were bankers, 18 per cent were merchants, and a third industrialists. By contrast, bankers and merchants made up only 14 per cent and 3 per cent of the wealthiest businessmen of Rhineland-Westphalia. Among the wealthy industrialists of this region, heavy industry played the greatest role, making up a third of the group, followed by textiles, clothing, and leather with a total of 17 per cent. Quantification is not possible as far as social life goes. The major sources here are autobiographies and biographies of wealthy businessmen.[36]

On the whole, wealthy Berlin businessmen associated mostly with other businessmen. The banker Carl Fürstenberg wrote an autobiography which contains lengthy passages on his social life. At his home, a focal point of Berlin society, the Berlin business world met and mixed with high society. He consciously tried to expand his circle of business friends. The people Carl Fürstenberg termed as 'friends' were mostly bankers, but included a few industrialists, and he had many acquaintances within the business community. His closest friends were Fritz von Friedländer-Fuld, Albert Ballin, director of the HAPAG shipping line, and Therese Simon-Sonnemann, owner of the *Frankfurter Zeitung*. Paul Schwabach also belonged to this circle. The Fürstenbergs thus brought a good many businessmen together socially.[37]

Eduard Arnhold, the department store owners Berthold Israel and Oskar Tietz, the bankers Paul Wallich and Weisbach, the Berlin speculator Max Esser, and Walther Rathenau, the son of the founder of the AEG – all Jews or converted Jews – also had numerous business friends.[38] The bourgeois orientation of Adolf Salomonsohn, who rose from humble, provincial beginnings to head the Disconto-Gesellschaft, a major Berlin bank, was particularly strong. His best friends were various fellow proprietors of the Disconto-Gesellschaft and the heavy industrialist Emil Kirdorf. At a reception held by the principal of the Disconto-Gesellschaft, Adolph von Hansemann, attended by officers and dignitaries, he is supposed to have said, 'in reality I am the grandest of those gathered here, for I have a value of my own, though not a single medal graces my dress-coat.'[39] Rentier Willy Ritter Liebermann von Wahlendorf, of a Jewish textile industrialist family, conveys the impression that there was an exclusive, close-knit Jewish *haute bourgeoisie* in Berlin, bound together by ties of friendship and marriage.[40] Turning to non-Jewish businessmen, Wilhelm von Siemens also associated mainly with other businessmen. Banker Carl von der Heydt had some ties with bankers, although they were not particularly strong. A director of the Deutsche Bank, Georg von Siemens, who was related to the owners of the Siemens Corporation, was something of a non-Jewish equivalent of Salomonsohn, avoiding contact with the aristocracy as far as he could.[41]

The everyday life of Berlin businessmen was generally characterized by daily contacts with other businessmen. They met for lunch at the Club of Berlin, which acquired the nickname 'Millionaires' Club', or at certain restaurants.[42] It is difficult to say in this class where a business relationship ended and socializing or friendship began. Friedländer-Fuld discussed both business matters and personal matters, such as his unsuccessful search for a wife, with Carl Fürstenberg. They parted over a business quarrel, but Fürstenberg

wrote that he regretted losing Friedländer-Fuld's personal friendship because of this.[43]

The extent of social contacts between the business elite and the
traditional Prussian elite in Berlin was particularly striking to
contemporary observers. One historian has seen this phenomenon
as the product of Jewish overcompensation – an attempt to overcome feelings of inadequacy by gaining the acceptance of the
'Junkers', resulting in the capitulation of the Jewish bourgeoisie
to the old guard.[44] Upon closer inspection, however, it becomes
evident that the Jewish elite of Berlin never really lost its sense of
identity at all, and that it cultivated connections which could be
mobilized to further its economic and political interests. Also, as
contemporary observers noted, aristocratic guests often fulfilled a
decorative function:

> for some, it is still an especially elevating feeling to surround
> oneself with military uniforms and noblemen. It flatters one's
> vanity to have Prince X and Count Y at one's home . . .
> Others use officers as fillers, as an attractive garnish. They
> invite them because they are clever and can dance well.[45]

According to Jules Huret, Jewish hostesses in Berlin usually invited
two or three officers to parties 'out of snobbishness'.[46]

A number of businessmen had personal contact with Kaiser
Wilhelm II, and thus enjoyed the opportunity to influence
decision-making directly at the highest level. These included Max
Esser, the Hamburg bankers Max Warburg and Max von
Schinckel, the director of the Northern German Lloyd, Heinrich
Wiegand, the owner of the Schultheiss Brewery in Berlin, Richard
Roesicke, Emil and Walther Rathenau, Fritz von Friedländer-Fuld,
and the Berlin bankers James Simon, Franz von Mendelssohn,
Paul Schwabach, Arthur von Gwinner, and Carl Fürstenberg, and
Eduard Arnhold. The heavy industrialist Carl Ferdinand Baron
von Stumm-Halberg, Albert Ballin, and Friedrich Alfred Krupp
were particularly intimate friends or personal advisers of the
Kaiser. The historian Isabel Hull, indeed, believes that Krupp
and Ballin had a good deal of influence over Wilhelm. She writes:
'The Kaiser regarded Krupp as his industrial counterpart, a kind
of bourgeois king whose meaning to Germany's strength, internal
and external, was practically as important as his own.'[47] Apart
from these three, however, businessmen were not part of Wilhelm
II's immediate entourage. And contact with the Kaiser did not

necessarily secure an entrée to court circles. Jewish businessmen in particular usually met Wilhelm II at hunts or luncheons, or received him in their homes, but they were not invited to court receptions or balls. Admiral Fritz Hollmann was one of the few members of the entourage who genuinely enjoyed the company of businessmen.[48] Even a titled non-Jewish banker such as Carl von der Heydt found these social barriers impenetrable:

> As commoners, we were excluded from the court, which means that we could not be part of court society, by which is meant the exclusive circle of the high nobility which congregated at court, the diplomats, the highest court officials and a few very wealthy noble houses.[49]

Carl Fürstenberg's son Hans gained the impression that the divisions between the bourgeois society of Berlin and court society grew deeper in the years before the outbreak of the First World War.[50]

A few bourgeois millionaires, of course, did gain entrance to court circles, for example the Krupps, Adolph von Hansemann of the Disconto-Gesellschaft, the Cologne metal industrialist Theodor Guilleaume, and Heinrich Wiegand.[51] Perhaps the most unusual case is that of Walther Rathenau, who was a welcomed guest in the cultivated salons of 'more European than bureaucratic orientation', where the circle around Empress Augusta congregated and which 'set the tone' at the court around the turn of the century. Count Kessler, a friend of Rathenau's, saw Rathenau's social and intellectual powers as the decisive factor in his successes here, whereas Alfred Kerr, who also knew Rathenau personally, believed it was his wealth that gained him an entrée into these lofty spheres.[52] For the great majority of businessmen, however, these circles and the court were entirely inaccessible.

In Carl Fürstenberg's home, high officials, influential personalities, and diplomats – German ambassadors abroad and representatives of foreign powers with which Fürstenberg's bank did business – were frequent visitors. Members of the traditional Prussian elite were rarely present at his parties unless they were valuable connections for the bank. Two Field Marshals fall into the non-utilitarian category, but this may be seen as part of a clever public relations strategy aimed at cultivating ties with an elite network which as a whole occupied a key position in political decision-making in Germany.[53]

Two other very wealthy Berlin Jews, Paul Schwabach and Fritz von Friedländer-Fuld, socialized with some of the politically best-informed aristocrats in the capital – ministers, state secretaries, ambassadors.[54] The information they picked up doubtlessly helped them to keep an eye on events at home and abroad that could have a major impact on their business ventures. To gain acceptance, they had to refrain from voicing opinions unpopular in these circles. 'The Friedländer salon, which took pains to avoid appearing to be a political salon, was a neutral territory where very different influential figures met.'[55] It seems doubtful, however, that Schwabach and Friedländer-Fuld sacrificed deep-felt political beliefs to the God of social ambition. Both were far from being radical: the former was conservative, the latter leaned more towards the National Liberal Party. If anything, this contact with persons in powerful positions gave them a chance to influence policy-making directly. Paul Schwabach passed on information concerning French and British foreign policy to the Foreign Office, and was entrusted with small diplomatic missions.[56] On one occasion, negotiations between the Foreign Office and the French Ambassador were conducted on Friedländer-Fuld's estate. Milly von Friedländer-Fuld (Fritz's wife) put the Foreign Office in contact with friends and relatives of hers abroad.[57]

Admittedly, social ambitions were at work here as well. Among the guests of the Friedländer-Fulds were also officers and the scions of the great Silesian landowning families – nobles whose friendship hardly could have furthered business interests. Lady Susan Townley recounts Milly von Friedländer-Fuld's unfulfilled social aspirations:

> But she could not force the portals of Berlin society, not even though she added a covered tennis-court and a riding-school to the already numerous amenities of her beautiful house on the Pariser Platz. She climbed and climbed, but when I left Berlin she had not succeeded in reaching the top, although to accomplish her end she had recourse to all sorts of expedients.

She is reported to have finally conquered the pinnacle of Berlin society on the eve of the First World War.[58]

We know all too little about the content of some relationships between Jewish millionaires and 'Junkers' in Berlin. Eduard Arnhold socialized with ambassadors, ministers, other high officials, 'dukes', and 'princes'. Banker Eugen Gutmann often invited officers to parties, as did the notorious stock market speculator Max Esser. Merchant banker Weisbach's guests included government officials.[59]

Non-Jewish businessmen in Berlin also mixed with the traditional, pre-industrial elite. Banker Carl von der Heydt socialized mainly with high officials and officers. He admiringly referred to the officer corps as an 'educational force'. At balls in his house, almost all the male dancers were in uniform. Wilhelm von Siemens, owner of the Siemens electrical company, associated with senior officials, officers, and members of the high aristocracy. His brother and associate, Arnold von Siemens, had social contact with chancellor Bernhard von Bülow, General Field Marshal Helmuth von Moltke, and Count Otto Schlippenbach.[60] Von der Heydt's admiration of the officer corps and the apparent absence of useful business connections here would seem to indicate that he genuinely sought the approval of the old guard. In socializing with Bülow and Moltke, the Siemens, by contrast, were almost certainly courting the state, not the Junker class.

The strength of ties between the worlds of business and culture was a striking characteristic of Berlin society, and of Jewish circles in particular. Jews of wealthy business families had played a major role in the great intellectual salons of the era 1780–1806.[61] In a number of Jewish families, the two realms were intertwined.[62] Typical of Fürstenberg's home was the large number of artists and intellectuals among his guests. Before his marriage, he often visited the home of Ernst Dohm, the editor-in-chief of the *Kladderadatsch*, a weekly known for its political satire, and was on friendly terms with Dohm's wife Hedwig, a well-known writer and advocate of female emancipation, and their daughters and sons-in-law, who were involved in artistic and literary pursuits. Fürstenberg was also a frequent guest of theatre director Adolf l'Arronge, whose home was at the centre of Berlin's theatre and literary life. Fürstenberg met his wife Aniela in the circle dominated by theatre critic Paul Lindau and his brother Rudolf, who was a writer and press secretary in the Foreign Office. After their marriage, Aniela Fürstenberg cultivated ties with some of the most prominent artists, composers, musicians, writers, scholars, scientists and architects of the Wilhemine period – among others, composer Richard Strauss, theatre director Max Reinhardt, writer Gerhart Hauptmann, and bacteriologist Robert Koch. According to Fürstenberg, his wife 'came as close to founding a salon as was possible in that era in Berlin'. Aniela tried to stimulate conversations on art, literature, and music at formal dinners by inviting outstanding conversationalists, such as the poet Gabriele Reuter and the pacifist Bertha von Suttner, and by placing scholars, journalists, and artists next to industrialists and government officials at the table.[63] This may have helped to mediate between the very disparate value systems and conventions of the bourgeois and noble guests. None the less, the genuineness of the Fürstenbergs' cultural interests is underlined by the fact that they socialized with controversial figures of this period such as Hauptmann and von Suttner.

The list of cultivated Berlin businessmen's homes – mostly Jewish – is long. The banking Mendelssohns (a branch of the family of composer Felix Mendelssohn-Bartholdy) kept up the family's musical tradition. Franz and Robert von Mendelssohn and Robert's wife Guillietta, an Italian, played instruments, performing occasionally at social gatherings with well-known musicians. Franz was a close friend of Josef Joachim, a violin virtuoso, and Joachim's former wife, the singer Alma Weiss. The actress Eleonora Duse stayed with Robert and Giulietta von Mendelssohn when in Berlin. Therese Simon-Sonnemann, the owner of the *Frankfurter Zeitung* and AEG director Felix Deutsch and his wife also had contact with the world of music.[64] Berlin was also a centre of art patronage, where wealthy patrons mixed socially with artists, for example in the home of artists Reinhold and Sabine Lepsius and the salon of Félice Bernstein, the widow of an economics professor. Many of the wealthy businessmen who supported the arts were Jewish, among others James Simon, Eduard Arnhold, Eugen Gutmann (a co-founder of the Deutsche Bank), Oskar Hainauer, the engineering industrialist Julius Freund, Franz and Robert von Mendelssohn, the heavy industrialist Oskar Huldschinsky, the bankers Markus Kappel, and Rudolf Mosse.[65] Amy Israel (née Salomon), the English-born wife of department store-owner Berthold Israel, cultivated the friendship of actors, musicians, and intellectuals. Very well-read, she 'terrified the more sedate wives of businessmen by quoting from contemporary French poets; she signed herself "Aimé" '.[66] Her son Wilfrid was a frequent guest in the house of Albert Einstein, who moved to Berlin in 1914. Banker Paul Wallich, a converted Jew, was a bibliophile who owned an unusually complete collection of works of German literature along with a good deal on Prussian history. His social circles included the poet and officer Fritz von Unruh, the daughter of painter Max Liebermann, several actors, feminist writer Hedwig Dohm, and the wife of writer Thomas Mann. At the stag dinners of the banker Weisbach, bankers mingled with high officials, men of learning, and artists. Publisher Samuel Fischer's strong ties with the most outstanding intellectual and literary circles of Berlin were a professional necessity.[67]

AEG founder Emil Rathenau grew up in an *haut-bourgeois* Jewish milieu in Berlin which was characterized by 'elegance', 'an active social life', and 'learning'. Rathenau turned his back on this world, and from the 1880s, when he was building up his empire, hardly found time for activities outside of his work. The theatre (aside from light entertainment), literature, art, and music meant nothing to him. He was rather unsociable. His wife Mathilde (née Nachmann), born into the same segment of Jewish society as her husband, was herself interested in art and music, and her husband's spartan mentality caused her great suffering. Her granddaughter went so far as to write that Mathilde Rathenau went through 'all the stages of embitterment, loneliness and desperation'.[68] Her son Walther returned so to speak to the world of his grandparents, but then outgrew it, becoming a unique figure in Wilhelmine society, a businessman-philosopher who, though he did not convert, occupied a position of great distinction at court, in business circles, and among intellectuals. It would be futile to attempt a complete catalogue even of his best-known, so numerous were they. In this connection Maximilian Harden, critical intellectual and journalist, should be mentioned, because it was Rathenau who brought Harden together with businessmen such as Carl Fürstenberg, banker Fritz Andreae, Felix and Lili Deutsch, Hermann Rosenberg, heavy industrialists Emil Kirdorf and Hugo Stinnes, and Albert Ballin.[69]

Turning to non-Jewish businessmen, Carl von der Heydt was also interested in cultural life. An art collector, he received artists, men of learning, and writers such as Rainer Maria Rilke, Hermann Sudermann, the sculptor Georg Kolbe, and the museum director Wilhelm von Bode in his home, and his balls included interludes for short recitals or literary recitations. 'And yet these interests were far from giving our house its characteristic stamp,' he admitted. The banker Fritz Andreae, married to Walther Rathenau's sister, was a patron of the arts and scholarship.

An exception to this pattern is the (non-Jewish) Deutsche Bank director Carl Klönne. Of middle-class background, he remained 'simple and unpretentious', was interested only in his profession, and had no hobbies. Intellectual interests also did not necessarily have an impact on social life, as can be seen with the example of Salomonsohn, who was Jewish. An avid reader, he conducted autodidactic studies of wide-ranging subjects, such as the philosophy of Immanuel Kant, military science, geography, law, and natural science. These interests remained quite private, however.[70]

Ties with the non-business bourgeois upper class appear to have been mostly confined to scholars, intellectuals, journalists, and government officials, and were thus closely linked with the cultural interests of businessmen on the one hand and with attempts to influence officialdom on the other. There are exceptions. Rudolf Mosse's friends included the prominent doctor and left-liberal politician Rudolf Virchow and the parliamentarians Traeger and Rickert. Wilhelm von Siemens' guests included an occasional doctor or engineer. Oskar Tietz, who in 1911 owned a fortune of roughly 25 million Marks, had started business as the owner of a small shop. A shift in the family's social life took place in the 1890s, coinciding with a move to a wealthy area of Munich, then to Berlin. While the family's guests had formerly included visiting manufacturers and poor Jewish students and soldiers, the Tietz family now associated with politicians, lawyers, big industrialists, bankers, and journalists. The wealthy elite of Berlin had clearly lost virtually all ties with the middle class proper.[71]

For most, social life in Berlin typically involved a heavy burden of social obligations, daily outside contacts, and major expenditure on entertainment. Social competition had grown quite keen in the Imperial capital. Large-scale capitalists had to stay on a social merry-go-round that was turning faster and faster or risk losing business connections and influence on decision-making. The Fürstenbergs held a weekly formal reception, received guests on a more informal basis every afternoon, and went to dinner parties virtually every night when not themselves giving a party. Most society women were 'at home' on a particular day of the week. The Siemens brothers seem to have seen their social obligations primarily as an onerous burden. Intimidated by the more sophisticated of his guests, Wilhelm von Siemens felt ill at ease at the magnificent festivities arranged by his wife.[72] Arnold von Siemens wrote to his brother in 1906, 'Nothing exciting has been going on here; the social season is in full swing, pleasantly interrupted at the moment by the official mourning for the King of Denmark. The young girls think differently of it, though.'[73] Marie von Bunsen wrote about Arnold von Siemens: 'He was polite and friendly to all his guests, but he probably took little pleasure in them.'[74]

Nevertheless, the charming, sophisticated host or hostess was common in this class. Paul Wallich's father, the retired banker Hermann Wallich, was according to his daughter-in-law an entertaining host and owner of a wine cellar of city-wide fame. The prominent role of the women in social life was characteristic in these circles. Not every partner or director was personally responsible for representing the company socially. This 'division of labour' within the company depended a great deal on the social abilities of the businessman's wife. These women presented themselves to the world as *grandes dames* – charming, ostentatious, and arrogant. They could afford to be eccentric. Aniela Fürstenberg, described by a contemporary as 'aristocratic, with an air of superiority',[75] took delight in organizing social functions that bore the stamp of her personality. Amy Israel was a similar figure:

> No quiet bluestocking, Amy had no compunction about displaying the Israels' great wealth. The Israels entertained in the formal style which Berlin Jewry believed was English, with a butler and a team of other servants. Artists, opera singers and diplomats, as well as business friends, were always Amy's guests on her birthday, 1 January, when she wore her favourite emerald necklace. She was an eccentric rather than an elegant woman, one of the first to wear trousers.[76]

The wife of publisher Samuel Fischer was, according to her daughter, another great Berlin hostess:

> As the heart of the large publishing house, she for many years stood in the centre of Berlin's intellectual and cultural life. Her activities and her personal aura were probably similar to those of the famous women of the Romantic movement, who were vivid models for her. Our house on Edener Street became in this way the home of the family of authors.[77]

The police reported of Milly von Friedländer-Fuld: 'Frau Friedländer is an elegant woman-of-the-world, kind – when it suits her; her demeanour is not far removed from arrogance, but she knows how to fascinate her guests.'[78] Léonie von Schwabach was described by a contemporary as 'the most charming of women'. Only with her help was her husband Paul able to conquer a place in society.[79] An intimate of Kaiser Wilhelm II wrote of her: 'She treated other women with extreme politeness, but with a mixture of disdain and of contempt that was most interesting to watch.' The same observer wrote of Ellen von Siemens:

> She is one of Berlin's greatest *élégantes*, and is to be met in the most fashionable circles of the capital . . . Her pretty, smart figure can be seen on the race-courses and on first nights at fashionable theatres, as well as at Court balls, where she was admitted by the special order of the Emperor, with whom she is a great favourite. Frau Siemens gives receptions that are considered events of the winter season.[80]

These women clearly felt themselves to be part of an elite, and they presented themselves to the world as such.

A great deal of money was spent on entertaining and conspicuous consumption in Berlin. Around the turn of the century, a society matron told the French journalist Jules Huret that the German upper class was spending three times as much on travel, pleasure, comfort, and formal attire as it had ten or fifteen years earlier.[81] An intimate of the Kaiser attributed this development to Wilhelm II's attitudes:

> The Emperor's broadness of view resulted in Berlin becoming like Paris, the only passport necessary to obtain a leading part in its entertainments and enjoyments being the possession of an unlimited amount of money and perfect knowledge of the art of spending it with advantage to oneself and to others.[82]

Expensive clothes, Parisian fashions in particular, were popular among members of the wealthy Berlin bourgeoisie. Oysters and caviar on toast and the finest vintage wines were served.[83] The wedding of Friedländer-Fuld's daughter 'was one of the most sumptuous that has ever been witnessed in Berlin.'[84]

Even thrift was used with calculation in this wealthy Berlin milieu. One variation might be termed 'ideological' or 'outward' parsimony. Werner Weisbach, son of a Berlin banker, contrasts Walther Rathenau's elegant, dandified way of dressing and luxurious lifestyle with his spartan pose. On one occasion, Rathenau slapped Weisbach on the shoulder and told him, 'one must be simple, my young friend, simplicity is one of the important things in life'. Fürstenberg called an unnamed Berlin millionaire who claimed to lead a 'simple, middle-class' life an *'Einfachheits-Protz'* (simplicity show-off).[85] This was not typical behaviour, however, frugality in private being far more common. Department store-owner Berthold Israel was driven to work in a shabby car and ate sandwiches brought from home, though the family used a Mercedes or Rolls Royce on formal occasions. Werner Weisbach's father tried to teach his son simplicity and thrift, contrasting the worthlessness of money and personal property with the value of hard work, public reputation, and success. Spending large sums on other things, Weisbach senior scrutinized his son's petty expenditures, trying to cut down on 'waste'. On the other hand, he constantly encouraged his son to dress well, stressing that this was important if one was to make a good impression. Eduard Arnhold stressed the importance of punctuality, neatness, fulfilment of duty, and modesty. While Carl and Aniela Fürstenberg were at elegant dinner parties, their children sat at home, eating a simple meal. According to his granddaughter, Emil Rathenau was miserly with others as well as with himself. None the less, he built a magnificent house (see p. 53).[86] These examples support Veblen's thesis that the consumption of luxury goods is primarily a way of defining social status.

> Through this discrimination in favour of visible consumption it has come about that the domestic life of most classes is relatively shabby, as compared with the éclat of that overt portion of their life that is carried on before the eyes of observers.[87]

If 'middle-class virtues' such as thrift lived on in a couple of families, if we are to believe their memoirs, this was rare. Adolf Salomonsohn was described by his son as frugal and dedicated to the work ethic, the mother as proud of her husband's position, but above worldly 'tinsel and trinkets' and free of all arrogance and conceit.[88] Georg Tietz writes that his family's life-style retained a middle-class simplicity after they became wealthy.[89] Georg von Siemens is a similar case.

> Often enough on trips, he was placed in the smallest, worst room by the porters and reception desk managers because of his unassuming suit and luggage. Then at some point, it

was discovered who they had before them; suddenly all the employees became polite and the best rooms were available.[90]

He retained a dislike of conspicuous consumption and a lifestyle geared to social obligation, as the following lines in a letter to his daughter, who was staying at the home of Sir Ernest Cassel, demonstrate:

> I am happy for you to have the chance to see a magnificent house. One learns that magnificence usually destroys the home atmosphere, and that one cannot have both things. Judging from your letter, I would guess that you would choose the warm home atmosphere. That pleases me greatly. A warm home atmosphere can be created with limited means through the inner character of the people involved. The first prerequisite is the host's affability. In so-called magnificent homes, those present each play roles as in the theatre . . .[91]

Carl Klönne and, in a sense, Emil Rathenau also belonged to this group. This difference in mentality may be explained by the background of these individuals. Salomonsohn, Klönne, and Tietz were of middle-class origins; Rathenau's family had gone bankrupt. In Siemens' case, individual circumstances were probably of greater importance than social background: his parents are supposed to have been unsociable.[92]

In Berlin, as elsewhere in Germany, wealthy businessmen socialized mainly with each other. Nevertheless, social ties with the traditional Prussian elite were important, since any attempt to influence the state had to be directed at this elite. Bankers were particularly dependent on the state for business and for inside information on affairs at home and abroad. Berlin was also a cultural centre, and one in which Jews played a major role. This accounts in large part for the cultural orientation of social life in elite business circles in Berlin. Like Fontane's Jenny Treibel,[93] wealthy Berlin business families hardly associated with the middle class, shunning all but its most illustrious representatives. The Berlin style of entertaining corresponded to this social exclusivity, involving conspicuous luxury and waste, an atmosphere of competition between hostesses vying nightly for the attention of society, and the public display of social graces. The women of this class fulfilled an important function, and – though of course dependent upon their husbands' and fathers' status – enjoyed a degree of independence and public visibility that was quite untypical for Germany in this era.

IV

The second business centre to be discussed here is the Rhine Province and Westphalia. Parallels might be drawn between the Krupps and Carl Fürstenberg as far as connections with the aristocracy are concerned. As munitions manufacturers, the Krupps were heavily dependent on state contracts. Accordingly, guests at the Villa Hügel included generals, admirals, high officials, and German and foreign diplomats, as well as lawyers, engineers, company directors, and other businessmen. Members of the high aristocracy of the Rhineland were often invited to balls, but usually declined. After F. A. Krupp's death, his wife Margarete, daughter of General von Ende, favoured officers over engineers.[94] The Krupps' social life was untypical, however. Only an occasional civil servant or major is mentioned as a friend or guest of other heavy industrialists of this region. There was little contact with the nobility. Munitions industrialist Heinrich Ehrhardt is unusual in this respect, since he received frequent visits from the Duke of Saxe-Coburg Gotha. On the whole, however, Ehrhardt devoted much less time and energy to public relations than did the Krupps. As a result the latter got government backing for their attempts to win foreign markets, while Ehrhardt did not.[95] Social bonds among businessmen were all-important in the western provinces. Paul Reusch's personal correspondence and guest list show that the overwhelming majority of his friends and acquaintances were businessmen. Peter Klöckner, August Thyssen, Emil Kirdorf, and Bruno Schulz-Briesen also associated mainly with businesmen. Thyssen and Reusch's guests also included an occasional engineer or other middle- to high-ranking employee in private industry. Social contacts with the non-business middle class or bourgeois upper class played a minor role here.[96] While old business families of the Rhineland, such as the vom Raths, belonged to the patrician upper class, new business families were often excluded from these select circles, at least initially. The Jewish banker Louis Levy, for example, converted to Catholicism and adopted the surname of his father-in-law, who was Catholic (Hagen). The latter, a merchant and manufacturer, tried without much success to introduce Levy/Hagen into the high society of Cologne. This may have changed when Louis Hagen was elected president of the Chamber of Commerce in 1914. The General Director of the Bayer pharmaceutical corporation, Carl Duisberg, was at first ignored by the old bourgeois elite of Elberfeld.[97]

The world of art, music and scholarship had a limited impact on the social connections, outside interests, and recreational activities of businessmen in the Rhineland and Westphalia. Though the Krupps were patrons of the arts, artists, scholars, writers, and theatre people were seldom invited to parties at the Villa Hügel. F. A. Krupp once told the Kaiser, 'My fortune is my curse. Without it I would have dedicated my life to art, literature, and science.' His principal hobby was biology. The historian Willi Boelcke considers him a dilettante par excellence, and his understanding of art appears to have been superficial. Certainly it is clear that Krupp's interests did not lead to friendships with scholars and artists.[98] August Thyssen was a fanatical worker with virtually no outside interests. He owned few books. He commissioned Rodin to execute a number of sculptures, which he exhibited in his home, but he also hung popular works of art, of which Huret for one had a poor opinion: 'One could weep when one sees these horrid things!'[99] Klöckner had no hobbies and did not enjoy music. Hugo Stinnes was obsessed with his work, according to his son. Though interested in a few subjects outside his work, he found no time to read books. Business was the only subject of conversation at his table.[100] Munitions manufacturer Heinrich Ehrhardt writes in his autobiography that he bought paintings, enjoyed music 'without being musically talented', attended concerts, opera, and the theatre, and read 'good books', though he was not a 'theatre man or literature snob'. 'I saw, read, heard and bought things that according to my simple judgment were pleasing to me, were beautiful.' Nature meant more to him than cultural pursuits, however. Though Ehrhardt pays tribute to middle-class notions of culture here, these passages make clear that he was not at home in the world of art, music, and ideas.[101] There may have been exceptions among the businessmen of the Rhineland and Westphalia. Emil Kirdorf collected contemporary works of art and books.[102] Paul Reusch's main interest outside of his work was history, and he became a close friend of historian Oswald Spengler shortly after the First World War. He read out of history books to his wife. A rare edition of the poet Friedrich Hölderlin's works was his 'talisman', but he does not appear to have had a large collection of books. He owned paintings, but 'did not in the sense of the art dealers own a valuable "collection"'. The way he displayed works of art in his home tells us something about his attitude towards art: a porcelain Chinese horse of the classic period stood along side ordinary figures of the nineteenth century. Compared with the Berlin bourgeoisie, his interests – perhaps aside from history – seem superficial, and Spengler was his only intellectual friend, as far as we know.[103] The cultural values of the non-Jewish bourgeoisie evidently varied significantly from those of the Jewish bourgeoisie, which was the main force behind ties between *Bildung* and *Besitz* (learning and wealth) in Berlin.[104]

The Krupps' daily life was geared to professional and social obligations to an even greater extent than was the case with the wealthy business elite of Berlin. Guests were received every day. Breakfast time was the only time of day when the family could be alone, yet private conversations were often not possible, because organizational matters, such as the menu, wine selection, and the seating arrangement for evening functions, had to be discussed. In the afternoon, when F. A. Krupp returned home from work, visitors were often waiting to see him. F. A. Krupp was, according to an employee of the Villa Hügel, a '*Lebenskünstler (bon vivant)* with an artistically schooled eye and refined taste' who offered his guests every possible amenity. He was a sociable person who enjoyed relaxing with friends after work; he especially liked small, informal gatherings. With Gustav Krupp von Bohlen und Halbach, who became head of the corporation with his marriage to Bertha Krupp in 1906, the style of social gatherings changed somewhat. At dinner parties, the food was served quickly, and every hint of 'cheerful casualness' was gone. He performed the role of host correctly, but without enthusiasm: 'Despite his reserve and dedication to duty, he can, when it is called for, be kind and courteous, a true diplomat of the old school.'[105]

Reusch loved 'social life, a cultivated conversation, a good wine and a heavy cigar'.[106] Peter Klöckner entertained frequently, and his son-in-law wrote of Klöckner's wife: 'Impressive in appearance, demeanour, and in general, my mother-in-law was the perfect embodiment of what one would imagine a *grande dame* to be.'[107] Hugo Stinnes, could, according to his son, be charming, and was a wine connoisseur. After his divorce, August Thyssen lived a fairly isolated existence, and was often alone in the evening. None the less, he felt obliged to do some formal entertaining, and spared no expense on these occasions. A brunch at his home included caviar, salmon, ham and asparagus, roast meats, and pineapple ice cream. Though it was a spring day, his male guests (mainly businessmen) wore tails, his female guests embroidered crèpe-de-chine, black tulle, spangled dresses, and a great deal of jewelry. Carl Duisberg occasionally brought delicacies in from Berlin or Hamburg for his guests. Max Liebermann, who executed a portrait of Duisberg, wrote that Duisberg was a 'rarity in Germany', namely a *Genussmensch* (a pleasure-seeking person). None the less, the Duisbergs entertained less than was usual in Berlin, often spending the evening alone as a family. Another example for this part of Germany is the tobacco manufacturer Arnold Böninger, who enjoyed parties and acquired the nickname 'Marquis' because of his elegant appearance.[108]

As in the case of Berlin, a few examples of very private lives can also be found among the industrialists of the Rhineland and Westphalia. Coal mining director Bruno Schulz-Briesen spent his free time with his family and hiking. Karl Röchling, a heavy industrialist in Saarbrücken, was a 'folksy' man who after work played billiards with friends in a pub or went swimming. He was a 'friend of the simple, solid way of life'.[109] Gustav Knepper, who headed the coal-mining operations of the Deutsch-Luxemburgische Bergwerks- und Hütten-AG, played cards and sang in a men's choir in his spare time. Düsseldorf steel industrialist Carl Poensgen was interested mainly in gardening and did little entertaining.[110]

Further examples of private thrift coupled with public luxury can be found for the Western provinces. F. A. Krupp's daughters Bertha and Barbara were given a spartan upbringing. In Gustav Krupp von Bohlen und Halbach's time, the temperature in Villa Hügel was not allowed to rise above 18° C, and he kept a record of all his petty personal expenditures. His wife told the French journalist Jules Huret that she 'loved simplicity'.[111] A number of anecdotes attest to August Thyssen's frugality.[112] When at home, Hugo Stinnes ate fried eggs with bacon 'about three times a day', wore inexpensive, outmoded suits, and gave his children a very small allowance.[113]

The wealthy business elite of Rhineland-Westphalia was to a large extent socially isolated. Only the two munitions manufacturers, Krupp and Ehrhardt, associated with the traditional pre-industrial elite. This was a product of their dependence on state contracts. This business class presented itself to society as an elite, sparing no expense on entertainment, and cultivating an image as *bon vivant*, connoisseur, or *grande dame*. Exceptions may be found among newcomers to this class and businessmen living in small towns, where there was no upper class to compete with.

V

As a sector of the business elite became part of the Wilhelmine upper class, a relatively superficial process of assimilation took place. More significantly, a new upper-class bourgeois mentality emerged, as the class that had turned Germany into the most economically dynamic nation in Europe claimed its place in the German ruling class. This reorientation has been discussed in relation to various aspects of material and social life. With the move to exclusive suburbs, contact between the factory owner and his workers (or between the banker or merchant and his office workers) was lost, contributing to the decline of patriarchal structures in business. Businessmen were also increasingly able to insulate themselves from the working class. The social segregation taking place here – part of a more general process of segregation in German big cities – contributed to the cohesion of the bourgeois upper class, and of the wealthy business elite in particular, which showed a marked tendency to cluster in particular residential areas. A very high standard had established itself in the nineteenth century with regard to the wealthy businessman's home. The wealthy business elite of the Wilhelmine era lived almost universally in mansions or apartments as large as mansions. Along with landed estates and summer homes, the villa was part of an elite lifestyle that clearly distinguished this class from the middle class. Typically, these houses and their grounds made use of elements of aristocratic style. This was an architecture of legitimation (*vis-à-vis* social peers), as well as an architecture of domination. The businessman's villa, and especially his summer homes, were also luxuries meant to be enjoyed. The landed estate also served as legitimation and luxury, in addition to representing a diversification of investment. The purchase even of East Elbian estates was not normally indicative of real feudalization, for it did not draw businessmen or their sons away from the business world in significant numbers or bring about the adoption of Junker values.

A great deal of money was spent in business circles in the

Wilhelmine era on entertaining, clothing, and other forms of conspicuous consumption. This was part of an attempt to outdo the
'next class above them' – the wealthiest segment of the aristocracy.
The idea that social prestige could be bought was fairly new in
Germany. This attitude shows how strong capitalist values had
become. This class – with the exception of a few newcomers whose
self-image was still very middle class – presented itself to society
as an elite. This is especially marked in the case of the wives.
These women behaved in a way thought of as 'aristocratic', but
here again the bourgeoisie was using the existing forms for its own
purposes.

Upper-class bourgeois patterns predominated as far as the style
of entertaining and general lifestyle are concerned in both Berlin
and the western provinces. Elegance, luxury, and the cultivation of
social graces went hand-in-hand with an active social life. Reusch,
Thyssen, Klöckner, Stinnes, Duisberg, and Böninger are examples
from the Rhineland and Westphalia. This style had little to do
with aristocratization: ties with the nobility were virtually non-
existent here. A second group, consisting of Ehrhardt, Schulz-
Briesen, Röchling, Knepper, and Poensgen, led more private lives,
doing little entertaining and engaging in forms of recreation that
were intended less for the eyes of society than for their own enjoyment. This 'type' was to be found in Berlin as well, represented
by Georg von Siemens for one. Though social ties with the middle
class are not mentioned in the sources, middle-class patterns of
behaviour lived on in this group, a relic of the class from which
the business elite had evolved, and more directly a consequence
of the predominantly non-elite or small-town origins of this group.
Frugality had a strategic function in this class as a whole, however.[114] It was used to inculcate children with bourgeois self-discipline, and was often a mechanism of self-justification, a way of
proving to oneself that – despite luxury – one had not fallen into
a state of decadence. Here, traditional bourgeois values retained
a private meaning.

The pattern of social contacts reveals a high degree of social
cohesion among the heavy industrialists of the Rhineland and
Westphalia. In Berlin, the social network encompassed not only
business circles, but parts of the traditional, pre-industrial elite as
well, in addition to intellectuals and artists. Social ties with high
officials, diplomats, and the like were more common in Berlin
because these groups were concentrated in the capital. Another

explanation for this difference was the prevalence in Berlin of banking, which was particularly dependent on these ties with the state. Of overwhelming importance in the Western provinces were friendships among businessmen; this was somewhat less the case in Berlin, owing to the importance of cultivating connections with the state in the capital and the cultural leanings of the Jewish bourgeoisie. Impressionistic evidence would seem to indicate that the intellectual and aesthetic interests of businessmen in Rhineland-Westphalia were less 'authentic', which is to say, not based on marked personal interest and knowledge, not reinforced with ties of friendship and kinship, and without historic precedent (such as the Berlin salons of the Romantic era). Art patronage and social ties in this direction were probably more exclusively status symbols in the Rhineland and Westphalia. Various industrialists of this region socialized with employees in private industry, engineers in particular, whereas business circles in Berlin were in this sense more exclusive. Members of the free professions, university professors, mayors, and local politicians played a certain role in the social lives of Reusch, Klöckner, and Kirdorf, while in Berlin ties to these groups were almost non-existent. The social life of Wilhelmine businessmen was limited to very exclusive circles, the composition of which varied from one part of Germany to another. Surging forward into the Wilhelmine upper class, the business elite had broken away from the middle class, but without renouncing its identity or fusing with the nobility.

NOTES

This chapter summarizes parts of a larger project which is to be submitted as a doctoral dissertation at the Free University of Berlin. Research for this article was supported in part by a grant from the International Research & Exchanges Board (IREX), with funds provided by the National Endowment for the Humanities and the United States Information Agency. None of these organizations is responsible for the views expressed.

1 The inability of the bourgeoisie to unify Germany under a constitutional system in the revolution of 1848–9 and the unification of Germany under the aegis of the militaristic, monarchical Prussian state in 1870–1 are seen as decisive turning-points by a number of historians. A further motivation for bourgeois realignment pointed to by some is fear of proletarian revolution. See references to secondary literature in Dolores L. Augustine-Pérez, 'Very wealthy businessmen in Imperial Germany', *Journal of Social History*, 22 (1988), 299–321.

2 The group under study includes all entrepreneurs in industry, trade and commerce, and banking who owned a fortune of 6 million Marks or more. Who was an entrepreneur was defined not according to function, but rather according to position (owner, member, or chairman of the board, etc.). Thus, rentiers and persons with other professions were included if they sat or had ever sat on the board of directors of a corporation, providing that it can be assumed that their fortunes were primarily derived from industry, commerce, or banking.

3 Rudolf Martin, *Jahrbuch der Millionäre Deutschlands*, 18 vols (Berlin, 1912–14). Data was supplemented with information from numerous reference works, such as the *Neue Deutsche Biographie*, 13 vols (Berlin, 1953–82). The most important archive for the quantitative study was the 'Institut zur Erforschung historischer Führungsschichten' in Bensheim, West Germany. The state archives of the GDR in Potsdam, Merseburg, Leipzig, and Dresden also yielded a considerable body of data. Further material was gained through correspondence with descendants of the persons under study, genealogists, and public archives in West Germany.

4 See David Blackbourn, 'The discreet charm of the bourgeoisie: reappraising German history in the nineteenth century', in David Blackbourn and Geoff Eley, *The Peculiarities of German History* (Oxford and New York, 1984), 230–7; Hartmut Kaelble, 'Wie feudal waren die deutschen Unternehmer im Kaiserreich? Ein Zwischenbericht', in Richard Tilly (ed.), *Beiträge zur quantitativen vergleichenden Unternehmensgeschichte* (Stuttgart, 1985), 148–71.

5 Many social historians define the lower middle class of this period as consisting of farmers, master craftsmen, merchants, the petit bourgeoisie (shop and restaurant owners, etc.), small-scale businessmen, middle-grade civil servants (who had no university education), white-collar workers, factory foremen, and non-commissioned officers and lieutenants. The upper middle class includes top and middle management, medium-scale capitalists, university educated civil servants (including teachers at college-preparatory schools and university professors), Protestant ministers, members of the free professions (doctors and lawyers, for example), and commissioned officers below the rank of general. We certainly must include the high nobility, big land-owners, generals and other top-ranking officers, and top government officials in the upper class. As will be shown in this chapter, large-scale industrialists, and great merchants and bankers became part of the upper class in this era. For a systematic classification of professions, see Peter Lundgreen, Margret Kraul, and Karl Ditt, *Bildungschancen und soziale Mobilität in der städtischen Gesellschaft des 19. Jhs.* (Göttingen, 1988), appendix II, 319–64. (They define the upper middle class as part of the upper class.) For a literary treatment of the exclusivity of the business elite *vis-à-vis* the more middle-class professoriate, see Theodore Fontane's novel *Jenny Treibel*, Ulf Zimmermann, trans. (New York, 1977).

6 Thorstein Veblen, *The Theory of the Leisure Class. An Economic Study of Institutions* (cited according to the London edition, 1970), 42, 81.
7 See Reinhard Bentmann and Michael Müller, *Die Villa als Herrschafts-architektur. Versuch einer kunst- und sozialgeschichtlichen Analyse* (Frankfurt-on-Main, 1970), esp. 121. On pollution in Hamburg, see Richard J. Evans, *Death in Hamburg. Society and Politics in the Cholera Years 1830–1910* (Oxford, 1987), 109–79.
8 See Carl-Friedrich Baumann, 'August Thyssen – ein Bürger Mülheims', *Zeitschrift des Geschichtsvereins der Stadt Mülheim a.d. Ruhr*, 61 (1989), 17–18.
9 Examples in Helmuth Croon, 'Die wirtschaftlichen Führungs-schichten des Ruhrgebiets in der Zeit von 1890 bis 1933', *Blätter für deutsche Landesgeschichte*, 108 (1972), 155; Richard Nutzinger, *Karl Röchling 1827–1910. Das Lebenswerk eines Grossindustriellen* (Völklingen and Saarbrücken, 1927), 151–3; Theodor Heuss, *Robert Bosch, Leben und Leistung*, 5th edn (Tübingen, 1946), 190.
10 On the history of individual suburbs, see Dittmar Machule and Lutz Seiberlich, 'Die Berliner Villenvororte', *Berlin und seine Bauten*, pt 4, vol. A (Berlin, Munich, and Düsseldorf, 1970), 93–114; Julius Posener and Burkhard Bergius, 'Individuell geplante Einfamilienhäuser 1896–1968', ibid., pt 4, vol. C (Berlin, Munich, and Düsseldorf, 1975), 1–42.
11 On Hamburg, see Evans, *Death*, 56–63, 125–6; Clemens Wischermann, *Wohnen in Hamburg vor dem Ersten Weltkrieg* (Münster, 1983), 310–11; Heinrich Merck, *Vom gewesenen Hamburg. Nach eigenen Erinnerungen aufgezeichnet* (Hamburg, 1953), 63. Examples of country homes in Lamar Cecil, *Albert Ballin. Business and Politics in Imperial Germany, 1888–1918* (Princeton, 1967), 143; Gertrud Wenzel-Burchard, *Granny. Greta Warburg und die Ihren. Hamburger Schicksale* (Hamburg, 1975), 33–4; Jacques Attali, *Siegmund G. Warburg. Das Leben eines grossen Bankiers* (Düsseldorf and Vienna, 1986), 71; Max M. Warburg, *Aus meinen Aufzeichnungen* (private print, New York, 1952), 15–16; Mary Amelie Sloman, *Erinnerungen* (Hamburg, 1957), 86–8. Examples for Essen, Cologne, and Frankfurt in Paul Brandi, *Essener Arbeitsjahre. Erinnerungen des Ersten Beigeordneten Paul Brandi* (Essen, 1959), 15; Horst A. Wessel, 'Die Unternehmerfamilie Felten & Guilleaume', *Rheinisch-Westfälische Wirtschaftsbiographien*, 13 (Münster in Westfalen, 1986), 73–5; Maria Lanckoronska. *Li(e)ber Beda. Memoiren einer Individualistin* (Frankfurt-on-Main, 1977), 22. On the Tiergarten, see Erich Achterberg, *Berliner Hochfinanz. Kaiser, Fürsten, Millionäre um 1900* (Frankfurt-on-Main, 1965), 43–6. On Fürstenberg, see Carl Fürstenberg, *Die Lebensgeschichte eines deutschen Bankiers, 1870–1914*, Hans Fürstenberg (ed.) (Berlin, 1931), 504. On Finck, see Bernhard Hoffmann, *Wilhelm von Finck. 1848–1924. Lebensbilder eines deutschen Bankiers* (Munich, 1953), 183.
12 StA Potsdam, Polizeipräsidium Berlin Pr. Br. Rep. 30 Berlin C Tit. 94, *passim.*
13 On Fürstenberg, see Fürstenberg, *Lebensgeschichte*, esp. 231–3, 329, 450–1, 504; on the departure of aristocrats from Berlin, see Lamar

77

A. Cecil, 'Jew and Junker in Imperial Berlin', *Leo Baeck Institute Year Book* 10 (1975), 54–5.

14 On Berlin and its suburbs, see Heinrich Johannes Schwippe, 'Prozesse sozialer Segregation und funktionaler Spezialisierung in Berlin und Hamburg in der Periode der Industrialisierung und Urbanisierung', in Heinz Heineberg (ed.), *Innerstädtische Differenzierung und Prozesse im 19. und 20. Jahrhundert* (Cologne and Vienna, 1987), 195–224; Burkhard Hofmeister, 'Wilhelminischer Ring und Villenkoloniengründung', in ibid., 105–17; Alfred Kerr, *Walther Rathenau. Erinnerungen eines Freundes* (Amsterdam 1935), 34–5; Achterberg, *Berliner*, 43–6. On Marienburg, see Erwin Maruhn, 'Der Kölner Stadtteil Marienburg. Strukturwandel eines Villenvorortes von der Gründerzeit bis zur Gegenwart', *Jahrbuch des Kölnischen Geschichtsvereins*, 52 (1981), 131–47; Frank Thomas and Sofie Trümper, *Bayenthal-Marienburg. 150 Jahre Leben und Arbeiten am Rhein* (Cologne, 1985), 106–11. On Hamburg, see Evans, *Death*, 56–63; Wischermann, *Wohnen*, 310.

15 For examples of vacation homes, see Ursula von Mangoldt, *Auf der Schwelle zwischen Gestern und Morgen. Begegnungen und Erlebnisse* (Weilheim, 1963), 56; Carl von der Heydt, *Unser Haus* (private print, without place of publication, 1919), 43; Karl Helfferich, *Georg von Siemens. Ein Lebensbild aus Deutschlands grosser Zeit*, 3 vols (Berlin, 1923), 3:251; Johanna Arnhold (ed.), *Eduard Arnhold. Ein Gedenkbuch* (Berlin, 1928), 29; Heinrich Ehrhardt, *Hammerschläge. 70 Jahre deutscher Arbeiter und Erfinder* (Leipzig, 1922), 70; Brandi, *Essener Arbeitsjahre*, 18; Hans Achinger, *Wilhelm Merton in seiner Zeit* (Frankfurt-on-Main, 1965), 243. On summer homes in Bavaria, see Martin, *Jahrbuch*, vol. 4. For examples of bringing along work, etc., see Julius Meisbach, *Friedrich Alfred Krupp, wie er lebte und starb* (Cologne, 1903), 16, 19; Andreas Kohlschütter (ed.), *Ein Genie in chaotischer Zeit. Edmund H. Stinnes über seinen Vater Hugo Stinnes (1870–1924)* (Bern, 1979), 44; Achinger, *Wilhelm Merton*, 247; letter from Wilhelm von Siemens to Arnold von Siemens, 1 July 1896, Siemens Archive SAA Lr 563.

16 Peacocks roamed the parks of Hamburg merchant Robert Sloman and of August Thyssen. Heavy industrialist Paul Reusch set up statues of 'great Germans' in his park, modelled on King Ludwig I of Bavaria's 'Valhalla' near Regensburg. See Sloman, *Erinnerungen*, 88; Hjalmar Schacht, *76 Jahre meines Lebens* (Bad Wörishofen, 1953), 185; Erich Maschke, *Es entsteht ein Konzern. Paul Reusch und die GHH* (Tübingen, 1969), 37–8. On servants, see Percy Ernst Schramm, *Neun Generationen. Dreihundert Jahre deutscher 'Kulturgeschichte' im Lichte der Schicksale einer Hamburger Bürgerfamilie (1648–1948)*, 2 (Göttingen, 1964), 421–2.

17 See Hartwig Suhrbier, 'Abseits von Villa Hügel. Herrschaftsarchitektur im Ruhrgebiet', *Kritische Berichte*, 4 (1976), 5; Wolfgang Richter and Jürgen Zännker, *Der Bürgertraum vom Adelsschloß. Aristokratische Bauformen im 19. und 20. Jahrhundert* (Reinbek, 1988), esp. 87, 99, 107–8; Andreas Ley, *Die Villa als Burg* (Munich, 1981), 27–58. This is not an exhaustive explanation of the popularity of the castle in the Wilhelmine bourgeoisie. An important aspect was, according to

Ley, enthusiasm for the Middle Ages, originating in the Romantic movement and spurred by nationalism, which saw the Gothic style as intrinsically German. Paradoxically, the popularity of medieval architecture in England also contributed to its spread in Germany.

18 See Bentmann/Müller, *Villa*, esp. 93, 121.

19 Knut Borchardt, 'Der Unternehmerhaushalt als Wirtschaftsbetrieb', in Tilmann Buddensieg (ed.), *Villa Hügel. Das Wohnhaus Krupp in Essen*, (Essen and Berlin, 1984), esp. 11, 14; Michael Stürmer, 'Alltag und Fest auf dem Hügel', in ibid., 257, 262.

20 See his introduction to *Landhaus und Garten. Beispiele neuzeitlicher Landhäuser nebst Grundrissen, Innenräumen und Gärten*, 2nd edn (Munich, 1910), xx.

21 See Stadtarchiv Köln, Abt. 1068 (Mallinckrodt), Kasten 77; Henri Wilmin, *Die Familie Adt und ihre Industriebetriebe. Die Familie Adt in Forbach*, Axel Polleti trans. (Bad Orb, 1979), 56; Thyssen-Archiv A/9577, letter from August Thyssen dated 19 Dec. 1902; Mangoldt, *Auf der Schwelle*, 18.

22 One possible example would be the house Fritz Thyssen occupied from 1899 to 1912, judging by a photograph (Thyssen-Archiv F 403). Fritz Thyssen was, however, only the heir apparent. His father, August Thyssen, represented the company in society and owned a house that was appropriate for formal entertaining.

23 On Thyssen, see Paul Arnst, *August Thyssen und sein Werk* (Leipzig, 1925) 69–70; Schacht, *76 Jahre*, 184–5 (my translations here and below); Jules Huret, *In Deutschland*, E. von Kraatz, trans. (Leipzig, Berlin and Paris, 1907), pt 1, *Rheinland und Westfalen*, 253–4.

24 Hildegard Wallich, *Erinnerungen aus meinem Leben* (Altenkirchen, 1970), 109; Fürstenberg, *Lebensgeschichte*, 504; Wenzel-Burchard, *Granny*, 18; Georg Tietz, *Hermann Tietz. Geschichte einer Familie und ihrer Warenhäuser* (Stuttgart, 1965) 118; Elsabea Rohrmann, *Max von Schinckel, hanseatischer Bankmann im wilhelminischen Deutschland* (Ph.D. Dissertation, Hamburg, 1971), 78.

25 Posener and Bergius, 'Individuell', 5–11.

26 Evans, *Death*, 126.

27 Augustine-Pérez, 'Very wealthy', 306.

28 See Hans Rosenberg, 'Die Pseudodemokratisierung der Rittergutsbesitzerklasse', in *Moderne deutsche Sozialgeschichte*, Hans-Ulrich Wehler (ed.) (Königstein and Düsseldorf, 1981), 287–308; Hoffmann, *Wilhelm von Finck*, 99–103, 172, 184; Genealogical collection of the Institut zur Erforschung historischer Führungsschichten in Bensheim, File Wilhelm Finck; Georg Siemens, *Carl Friedrich von Siemens. Ein grosser Unternehmer* (Munich, 1960), 77; Helfferich, *Georg von Siemens*, 250–1; Arnhold, *Eduard Arnhold*, 36; Friedrich Schulz (ed.), *Geschichte der Familie Ackermann aus Gödern* (Leipzig, 1912), 126–7.

29 Wallich, *Erinnerungen*, 112; see also 111, 137.

30 Arthur von Gwinner, *Lebenserinnerungen*, Manfred Pohl (ed.) (Frankfurt-on-Main, 1975), 109. On Friedländer-Fuld and Schwabach, see Fürstenberg, *Lebensgeschichte*, 399; Lali Horstmann, *Unendlich viel ist uns geblieben* (Munich, 1954), 11–12.

31 Polizeipräsident Berlin to Handelsministerium 1909, StA Potsdam Pr. Br. Rep. 30 Berlin C Tit. 94, Nr. 10123.

32 This figure slightly overestimates the importance of Berlin and Rhineland-Westphalia because Martin's work omitted Baden, the Grand Duchy of Hesse (the Prussian province of Hesse-Nassau was included), Alsace-Lorraine (then part of Germany, now belonging to France), the Thuringian states, and a few minor principalities.

33 See Cecil, 'Jew', 47–58; Friedrich Zunkel, *Der rheinisch-westfälische Unternehmer 1834–1879. Ein Beitrag zur Geschichte des deutschen Bürgertums im 19. Jh.* (Cologne and Opladen, 1962); Bernd Faulenbach, 'Die Herren an der Ruhr. Zum Typus des Unternehmers in der Schwerindustrie', in Lutz Niethammer, Bodo Hombach, Tilman Fichter, Ulrich Borsdorf (eds), *Die Menschen machen ihre Geschichte nicht aus freien Stücken, aber sie machen sie selbst* (Berlin and Bonn, 1984), 76–88.

34 Sixty per cent of the Berlin businessmen in the *Yearbook of Millionaires* were ethnic Jews. Ideally, an ethnic definition of Jewishness would include converted Jews, and Christians whose family was Jewish a couple of generations back – such as the Mendelssohns – to the extent that these individuals considered themselves to be Jewish or demonstrated solidarity with the Jewish community. In actual practice, it is very difficult to use self-definition as a criterion in a quantitative study. Thus, converted Jews and Christians of Jewish families were considered to be Jews for the purposes of the present study. For a similar definition of Jewishness, see Werner E. Mosse, *Jews in the German Economy. The German-Jewish Economic Elite 1820–1935* (Oxford, 1987), 1–2. Mosse points out that the Judaic religion constituted just one element of Jewish identity in this era, along with social origins, endogamy, family and business networks, and traditions.

35 In another 5 per cent of the cases, the person was known to be Christian, but it was unknown if he was Protestant or Catholic. 5 per cent were Jewish. Figures refer to the *Yearbook of Millionaires* study.

36 Not necessarily persons among the 502 wealthiest, but at least millionaires.

37 Fürstenberg, Ballin, and Simon-Sonnemann spent three weeks each year together in a spa. Politics was the main subject of their conversations. Fürstenberg's wider circle of friends included Walther Rathenau, Maximilian Harden (to be discussed below), and Wilhelm Knappe (who was part of a social circle consisting of Foreign Ministry officials). In his autobiography, Fürstenberg also describes as 'friends' the bankers Max Steinthal, Julius von Peters, Julius Stern, Alfred Benvenisti, Robert Müser, and Paul Schwabach, various bankers in Italy, Austria, and France, Emil Rathenau, August Thyssen, and AEG director Felix Deutsch. Fürstenberg mentions numerous acquaintances who were businessmen. He describes his relationships with officials, noblemen, diplomats, and officers on the whole in more distanced language. See Fürstenberg, *Lebensgeschichte*, esp. 254, 262, 263, 308, 315, 350, 355, 369, 371, 436, 509ff; Hans Fürstenberg,

Carl-Fürstenberg-Anekdoten. Ein Unterschied muss sein (Düsseldorf and Vienna, 1978), 14–15.

38 Arnhold's best friends were heavy industrialist Gustav Krupp von Bohlen und Halbach and Adolf von Harnack, the president of the Kaiser Wilhelm Society. Paul Wallich's social life in the years 1910–12 was centered on banking and intellectual circles. On Arnhold, see Arnhold, *Eduard Arnhold*, 43. On Israel, see Naomi Shepherd, *Wilfrid Israel. German Jewry's Secret Ambassador* (London, 1984), 20–1. On Tietz, see Tietz, *Hermann Tietz*, 49. On Wallich and Weisbach, see Paul Wallich, *Lehr-und Wanderjahre eines Bankiers*, in *Zwei Generationen im deutschen Bankwesen 1833–1914* (Frankfurt-on-Main, 1978), 343–5; Werner Weisbach, *'Und alles ist zerstoben.' Erinnerungen aus der Jahrhundertwende* (Vienna, Leipzig, and Zurich, 1937), 109. On Rathenau, see Peter Berglar, *Walther Rathenau. Seine Zeit. Sein Werk, Seine Persönlichkeit* (Bremen, 1970), 311.

39 Georg Solmssen, *Gedenkblatt für Adolf und Sara Salomonsohn zum 19. März 1931* (private print, Berlin, 1931), 19, see also 10–12.

40 See Willy Ritter Liebermann von Wahlendorf, *Erinnerung eines deutschen Juden 1863–1936*, Ernst Reinhard Piper (ed.) (Munich and Zurich, 1988), esp 49, 67, 83–4.

41 The information on Wilhelm von Siemens is partly based on a collection of visiting cards (Siemens Archiv, SAA 4/LC 999). See also Carl Dietrich Harries, 'Nachruf für Wilhelm von Siemens', *Wissenschaftliche Veröffentlichungen aus dem Siemens-Konzern*, 1 (Sonderabdruck, 1920), 6, 9 (also Siemens Archive). Harries was Wilhelm von Siemens' brother-in-law. On von der Heydt, see von der Heydt, *Haus*, 30. On Georg von Siemens, see Helfferich, *Georg von Siemens*, 240.

42 On the Club of Berlin, see Gwinner, *Lebenserinnerungen*, 54–6; Max I. Wolff, *Club von Berlin. 1864–1924* (Berlin, 1926), esp. 20–9, 89, 99; Wallich, *Lehr- und Wanderjahre*, 352–3. On a restaurant where businessmen met, see Fürstenberg, *Lebensgeschichte*, 397.

43 See ibid., 255, 262, 497.

44 Cecil, 'Jew and Junker'.

45 Fedor von Zobeltitz, *Chronik der Gesellschaft unter dem letzten Kaiserreich*, 2 (Hamburg, 1922), 210.

46 Jules Huret, *En Allemagne. Berlin* (Paris, 1909), 346–7.

47 Isabel V. Hull, *The Entourage of Kaiser Wilhelm II, 1888–1918* (Cambridge, 1982), 159–60; see also 157–74. See Jaeger, *Unternehmer*, 172–8; Polizeipräsident Berlin to Handelsministerium, 1899, StA Potsdam, Pr. Br. Rep. 30 Berlin C Tit. 94, Nr. 9748; Attali, *Siegmund G. Warburg*, 83; Arnold Petzet (ed.), *Heinrich Wiegand. Ein Lebensbild* (Bremen, 1932), 211; Rohrmann, *Max von Schinckel*, 190; H.S. Art'l, *Richard Roesicke. Sein Leben und Wirken dem Volke dargestellt* (Berlin, 1904) 25; Ernst Feder, 'James Simon. Industrialist, art collector, philanthropist', *Leo Baeck Institute Year Book*, 10 (1965), 6; Fritz Stern, *Gold and Iron. Bismarck, Bleichröder and the Building of the German Empire* (New York, 1977), 544; Arnhold, *Eduard Arnhold*, 45–6; Fürstenberg, *Lebensgeschichte*, p. 439; Fritz Hellwig, *Carl Ferdinand Freiherr von Stumm-Halberg 1836–1901* (Heidelberg and Saarbrücken, 1936), 429, 515;

Cecil, *Albert Ballin, passim*; nine of the fifteen businessmen named here were Jewish.

48 See Cecil, *Albert Ballin*, 99.

49 Von der Heydt, *Haus*, 30–1.

50 See Fürstenberg, *Anekdoten*, 14.

51 See Solmssen, *Gedenkblatt*, 23–4; Huret, *In Deutschland*, vol. 1: *Rheinland und Westfalen*, 356; Wessel, 'Unternehmerfamilie', 73, 81; Petzet, *Heinrich Wiegand*, 211.

52 See Harry Graf Kessler, *Walther Rathenau. Sein Leben und sein Werk* (Berlin, 1928), 55–6; Kerr, *Walther Rathenau*, 92.

53 See Fürstenberg, *Lebensgeschichte*, 332–3, 337, 427, 510ff.

54 On Schwabach, see Rudolf Vierhaus (ed.), *Das Tagebuch der Baronin Spitzemberg, geb. Freiin von Varnbüler. Aufzeichnungen aus der Hofgesellschaft des Hohenzollernreiches*, 3rd edn (Göttingen, 1963), esp. 475. On Friedländer-Fuld, see Bogdan Graf von Hutten-Czapski, *Sechzig Jahre Politik und Gesellschaft* 2 (Berlin, 1936), 63; Werner Frhr. von Rheinbaben, *Viermal Deutschland. Aus dem Erleben eines Seemanns, Diplomaten, Politikers 1895–1954* (Berlin, 1954), 76; Huret, *En Allemagne. Berlin*, 313.

55 Von Hutten-Czapski, *Sechzig Jahre*, 2:63.

56 See Hans Jaeger, *Unternehmer in der deutschen Politik (1890–1918)* (Bonn, 1967), 181.

57 The information on political persuasion is to be found in StA Potsdam, Polizeipräsidium Berlin Rep. 30 Berlin C Tit. 94, Nr. 9940 and Nr. 13431. See von Hutten-Czapski, *Sechzig Jahre*, 63.

58 Lady Susan Townley, *'Indiscretions' of Lady Susan* (New York, 1922), 45–6. See also Lord Edward Gleichen, *A Guardsman's Memories. A Book of Recollections* (Edinburgh and London, 1932), 276–7.

59 On Arnhold, see Arnhold, *Eduard Arnhold*, 43; Marie von Bunsen, *Zeitgenossen die ich erlebte 1900–1930* (Leipzig, 1932), 72. On Gutmann, see Polizeipräsident Berlin to Handelsministerium, 1898, StA Potsdam, Pr. Br. Rep. 30 Berlin C Tit. 94, Nr. 10239. On Weisbach, see Weisbach, *Und alles*, 109. On Esser, see Polizeipräsident Berlin to Handelsministerium, 1896, StA Potsdam, Pr. Br. Rep. 30 Berlin C Tit. 94, Nr. 9748.

60 See von der Heydt, *Unser Haus*, 29, 30, 35–7. On Siemens, see note 41. On Arnold von Siemens, see von Bunsen, *Zeitgenossen*, 42–4.

61 See Deborah Hertz, *Jewish High Society in Old Regime Berlin* (New Haven and London, 1988).

62 Among the Jewish families in which intellectuals, artists, and the like were to be found were the Fürstenbergs and the Mendelssohns. Max Liebermann, the best-known German painter of the Wilhelmine era, was a member of a family of textile industrialists, and he was related to the Rathenaus. See Hans Fürstenberg, *Erinnerungen. Mein Weg als Bankier und Carl Fürstenbergs Altersjahre* (Düsseldorf and Vienna, 1968), 16–18; Gisela Gantzel-Kress, 'Noblesse oblige. Ein Beitrag zur Nobilitierung der Mendelssohns', *Mendelssohn-Studien*, 6 (1986), 163–81. For a valuable treatment of the role of Jews in German cultural life, see Peter Gay, *Freud, Jews and other Germans* (New York, 1978).

63 See Fürstenberg, *Lebensgeschichte*, esp. 95, 99–100, 142, 216–17, 317, 334, 398–9; quote on 399.

64 On the Mendelssohns, see Wilhelm Treue, 'Das Bankhaus Mendelssohn als Beispiel einer Privatbank im 19. und 20. Jahrhundert', *Mendelssohn-Studien* 1 (1972), 54–5, 57–8; Cécile Lowenthal-Hensel, 'Franz von Mendelssohn', *Mendelssohn-Studien*, 6 (1986), 259; Felix Gilbert (ed.), *Bankiers, Künstler und Gelehrte. Unveröffentlichte Briefe der Familie Mendelssohn aus dem 19. Jahrhundert* (Tübingen, 1975), 229. On Simon-Sonnemann and Deutsch, see Fürstenberg, *Lebensgeschichte*, 492, 512.

65 See Sabine Lepsius, *Ein Berliner Künstlerleben um die Jahrhundertwende* (Munich, 1972), 157, 175, 177–8; Irmgard Wirth, 'Juden als Künstler und Kunstförderer in Berlin im späten 19. und 20. Jahrhundert', *Emuna*, 9 (1974), 36; Arnhold, *Eduard Arnhold*, 43, 197, 218; Weisbach, '*Und alles*', 367, 370–2.

66 Shepherd, *Wilfrid Israel* 20–1.

67 See ibid., 24–5; H. Wallich, *Erinnerungen*, 111, 121–2; Wallich, *Lehr- und Wanderjahre*, 343–5; Weisbach, '*Und alles*', 109; Brigitte B. Fischer, *Sie schrieben mir oder was aus meinem Poesiealbum wurde* (Stuttgart and Zurich, 1978), 40.

68 Mangoldt, *Auf der Schwelle*, 12, see also 13–18; Kessler, *Walther Rathenau*, 9–12, 18; Etta Federn-Kohlhaas, *Walther Rathenau. Sein Leben und Wirken*, 2nd edn (Dresden, 1928), 24; Felix Pinner, *Emil Rathenau und das elektrische Zeitalter* (Leipzig, 1918), 358–61.

69 See Helmuth M. Böttcher, *Walther Rathenau. Persönlichkeit und Werk* (Bonn, 1958), 37; Kessler, *Walther Rathenau*, 59; Hans Dieter Hellige, 'Rathenau und Harden in der Gesellschaft des Deutschen Kaiserreichs', in *Walther Rathenau. Maximilian Harden. Briefwechsel 1897–1920* (Munich and Heidelberg, 1983), 146.

70 On Heydt, see von der Heydt, *Haus*, 28–30, 38–9. On Andreae, see Mangoldt, *Auf der Schwelle*, 11. On Klönne, see Erich Achterberg and Maximilian Müller-Jabusch, *Lebensbilder Deutscher Bankiers aus fünf Jahrhunderten*, 2nd edn (Frankfurt-on-Main, 1964), 244. On Salomonsohn, see Solmssen, *Gedenkblatt*, 5–7, 26; Kurt Zielenziger, *Juden in der deutschen Wirtschaft* (Berlin, 1930), 119.

71 On Mosse, see 'Rudolf Mosse', 250, 253. On Siemens, see references in note 41. On Tietz, see Tietz, *Hermann Tietz*, 37, 49.

72 On Fürstenberg, see *Lebensgeschichte*, 315, 396. On 'receiving', see von der Heydt, *Haus* 39. On the Siemenses, see Harries, 'Nachruf', 6.

73 Siemens Archive SAA Lr 563.

74 Von Bunsen, *Zeitgenossen*, 43.

75 Kerr, *Walther Rathenau*, 36. On Hermann Wallich, see Wallich, *Erinnerungen* 110–11.

76 Shepherd, *Wilfrid Israel*, 20–1. On Aniela Fürstenberg, see Fürstenberg, *Lebensgeschichte*, 398.

77 Fischer, *Sie schrieben*, 40.

78 Polizeipräsident Berlin to Handelsministerium, 1901, StA Potsdam, Pr. Br. Rep. 30 Berlin C Tit. 94, Nr. 9940.

79 Comte Paul Vasili (pseud.) (according to Cecil, Catherine Princess Radziwill), *La Société de Berlin* 12th edn (Paris, 1884), 160.
80 Count Axel von Schwering (pseud.), *The Berlin Court under William II* (London, 1915), 220, 221.
81 See Huret, *En Allemagne*, 104.
82 Schwering, *Berlin Court*, 254–5.
83 See Huret, *En Allemagne*, 104–5; von Bunsen, *Zeitgenossen*, 72–3; Siemens Archive SAA 4/Lc 731, vol. 2, p. 462.
84 Schwering, *Berlin Court*, 218–19.
85 Weisbach, '*Und alles*', 386; Fürstenberg, *Anekdoten*, 54.
86 See Shepherd, *Wilfrid Israel*, 18, 21; Weisbach, '*Und alles*', 117; Arnhold, *Eduard Arnhold*, 16; Fürstenberg, *Erinnerungen*, 8; Mangoldt, *Auf der Schwelle*, 13–18.
87 Veblen, *Theory*, 86.
88 Solmssen, *Gedenkblatt*, 3–4, 25.
89 Tietz, *Hermann Tietz*, 37, 49.
90 Helfferich, *Georg von Siemens*, 241.
91 ibid., 336–7.
92 See ibid., 345–6.
93 See Fontaine, *Frau Jenny Treibel*.
94 See Willi A. Boelcke (ed.), *Krupp und die Hohenzollern in Dokumenten. Krupp-Korrespondenz mit Kaisern, Kabinettschefs und Ministern 1850–1918*, 2nd edn (Frankfurt-on-Main, 1970), 109; Meisbach, *Friedrich Alfred Krupp*, 14, 16; Stürmer, 'Alltag', 263–4; Huret, *In Deutschland*, 355–6; Gert von Klass, 'Bertha Krupp von Bohlen und Halbach', *Beilagen zu den Krupp-Mitteilungen* (29 Mar. 1956), 9; Gert von Klass, *Die drei Ringe. Lebensgeschichte eines Industrieunternehmens* (Tübingen and Stuttgart, 1953), 230.
95 See Jaeger, *Unternehmer*, 176; Heinrich Ehrhardt, *Hammerschläge. 70 Jahre deutscher Arbeiter und Erfinder* (Leipzig, 1922), 70.
96 On Reusch: Haniel-Archiv 3001938/0, 40010128/52, 30019390/0b, 30019390/36, 30019390/51, 400101290/160, 400101290/159. On Thyssen, see Huret, *In Deutschland*, 253–5; Josef Winschuh, 'Der alte Thyssen', in *Die heitere Maske im ernsten Spiel. Eine Freundesgabe für Volkmar Muthesius. Zum 19. März 1960* (Frankfurt-on-Main, 1960), 109, 113; Wilhelm Treue, *Die Feuer verlöschen nie. August Thyssen-Hütte 1890–1926* (Düsseldorf and Vienna, 1966) 161; Günter Henle, *Weggenosse des Jahrhunderts. Als Diplomat, Industrieller, Politiker und Freund der Musik* (Stuttgart, 1968) 67–8. On Klöckner, see Henle, *Weggenosse*, 52; Jakob Reichert, 'Peter Klöckner', *Rheinisch-Westfälische Wirtschaftsbiographien*, 7 (Münster in Westfalen, 1960), 101–2. On Kirdorf, see Walter Bacmeister, *Emil Kirdorf. Der Mann. Sein Werk*, 2nd edn (Essen, 1936), 160. On Ehrhardt, see Ehrhardt, *Hammerschläge*, 70. On Schulz-Briesen, see Max Schulz-Briesen, 'Bruno Schulz-Briesen', in *Rheinisch-Westfälische Wirtschaftsbiographien* (Münster in Westfalen, 1941, reprint 1974), 4; 129, 131.
97 On Levy/Hagen, see Hermann Kellenbenz, 'Louis Hagen, insbesondere als Kammerpräsident', in *Rheinisch-Westfälische Wirtschaftsbiographien*, 10 (Münster in Westfalen, 1974), 140; Zentrales Staatsarchiv,

Dienststelle Merseburg, Geheimes Zivilkabinett, 2.2.1. Nr. 1596, Bl. 5; on Duisberg, see Curt Duisberg, *Nur ein Sohn. Ein Leben mit der Grosschemie* (Stuttgart, 1981), 14–15.

98 Quotation in William Manchester, *The Arms of Krupp. 1587–1968* (Boston and Toronto, 1968), 190. For general comments on the relationship between business and the arts in the Ruhr district, see Paul Hermann Mertes, 'Zum Sozialprofil der Oberschicht im Ruhrgebiet. Dargestellt an den Dortmunder Kommerzienräten', *Beiträge zur Geschichte Dortmunds und der Grafschaft Mark*, 67 (1971), 186 and Brandi, *Essener Arbeitsjahre*, 18. On the Krupps, see Boelcke, *Krupp*, 109, 151.

99 Huret, *In Deutschland*, 255; see also Winschuh, 'Thyssen', 113; Arnst, *August Thyssen*, 70.

100 On Klöckner, see Reichert, 'Peter Klöckner', 101. On Stinnes, see Kohlschütter, *Ein Genie*, esp. 32, 37, 42, 44, 51.

101 Ehrhardt, *Hammerschläge*, 117–18.

102 See Bacmeister, *Emil Kirdorf*, 162.

103 Edgar Salin, 'Paul Reusch', in Edgar Salin, *Lynkeus – Gestalten und Probleme aus Wirtschaft und Politik* (Tübingen, 1963), 51,55; see Bodo Herzog, 'Die Freundschaft zwischen Oswald Spengler und Paul Reusch', in Anton Mirko Koktanek (ed.), *Spengler-Studien. Festgabe für Manfred Schröder zum 85. Geburtstag* (Munich, 1965), 77, 81–2; Maschke, *Es entsteht*, 37, 38.

104 There are a few examples of highly cultivated, non-Jewish business families, such as the Reisses in Mannheim. On the whole, though, the differences between Jews and non-Jews are in this respect quite marked.

105 Von Klass, *Die drei Ringe*, 324, 325, see also 230; Meisbach, *Friedrich Alfred Krupp*, 11–16; von Klass, 'Bertha', 9; Wilhelm Berdrow, *Alfred Krupp und sein Geschlecht. Die Familie Krupp und ihr Werk von 1787–1940 nach den Quellen des Familien- und Werksarchivs geschildert* (Berlin, 1943), 208.

106 Maschke, *Es entsteht*, 55.

107 Henle, *Weggenosse*, 52.

108 On Stinnes, see Kohlschütter, *Ein Genie*, 32, 42. On Thyssen, see Huret, *In Deutschland*, 253–4; Treue, *Die Feuer*, 161. On Duisberg, see Hans-Joachim Flechtner, *Carl Duisberg. Eine Biographie*, 2nd edn (Düsseldorf, 1981), 171; on Böninger, see Walter Ring, *Geschichte der Duisburger Familie Böninger* (Duisburg, 1930), 278, 382.

109 Nutzinger, *Karl Röchling*, 148, 151; on Schulz-Briesen, see Schulz-Briesen, 'Bruno Schulz-Briesen', 129, 131.

110 On Knepper, see Walter Bacmeister, *Gustav Knepper: Das Lebensbild eines grossen Bergmanns* (Essen and Rüttenscheid, 1950), 32; on Poensgen, see Lutz Hatzfeld, 'Ernst Poensgen (1871–1949)', in *Rheinische Lebensbilder*, 7 (Cologne, 1977), 205, 208.

111 See von Klass, 'Bertha', 3; Manchester, *Arms*, 226; von Klass, *Drei Ringe* 322–4; Huret, *In Deutschland*, 355–7.

112 See Baumann, 'August Thyssen', 15–16.

113 See Kohlschütter, *Ein Genie*, 37, 44, 51.

114 Richard Evans points to an example for Hamburg in Evans, *Death*, 96.

3

The titled businessman: Prussian Commercial Councillors in the Rhineland and Westphalia during the nineteenth century

Karin Kaudelka-Hanisch

I

Research on the social history of the Prussian-German bourgeoisie has been strongly influenced by the 'feudalization' thesis. After the failure of the 1848–9 revolution, and the achievement of German unification by military means under Prussian auspices, the bourgeoisie – so the argument runs – was prompted to give up its oppositional role and form an alliance with the old pre-industrial elites in state and society. It was pushed in the same direction by its fears of a working class that was growing in size and importance. Nineteenth-century German society was thus markedly less 'bourgeois' than its counterparts in western Europe, a view that has been fundamental to arguments about a German *Sonderweg*. It is argued that this 'feudalization', to which the economic bourgeoisie was particularly subject, found expression in a number of ways: in the shift from modestly bourgeois styles of life to conspicuous consumption, in intermarriage, increasing social contacts, and other forms of intermingling with the rural aristocracy, and in a growing bourgeois fondness for titles, orders, and other badges of feudality.

Werner Sombart was one of the first contemporary observers to suggest that the economic bourgeoisie inclined towards 'feudal' values and patterns of behaviour. In his words,

> the bourgeois who have become rich try to forget their origins
> as soon as possible, and to rise into the landed aristocracy or
> at least into the ranks of feudal estate owners. The capitalist
> enterprise, on which the wealth of the family was originally

founded, is sold. The sons and grandsons buy themselves into land, entail the estate, marry into old aristocratic families, have their offspring join the Saxoborussian student corporation and serve in a guards regiment, and no longer think of preparing a son for any kind of career in business.[1]

After the Second World War, Friedrich Zunkel was prominent among those who made the same case. In his classic study of Rhenish and Westphalian entrepreneurs, he argued that the bourgeoisie had increasingly adopted the norms and styles of life of the aristocracy, and thus differentiated itself sharply from its west European neighbours. In comparison to England, where the aristocracy itself proved more flexible, and France, where the power of the old elite was broken by the revolution of 1789, Germany had followed a 'special road' (*Sonderweg*) to modernity.[2]

This approach has been questioned recently by David Blackbourn and Geoff Eley, and by Arno J. Mayer, although from different positions. Mayer talks of a 'persistence of the old regime' throughout Europe in the economic, political, and cultural spheres, and ascribes a general lack of self-confidence to the bourgeoisie *vis-à-vis* pre-industrial elites.[3] Blackbourn and Eley also see no fundamental differences between Germany and western Europe, although in their case this is because they place more emphasis generally on the powerful presence of the bourgeoisie. For them, there were numerous signs of growing bourgeois social influence, while the assumption by the bourgeoisie of older status symbols – where this occurred – signified not so much feudalization as the formation of a new ruling elite.[4] Among German historians, Hartmut Kaelble has also cast serious doubt on the feudalization thesis. In his view, the adoption of aristocratic patterns of behaviour by the industrial bourgeoisie should not necessarily be interpreted as a loss of bourgeois identity; it represented rather the tendency of new elites to secure and legitimize their position by appropriating what was originally associated with established elite groups.[5]

There are really two points at issue. The first is how far German development diverged significantly from the putative western European 'norm', the second how bourgeois or 'feudalized' European societies were in the nineteenth and early twentieth century. The debate about feudalization is certainly not the only social-historical angle of approach to the history of businessmen, but comparisons on the basis of precise, statistically supported enquiries into marriage patterns, the occupational choices of children, values, and social contacts nevertheless promise to provide better answers to many unresolved questions.[6]

Recent quantitative work has not, in general, provided evidence of the attraction exerted on the economic bourgeoisie by what Kaelble calls the 'aristocratic model'. Wilhelm Stahl, looking at businessmen from German-speaking Europe who had entries in the *Neue Deutsche Biographie*, found that a high proportion of their sons also became entrepreneurs: rather more than half the sons of Stahl's sample of 109 were engaged in business, 11 per cent became landowners or officers, 8 per cent officials, and 16 per cent entered the free professions.[7] Kaelble has found a similarly high level of self-recruitment.[8] In his study of Westphalian industrialists, Toni Pierenkemper has shown that these also had fathers and fathers-in-law who came predominantly from the upper reaches of business. Of the 56 fathers-in-law, 28 were entrepreneurs, 3 were engineers or craftsmen, 15 came from 'traditional occupations' (estate owner, officer, official), 4 from academic professions, and 5 from agriculture. Of the 175 heavy industrialists whose father's occupation could be determined, 93 had business and 10 technical backgrounds, 47 came from traditional occupations, 12 were from academic life and 10 engaged in agriculture.[9] Such 'tendencies to group-specific endogamy'[10] have also been demonstrated among entrepreneurs in the textile branch by Hans-Jürgen Teuteberg. The majority of the businessmen investigated by him came from industrial families, usually in textiles, and married into the same group. In the following generation, 21 of the 45 sons-in-law of textile entrepreneurs were themselves the sons of factory owners or businessmen, the remainder having fathers who were officers, academics, higher officials, or estate owners.[11]

Other studies have produced similar findings. Hansjoachim Henning, for example, has compared the social background, marriage patterns, and social contacts of the business elite – largely those with the title Commercial Councillor – with those of middle-ranking businessmen. While the latter had close links to master craftsmen and middle-ranking officials, the former demonstrated a marked degree of social self-sufficiency. In the period 1860–90, 75 per cent of the top businessmen came from that same social group. This tendency continued after the turn of the century, although it became somewhat less marked. Marriage partners were also chosen predominantly from within the same group, and a clear distance was maintained from other bourgeois groups. Private social contacts were generally with their own kind, although they did mix with the educated middle class and local officials in associations and on occasions such as factory celebrations. Henning talks of the top businessmen as a new elite shaped by industry and concerned to maintain its social autonomy. This relatively small group displayed some patterns of behaviour modelled on those of the nobility, but had no personal or social links to the aristocracy.[12] The findings of Dolores Augustine's study of German business multi-millionaires point in the same direction.[13]

When it comes to choices of occupation and marriage partner, two of the most important indicators of bourgeois attraction to the aristocracy, the evidence therefore indicates that the links between nobility and bourgeoisie were slight. More plausible are arguments that emphasize the special relationship of the German bourgeoisie to the state. Kaelble has suggested, for example, that many phenomena generally seen as evidence of the bourgeois propensity to ape the aristocracy were in fact expressions of a new bourgeois loyalty towards the state. That, in his view, is how we should explain the importance of the reserve officer corps and the high respect shown by the bourgeoisie towards officials and officers – the last of which found very specific expression in choices of occupation and marriage partner by the sons of the bourgeoisie.[14] The same point has been made by Jürgen Kocka and others.[15]

One way of considering arguments of this kind is to look at the elevation of members of the bourgeoisie into the nobility.[16] Another approach is to examine the bourgeois acquisition of titles from the state. The title designed specifically for businessmen in Prussia was Commercial Councillor. Research on these has been patchy. Articles have appeared on holders of the title in Essen and Dortmund,[17] and Werner Mosse's recent book on Jews in the modern German economy includes a chapter on those who became Commercial Councillors.[18] There are in addition scattered references to the subject throughout the general literature on business history. The present chapter, drawing on research done under the aegis of a larger comparative project on the bourgeoisie, offers the first systematic long-term analysis of those who became Prussian Commercial Councillors.

The intention is to pose a series of questions about the economic elite, as defined by the possession of this title. How was it formed and what was its social composition? What was the position of

Commercial Councillors compared to the local elite as a whole, in terms of economic power, social status, and political influence? Was the title an effect or a cause of success? Finally, what does acceptance of the title Commercial Councillor tell us about the attitude of its recipients towards the state? In order to answer these questions, I have used a variety of sources to construct a collective biography of the group in question, similar to that employed in the large-scale Cologne project on German parliamentarians in the years 1848 to 1933.[19] These sources include contemporary discussions about the practice and significance of the title, and many scattered references in biographies and works such as histories of firms. But the principal evidence comes from the records of central and local government authorities, as well as chambers of commerce, on the granting of the title. For the period 1830–1918 I have identified all those who received the title Commercial Councillor in the Prussian province of Westphalia, together with the administrative district of Düsseldorf in the Rhine Province. This provides a total of 673 businessmen. For comparative purposes, I have also looked at a control group of Councillors from Berlin and the surrounding area, and from the agrarian-dominated province of East Prussia.

On the basis of this quantitative evidence it is possible to reconstruct who became Councillors during this period, and to look at possible changes over time. No less important, it is also possible to identify regional and denominational differences among those who were granted the title, as well as their family backgrounds, the economic branches from which they came, and other variables.

II

Before presenting the results of this research, a word is necessary on the origin of the title Commercial Councillor and the means by which the honour was obtained. Under the form of Prussian administration that existed up to the early nineteenth century, Commercial Councillors exercised a quasi-bureaucratic role within the state councils of commerce (*Kommerzkollegien*). They were appointed onto these bodies to sit alongside civil servants and give their expert advice on economic questions. But the growing separation of state and civil society brought changes. In the economically liberal climate of the early nineteenth century, the state no longer sought to incorporate businessmen within its own apparatus, but confined itself to setting the framework within which economic activity was conducted. The result was the emergence of a state economic ministry on the one hand, and the formation of self-regulating bodies – such as chambers of commerce – to represent the interests of business on the other.[20] With the dissolution of the old corporate administration of the economy in the Prussian reforms of 1807, the original meaning of the Commercial Councillor title became obsolete.[21]

The title remained, but became a means by which the state gave honorary recognition to deserving members of the commercial and business classes. After the failure of the liberal reform ideas of Stein and Hardenberg, who had considered the possible participation of citizens in the administration ('National representation'), titles acquired a new function that was quite at odds with the intentions of the reformers. They became a relatively cheap substitute for the failed attempt to offer the bourgeoisie direct political participation. A title was understood by contemporaries as an official or honorific name which distinguished the bearer from others, by virtue of office, standing, or worthiness.[22] While senior bureaucrats received official titles (*Amtstitel*), Commercial Councillor was the highest honorary title not connected with office that could be bestowed on merchants, manufacturers, and industrialists.[23] Titular councillors were divided into a first class (Privy Councillor, or *Geheimer Rat*) and a second class (simple Commercial Councillor, or *Kommerzienrat*), which corresponded to the fourth and fifth ranks respectively of senior officials in the provincial administration.[24] In the nineteenth century it was within the gift of the King of Prussia to grant a businessman 'the rank (*Charakter*) of Royal Prussian [Privy] Councillor', subject to criteria laid down by decree.[25] Punishment was inflicted by the king for unauthorized use of the title, and the title was revoked in cases such as dishonest business practices. Loss of the title also followed automatically from the loss of civil rights (*bürgerliche Ehrenrechte*).[26] No general regulations for the granting of the title have survived for the period before 1890, although it was already being conferred in the first decades of the nineteenth century.[27] The designation Commercial Councillor was not brand new, and an obvious line of continuity links it to the title formerly held by businessmen within the corporate Prussian administration, even though its functional significance disappeared when the latter was reformed. Within the modern nineteenth-century state, under a system of constitutional monarchy, the title remained although its meaning had changed. It signified the closeness of the economic bourgeoisie in Germany to the state, and the specific means by which the state honoured prominent businessmen.

How did someone become a Commercial Councillor? The procedure for conferring the title was through official channels. Suggestions made by private individuals, bodies such as chambers of commerce, or local officials (district administrators, mayors) were passed through the competent individuals in the different rungs of the provincial administration and eventually to the Minister of Trade and Industry. It was normal to take up doubts or queries with the lower-level authorities, and in cases where the senior district or provincial officials felt that a particular proposal had no chance of success it would not be passed on to the top. From the later nineteenth century it became increasingly common for the ministry to seek information from the Imperial Bank (*Reichsbank*) about the financial circumstances of a candidate for the title. When the minister was persuaded by the information at his disposal that the individual concerned was worthy of the rank, he put forward a proposal to the king through the civil cabinet. The royal assent was seldom refused, and a patent would be drawn up over the counter-signature of the minister and the title granted after payment of the appropriate stamp duty.[28]

The suitability of candidates for the title was scrutinized in this way because they had to satisfy a set of strict criteria. Ministers of Trade set out the necessary qualifications for a potential Commercial Councillor in a number of confidential decrees, only some of which are extant. One of these originated from Hans von Berlepsch in 1890:

> In addition to personal worthiness, a prominent standing in commerce or industry and the general meritoriousness of a merchant or industrialist, the possession of very considerable means is also required as an essential precondition for obtaining the title. This wealth must be sufficient that there is felt to be no question whatever about the financial position of the person in question even under adverse business conditions.[29]

'Meritoriousness' (*Verdienstlichkeit*) was interpreted as a strong commitment to voluntary activity for the public good. This might take the form of membership and activity within bodies such as chambers of commerce, regional or supra-regional business federations like the Association of German Iron Manufacturers *(Verein deutscher Eisenhüttenleute)*, or organizations concerned with the improvement of communications such as a railway council *(Eisenbahnrat)*. The claim might equally rest on the assumption of honorary political posts at communal, provincial, or national level, or in charitable activity in a variety of spheres – the founding of a technical school, endowing a children's home, church, museum, or hospital, setting up a foundation for the needy or for injured miners, making donations of land or valuables to a town hall. By the time of the relevant decree of 22 January 1904,[30] if not before, importance was also attached to industrial welfare and schemes for the social security of workers, although activities in this sphere were ranked behind service to the common good in the recommendations passed on by the minister to the king. As far as the criterion of considerable wealth was concerned, the primary consideration was not the size of the fortune, but the long-term security and 'solid foundations' *(Fundierung)* of a recipient's position. This was demonstrated in the case of Fritz Baare, the executive General Director of the Bochum mining and steel combine, the *Verein für Bergbau und Gussstahlfabrikation.* In 1899, the senior district administrator *(Regierungspräsident)* of Arnsberg took the view that Baare's personal wealth of 700,000 Marks was insufficient to warrant the granting of a title. But the fact that Baare, as general director of the Bochum combine, possessed a high income and a secure position encouraged the authorities to turn a blind eye to his relatively meagre personal wealth, and he became a Commercial Councillor the same year.[31]

Despite the laying down of the requirements expected of someone aspiring to the title, individual cases continued to raise uncertainties and doubts in the minds of the authorities. It was these which the ministerial decree of 28 March 1911 was intended to resolve.[32] The minister emphasized once again that only active businessmen could receive the title, not those who had given up their commercial or industrial activities, however recently. Potential Councillors should have earned their standing primarily in the field of business, while other activities such as those undertaken for the public good, although desirable, were not to be given preferential attention. What should be prevented above all was the appearance that the conferment of the title was linked to the donation of particular sums of money. There should thus be the maximum possible interval between such donations and the bestowing of the title, in order to avoid giving the impression that the title of Commercial Councillor could be acquired simply through the payment of a certain sum of money.[33] Finally, according to the minister's guidelines, only under exceptional circumstances should there be more than one Commercial Councillor in the same firm at a given time, and only those who had already been Councillors for ten years should be elevated to the rank of Privy Councillor.

It is clear from the sources that without being explicitly referred to, political criteria – i.e. loyalty towards government and ruling house – continued to play an important role in the granting of titles. Thus, the Mönchen-Gladbach textile industrialist Franz Brandts, a Catholic, was still being refused the title in 1888 because as a supporter of the Catholic Centre Party he had shown himself too 'ultramontane in his attitudes'.[34] Previous political support for the Progressive Party was also frequently an obstacle, although this could be fairly easily made good by those who 'laundered' their views in a National Liberal direction. Before the formal patent to the title was drawn up, particularly close attention was paid in the years before the First World War, through discreet enquiries, to whether the would-be recipient was prepared to pay the appropriate sum of stamp duty. Until 1909 the tariff for any title was 300 Marks. After the changes to the 1895 law on stamp duty introduced by the financial reform of 26 June 1909, the title of Commercial Councillor henceforth cost 3,000 Marks, that of Privy Councillor, 5,000 Marks.[35]

III

In the nineteenth and early twentieth century, applications for the titles of Councillor or Privy Councillor of Commerce were made on behalf of 673 merchants and manufacturers in the Prussian province of Westphalia and the Düsseldorf district of the Rhine Province. Of these, 256 came from Westphalia, 417 from the district of Düsseldorf. The number of applications rose from around 1890, and still more steeply after the turn of the century, so that there were as many applications in the years 1900–18 as there had been in the whole of the previous sixty years.[36]

In our sample, the earliest grants of the Commercial Councillor title were made to three businessmen from Elberfeld in 1834, Joh. Adolf Carnap, August von der Heydt, and Wilhelm Kaspar

Table *3.1* Applications for titles 'Commercial Councillor' and 'Privy Commercial Councillor' in Rhineland-Westphalia, 1830–1918

1830–9	7
1840–9	37
1850–9	34
1860–9	57
1870–9	74
1880–9	74
1890–9	107
1900–9	229
1910–18	170

(N = 673)

Meckel. The first to be honoured as a Privy Councillor was Friedrich Diergardt, a textile industrialist from Viersen, in 1842. In fifty-two cases the title Privy Councillor was granted, in contravention of the guidelines, less than ten years after the conferment of the lesser title. This occurred with particular frequency in the Düsseldorf district, and mainly in the period after 1890. Compared with the overall sample, this speedy elevation to Privy Councillor affected mining entrepreneurs more than other branches, Catholics more than Protestants, liberal-minded rather than conservative industrialists.

The majority (57.7 per cent) of the Westphalian and Düsseldorf Councillors came from the same town in which they were engaged in business, and almost three-quarters came from the same administrative district. That the regional mobility of the group should have been so low is no surprise, for setting up a business naturally had a strongly negative effect on geographical mobility. And given that many concerns were run with the help of (or inherited by) sons, sons-in-law, and other relations, their lack of mobility is also registered in the findings that show a high degree of local rootedness (*Bodenständigkeit*). The 'settled' pattern among the Commercial Councillors was representative of Rhenish and Westphalian businessmen generally. It applied particularly to areas with a strong and developed industrial tradition like Westphalia and the Bergisches Land, and was to be found in the mining and iron branches as well as among entrepreneurs in the cotton and linen sectors.[37]

The social background of the businessmen granted titles was predominantly within the economic bourgeoisie. In Westphalia and Düsseldorf, more than half (54.8 per cent) had a businessman as a father, and a further third (33.8 per cent) came from commercial families. Other social backgrounds were relatively uncommon: 6.4 per cent had their origins in the free professions, 4.5 per cent had official backgrounds, only 0.6 per cent came from craftsmen's families. Compared to the social origins of businessmen as a whole, the high degree of social self-recruitment among title-holders is striking. This applied to 88.6 per cent of the Commercial Councillors, against a general figure of between two-thirds and three-quarters. The difference can be seen in individual branches. In heavy industry, 80.7 per cent of Councillors came from business backgrounds, compared with the figure of 53.1 per cent given by Pierenkemper for all heavy industrialists.[38] The difference is there, if less strikingly, even in the unusually homogeneous group of Westphalian textile industrialists. Over the period 1880–1913, 85 per cent of all entrepreneurs in this branch came from merchant, merchant-capitalist, or manufacturing families;[39] Commercial Councillors in textiles exceed even this, with a figure of 90.9 per cent. Although time-spans and geographical boundaries do not coincide exactly in these comparisons, it is safe to assume that the degree of self-recruitment among titled businessmen was greater than it was among their untitled peers. Commercial Councillors had an even more homogeneous social background than the economic bourgeoisie as a whole.

What does our sample reveal about the choice of occupation and marriage partner among the sons and daughters of the entrepreneurial elite? The business history literature habitually emphasizes that members of the economic bourgeoisie tended to relinquish entrepreneurial activity as soon as possible and live as *rentiers*. The lack of quantitative research to support this proposition has already been mentioned. The evidence from the present enquiry certainly points in the opposite direction. In the 174 cases about which we have information, the overwhelming majority of Councillors' sons became industrialists, while industrialists and merchants constituted the most favoured group among which daughters sought marriage partners.

The broader occupational range of daughters' marriage partners, compared with the occupations of sons, is unsurprising. Whom daughters married was of secondary importance from the point of view of keeping up the business. The needs of the firm nevertheless put pressure on both sons and daughters. Male children seldom had a truly free choice of what they did in life, especially an only

Table *3.2* Occupation of sons and marriage partners of daughters of Commercial Councillors, Rhineland-Westphalia 1830–1918 (%)

	Sons	Sons-in-law
Industrialists	66.7	31.6
Free Professionals	13.3	21.0
Officers	6.7	12.3
Landowners	6.7	7.0
Officials	3.3	19.3
Merchants	3.3	8.8

(N = 174)

son and heir who was gifted. They were 'destined for the business' and in the event of a conflict had to subordinate their own ideas to its interests.[40] Take the case of Wilhelm Endemann of Bochum, whose father owned a brewery and was also an agriculturalist, publican, and baker. Under pressure from his father, he gave up plans to study theology and went into the family business in 1825 at the age of 16.[41] As a historian has recently observed, handing on the business to one's own sons represented 'one of the central entrepreneurial strategies of the large bourgeoisie in the nineteenth century'.[42] At the same time, the marriage of a daughter also frequently formed part of a larger dynastic design. Businessmen looked for equality of social and financial standing in the families into which their daughters married.[43] The importance of forging good business connections was uppermost, and efforts were often made to marry daughters into manufacturing circles in the same locality and engaged in the same branch of production.[44]

What of the distribution of titles by industrial sector? Table 3.3, shows textile industrialists very clearly in first place, followed by heavy industrialists, and those concerned with food production and commerce. Three-quarters of all Commercial Councillors came from these four sectors, with other branches poorly represented.

Over time, mining and heavy industry showed the most marked improvement in their share. Mining entrepreneurs showed a steady rise from 2.7 per cent of all Councillor titles before 1850 to 4.5 per cent in 1850–70, 5.5 per cent in 1870–90, and 7.6 per cent after 1890; the share of heavy industrialists nearly tripled from the period before 1850 to the years 1870–90, from 7.7 to 21.1 per cent, then rose again to 23.8 per cent after 1890. The foodstuffs and luxury foods sector showed a modest increase from 7.7 per

Table *3.3* Distribution of Commercial Councillors by sector, Rhineland-Westphalia, 1830–1918 (%)

Textiles	32.4
Heavy Industry	21.3
Foodstuffs	11.6
Commerce	9.6
Mining	6.6
Banking	6.5
Chemicals	4.5
Paper/Printing	4.1
Stone/Quarrying	1.5
Leather	0.8
Transport	0.6
Electrical	0.2
Insurance	0.2
Other	0.3

cent before 1850 to 12.5 per cent in 1870–90, before falling back slightly to 11.8 per cent after 1890. The share of both the textile and banking sectors reached a high point in the decades preceding German unification and declined thereafter, the former from 43.9 per cent in 1850–70 to 28.1 per cent after 1890, the latter from 15.1 per cent to 5.8 per cent between the same dates. The share taken by those involved in commerce more than halved (from 17.9 to 7.6 per cent) between the period before 1850 and the years 1850–70, fell again slightly to 7 per cent in 1870–90, then rose to 9.9 per cent after 1890. Before the turn of the century the textile sector very plainly had the largest share of those who became Commercial Councillors and retained its leading position through to 1918. In the period before 1850, commerce and then banking were in second place. In the two decades before unification banking moved clearly into second place ahead of commerce (this was the era when the great banking houses were founded),[45] with heavy industry in third place, and the food sector in fourth. The last two each moved up a place in the period 1870–90, a position they retained in subsequent years while banking was relegated to a lowlier place in the league table.

Commercial Councillors in Westphalia and the Düsseldorf district were generally to be found in fewer than 1 per cent of the firms in a given sector.[46] Mining was the exception, especially in Rhenish districts. In the Arnsberg district 1.8 per cent of all mine owners bore the title; in the Düsseldorf district the figure was as high as 5.9 per cent. Most concerns with Commercial Councillors were private firms. Only a few, in the iron and steel, chemical, and food branches, were publicly quoted companies.

Ministerial guidelines laid down that an aspiring Prussian Councillor of Commerce should possess wealth and income that were adequate and secure. How did their actual financial circumstances measure up to this? Table 3.4 gives the annual incomes of a sample of 329 Councillors, which ranged from 3,000 Marks to 1.89 million Marks. The majority earned between 50,000 and 500,000 Marks, with a median income of 130,000 Marks.

Table *3.4* Annual income of Commercial Councillors (in Marks), Rhineland-Westphalia 1830–1918

	Number	Percentage
Under 5,000	2	0.6
5–10,000	1	0.3
10–20,000	4	1.2
20–50,000	38	11.6
50–100,000	72	21.9
100–200,000	93	28.3
200–500,000	91	27.7
500,000–1,000,000	22	6.7
1–2,000,000	6	1.8

(N = 329)

Two-thirds of the Councillors owned fortunes of between 1 and 5 million Marks. On the other hand, 20 per cent were non-millionaires, and thus did not meet the requirement laid down in 1909 that Councillors should have assets of at least a million Marks.[47] Almost all could nevertheless demonstrate personal wealth exceeding 500,000 Marks. That is shown by Table 3.5, giving details of 319 Commercial Councillors.

Individual cases show that the minimum figure lay around the 100–200,000 Mark level. The evidence suggests that the Duisburg soap manufacturer Eduard Gallenkamp, who had assets of only 100,000 Marks, probably failed in his efforts to acquire the title in 1874. The same is true of the linen manufacturer August Sternenberg, from Schwelm in Westphalia, whose personal wealth amounted to a mere 200,000 Marks when he failed to be granted the title in 1903.[48] At the other end of the scale, the wealthiest Commercial Councillor in Westphalia was Gustav Selve from

Table *3.5* Personal wealth of Commercial Councillors,
Rhineland-Westphalia, 1830–1918

	Number	Percentage
100–200,000	2	0.6
200–500,000	17	5.3
500,000–1,000,000	45	14.1
1–2,000,000	114	35.7
2–5,000,000	105	33.2
5–10,000,000	23	7.2
10–20,000,000	10	3.1
Over 20,000,000	2	0.6

(N = 318)

Altena, who was worth 30 million Marks;[49] his counterparts in the Rhineland were the Langenberg soap manufacturer Adalbert Colsman, and the joint owner of the Düsseldorf firm of Haniel and Lueg, Franz Haniel. Both had fortunes of around 20 million Marks when they became Privy Commercial Councillors.[50]

A breakdown of our sample by religious denomination also yields clear results. The great majority of Councillors were Protestant (73.4 per cent); only around one in five was Catholic and about one in twenty Jewish. Although the Catholic proportion rose at the end of the nineteenth century – from 5.9 per cent of Councillors in 1850–70, to 18.6 per cent in the following two decades and 23.8 per cent after 1890 – they remained strongly underrepresented by comparison with their share of the population. In the middle of the century Catholics made up 42.89 per cent of the population in Westphalia and 23.47 per cent in the Rhine Province. Businessmen were, however, disproportionately Protestant. The extreme case was Krefeld, where the population was over 70 per cent Catholic, but the textile manufacturers and merchant-capitalists (*Verleger*) were exclusively Protestant.[51] In the period around 1900, Protestants constituted 38.5 per cent of the population in Rhineland-Westphalia, but provided 78.1 per cent of the entrepreneurs; Catholics, conversely, made up two-thirds of the population but provided only one entrepreneur in seven.[52] The position was similar in the German Empire as a whole, although the discrepancy was somewhat less extreme: Protestants accounted for 62.5 per cent of the population but 73.3 per cent of the businessmen, Catholics for 36.1 per cent of the population, and only 11.9 per cent of the businessmen.

The evidence of a very marked overrepresentation of Protestants among Commercial Councillors tends therefore to confirm Max Weber's thesis about the 'predominantly Protestant character of capital ownership and entrepreneurship'.[53] This has been constantly propounded but seldom backed up by quantitative research. Historians have frequently referred to the dominance of Protestant entrepreneurs in the Bergisch, Märkisch, and Ravensberg regions, and to the fact that the leading industrialists of the Ruhr as well as the majority of the textile manufacturers on the Catholic Lower Rhine were likewise Protestant.[54] Attempts have been made to explain this preponderance of Protestants in the economic bourgeoisie in terms of the 'minority' argument:

> When a religious minority was formed, the 'traditional roads to riches, standing and power' were . . . not infrequently barred to them, so that energy and effort were constantly demanded of them, group cohesion grew, and the credit that was loyally extended to fellow-believers made business on a supra-regional basis easier.[55]

This argument certainly explains the high proportion of Protestant businessmen in regions with a predominantly Catholic character like the Prussian west. But the converse is not true: the Catholic minority in heavily Protestant regions did not generate a disproportionately large number of Catholic businessmen, and there too Protestant entrepreneurs predominated. The 'minority' argument alone does not explain the Protestant-Catholic discrepancy. As Weber himself noted, the main cause has to be sought in the permanent inner characteristics of a religious community, not in the external position in which its members find themselves at a given time.[56] This was the basis of the celebrated thesis on the Protestant ethic and the spirit of capitalism, whereby the values and forms of behaviour encouraged by Protestantism (and especially by the Protestant sects) initially provided an essential precondition for successful economic activity. It is clear, conversely, that the under-representation of German Catholics among businessmen has to be seen against a background of a traditional scepticism within the Catholic milieu towards secularization, economic liberalism, capitalism, and the materialism associated with the rising industrial system.[57]

When it comes to party-political sympathies, we have information for only about a quarter (179) of the whole sample. Table

3.6 shows that the Councillors in question leaned overwhelmingly towards the National Liberal and Conservative parties.

Table *3.6* Party-political sympathies of Commercial Councillors, Rhineland-Westphalia, 1830–1918

	Number	Percentage
National Liberal	99	55.3
Conservative	45	25.1
Free Conservative	16	8.9
Centre	13	7.3
Liberal	4	2.2
Left Liberal	2	1.1

(N = 179)

Support for the Conservatives among Commercial Councillors declined in the course of the nineteenth century, although it rose somewhat for the Free Conservatives. The most striking change, however, was the growth in support for liberal parties, and above all for the National Liberals. In the period 1850–70, only 14.3 per cent of Councillors about whom we have information were liberal sympathizers. This figure rose to 41.3 per cent in 1870–90, and 70.3 per cent after 1890. The Centre Party, founded in 1870, enjoyed strong support from Councillors in the Catholic region around Münster (45.5 per cent, almost as many as the liberals), while the Conservatives continued to enjoy high levels of support in the Minden district (52.9 per cent over the whole period). The party sympathies of titled businessmen generally reflected what research has shown to be those of the economic bourgeoisie as a whole. The dominant inclination was towards moderate liberalism, which tended after 1850 to accept and support the existing state system and social order. Above all, the National Liberals, whose 1884 programme was strongly geared to business interests, developed into the classic party of the German economic bourgeoisie. As the banker Carl Fürstenberg later recalled, 'At that time National Liberalism was just about the only thing which had a claim to respect in the Prussian business world.'[58]

IV

Commercial Councillor was evidently a most acceptable and popular title to possess, and businessmen applied for it with notable self-assurance. 'If I do not receive this title soon, there is little point in remaining active in business, which I do not need to do', was how Julius Schmits of Elberfeld put it in an application of 1894.[59] As far as we know, the title was seldom refused when offered. Julius van der Zypen of Cologne declined the simple title in 1898 on the grounds that it was 'inadequate'; he successfully demanded to be made a Privy Councillor straight away.[60] The bestowing of an order seems to have been a less attractive alternative. The practice of conferring titles shows that orders were frequently seen as a kind of surrogate for businessmen not considered worthy of the Commercial Councillor title. On the other hand, many Councillors were holders of the Order of the Red Eagle or the Order of the Crown. The elevation of businessmen into the nobility as a more exalted alternative to the Councillor title seems not to have been an issue, judging from our sources. Of the 673 Councillors from Westphalia and the Düsseldorf district, just 9 were ennobled, including 5 members of the ancient Essen family of Waldthausen, whose noble status went back to the year 1569 and was confirmed in 1903. In three cases ennoblement followed conferment of the Privy Councillor title. Rudolf Baum of Elberfeld became a Councillor in 1901, a Privy Councillor in 1912, and was ennobled in 1913. Friedrich Diergardt became a Councillor in 1837, a Privy Councillor five years later, and entered the nobility in 1860. Gustav Mevissen received the Councillor title in 1855, became a Privy Councillor in 1859, and was ennobled in 1884. However, numerous other businessmen were never ennobled, including some figures of national importance such as Krupp, Klöckner, Thyssen, Haniel, and Delius.

If a businessman was to receive recognition by the state, the title of Commercial Councillor was thus viewed by both sides as the most appropriate and keenly coveted. It is therefore understandable if there were attempts to acquire the title 'at any price', whether through the normal route or via the 'traffic (*Schacher*) in Councillor titles' that had already attracted the hostility of contemporaries. Newspaper advertisements and the critical commentary they drew suggest that the sale of titles went on, although cases in which the title was effectively bought were almost certainly exceptional. Levin Schücking's novel *Held der Zukunft* was already referring to the sale of titles in 1855.[61] In his memoirs of Berlin, Adolf von Wilke held that talk of titles for sale was exaggerated and the product of envy, but in an article published in 1889 with the title 'Prussian Royal Titles are For Sale', Uli Schanz referred to newspaper advertisements which offered to procure titles.[62] Other critics talked of a going rate for the Commercial Councillor title of between 30,000 and 60,000 Marks.[63] A 'full price-list' is even supposed to have existed, in which the Commercial Councillor title cost 30,000 Marks, with lesser titles going down to 7500 Marks and no payment in advance required.[64] It may be that some disappointed aspirants, failing in their efforts to acquire the title through the normal means, were driven to this expediency by thwarted ambition.[65] But those who had come by their titles honestly were inevitably troubled by the 'humiliating awareness . . . that what they had achieved by ability could have been more easily acquired with hard cash'.[66] The alleged abuse was bitterly satirized by one writer in the following words: 'Every wife should give her husband a title . . . for Christmas. So buy now, ladies and gentlemen, and don't delay!'[67]

This contemporary debate, which was mainly critical in tone, suggests a powerful longing among the bourgeoisie for recognition in the form of titles and orders. The craving for titles was already being described in 1846 as an 'epidemic' (*Titelseuche*) that was particularly widespread in Germany.[68] With the growth in the number of titles conferred around the end of the century, such criticism became more common.[69] In fact, the relevant files give a revealing glimpse into the expectations of those who sought the Councillor title. Applicants frequently refer to its acquisition as an 'ardent desire', a 'particular source of gratification', and 'a matter of great consequence'; the conferment of the title was 'eagerly awaited' as bringing 'great happiness'. As a contemporary wrote, 'for some worthy (*bieder*) Germans the longing for the title Commercial Councillor and even more for the title of Privy Councillor, causes sleepless nights'.[70] There were those who argued, from the perspective of the bourgeois ethos of achievement (*Leistungsethos*) that the title had been granted to too many who were unworthy of it: the inflation of the title had caused it to degenerate into a negative honour, something that was purely decorative once mediocrity had become the criterion.[71] The title was also devalued in the eyes of some because non-experts determined who should receive it, while from an austerely democratic standpoint it was meaningless because conferred by authority.[72]

These contemporary criticisms of the longing for titles, whether made directly or expressed in the fiction of the period,[73] unsurprisingly found no echo in the behaviour of those who applied for the Commercial Councillor title. In none of the 673 cases in my sample was the honour refused, although it is known that a few recipients attached no value to titles or honours and ignored their Councillor title.[74] The demand that 'commerce should have nothing whatsoever to do with any titles which it does not need, for it has long outgrown the protection of the bureaucracy' seems to have found little resonance, despite the claim that prominent and influential merchants refused titles.[75]

What did make the title attractive? One observer noted that 'it may not always be vanity which prompts the craving for titles and orders, for business interests also play a not inconsiderable role in this'.[76] Lewinsohn spoke of the title possessing 'real goodwill value in business', easing contacts and securing orders that would not otherwise have been obtained.[77] For Avenarius, the title had a 'monetary value' and served as a 'guarantee of financial security'.[78] It was a testimonial from the state to the credit-worthiness of the individual concerned, for it was known in the business world that titles were granted only after exhaustive inquiries.[79] The title was therefore clearly of financial benefit by virtue of its business advantages.[80] If it brought benefits in business, it also gave rise to envy among competitors; but these could hardly withhold their congratulations 'because otherwise he wouldn't buy from them'.[81] But the title also brought increased social standing and greater influence with the authorities, as well as inspiring pride among relations, and these considerations played a major part in prompting businessmen to seek the title.[82]

V

The Commercial Councillor title and the circumstances in which it was granted belong to the larger social history of the German economic bourgeoisie, or 'aristocracy of money'. The subject also provides an ideal means of observing the relationship between state, aristocracy, and a bourgeoisie whose social position appeared not to match the economic power it had achieved in the course of a rapid process of industrialization. The business elite in particular clearly attached a high value to social acceptance and public appreciation of achievements it believed to be of general social benefit. The Prussian state offered an excellent means by which such public recognition could be expressed, in the form of a title reserved specifically for businessmen: Commercial Councillor. The title enjoyed great popularity among Prussian merchants and manufacturers, for it represented a high state honour for deserving citizens and a sign of belonging to a select group within the business community.

One important reason for the high regard in which Prussian titles, orders, and honours were held – and Privy Councillor of Commerce was the highest honorary title available to a businessman in Prussia – may be found in the fact that no such honours existed at the level of the German Empire. Those granted by Prussia, the largest and most powerful of the federal states within the Empire, whose king was also German Emperor, therefore assumed a particular importance. Moreover, by comparison with equivalent titles in other states such as Bavaria, Saxony, and Austria, the Prussian title of Commercial Councillor appears to have been granted on the basis of very strict criteria and obtained only with difficulty, with the result that it was accordingly very highly valued.[83] It is open to question whether it can really be regarded as 'a permanent yardstick of social ranking for the whole nineteenth century', as one author has claimed.[84] But possession of the title certainly denoted public recognition, economic potency, a good moral character, and finally social standing.[85] With businessmen around the turn of the century in mind, Friedrich Naumann spoke of a generation 'in which people would rather be called Herr Commercial Councillor than Herr Baron'.[86] For the word 'Councillor' – the suffix '-rat' in German – suggested equality of standing with the highly esteemed bureaucracy.[87]

In most European countries – Britain, France, the Netherlands, Belgium, Switzerland – there was no title equivalent to Commercial Councillor.[88] The use of the title in Prussia indicates a peculiarity of the German bourgeoisie, namely its strongly marked statism. The enthusiasm for the Councillor title suggests a relationship on the part of the business elite towards the state that was positive and supportive rather than critical or aloof. Whether this indicates some lack of 'bourgeois' values is more questionable, however, in view of the self-assurance with which businessmen regarded their own achievements. Closeness to the state and bourgeois self-confidence seem to have gone together. While the state undoubtedly sought the political integration of the bourgeoisie, the latter also benefited from the state's seal of approval. The bourgeoisie claimed that it worked in the general public interest, that its particular

107

interests were subordinated to the common good. It was able to represent the pursuit of its own interests in this way all the more effectively for having the approval and backing of the state. The Commercial Councillor title was one important means by which this recognition by the state was expressed.

NOTES

This chapter has been translated by David Blackbourn.

1 Werner Sombart, *Die deutsche Volkswirtschaft im 19. Jahrhundert* (Berlin, 1903), 469–70

2 Friedrich Zunkel, *Der Rheinisch-Westfälische Unternehmer 1834–1879* (Cologne, 1962). The relatively limited number of cases considered, their possible lack of representativeness, and the absence of statistical methods should all be noted in Zunkel's work.

3 Arno J. Mayer, *The Persistence of the Old Regime* (London, 1981).

4 David Blackbourn and Geoff Eley, *The Peculiarities of German History: Bourgeois Society and Politics in Nineteenth-Century Germany* (Oxford, 1984).

5 Hartmut Kaelble, 'Wie feudal waren die deutschen Unternehmer im Kaiserreich?', in Richard Tilly (ed.), *Beiträge zur quantitativen vergleichenden Unternehmensgeschichte* (Stuttgart, 1985), 148–71.

6 Other no less important approaches to entrepreneurial history are discussed in Jürgen Kocka, 'Familie, Unternehmer und Kapitalismus. An Beispielen aus der frühen Industrialisierung', in *Zeitschrift für Unternehmensgeschichte*, 24 (1979), 99–135.

7 Wilhelm Stahl, *Der Elitekreislauf in der Unternehmerschaft* (Frankfurt-on-Main, 1973).

8 Hartmut Kaelble, 'Long-term changes in the recruitment of the business elite: Germany compared to the U.S., Great Britain, and France since the Industrial Revolution', *Journal of Social History*, 13 (1980), 404–23.

9 Toni Pierenkemper, *Die westfälischen Schwerindustriellen 1852–1913. Soziale Struktur und unternehmerischer Erfolg* (Göttingen, 1979), 44ff.

10 Pierenkemper, *Die westfälischen Schwerindustriellen*, 46.

11 Hans-Jürgen Teuteberg, *Westfälische Textilunternehmer in der Industrialisierung. Sozialer Status und betriebliches Verhalten im 19. Jahrhundert* (Dortmund, 1980), 32.

12 Hansjoachim Henning, 'Soziale Verflechtungen der Unternehmer in Westfalen 1860–1914', *Zeitschrift für Unternehmensgeschichte*, 23 (1978), 1–30. Friedrich Zunkel has also shown that there was no intermarriage between businessmen and nobility. See *Der Rheinisch-Westfälische Unternehmer 1837–1879* (Cologne, 1962), 95.

13 'Heiratsverhalten und Berufswahl in den nichtagrarischen Multimillionärsfamilien in Deutschland vor 1914', unpublished MA dissertation, Free University Berlin, 1983. See also chapter 2 of the present book.

14 Kaelble, 'Wie feudal'.

15 Jürgen Kocka, 'Bürgertum und bürgerliche Gesellschaft im 19. Jahrhundert. Europäische Entwicklungen und deutsche Eigenarten', in Kocka (ed.), *Bürgertum im 19. Jahrhundert. Deutschland im europäischen Vergleich*, 3 vols (Munich, 1988), 1:11–76.

16 See Hans-Konrad Stein, 'Der preussische Geldadel des 19. Jahrhunderts. Untersuchungen zur Nobilitierungspolitik der preussischen Regierung und zur Anpassung der oberen Schichten des Bürgertums an den Adel', unpublished dissertation, Hamburg, 1982.

17 Hermann Schröter, 'Essener Kommerzienräte', *Die Heimatstadt Essen* (1959/60), 59–84; Paul H. Mertes, 'Zum Sozialprofil der Oberschicht im Ruhrgebiet, dargestellt an den Dortmunder Kommerzienräten, *Beiträge zur Geschichte Dortmunds und der Grafschaft Mark*, 67 (1971), 167–227. Schröter's article is based largely on material in the Essen municipal archive (*Stadtarchiv*); Mertes has used similar sources for Dortmund, but his article is mainly based on Prussian central government documents now located in Merseburg.

18 Werner Mosse, *Jews in the German Economy. The German-Jewish Economic Elite 1820–1935* (Oxford, 1987), 69–95.

19 At the *Zentrum für Historische Sozialforschung* (Centre for Historical-Social Research) in Cologne, a long-established project employing quantitative methods has been engaged in research into German parliamentarians. See, for example, Wilhelm Heinz Schröder (ed.), *Sozialdemokratische Reichstagsabgeordnete und Reichstagskandidaten 1898–1918. Biographisch-statistisches Handbuch* (Düsseldorf, 1986).

20 The status and degree of autonomy of organizations like the chambers of commerce has attracted a large literature. Some (like Thomas Nipperdey) see them as quasi-official bodies, others (like Wolfram Fischer and Hartmut Kaelble) emphasize that they were forerunners of modern industrial interest-organizations. See T. Nipperdey, 'Interessenverbände und Parteien in Deutschland vor dem Ersten Weltkrieg', in Hans-Ulrich Wehler (ed.), *Moderne deutsche Sozialgeschichte* (Cologne, 1976), 369–88; H. Kaelble, 'Industrielle Interessenverbände vor 1914', in Walter Rüegg and Otto Neuloh (eds), *Zur soziologischen Theorie und Analyse des 19. Jahrhunderts* (Göttingen, 1971), 180–92; W. Fischer, *Wirtschaft und Gesellschaft im Zeitalter der Industrialisierung* (Göttingen, 1972), 197.

21 Friedrich Facius, *Wirtschaft und Staat. Entwicklung der staatlichen Wirtschaftsverwaltung in Deutschland vom 17. Jahrhundert bis 1945* (Boppard, 1959), 30.

22 *Allgemeine deutsche Real-Encyklopädie für die gebildeten Stände. Conversations-Lexikon*, 14 (Leipzig, 1847), 309.

23 *Allgemeine deutsche Real-Encyklopädie für die gebildeten Stände. Conversations-Lexikon*, 10 (Berlin and Vienna, 1902).

24 Hermann Lorenz, *Die Amtstitel und Rangverhältnisse der höheren, mittleren und unteren Reichs- und Preuss. Staatsbeamten, der Hofbeamten, der Offiziere, Geistlichen, Lehrer, Rechtsanwälte, Bürgermeister und sonstigen Kommunalbeamten in Preussen sowie der Landesbeamten und Lehrer von Elsass-Lothringen, ferner Bestimmungen über Diplomprüfungen und über Erlangung und Führung akademischer Würden und endlich sachweise über die rangmässigen Wohnungs-*

geldzuschüsse, Tagegelder, Fahrkosten und Umzugskosten (Berlin, 1907), 27–9; Rudolf von Bitter (ed.), *Handwörterbuch der preussischen Verwaltung*, 2 (Leipzig, 1911), 342. After 1817 higher ministerial officials were divided into three classes. Cf. Lorenz, *Amtstitel*, 21ff.

25 See Zentrales Staatsarchiv [ZStA] Merseburg, Rep 120, CB 11, Nr. 1, Beiheft 1, p. 6: Allerhöchste Verordnung vom 27,10.1810; Prussian Constitution of 31 January 1850, articles 45, 47, 50; Heinrich Marquardsen, *Handbuch des öffentlichen Rechts der Gegenwart*, 2:pt 2 (Freiburg, 1887), 44–6; Ludwig von Rönne, *Das Staatsrecht der preussischen Monarchie*, 1 (Leipzig, 1899), 210–12; Robert Graf Hue von Grais, *Handbuch der Verfassung und Verwaltung in Preussen und dem Deutschen Reiche* (Berlin, 1914), 65; Paul Herre (ed.), *Politisches Handwörterbuch*, 2 (Leipzig, 1923), 237. We are dealing therefore with an act of government, a state honour, and not with a court title as Rudolf Braun suggests. See R. Braun, 'Zur Einwirkung sozio-kultureller Umweltbedingungen auf das Unternehmerpotential und das Unternehmerverhalten', in Wolfram Fischer (ed.), *Wirtschafts- und sozialgeschichtliche Probleme der frühen Industrialisierung* (Berlin, 1968), 247–84, esp. 264ff. In their political dictionary, Rotteck and Welcker referred to the conferring of rank as 'an empty title without office': Carl von Rotteck and Carl Welcker (eds), *Das Staats-Lexikon. Encyklopädie der sämmtlichen Staatswissenschaften für alle Stände*, 12 (Altona, 1848), 575.

26 E. Braun, 'Die Zurückziehung von Titeln, Orden und Ehrenzeichen nach dem Verwaltungsrecht in Preussen', *Archiv des öffentlichen Rechts*, 16 (1901), 533, 545; Eduard Hubrich, 'Die Entziehung verliehener Ehrentitel in Preussen', *Archiv des öffentlichen Rechts*, 22 (1907), 327–68; Lorenz, *Amtstitel*, 13–15.

27 An early beneficiary of the conferment of the title was the merchant Koch of Cologne in 1820: Hauptstaatsarchiv Düsseldorf-Kalkum [HStA-Düsseldorf-Kalkum] Regierung Düsseldorf, Präs, 394, Bl 14. The relevant files of the Prussian Ministry of Trade and Industry dealing with the conferring of titles begin immediately after the dissolution of the old corporate administration for the area of Berlin and Brandenburg (1810), slightly later for the Rhine Province (1820) and Westphalia (1828). The absence of any early regulations on the conferring of the title has been confirmed on my enquiry by the archives I have used.

28 See the extensive files of the Ministry of Trade and Industry and the Civil Cabinet in ZStA Merseburg. Also Lorenz, *Amtstitel*, 28ff; 'Wie erwirbt man den Kommerzienratstitel?', *Reichsbote*, 13 Nov. 1910.

29 Staatsarchiv [StA] Detmold, Landratsamt Warburg, M 2, 582: Erlass des Ministers für Handel und Gewerbe vom 8. Oktober 1890.

30 StA Detmold, Landratsamt Warburg, M 2 583.

31 Staatsarchiv [StA] Münster, Oberpräsidium, 1514, Bd. 2, Bl 85–6.

32 StA Detmold, Landratsamt Warburg, M 2, 583.

33 StA Münster, Kreis Hörde, Landratsamt, Nr. 7: Erlass des Ministers für Handel und Gewerbe vom 22, Juli 1914; StA Detmold, Landratsamt Warburg, M 2, 583. But see also below, pp. 104–5.

34 ZStA Merseburg, Rep 120, A IV, 13a, Bl 132.

35 StA Münster, Regierung Münster, 4662, B1 9.
36 Few applications were made during the First World War. Not until 1918, when German defeat became clear and the fall of the monarchy was feared (which did indeed lead to the abolition of the title) did the number of applications rise again.
37 Gerhard Adelmann, 'Führende Unternehmer im Rheinland und in Westfalen 1850–1914', *Rheinische Vierteljahresblätter*, 35 (1971), 335–52; Gerhard Adelmann, 'Die wirtschaftlichen Führungsschichten der rheinisch-westfälischen Baumwoll– und Leinenindustrie von 1850 bis zum Ersten Weltkrieg', in Herbert Helbig (ed.), *Führungskräfte der Wirtschaft im 19. Jahrhundert 1790–1914*, II (Limburg, 1977), 177–99; Karl Emsbach, *Die soziale Betriebsverfassung der rheinischen Baumwollindustrie im 19. Jahrhundert* (Bonn, 1982); Hans-Jürgen Teuteberg, *Westfälische Textilunternehmer in der Industrialisierung* (Dortmund, 1980).
38 Pierenkemper, *Die westfälischen Schwerindustriellen*, 44.
39 Hans-Ulrich Wehler, *Deutsche Gesellschaftsgeschichte, Band II: 1815–1844/49* (Munich, 1987), 188.
40 Silvia Oberhänsli, *Die Glarner Unternehmer des 19. Jahrhunderts*, dissertation, Zurich 1980 (Zurich, 1982), 84.
41 Cf. Wilhelm Endemann's 'curriculum vitae' of 6 October 1872, in StA Münster, Oberpräs, 1514, 1, B1 103–109. Dolores Augustine, 'Heiratsverhalten und Berufswahl', gives other examples of the 'costs' borne by the sons of businessmen.
42 Kaelble, 'Wie feudal waren die deutschen Unternehmer?', 156.
43 Georg Steinhausen, 'Häusliches und gesellschaftliches Leben im 19. Jahrhundert', in Paul Bornstein (ed.), *Am Ende des Jahrhunderts. Rückschau auf 100 Jahre geistiger Entwicklung*, 4 (Berlin, 1898), 73; Zunkel, *Der Rheinisch-Westfälische Unternehmer*, 95. Hartmut Zwahr has shown that in the case of Leipzig 'money marriages' were the rule initially among the bourgeoisie, whereas later social status came to assume more importance than simple material considerations. See H. Zwahr, 'Zur Klassenkonstitution der deutschen Bourgeoisie', *Jahrbuch für Geschichte*, 32 (1985), 41.
44 Max Barkhausen, 'Der Aufstieg der rheinischen Industrie im 18. Jahrhundert und die Entstehung eines industriellen Grossbürgertums', *Rheinische Vierteljahresblätter*, 19 (1954), 135–78, esp. 174; Adelmann, 'Führende Unternehmer', 348; Henning, 'Soziale Verflechtungen', 12; Pierenkemper, *Die westfälischen Schwerindustriellen*, 45ff.
45 These included the Schaffhausenscher Bankverein (1848), the Darmstädter Bank (1853), the Disconto Bank and the Berliner Handelsgesellschaft (1856), the Deutsche Bank (1870), and the Dresdner Bank (1872). For economic development in the western regions with which we are concerned, it was the banking network in Cologne that was crucial. It was the Cologne banks which provided capital for new firms from the 1840s, before banks then emerged in Düsseldorf, Elberfeld, and Essen to finance industry in the Rhineland-Westphalia area.
46 Figures on number of firms (*Hauptbetriebe*) from *Statistik des Deutschen Reiches*, 117 (Berlin, 1898, reprinted Osnabrück 1975), 286ff, 294ff, 302ff, 361ff.

KARIN KAUDELKA-HANISCH

47 Geheimes Staatsarchiv [GStA] Dahlem, Rep 90, Nr. 2002: cabinet sitting of 19 Mar. 1909.
48 StA Münster, Oberpräs, 1514, 3, Bl 23–24; ZStA Merseburg, Rep 120, A IV, zu 13: Bankberichte.
49 Cf. Mertes, 'Zum Sozialprofil', 186.
50 On Colsman, see ZStA Merseburg, Geh. Zivilkabinett, 2.2.1., 1596, Bl 179. On Haniel, see Rudolf Martin, *Jahrbuch des Vermögens und des Einkommens der Millionäre in der Rheinprovinz* (Berlin, 1913), 139. In 1913 Haniel was the highest-taxed individual in Düsseldorf, and Martin estimated his wealth at 55 million Marks in 1908 and 65 million Marks three years later. The firm Haniel and Lueg included foundries, a hammer mill, and an engineering works.
51 Zunkel, *Der rheinisch-westfälische Unternehmer*, 29.
52 These figures, and those that follow, are taken from Otto Kindermann, 'Das Sozialprofil deutscher Unternehmer im 19. Jahrhundert anhand der Neuen Deutschen Biographie', unpublished *Staatsarbeit*, Münster 1975.
53 Max Weber, *Gesammelte Aufsätze zur Religionssoziologie* (Tübingen, 1947).
54 Wehler, *Deutsche Gesellschaftsgeschichte*, II: 195; Adelmann, 'Führende Unternehmer', 348; Emsbach, 'Soziale Betriebsverfassung' 349. There were exceptions, however, such as Gustav Mevissen, the Thyssen and Klöckner families in the Ruhr, and the 'established class of Catholic textile magnates' in the Münsterland, such as the Kümpers in Rheine, Laurenz in Ochtrup, and Schwartz and Beckmann in Bocholt. See Adelmann, 'Führende Unternehmer', 348.
55 Wehler, *Deutsche Gesellschaftsgeschichte*, II: 195.
56 Weber, *Gesammelte Aufsätze zur Religionssoziologie*, 23.
57 See Jürgen Kocka, *Unternehmer in der deutschen Industrialisierung* (Göttingen, 1975), 37.
58 Carl Fürstenberg, *Die Lebensgeschichte eines deutschen Bankiers 1870–1914* (Berlin, 1931), 28.
59 HStA Düsseldorf-Kalkum, Regierung Düsseldorf, Präs, 478, Bl 161–3.
60 *Kölnische Volkszeitung*, 29 Dec. 1898.
61 First published in Prague, 1855. I am referring to the 1859 second edition, p. 11
62 Adolf von Wilke, *Alt-Berliner Erinnerungen* (Berlin, 1930), 233; Uli Schanz, *Königlich Preussische Titel sind käuflich zu haben* (n.p., 1889), copy in ZStA Merseburg, Rep. 120, CB II, Nr. 1b, Bd. 1, Bl 1.
63 'Die Verramschung von Titeln', *Die Welt am Montag*, 14 November 1910; W. Rassbach, *Wie kann man den Titel eines Königl. Preussischen Kommerzienrats erlangen?* (Magdeburg, 1900); A.B., 'Kommerzienrat', *Berliner Morgenpost*, 29 July 1906; Richard Lewinsohn, *Das Geld in der Politik* (Berlin, 1931), 29. See also Landeshauptarchiv [LHA] Koblenz, Bestand 403, Nr. 9893, Bl 183–5: Antrag auf Verleihung des Kommerzienratstitels an August Vorwerk (Barmen) 1908.
64 'Die Verramschung.'
65 M.D., 'Orden and Titel im Kaufmannsstande', *Der Einkäufer*, 5 May 1903.
66 'Kommerzienräte', *Berliner Tageblatt*, 30 Oct. 1906.

112

67 'Die Verramschung'.

68 F. Sass, *Berlin in seiner neuesten Zeit und Entwicklung* (Leipzig, 1846), cited in *Preußen. Zur Sozialgeschichte eines Staates* (Reinbek, 1981), 295; Richard Biermann, *Der Schwindel mit Hoflieferanten-, Kommerzienrats-, Geheimrats-, in- und ausländischen Doktortiteln sowie der sonstige Titel- und Ordenschacher in Deutschland . . .* (Fallersleben, 1914), 5.

69 Biermann, *Der Schwindel*, 5; Ferdinand Avenarius, 'Banalitäten', *Der Kunstwart*, 11(1898), H.8, 241–3; Ferdinand Avenarius, 'Titel', *Der Kunstwart*, 27(1914), H.19, 2; Lorenz, *Amtstitel* 75ff.

70 Josef Schlink, *Über die soziale Stellung des deutschen Technikers* (Berlin, 1879), 3–4.

71 Lorenz, *Amtstitel*, 76; Avenarius, 'Titel', 1–2.

72 Avenarius, 'Titel', 5.

73 Ilsedore Rarisch, *Das Unternehmerbild in der deutschen Erzählliteratur des 19. Jahrhunderts* (Berlin, 1977), 39, 55, 103.

74 Examples include Friedrich Harkort, honoured in 1847, Wilhelm Funcke (1902) and Karl Leverkus (1905).

75 A.B., 'Kommerzienrat'.

76 M.D., 'Orden und Titel im Kaufmannsstande',

77 Lewinsohn, *Das Geld in der Politik*, 28.

78 Avenarius, 'Titel', 3,6.

79 Cf. the decree of 8 Oct. 1890, cited in note 29.

80 Rassbach, *Wie kann man den Titel*.

81 A.B., 'Kommerzienrat'.

82 On influence with the authorities, see the material on Gustav Nahrhaft of Düsseldorf, who received the title in 1918, in: HStAD, Regierung Düsseldorf, Präs 479, Bl 332.

83 LHA Koblenz, Bestand 403, 9881, Bl 128–9: Letter of District Administrator Düsseldorf to Minister of Trade and Industry, 29 Dec. 1896. See also LHA Koblenz, Bestand 403, 9883, Bl 183–5: evidence in the case of August Vorwerk, 1908; Rudolf Morsey, *Die oberste Reichsverwaltung unter Bismarck 1867–1896* (Münster, 1957), 275. On the Commercial Councillor title in other states, including Bavaria, Saxony, Württemberg and Lippe-Detmold, see *Handbuch der deutschen Kommerzienräte, bearbeitet und herausgegeben auf Grund amtlicher Ernennungen*, 2nd edn (Berlin-Wilmersdorf, 1911/12).

84 Karlheinz Wallraff, 'Die "bürgerliche Gesellschaft" im Spiegel deutscher Familienzeitschriften', unpublished dissertation (Cologne, 1939) 41ff.

85 Eberhard Schmieder, 'Die wirtschaftliche Führungsschicht in Berlin 1790–1850', in Herbert Helbig (ed.), *Führungskräfte der Wirtschaft im 19. Jahrhundert*, pt II, 47; Pierenkemper, *Die westfälischen Schwerindustriellen*, 76; Mertes, 'Zum Sozialprofil', 168; Franz Mariaux, *Gedenkwort zum 100jährigen Bestehen der Harpener Bergbau AG* (Dortmund, 1956), 188; Emsbach, *Die soziale Betriebsverfassung*, 352. Theodor Fontane observed in 1889 that only that which had the 'state seal of approval' counted; then you 'are looked at with greater respect and better treated': Theodor Fontane, *Briefe an Georg Friedländer*, K. Schreinert (ed.) (Heidelberg, 1954), 103.

86 Friedrich Naumann, *Demokratie und Kaisertum* (first published 1900), section on 'the industrial aristocracy', in Naumann, *Werke*, 2 (Cologne-Opladen, 1964), 174–90, quotation p. 178. Michael Stürmer's allusion to titles for the 'middle ranks' who had risen can hardly refer to Commercial Councillors. See Stürmer, *Das ruhelose Reich. Deutschland 1866–1918* (Berlin, 1983), 4.

87 See Hansjoachim Henning, *Sozialgeschichtliche Entwicklungen in Deutschland von 1815 bis 1860* (Paderborn, 1977), 133.

88 Austria was, as we have seen, an exception. There the title was *Kommerzialrat*.

4

Family and class in the Hamburg grand bourgeoisie 1815–1914

Richard J. Evans

I

If there was any single institution that was central to the cultural life and value systems of the nineteenth-century German bourgeoisie, it was – the majority of historians seem agreed – the family. In previous centuries, the dynasticism of the Central European feudal aristocracy had led to marriage alliances being pressed into the service of the aggrandizement of landed property and the acquisition of political influence. Intrafamilial feuds and rivalries had been commonplace. The family had in many ways been a public institution, set in conscious opposition to the operation of private emotion and personal passion.[1] In the bourgeois nineteenth century, the family became the focal point of the emerging private sphere. Social commentators began to regard it as a central institution of civil society, even perhaps its fundamental, constitutive element. In the bourgeois world, it came to provide the intimacy and warmth, the emotional centre of life, the purpose for which men fought and strove for success in the competitive arena of industry and enterprise outside.[2]

Yet, as Karin Hausen has remarked, the growing flood of publications on the nineteenth-century German bourgeoisie has been accompanied by hardly more than a trickle of studies of the bourgeois family; the family continues to be regarded as an epiphenomenon of bourgeois society.[3] Thus while there are studies of the peasant family and the working-class family,[4] of maidservants and bluestockings, of feminist pioneers and women's emancipation,[5] of children,[6] and the old,[7] there is no German equivalent of the monographs such as Bonnie Smith's *Ladies of the Leisure Class*, on bourgeois women in nineteenth-century France, or Catherine Hall and Leonore Davidoff's *Family Fortunes*, on the role of family and gender in the English middle class from 1780 to 1850, which have been published in Britain and America in the past few years.[8]

Such studies as have been carried out on the bourgeois family in nineteenth-century Germany have tended to stress two major, widely accepted arguments. The first of these is that the importance of the family in public life declined with the growth of the competitive individualism that formed at least the theoretical basis for the economic and political activities of the bourgeoisie.[9] Correspondingly, it is usually argued, such cohesiveness as the bourgeois world achieved in these respects was gained above all through the free combination of individuals – overwhelmingly men – in the voluntary associations that sprang up all over Germany in the period from the 1830s onwards: the celebrated *Vereine*, about which so much has been written by historians.[10] Even the family business, it is often suggested, was important in Germany only in the early stages of industrialization, and became less significant later on because of the rapid pace of German economic growth and the very large scale of the business enterprises which emerged in its course.[11] The second generally accepted belief about the bourgeois family in nineteenth-century Germany is that its importance and functions were closely bound up with the 'separation of spheres' between men and women, between the masculine world of work and the feminine world of the home. The emergence of the family as a fundamental institution of bourgeois society rested on the increasing restriction of women to the private sphere. Their enforced subordination was a fundamental constituent part of bourgeois society.[12]

These arguments have been complicated by the fact that it has also been widely believed that substantial parts of the German bourgeoisie did not really lead a bourgeois lifestyle at all. In particular, it has frequently been assumed that the upper middle class or grand bourgeoisie did not properly exist as a discrete group on its own, or form part of a broader German middle class. On the contrary, many historians have claimed that it was to all intents and purposes absorbed into a new social elite, where it shared power – in a strictly subordinate capacity – with the established aristocracy, accepting aristocratic standards, values, and beliefs rather than aligning itself with the bourgeoisie proper.[13] But a growing quantity of detailed historical research has demonstrated that this was not the case. As Dolores L. Augustine has shown, for example, the wealthiest German businessmen married over-whelmingly into the families of other very wealthy businessmen. Only 12 per cent married women from the aristocracy. And only about a tenth of their sons went into a profession such as landown-ing, diplomacy, or the army officer corps, that could be described as aristocratic.[14] Similarly, H. Henning has shown in a study of Westphalian 'Commercial Councillors' (*Kommerzienräte*), that is, businessmen whose standing had been officially recognized by the government, that more than 85 per cent married the daughters of other businessmen. Less than 10 per cent married into the edu-cated middle class or *Bildungsbürgertum*, that is, the families of university-trained professionals and civil servants.[15]

This has been seen by some historians as a sign of the fragmen-tation of the German bourgeoisie into different groups which largely failed to intermarry,[16] but Henning also demonstrated that while higher civil servants in the province of Hanover, which was generally rather economically backward, did indeed tend to marry the daughters of other higher civil servants, the majority of their counterparts in the rapidly industrializing provinces of the Rhine-land and Westphalia mostly married the daughters of businessmen. In these areas, businessmen were relatively numerous compared to other groups in the bourgeoisie, so it should not be surprising that they tended to marry into each other's families as well as into the educated and professional middle class. Similarly, if relatively few senior civil servants or university professors were the children of businessmen in the early nineteenth century, this was not least because there were relatively few German businessmen at this time. As industrialization took hold later in the century, the num-bers of businessmen obviously underwent a rapid increase, both absolutely and in relation to the educated middle class, so that by about 1900 between a fifth and a third of judges and senior state officials came from the families of businessmen.[17]

Recent studies have also shown that long-accepted notions about the 'feudalization' of the German bourgeoisie, based on the tend-ency of middle-class Germans to buy up country estates, get them-selves commissions in the army reserve, lust after honours and titles, or ape the lifestyle of the nobility through indulging in customs such as duelling, place too much weight on evidence that is in reality capable of sustaining a variety of interpretations, as some of the other contributions to this book suggest.[18] If the German bourgeoisie did have a peculiarity in comparison with its equivalents in other countries, it was, historians have recently begun to argue, its fragmentation into different groups. Historians used to claim that the German bourgeoisie was weak because it had been absorbed into the aristocracy. Now they seem to be arguing that it was weak because it was not. Social isolation, it is now suggested, robbed the German bourgeoisie of powerful allies such as the British middle class enjoyed in the landed aristocracy, while its fragmentation into different groups enfeebled its sociocultural grip on the rest of society.[19]

One point that Henning's work does make clear is that there were substantial variations in the composition, influence, and behaviour of the bourgeoisie from one part of Germany to another. More local and regional studies are needed to build up a broader and more comprehensive picture. The present chapter draws on evidence from Germany's second city, the northern seaport of Hamburg, in order to submit some widely held historical views on the bourgeois family to critical scrutiny, and, beyond this, to use the history of the family as a kind of prism through which facets of the broader history of the German bourgeoisie are refracted. In some ways, of course, Hamburg was exceptional.[20] It was a self-governing state, first of all within the German Confederation and then in the Bismarckian Empire. It had its own constitution, its own political structures, and its own way of doing things, which only conformed gradually and hesitantly to the Prussian model as time went on. The city was ruled by an eighteen-man Senate, elected for life under complex rules which amounted to a system of self-recruitment subject to a partial right of veto by the legislature, the Citizen's Assembly or *Bürgerschaft*, which itself was elected by a small minority of propertied citizens. The Senate was led by its two most senior legally qualified members, the Burgomasters or *Bürgermeister*, and even after 1871 it controlled most aspects of Hamburg's internal affairs. Equally unusual in the German context was the dominance in the city's politics of liberal doctrines of free enterprise and *laissez-faire*.[21]

But if its politics diverged from German normality, this was not least because of Hamburg's unique combination of political autonomy and economic strength. Other self-governing cities such as Bremen or Lübeck lacked the financial weight to preserve their independence, while centres of bourgeois wealth and prosperity such as Frankfurt or Leipzig, above all after 1866, lacked the institutional elbow-room to convert their economic muscle into political power. The merchants, bankers, financiers, and (towards the end of the century) industrialists who held sway in Hamburg were in many respects not so very different from wealthy business-men in other parts of Germany. It was their political situation, and the scope which Hamburg's relative autonomy offered their ambitions, which was unusual. The social history of the grand bourgeoisie in Hamburg can thus be placed alongside the evidence presented in Lothar Gall's engrossing family history of the Basser-manns and Werner Mosse's fine study of German-Jewish business dynasties to help construct an account of the role played by the family in the political and economic life of the German middle and upper classes. Perhaps the best way of doing this is to take one particular example of a Hamburg grand bourgeois family and follow it through the nineteenth century. A major, little-used source is fortunately available in the shape of a genealogy compiled for the wealthy Amsinck family by the archivist and historian Otto Hintze in the early 1930s. Commissioned by the family in the Weimar Republic, the genealogy, which fills three large printed volumes, is of such richness that it is also to some extent a social history. It enables us to gain unrivalled insight into the economic and political functions of the family in the nineteenth-century German upper middle class.[22]

II

Like so many of Hamburg's leading families in the nineteenth century, the Amsincks were of foreign origin. They dated back to Willem Amsinck, a Dutch merchant who settled in Hamburg in 1576. The family's fortunes fluctuated a good deal during the next two centuries; and those descendants of the senior branch of the Amsincks of this period who remained in Hamburg lived in the nineteenth century in relatively modest circumstances, as engin-eers, booksellers, and small-time publishers. The fortunes of the successful younger branch of the family were founded by Wilhelm Amsinck (1752–1831), a lawyer, who concluded an advantageous marriage with Elizabeth Schuback, granddaughter of Burgomaster Nicolaus Schuback. Throughout the nineteenth century, the law was the one bourgeois profession which was accepted in the city as being equal in standing with the merchant community. Com-mercial law was a vital part of merchant enterprise, and the operations of the law of contract, salvage, insurance, liability, and debt could mean the difference between prosperity and bank-ruptcy. The great merchant families therefore encouraged those of their sons who seemed willing and able to go into the law. Half the seats in the Senate were reserved for lawyers, and only a legally trained Senator, as we have seen, could hold the office of Burgomaster. There were no senior civil servants in Hamburg until the very end of the nineteenth century, nor did the city possess a university (the lawyers took their degrees in Heidelberg or Bonn). The status of the medical profession for most of the century was relatively low. Thus the position of the legal and mercantile bourgeoisie in the city was more or less supreme.[23]

What bound the two together was among other things the family. In the prosperous and ambitious Hamburg grand bour-geoisie, this was a large and highly ramified institution. Burgo-master Wilhelm Amsinck – or Wilhelm I, as it is necessary to call him in view of the frequent occurrence of the name in the family's annals – had six children, including two sons, Johannes I (1792–1879), a merchant, and Wilhelm II (1793–1874), a lawyer. Of these two sons, Johannes I had no fewer than twelve children, only one of whom died in infancy: six sons and five daughters reached adulthood. Five of these sons went into business – Wilhelm III (1821–1909), Heinrich I (1824–83), Erdwin (1826–97), Martin Garlieb (1831–1905) and Gustav (1837–1909). The sixth, Johannes II (1823–99), who walked with a limp and was thus regarded by the family as neither suitable for a business career nor fit for the marriage market, remained a bachelor until the age of fifty-five and had no children. He became a doctor, thus neatly illustrating the subordinate place of this profession in the city's social hier-archy. With this exception, therefore, the businessman Johannes I's sons also went into business.

His lawyer brother Wilhelm II's sons, of whom there were a mere three, took a different direction. One of them, Wilhelm IV (1834–1900) married into the Prussian aristocracy and bought a Junker estate, Gut Glubenstein, in East Prussia. His brother Werner (1837–1913) also bought an estate in East Prussia, but failed to make a success either of it or of a second estate which he purchased in 1878. He sold off his landed property in 1890 and lived thereafter as a gentleman of independent means in Lübeck. The fact that both brothers took this course suggests some excep-tional factor in their upbringing. And indeed their father Wilhelm II, the lawyer, had purchased a noble estate in 1838. Though he continued to serve as Senate Syndic – one of four (later two) legal officials present as non-voting participants at every Senate meeting and charged with giving detailed advice on points of law – until 1860, he suffered from repeated illnesses, which were probably the reason why he was never elected to the Senate as a full member. Thus his purchase of a landed estate was dictated principally by the need to have a place away from the bustle of Hamburg to which he could retire during and after bouts of ill-health. His two sons spent much of their childhood and adolescence on the estate, and this clearly gave them a taste for the country life. All of this had little to do with any putative feudal yearnings on their part; it was not social ambition, but socialization, which led them to buy up Junker properties.

Of the other nineteenth-century Amsincks of the younger line, of whom in all forty-seven survived infancy and reached adulthood, one, Lydia, fourth child of Wilhelm III, married a Prussian army officer, Hans von Wolff, and another, Olga, fourth child of Heinrich I, married a Hamburg merchant, Hermann Burchard, who subsequently bought a castle with a landed estate in Bavaria. None of the others either married into the aristocracy or took on the ownership of landed estates. Nor did any of the Amsincks trouble to acquire a title, not even that of officer in the reserve. Titles of nobility, orders, and decorations were looked upon among the Hamburg elite as signifying deference to foreign, monarchical institutions, and alien to the proudly republican traditions of the city-state. Senators were expressly forbidden to accept them, and even a retired Senator who did so would be barred from using his Senatorial title as a consequence. When, at one point, early in the history of the Empire, Bismarck and the Imperial court started handing out honours to Hanseatic notabilities, the Burgomaster of Hamburg led a special delegation to Berlin to request them to desist. Whatever may have happened elsewhere, the Hamburg grand bourgeoisie maintained a rigorous stance of republican independence right to the end, even after increasing numbers of aristocratic or ennobled businessmen from other parts of the Reich began to settle in the city.[24]

If Wilhelm II Amsinck's two older sons took up landownership, then his third son Caesar (1849–1922) was much more in the conventional family mould. He became a lawyer, thus continuing the tradition of one lawyer in each generation of the family that stretched back to Wilhelm I – before which a lawyer had tended to appear in alternate generations.

Other great Hamburg families such as the Mönckebergs and the Schröders maintained a similar practice, with the majority of the sons going into business but roughly one in each generation going into the law. If this was one means by which these different professional segments of the grand bourgeoisie in Hamburg were welded together, another, equally important, was the marriage alliance. Five of the forty-seven nineteenth-century Amsincks married lawyers or the daughters of lawyers, most of whom belonged in turn to great merchant families themselves.[25] The practice of godparenthood (or fictive kinship), about which, however, Hintze's genealogy is largely silent, further cemented these cross-professional ties. Thus Martin Garlieb I (1831–1905), fifth son of Johannes I, was the godson of Burgomaster Martin Garlieb Sillem (who was also incidentally distantly related to the Amsincks by marriage).

The Amsinck family had particularly close ties to a small number of other great business families. Chief among these were the Gosslers. In 1818 Johannes I married Emilie Gossler, daughter of the merchant Senator Johann Heinrich Gossler; in 1900 his grandson Wilhelm V married Emmy Gossler (whose mother was also a member of the Gossler family); while in 1857 Wilhelm V's younger brother Martin Garlieb I married Susanne Gossler, daughter of the businessman Johann Hermann Gossler and his American wife. Sometimes such alliances could be quite close. Thus when Wilhelm III's first wife Emily Willink, who came from a substantial Hamburg merchant family, died in 1858, he proceeded after a decent interval to take her sister Laetitia Willink as his second. Werner Amsinck, Wilhelm III's youngest son, married the niece of his crippled physician uncle Johannes II's widow; both women were, incidentally, as Hintze points out, descendants of the poet Lessing. Similarly, another of Wilhelm II's sons, Johannes III, had a member of the Westphal family as his mother-in-law, while his first cousin Ida, daughter of Heinrich Amsinck (1824–83), married Otto Westphal, who became a merchant Senator in 1909. The ramifications of these family alliances were virtually endless, and would have been even more complicated to relate had Hintze not confined his detailed account solely to the male line, leaving the women's descendants largely unmentioned.

At any one time, several members of Hamburg's ruling Senate

were thus likely to be related, despite a rule which barred the closest relatives, such as fathers and sons, or brothers, from holding office at the same time. In the first half of the nineteenth century, as Hintze noted, for example, there were several relations of Wilhelm I Amsinck, Burgomaster from 1802 to 1831, in the Senate:

> His youngest son Wilhelm had begun his valuable service in the Senate in 1827 as fourth and junior Senate Syndic. The first Syndic was Dr. Jacob Albrecht von Sieren, whose wife was a niece of Burgomaster Amsinck; her sister was married to Senator Dr. Johann Ludwig Dammert (Burgomaster from 1843). Among the 24 Senators were also the merchant Johann Heinrich Gossler, the father-in-law of Burgomaster Amsinck's oldest son Johannes Amsinck, of the firm Johannes Schuback and Sons, a partner in which was Senator Martin Garlieb Sillem (Burgomaster from 1829), who had married the widow of Johannes Schuback, a brother-in-law of Burgomaster Amsinck.[26]

These ties, which would be celebrated at family festivals of one kind and another, from christenings to funerals, helped give the Senators, whether merchants or lawyers, a sense of common identity and eased their relations with one another in the business of guiding the city's fortunes.

Above all, the great merchant houses were able to keep a hold on the city governments, both by sending some of their members into the Senate as executive, legally trained Senators, and by constructing a network of family ties which subjected members of the Senate to constant ideological pressure. This helped counteract both the influence of smaller merchant houses over the Chamber of Commerce and the tendency of the legal Senators, because of their training and because of their sense of executive responsibility, sometimes to take a line which the great merchant families found objectionable or inconvenient. Generally speaking, the grand bourgeoisie therefore attached relatively little importance to occupying the position of merchant Senator, although here too, on occasion, the upper reaches of the mercantile community were able to exert a powerful influence over the city's affairs. When contemporaries claimed that Hamburg was ruled by the 'pepper-sacks' and 'coffee kings', therefore, it did not mean this to be taken literally. Hamburg was ruled by lawyers. But there was seldom much doubt as to where the lawyers' family allegiances lay.[27]

III

The economic functions of such family links were just as important as the political ones. To begin with, there was the family firm. In the Amsincks' case, this went by the name of Johannes Schuback & Sons. Johannes I inherited it in 1837 through his mother, the last surviving member of the Schuback family. As part of the settlement, Johannes made over a separate inheritance from Martin Garlieb Sillem, who had been a partner in the firm and was married to the widow of the last of the male Schubacks, to the Sillem family. The company was principally involved in shipowning, which was beginning to boom as Hamburg became the chief port of entry into Central Europe for the products of the British industrial revolution and a centre of growing importance for trade with the newly liberated South American states. Johannes I laid down the basis for the firm's fortunes in a classically patriarchal manner. He carried on working until his death at the age of 88, in 1879, and is said to have banned smoking, gas lighting, and beards from his office. In 1849 he made his sons Wilhelm III and Heinrich I, aged 28 and 25 respectively, partners in the firm. There was also a branch of the company in New York, where Johannes I's fourth son Erdwin was sent to set up business. Freed of family supervision, Erdwin, who seems to have been the nearest thing the Amsincks ever came to having a black sheep in the family fold, engaged in reckless speculation, and his more sober young brother Gustav was sent out to join him. While Gustav married an American and enjoyed a successful career on the boards of several banks in London, Hamburg, and New York, Erdwin was obliged to give up the business in 1874 to his brother and subsequently to his nephew by marriage, August Lattmann. Erdwin returned to Europe and lived quietly as an art collector in Hamburg until his death in 1897.

Subsequent partnerships in the firm of Johannes Schuback & Sons went to Wilhelm III's sons Johannes III in 1891, Wilhelm V in 1895, Carl in 1898, and Werner in 1908. Their cousin Heinrich II, son of Heinrich I, also became a partner in 1887, but he was one of the less business-minded of the family, and spent most of his energies on racehorse owning. Nor was he one of the luckier Amsincks; his father-in-law Senator Octavio Schröder went mad, and he himself died of typhoid at the age of 29. The family also acquired an interest in the trading house of Willink, through the marriages of Wilhelm III, whose brother Heinrich I represented the family on the board of shareholders' deputies, as he also did with the firm of Peter Siemsen, husband of Heinrich's sister. Heinrich, indeed, came in the course of time to serve as the representative of the family firm on a number of company shareholders' boards, making something of a specialism of this activity.

Meanwhile, significant developments were taking place in Hamburg's business world. The rise of mass emigration from Central and Eastern Europe to the Americas, and the transition from sail to steam ships, led to a huge expansion and concentration of the city's shipowning sector.[28] The Amsincks took an eager part in this development, and not simply through the family firm. For whatever reason – perhaps because as the fifth son of Johannes I, he would probably never have risen above a position subordinate to that of his brothers in the firm – Martin Garlieb I set up in business on his own. After learning his trade by helping to build Isambard Kingdom Brunel's celebrated steamship *The Great Eastern* in Glasgow, he returned to Hamburg and set up a shipyard in 1857. The capital was put up by his brothers Heinrich and Wilhelm from the family firm, which suggests that Martin Garlieb was setting up on his own as part of a family agreement. By 1881 he had become a substantial shipowner, with seventeen vessels in service, the fourth largest merchant fleet in Hamburg at the time. His son, Martin Garlieb II, duly joined the company in his turn, but the fleet was all sail, and as the day of the clipper finally came to an end, the company began to go into a decline. It was eventually liquidated in 1907. Martin Garlieb I's younger son Theodor was more successful, becoming a member of the executive board of directors (*Vorstand*) of the 'Hamburg-South' steamship line, which traded with Latin America. But it was his third son Arnold who achieved the greatest success, illustrating in the process the advantages of a good match. Arnold married Thekla Bohlen, who was the daughter of J. F. Bohlen and his wife Lulu Woermann. The Woermann line, which traded with Africa, was one of Hamburg's biggest shipping companies. Bohlen was already a partner, and Arnold Amsinck duly joined him, subsequently becoming chairman of the board of directors (*Vorstandsvorsitz*) of the company and of the German East Africa Line as well.

It was with the Hamburg-America Line that the Amsincks scored their greatest success. The family firm, Johannes Schuback & Sons, owned a substantial block of shares in the company, and together with the banking houses of Godeffroy and Merck and the shipping lines of Laeisz and Woermann was regularly elected to the *Direktion*, which collectively represented the interests of the shareholders. It was usually Heinrich I Amsinck who, as in other cases, took the leading role here, and served as the family representative on the supervisory board (*Aufsichtsrat*) of the Hamburg-America Line. By the turn of the century this had become the largest shipping company not just in Hamburg or Germany, but in the entire world.[29] With resources such as these at their disposal, it was not surprising that several of the Amsincks featured in Rudolph Martin's *Yearbook of German Millionaires*, published shortly before the First World War.[30] Their wealth had been acquired and augmented not least by family connections. Marriage into a mercantile, banking, or shipping dynasty, whether it was achieved by a male Amsinck (as in the case of the Willinks) or a female (as in the case of the Siemsens), appears to have brought with it at the very least the opportunity to acquire a block of shares, and quite often a partnership as well, as in the case of the Woermanns. If the other family line should die out – something that was clearly never even the remotest possibility with the Amsincks themselves – then it might even lead to a complete takeover of the company concerned, as with the Schubacks. Family capital was also important in helping to finance independent ventures launched by members of the family acting on their own, as in the case of Martin Garlieb I's shipping venture. Even in the age of large-scale corporate capitalism which dawned with the massive and complex operations of the Hamburg-America Line, family fortunes continued to flourish and family connections continued to be important.

The story of the Amsincks – and it could be retold for many other mercantile dynasties in nineteenth-century Hamburg – suggests that in the grand bourgeoisie at least, the role of the family in political and economic life continued to be not only significant but also publicly recognized right up to the First World War. Family ties helped ease the emergence of big business, they softened the contours of competitive capitalism, they drew together the disparate strands of the professional, mercantile, financial, and industrial grand bourgeoisie. Thus shipowners like the Woermanns, bankers like the Gosslers, factory-owners like the Trauns, merchants like the Westphals, and lawyer-politicians like the Sievekings, were all related to the Amsincks by marriage, and – by this and other means – to each other as well. Such ties no doubt helped when it came to setting up an Employers' Association at the end of the 1880s to resist the growing demands of the workers for better pay and conditions. They also meant that the concentration of wealth in Hamburg, in the hands of a small number of interrelated families, and the dominance of these families over the city's political institutions, were peculiarly obvious to the world, and thus increasingly vulnerable to criticism as time progressed.

IV

Alongside the slowly mutating public functions of the family in the Hamburg grand bourgeoisie, there also developed a more intimate, private sphere, within the home. Although it has sometimes been argued that this was the sphere in which the women of the bourgeoisie came into their own,[31] the fact is that male authority ruled supreme here too. It rested in the first place on the customary disparity in ages between husband and wife. Hintze's genealogy of the Amsincks reveals the family to have been broadly typical of the nineteenth-century bourgeoisie in this respect. The case of Wilhelm III Amsinck, it is true, was probably somewhat extreme. Born in 1821, he did not marry until he was 36 years of age. His first wife, Emily Willink, was just 17, and she died in childbirth a year later. As we have seen, Wilhelm III went on to marry his first wife's younger sister Laetitia Willink. At the time of Emily's death, Laetitia was only 13 years old, so Wilhelm was obliged to wait until she was 18 before taking her as his second wife. The age gap between the couple was thus no less than twenty-four years. By the time Laetitia had reached the age of 35, she had given birth to eleven children. When the youngest of them came into the world, his father was already in his sixties.

A similar, only slightly less dramatic example was that of Erdwin Amsinck, who failed in business in New York; his wife Antonie Lattmann was a good twenty-two years younger than he was. But the male Amsincks generally tended to marry late. Wilhelm III's sons, for example, all married when they were about 30; his uncle Heinrich married in his mid-thirties; and his cousin Caesar when he was 38. The basic reason for such tardiness was that, like virtually all the scions of the Hamburg mercantile grand bourgeoisie, the young male Amsincks were usually first apprenticed to a non-family merchant house in Hamburg for a while,

127

then sent to represent the family business overseas, in London, New York, or even further afield, often for a number of years. This was thought to provide them with all that was needed to understand the mechanics and principles of large-scale maritime trading. By the time they returned to Hamburg, they were usually already in their mid-to-late twenties. Even then it might be some time before they obtained a partnership in the family firm. Without a secure financial position such as this would offer, marriage and the establishment of an independent household were unthinkable, given the costs of buying or renting a suitably furnished and situated house, employing servants, bringing up and educating children, keeping a horse and carriage, and so on. A characteristic sequence of events could be observed in the case of Werner Amsinck, born in 1880, who spent his early twenties abroad, became a partner in the Schuback firm in 1908, and married the following year. Similarly, his brother Carl, born in 1872, married in 1902, five years after he had obtained his partnership. The exception, once again, was the energetic Martin Garlieb I, whose wife, Susanne Gossler, was only four years younger than he was. He married when he was 26, without having become a partner in the family firm, and this may well have contributed to his decision to set up in business on his own in the year of his wedding.

The women of the Amsinck family, by contrast, tended to marry young. Typical examples were Ida Amsinck, born in 1860, married at the age of 21, Elisabeth, born in 1876, married at 24, or Emily, born in 1858, married at 19. Here the family strategy was to marry the daughters off early in order to reduce the burden on the family purse. The customary disparity in age between spouses, a well documented feature of the bourgeois family in the nineteenth century, almost certainly implied a substantial degree of patriarchal power on the part of the older and more experienced husband.[32] Although day-to-day dealings with the servants were usually the wife's business, for example, it was generally the husband who had the last word on matters of discipline and hiring and dismissal.[33] It was the husband who acted as final authority on financial matters, including the household budget; and the law, above all after the introduction of the new Civil Code in 1900, gave him extensive powers over the management of the couple's life and the upbringing of the children, and explicitly accorded him the power of decision in all matters affecting married life.[34] Women were able to undertake some public activities in the field of charity and philanthropy, although in the current absence of research on the topic in the German context, little is known about them. However, the subscription lists for charities in nineteenth-century Hamburg, and memoirs and reports of philanthropy in times of disaster such as the great cholera epidemic of 1892, suggest that women only occupied a subordinate or even symbolic role, and that in the grand bourgeoisie at least, they mainly acted in this sphere in concert with their husbands.[35] Only rarely did women from the great Hamburg families, such as Amalie Sieveking, make a name for themselves with charitable activities of their own; these sometimes had a distinctive feminist slant which marked out the women concerned as non-conformists.[36] It was above all the Protestant Church which offered bourgeois women the opportunity to engage themselves outside the home under male leadership. However, the rash of women's patriotic, charitable, and other associations founded from the mid–1890s onwards was part of the general entry of women into the public sphere, spearheaded by the feminists, and thus signalled the breakdown of the 'separation of spheres' on which the classical model of the bourgeois family rested.[37]

V

In the general social life of the nineteenth-century Hamburg grand bourgeoisie, the family was only one of a number of factors. Many other informal social institutions played a vital role in cementing this social group together and giving it a cohesive sociopolitical ideology. The great and wealthy merchants frequently threw dinner-parties for influential citizens, but these were strictly men-only affairs, where up to thirty gentlemen – Senators, officials, clergymen, lawyers, merchants, and politicians – would be present, without a woman in sight.[38] Similarly, at lunchtime, the city elite, including members of the Senate, congregated at the Exchange (*Börse*), where equally important informal business would be done. The Lawyers' Club and the Doctors' Club and similar institutions catered for the professions,[39] while the great merchant and banking houses ensured that the professionals would not become too independent by retaining Senatorial management of health services and providing lay judges – among whom a number of the Amsinck family could be counted – on the Commercial Court.[40]

The social ties that bound the Hamburg grand bourgeoisie together were pulled tighter by the influence of neighbourhood.

Early in the nineteenth century, the wealthy families lived within the city walls, cheek-by-jowl with the poorer classes, although even at this period, they gave preference to certain streets. It was common for the family home to be located in the same building as the warehouse and office, though the invisible lines of demarcation between the different parts of the building were very clear.[41] As the city expanded in the second half of the century, however, the rich moved out into vast new villas constructed in the districts of Harvestehude and Rotherbaum, alongside the Alster lake, just outside the old city walls, away from the river, while offices and warehouses moved into more spacious accommodation in the newer parts of the harbour, which could take larger ships than those which formerly made their way into the old city boundaries. By 1897, the majority of the serving Senators lived in Harvestehude, and the district also contained the houses of members of the Amsinck, Gossler, Westphal, Sieveking, Merck, Godeffroy, Burchard, Mönckeberg, Ruperti, and Petersen families.[42] This substantially increased the distance between the elite and the rest of the population, and indeed memoirs of those who grew up in elite households in the late nineteenth century make it clear that the children of the grand bourgeoisie hardly ever ventured into the city centre or other areas where they might encounter the offspring of the masses.[43] The concentration of this social class into a single, relatively small area – still more, the custom of owning summer houses further out in the countryside, and passing the time on summer weekends or during the summer holiday in a series of mutual visits[44] – added a further influence to the web of informal social ties that bound the grand bourgeoisie together.

The values and beliefs which these social networks fostered were bourgeois in their very essence. Hard work was seen as the foundation of success; and not even the closest family ties were enough to excuse laziness, failure, or dilettantism. If nothing else, the training of the young scions of the grand bourgeoisie, as junior clerks in non-family offices, then as representatives of the family firm abroad, with a partnership on offer only to those who proved their competence or their willingness to contribute to the family fortune, was enough to school them in the bourgeois virtues of efficiency, industriousness, and self-reliance.[45] A touch of ostentation might be allowed in the construction and ornamentation of a new villa, but the open display of wealth was frowned on as vulgar, so that while *nouveaux riches* were sometimes admitted into the charmed social circles of the grand bourgeoisie, they were sure to be cold-shouldered if they failed to conform to the traditional reticence and modesty of the Hamburg mercantile elite.[46] Even the possession of a title of nobility was looked on with suspicion.[47]

Virtually everything was subordinated to the interests of business, even, as we have seen, social occasions such as dinners. Free trade was a dogma which no one dared to question; and although the great merchant houses were favourably inclined towards Hamburg's entry into the German Customs Union which took place in 1888, their enthusiasm was based not least on the concession wrung from Bismarck of a large free port covering the greater part of the harbour; political parties which favoured high tariffs, such as the Anti-Semites, never won much support in the city, although anti-Semitic sentiment continued to exist in organizations such as the Commercial Clerks' Union, which had its headquarters in Hamburg. In national political terms the mercantile elite was overwhelmingly liberal, and within the city it set great store on minimizing the intervention of the state in economy and society, so that there was not only no university, but also no professional civil service and until 1871 no state school system in the city. The medical profession was under continual pressure from the elite not to undertake preventative measures against diseases such as cholera or smallpox which might cost the state money or damage trade through quarantines.[48] If trade flourished, it was argued, then every other form of business and enterprise within the city would flourish too.[49]

In this way, as well as through a vast range of voluntary bodies ranging from parish councils to poor relief committees, the grand bourgeoisie sought to ally itself with other social groups among the middle and lower-middle classes in the city, from doctors and schoolteachers to shopkeepers and master-artisans. After 1860 indeed the Senate was forced to share power with an elected Citizens' Assembly in which these other groups – above all, the property-owners, those who earned a substantial part of their living by renting out apartments – were powerfully represented. Despite the enormous hierarchy of wealth within this coalition of dominant groups, ranging from millionaires like the Amsincks down to artisans earning no more than 2–3,000 Marks a year, and despite the social gulf that separated its constituent parts, it none the less worked together in the management of the city's affairs, as far as possible reconciling conflicting interests as it went along. Defined in political terms as Hamburg's citizens, those in possession of voting rights for the city elections, they numbered some 23,000 men and their families at the beginning of the 1890s and about 44,000 men and their families a decade later, or in other words about 75,000 people out of a population of 600,000 in 1890 and 145,000 out of a population of 750,000 at the turn of the century.[50] The rest of the population, encompassing the lower levels of the petty bourgeoisie and the mass of the working class, were not admitted to political rights; indeed, they were seen as a threat, to be countered increasingly by police repression and the operation of a variety of measures of propaganda and indoctrination. It was the contrast with these disfranchised masses, even more, the fear of urban unrest and the revolutionary rhetoric of the Social Democrats, for whom the majority of Hamburg's Reichstag electors, endowed with the benefit of universal manhood suffrage, voted, that arrayed the city's propertied classes, from the master-artisan to the millionaire, together in defence of their own position.

In this process, the grand bourgeois families came gradually to acquire a symbolic significance. Despite all the criticisms that had been levelled at them for their egoism and their neglect of the interests of the majority in the cause of mercantile profit, they represented ideals of continuity and stability which the Social Democrats, coming to power in the city in the 1918 revolution, found it only too tempting to employ. Although they had an absolute majority in the 1919 election in the city, the Social Democrats nevertheless decided to share power with the bourgeois parties, and to install a member of one of the old grand bourgeois families in office as First Burgomaster. A similar policy was followed by the Nazis, who gave the – now purely symbolic – office of Second Burgomaster from 1933 to 1945 to Wilhelm Amsinck Burchard-Motz. Even the British, when they occupied the city in 1945, pursued the same line, appointing as First Burgomaster the brother of the last liberal Burgomaster in the Weimar Republic.[51]

The grand bourgeois family in Hamburg thus retained its public significance surprisingly late into the twentieth century. It was far more than an institution belonging merely to the private sphere. Indeed, the bourgeois dynasticism of nineteenth-century Hamburg, like its counterpart in nineteenth-century France,[52] was a relatively new historical phenomenon. Many of the leading families, like the Amsincks, rose to prominence during the Napoleonic period. Their immense wealth was not least a product of the economic growth which the city enjoyed as a result of the British industrial revolution. Their social exclusivity stood in sharp contrast to the relative openness of Hamburg society in the age of the Enlightenment.[53] And the extraordinary fecundity which enabled them to intermarry on such a large scale was another novelty; the relative absence of infant mortality in the family testified to improved standards of hygiene and nutrition among the well-off and the relative decline of major epidemics apart from those, such as cholera and smallpox, which mainly affected the poor.[54] The women of the great bourgeois families were relegated to the sidelines in all this; their world was indeed mainly the home, and if they kept up ties with other members of the family through visits and correspondence, it was mainly with other female members of the family in the same situation as themselves. Bourgeois ideals of self-reliance, independence, and civil rights applied to them as little as they did to the proletariat; and despite a long prehistory dating back to before the 1848 revolution, it was not until almost the end of the century that the contradictions in the family regime of bourgeois society which these ideals opened up began to become a serious threat to the doctrine of separate spheres upon which the regime rested.[55]

The family ties and other informal social institutions which bound together the different economic and professional components of the Hamburg grand bourgeoisie suggest that the argument that the German bourgeoisie was fragmented above all by occupational differences may be not least the product of historians' research strategies, as they opt to study one group or the other, such as lawyers or industrialists, rather than examine their social relations with one another – something that is probably only possible in a local context. There were, of course, features of life in nineteenth-century Hamburg that gave the bourgeoisie a greater degree of cohesiveness than it possessed elsewhere in Germany. In this respect the absence of a large and powerful body of higher civil servants in the city, where the administration was run on a voluntary basis by bodies of prominent citizens known as 'Deputations', was crucial. Similarly the absence of a university in Hamburg weakened the educated middle class in comparison to its place in cities like Berlin. The fact that there was no royal or princely court in the city, that the social tone was not set by officers and aristocrats, not only gave the grand bourgeoisie more room for manoeuvre but also meant that there was relatively little anti-Semitic prejudice in Hamburg society. Coupled with the almost exclusively Protestant complexion of the city's population, this meant that the Hamburg bourgeoisie was less divided by religious and ethnic rivalries than were its counterparts elsewhere.[56]

Nevertheless, when all these individual features of Hamburg society are admitted, it remains likely that the role of informal social institutions such as the family was important in binding together the bourgeoisie, to a greater or lesser degree, in other German cities as well. Research on the family life and marriage strategies of various groups within the German bourgeoisie is beginning to reveal a number of variations in the pattern, but the basic features are generally rather similar: family and kinship ties used in business, for example, or late marriage among the males of a bourgeois family, dependent on the acquisition of economic independence.[57] The family proved surprisingly tenacious in its influence on the social and economic world of the German bourgeoisie. In its internal constitution, too, the subordination of the bourgeois housewife and the confinement of women to the private sphere continued to characterize the bourgeois family in general, despite being confronted with a variety of challenges, right up to the end of the century. The precise nature of women's role within the bourgeois family, however, remains to be investigated; and the vast mass of personal correspondence, diaries, and memoirs bequeathed to posterity by the women of the German bourgeoisie still awaits the attention of the historian.

NOTES

I am grateful to David Blackbourn for his comments on an earlier draft of this Chapter.

1 Jürgen Kocka, 'Bürgertum and Bürgerlichkeit als Probleme der deutschen Geschichte vom späten 18. zum frühen 20. Jahrhundert', in Kocka (ed.), *Bürger und Bürgerlichkeit im 19. Jahrhundert* (Göttingen, 1987), 21–63, here 43–4; Heinz Reif, 'Zum Zusammenhang von Sozialstruktur, Familien- und Lebenszyklus im westfälischen Adel in der Mitte des 18. Jahrhunderts', in Michael Mitterauer and Reinhard Sieder (eds), *Historische Familienforschung* (Frankfurt-on-Main, 1982), 123–55; Heide Rosenbaum (ed.), *Seminar: Familie und Gesellschaftsstruktur. Materialien zu den sozioökonomischen Bedingungen von Familienformen* (Frankfurt-on-Main, 1978), 437–79; Lawrence Stone, *The Family, Sex and Marriage in England 1500–1800* (London, 1981).

2 Ute Frevert, 'Einleitung' in Frevert (ed.), *Bürgerinnen und Bürger. Geschlechterverhältnisse im 19. Jahrhundert* (Göttingen, 1988), 1116; Frevert,

'Bürgerliche Meisterdenker und das Geschlechterverhältnis. Konzepte, Erfahrungen, Visionen an der Wende vom 18. zum 19. Jahrhundert', ibid., 17–48; Ingeborg Weber-Kellermann, *Die deutsche Familie. Versuch einer Sozialgeschichte* (Frankfurt-on-Main, 1974), 97–177; Heide Rosenbaum, *Formen der Familie. Untersuchungen zum Zusammenhang von Familienverhältnissen, Sozialstruktur and sozialem Wandel in der deutschen Gesellschaft des 19. Jahrhunderts* (Frankfurt-on-Main, 1982), 255–380. A valuable and influential study of the bourgeois family was published by Margarethe Freudenthal in Würzburg in 1934: *Gestaltwandel der städtisch-bürgerlichen und proletarischen Hauswirtschaft unter besonderer Berücksichtigung des Typenwandels von Frau and Familie, vornehmlich in Südwest-Deutschland zwischen 1760 und 1933, I. Teil: Von 1760 bis 1910* (PhD, Frankfurt-on-Main, 1933) (pt 2 never appeared). For interesting sidelights on the bourgeois family, see Hermann Zinn, 'Entstehung und Wandel bürgerlicher Wohngewohnheiten und Wohnstrukturen' and Gottfried Korff, 'Puppenstuben als Spiegel bürgerlicher Wohnkultur', both in Lutz Niethammer (ed.), *Wohnen im Wandel. Beiträge zur Gechichte des Alltags in der bürgerlichen Gesellschaft* (Wuppertal, 1979), respectively 13–27 and 28–43.

3 Karin Hausen, ' "eine Ulme für das schwanke Efeu." Ehepaare im Bildungsbürgertum. Ideale und Wirklichkeiten im späten 18. und 19. Jahrhundert', in Frevert (ed.), *Bürgerinnen*, 85–117, here 87–8. For an early survey of the field, see Hausen, 'Historische Familienforschung', in Reinhard Rürup (ed.), *Historische Sozialwissenschaft. Beiträge zur Einführung in die Forschungspraxis* (Göttingen, 1977), 59–95.

4 For example, Richard J. Evans and W. R. Lee (eds), *The German Family* (London, 1981), in which only peasant and working-class families are discussed.

5 Cf. the varying space allotted to these subjects and to the everday life of the majority of ordinary women in Ute Frevert, *Frauen-Geschichte. Zwischen Bürgerlicher Verbesserung und Neuer Weiblichkeit* (Frankfurt-on-Main, 1986), reflecting the current state of research.

6 Jürgen Schlumbohm (ed.), *Kinderstuben. Wie Kinder zu Bauern, Bürgern, Aristokraten wurden, 1700–1850* (Munich, 1983), 302–430; Gerd Hardach and Irene Hardach-Pinke (eds), *Kinderalltag. Deutsche Kindheiten in Selbstzeugnissen 1700–1900* (Reinbek, 1981).

7 Peter Borscheid, *Geschichte des Alters* (Munich, 1988); Helmut Konrad (ed.), *Der alte Mensch in der Geschichte* (Vienna, 1982).

8 Bonnie G. Smith, *Ladies of the Leisure Class. The Bourgeoises of Northern France in the Nineteenth Century* (Princeton, 1981); Leonore Davidoff and Catherine Hall, *Family Fortunes. Men and Women of the English Middle Class 1780–1850* (London, 1987). Sabine Meyer, *Das Theater mit der Hausarbeit. Bürgerliche Repräsentation in der Familie der Wilhelminischen Zeit* (Frankfurt-on-Main, 1982) is too sweeping in its attempt to demonstrate that bourgeois women did not live a life of leisure. Lothar Gall, *Das deutsche Bürgertum* (Berlin, 1989) is a 'family saga' with much illuminating detail, but relatively little analysis of the family as an institution. W. E. Mosse, *The German-Jewish Economic Elite 1820–1935:*

A Socio-Cultural Profile (Oxford, 1989), is good on marriage strategies and the functions of the family among wealthy Jewish businessmen.

9 Cf. C.B. Macpherson, *The Political Theory of Possessive Individualism* (Oxford, 1966), and Kocka's periodization of the history of the German bourgeoisie in Kocka (ed.), *Bürgertum im 19. Jahrhundert* (Munich, 1988) 1: 47–54.

10 Cf. the Introduction to the present volume; Thomas Nipperdey, 'Verein als soziale Struktur im späten 19. Jahrhundert', in Nipperdey, *Gesellschaft, Kultur, Theorie* (Göttingen, 1976); Otto Dann (ed.), *Vereinswesen und bürgerliche Gesellschaft in Deutschland* (Munich, 1984); Christiane Eisenberg, 'Arbeiter, Bürger und der "bürgerliche Verein" 1820–1870: Deutschland und England im Vergleich', in Kocka (ed.), *Bürgertum*, 2: 187–219.

11 Jürgen Kocka, 'Familie, Unternehmer und Kapitalismus. An Beispielen aus der frühen deutschen Industrialisierung', *Zeitschrift für Unternehmensgeschichte*, 24 (1979), 99–123.

12 Cf. note 2, above; also Karin Hausen, 'The polarisation of the "character of the sexes" ', in Evans and Lee (eds), *The German Family*, 25–50; and Jürgen Habermas, *Strukturwandel der Öffentlichkeit*, 5th edn (Neuwied, 1971).

13 See above, Introduction, pp. 12–14.

14 Dolores L. Augustine Pérez, 'Very wealthy businessmen in Imperial Germany', *Journal of Social History*, 21 (1988), 299–300.

15 H. Henning, *Das westdeutsche Bürgertum in der Epoche der Hochindustrialisierung 1860–1914*, 1 (Wiesbaden, 1973; vol. 2 has so far not appeared); Henning, 'Soziale Verflechtungen der Unternehmer in Westfalen 1860–1914', *Zeitschrift für Unternehmensgeschichte*, 23 (1978), 1–30.

16 Hartmut Kaelble, 'Französisches und deutsches Bürgertum 1870–1914', in Kocka (ed.), *Bürgertum*, 1: 107–40 esp. 117–27.

17 Cf. the discussion in Rosenbaum, *Formen der Familie* 334–6; also W. Stahl, *Der Elitekreislauf in der Unternehmerschaft* (Frankfurt, 1973), 280–1, 306–7; Hans-Jürgen Teuteberg, *Westfälische Textilunternehmer in der Frühindustrialisierung* (Dortmund, 1980), 33–4; Toni Pierenkemper, *Die Westfälischen Schwerindustriellen 1852–1913* (Göttingen, 1979), 45–6, 59–60, 73–4; Hartmut Kaelble, *Soziale Mobilität und Chancengleichheit im 19. und 20. Jahrhundert* (Göttingen, 1983), 50, 76, 90; Kaelble, 'Französisches und deutsches Bürgertum', 121; H. Henning, *Die deutsche Beamtenschaft im 19. Jahrhundert* (Stuttgart, 1984), 111–12.

18 See chapters 2, 3, 5 and 9 of the present volume; also Hartmut Kaelble, 'Wie feudal waren die deutschen Unternehmer im Kaiserreich?' in Richard Tilly (ed.), *Beiträge zur quantitativen deutschen Unternehmensgeschichte* (Stuttgart, 1985), 148–74; Ute Frevert, 'Bürgerlichkeit und Ehre. Zur Geschichte des Duells in England und Deutschland', Kocka (ed.), *Bürgertum*, 3: 101–40.

19 Kocka, 'Bürgertum', in Kocka (ed.), *Bürgertum*, 1: 59; Kaelble, 'Französisches und deutsches Bürgertum', 117–27 ('Die geringere soziale Verflechtung des Bürgertums in Deutschland').

20 Percy Ernst Schramm, *Hamburg. Ein Sonderfall in der Geschichte Deutschlands* (Hamburg, 1964).

21 Eckart Klessmann, *Geschichte der Stadt Hamburg* (Hamburg, 1981); Werner Jochmann and Hans-Dieter Loose (eds), *Hamburg. Geschichte der Stadt Hamburg und ihrer Bewohner*, 2 vols, (Hamburg, 1982–8); Hans-Wilhelm Eckardt, *Privilegien und Parlament. Die Auseinandersetzungen um das allgemeine und gleiche Wahlrecht in Hamburg* (Hamburg, 1980).

22 Otto Hintze, *Die Niederländische und Hamburgische Familie Amsinck*, 3 (Hamburg, 1932).

23 See Richard J. Evans, *Death in Hamburg. Society and Politics in the Cholera Years 1830–1910* (Oxford, 1987), ch. 1, esp. pp. 12–27, for a further description.

24 ibid., 34–5, 560–1; Renate Hauschild-Thiessen, *Bürgerstolz und Kaisertreue. Hamburg und das Deutsche Reich von 1871* (Hamburg, 1979), 97–106.

25 Olga Amsinck, daughter of Johannes I, married the judge and some-time Senator Friedrich Seiveking; Emily Amsinck, daughter of Wilhelm III, married the lawyer and later Burgomaster Johann Heinrich Burchard; her brother Wilhelm V married the daughter of Dr Oskar Gossler, lawyer and President of the Maritime Office (*Seeamt*); Amanda Amsinck, daughter of Heinrich I, married state prosecutor Dr Wilhelm Danzel; Caesar Amsinck, himself a lawyer, married a judge's daughter. See also Evans, *Death in Hamburg*, 18–21.

26 For a comparable example from the 1880s, see the accompanying genealogical table to Hildegard von Marchtaler, *Aus Alt-Hamburger Senatorenhäusern. Familienschicksale im 18. und 19. Jahrhundert* (Hamburg, 1958). The twenty-four Senators were reduced in number to eighteen by the constitutional reform of 1860 (cf. Eckardt, *Privilegien*).

27 Cf. the note of pride with which Carl August Schröder, *Aus Hamburgs Blütezeit* (Hamburg, 1921), 98–9, recalled that on his formal introduction into the Senate in 1899, Burgomaster Mönckberg alluded in his speech of welcome to the fact that their common great-grandfather had been elected to the Senate exactly a hundred years previously.

28 For a brief summary, see Evans, *Death in Hamburg*, 28–32, and more generally, Volker Plagemann (ed.), *Industriekultur in Hamburg. Des Deutschen Reiches Tor zur Welt* (Munich, 1984).

29 Cf. Lamar Cecil, *Albert Ballin. Business and Politics in Imperial Germany 1888–1918* (Princeton, 1971).

30 Rudolf Martin, *Jahrbuch des Vermögens und Einkommens der Millionäre in den drei Hansestädten* (Berlin, 1912).

31 Marina Cattaruzza, 'Das "Hamburgische Modell" der Beziehung zwischen Arbeit und Kapital. Organisationsprozesse und Konfliktverhalten auf den Werften 1890–1914', in Arno Herzig *et al.* (eds), *Arbeiter in Hamburg. Unterschichten, Arbeiter und Arbeiterbewegung in Hamburg seit dem ausgehenden 18. Jahrhundert* (Hamburg, 1983), 247–60; Michael Grüttner, *Arbeitswelt an der Wasserkante. Sozialgeschichte der Hamburger Hafenarbeiter 1886–1914* (Göttingen, 1984), 22–5; Klaus Saul, ' "Verteidigung der bürgerlichen Ordnung" oder Ausgleich der Interessen? Arbeitgeberpolitik in Hamburg-Altona 1896 bis 1914', in Herzig *et al.* (eds), *Arbeiter in Hamburg*, 261–82.

32 Cf. Hausen, ' "eine Ulme" ', in Frevert (ed.), *Bürgerinnen*, 92–8.

33 For an illuminating study of family life in the Swiss grand bourgeoisie

RICHARD J. EVANS

around the turn of the century, with many German parallels, see Ursi Blosser and Franziska Gerster, *Töchter der guten Gesellschaft, Frauenrolle und Mädchenerziehung im schweizerischen Grossbürgertum um 1900* (Zürich, 1985).

34 Marianne Weber, *Ehefrau und Mutter in der Rechtsentwicklung* (Tübingen, 1907).

35 See, for example, the extensive and detailed account of philanthropic activities in the cholera epidemic of 1892 in L. von Halle *et al.*, *Die Cholera in Hamburg in ihren Ursachen und Wirkungen Eine ökonomisch-medicinische Untersuchung* (Hamburg, 1895); or the *Jahresberichte des Armenpflegevereins zu Harvestehude* (copies in Staatsarchiv Hamburg).

36 On the absence of a Protestant tradition of female philanthropy in Germany, see Catherine M. Prelinger, 'The Nineteenth-century deaconessate in Germany: the efficacy of a family model', in Ruth-Ellen B. Joeres and Mary Jo Maynes (eds), *German Women in the Eighteenth and Nineteenth Centuries. A Social and Literary History* (Bloomington, Indiana, 1986), 215–29, esp 226.

37 See Frevert, *Frauen-Geschichte*, 112–20, and Richard J. Evans, *The Feminist Movement in Germany 1894–1933* (London, 1976), 74–5, for changing attitudes towards women in the public sphere.

38 Staatsarchiv Hamburg, Familienarchiv Buehl, 2c: Lebenserinnerungen des Stadtrates Dr Adolf Buehl, p. 55.

39 *Führer durch Hamburg zum III. Allgemeinen Deutschen Journalisten- und Schriftstellertage 1894* (Hamburg, 1894), 48, for a description of social life at the Exchange; see also J. Michael *Geschichte des Ärztlichen Vereins und seiner Mitglieder* (Hamburg, 1896), and the numerous stories of social and professional life among lawyers in Carl August Schröder, *Aus Hamburgs Blütezeit* (Hamburg, 1921).

40 For health services, see Evans, *Death in Hamburg*, 208–11, 221–5, 530–1. Members of the Amsinck family serving as lay judges on the Commercial court are listed in Hintze, *Familie Amsinck*, 3.

41 Percy Ernst Schramm, *Hamburg, Deutschland und die Welt* (Munich, 1943), 348. Schramm's writings, which include his own family history, *Neun Generationen* (Göttingen, 1964), are a valuable source for the history of the Hamburg grand bourgeoisie.

42 Evans, *Death in Hamburg*, 53–4.

43 See the childhood memories of Heinrich Merck, in Staatsarchiv Hamburg, Familienarchiv Merck, II 9 Konv. 4a, Heft II–III.

44 C.K.G. Behrmann, *Erinnerungen* (Berlin, 1904), 268–9

45 Julius von Eckardt, *Lebenserinnerungen* (Leipzig, 1910), 1: 204–5.

46 Buehl, Staatsarchiv Hamburg, Familienarchiv Buehl 2c, provides illuminating examples of this.

47 Renate Hauschild-Thiessen, *Bürgerstolz und Kaisertreue* (Hamburg, 1979), 98.

48 Evans, *Death in Hamburg*, 9, 26–7, 37, 253, 277–9, 310.

49 Renate Hauschild-Thiessen, *150 Jahre Grundeigentürmer-Verein in Hamburg von 1832 e. V* (Hamburg, 1982), 75–6, quoting Senator Heinrich Geffken (1847).

50 Eckardt, *Privilegien*, for a full account of the voting system.

138

51 Evans, *Death in Hamburg*, 557.
52 For the famous 'two hundred families' popularly supposed to have run nineteenth-century France, see Theodore Zeldin, *France 1848–1945, 1: Ambition, Love and Politics* (Oxford, 1973), 12–13.
53 Franklin Kopitzsch, *Grundzüge einer Geschichte der Aufklärung in Norddeutschland* (Hamburg, 1984).
54 Evans, *Death in Hamburg*, 176–82.
55 Cf. the contribution to this volume by Ute Frevert, 255–92.
56 For a useful discussion of how local conditions could affect marriage patterns, in this case among the Jewish grand bourgeoisie, see Mosse, *German-Jewish Economic Elite*, 181–3.
57 ibid.; also Gall, *Bürgertum*.

5

The industrial bourgeoisie and labour relations in Germany 1871–1933

Dick Geary

I

'A German employer regarded himself as a patriarch, as master in his own house *in pre-industrial terms*' (my italics).[1] This view of the distinguished economic historian Knut Borchardt is repeated by Hans-Ulrich Wehler in his criticism of Geoff Eley's emphasis on the modernity and dynamism of German capitalism in the Wilhelmine period.[2] Wehler writes: 'He [Eley] lacks any understanding of the influence of social-cultural factors, for example of the old paternalistic "master in my own house" ideology which formed and legitimised social relations in the factory, where it was not just a case of the rule of naked capitalists.'[3] That the industrial bourgeoisie of Imperial Germany had somehow adopted 'feudal' attitudes is a view to be found not only amongst latter-day commentators but also amongst contemporaries such as Heinrich Mann, whose novel *Der Untertan* portrays a title-hungry entrepreneur, and the Social Democratic Reichstag deputy Wendel, who declared in 1914: 'Historical development has produced a situation in which the bourgeois class has become feudalized and militarized.'[4]

Grounds for such a belief have been sought in the intermarriage of industrialists and landowning aristocrats, the purchase of East Elbian *Rittergüter* by wealthy bourgeois, and the increasing political cooperation of landed and business interests in organizations such as the Agrarian League and the Central Association of German Industrialists, especially in the umbrella organization, the 'Cartel of Productive Estates', in 1913.[5] Whether this process is best regarded as 'feudalization' or rather the 'embourgeoisement of the aristocracy' is at the centre of a debate that informs much of this book. What this chapter attempts to do is first of all examine the claim that the paternalism of employers in Imperial Germany was somehow 'feudal', based on 'pre-industrial' attitudes, and to suggest that it was not. The second part of the chapter then examines employers' attitudes in the Weimar Republic and hopes to show that employer hostility to the prevailing political system was not the function of some 'traditional' conservative ethic but reflected modern concerns and conflicts over the distribution of the national product in a welfare state at a time of economic crisis.

II

Historians have normally identified two aspects of employer paternalism in Germany: on the one hand a caring attitude towards employees, characterized by various company welfare schemes, and on the other an authoritarian stance which demanded obedience from the labour force and refused to countenance any concessions to their workers which interfered with managerial prerogatives in the factory. It is certainly true that a host of company welfare schemes were developed in Germany before 1914. The BASF factory at Ludwigshafen created sickness and accident insurance schemes for its labour force. The same company set up a savings bank for its workers, as did Krupp in Essen and several firms in the Augsburg textile industry. Schools to teach wives and daughters domestic science, convalescent homes, libraries, cheap company stores, all these institutions were established by engineering and chemical firms for their labourers and their families. Most famously of all, the larger firms often built housing for their employees, as in the case of Krupp in Essen, where the company owned no fewer than 1,045 dwellings by 1906. In general the standard of this accommodation was higher and the rents lower than in the private sector.[6]

Several different factors help to explain this development. Sometimes religious, ethical, and social-reformist motives played a part; or at least, so the employers claimed.[7] However, a closer examination of the central operation of company welfare schemes suggests other and more important motives were at work. In the first place such schemes and/or the occupation of a company dwelling were often targeted not at the workforce in general but only at certain valued groups: members of the so-called 'yellow' (i.e. company) unions, workers with a long history of service to the firm, skilled or white-collar employees. This suggests that one factor behind employer paternalism was the need to attract, create, and retain a solid core of workers with special skills in circumstances of very high labour turnover.[8] Additionally the application of benefits to some but not all sections of the workforce could serve to divide, or at least accentuate existing divisions amongst, the workers, rendering collective action on their part highly improbable.[9] Above all, welfare benefits and company housing, and the threat of their withdrawal, became a central mechanism in the preservation of employer control over labour. That is, even the 'welfare' aspects of employer paternalism were closely related to its more authoritarian, 'master in my own house' aspect.

This somewhat uncharitable view is given succour by the fact that the rent and labour contracts of those living in company housing were often inseparable, with workers leaving the firm or being dismissed having to evacuate their dwellings, sometimes on the very same day. Sometimes contributions towards company pension and insurance schemes were deducted directly from the wage-packet and on occasion forfeited when workers were dismissed, especially if this were for participation in industrial action or political agitation.[10] Thus, as contemporary trade union leaders and Social Democratic politicians claimed, these various private welfare schemes were but ways of robbing the worker of his freedom.[11] Such scepticism concerning the motives of German industrialists is further fuelled by the fact that those same Bochum employers who built company housing for their workforce opposed municipal housing schemes; that Krupp, the 'welfare employer' extraordinary, criticised *state* welfare measures; and that Stumm-Halberg, paternalist 'King of Saarabia', joined him in that criticism.[12] The point is of course clear: whereas company welfare tied the employee to his employer, state welfare provisions gave the worker an independence that the bosses thought all too dangerous. Thus 'paternalism' went hand in hand with a desire to control the labour force; and under such circumstances the concept of 'feudal' or 'pre-industrial' attitudes becomes an irrelevance.

It cannot be denied that Wilhelmine employers placed great emphasis on the loyalty of their workforce; something which is scarcely surprising given the massive expansion of German industry in this period, the high levels of labour turnover, and the consequent pressing need to attract and retain workers. Without company housing there would have been no one to man the pits of the Ruhr. But many German employers went much further than simply requesting 'loyalty'. They demanded the right to absolute control over their workers within the factory, and sometimes even outside it, and refused to recognize or have dealings with trade unions. Even the offer by state authorities to arbitrate in major industrial disputes was rejected by industrialists, at least initially.[13] This refusal to negotiate with workers or their representatives was perhaps most marked in those industries which at the same time introduced the most extensive company welfare schemes (iron, steel, chemicals) and finds elegant expression in the relative absence of collective wage agreements in Germany before the First World War. There were scarcely any such agreements in mining and chemicals; and in 1913 only about 16 per cent of the Reich's labour force was covered by them.[14]

In their desire to maintain exclusive control, German industrialists had recourse to a vast armoury of weapons to keep out both trade union organizers and political 'agitators'. Some paid bonuses to workers who informed on their colleagues who joined unions. Textile manufacturers in Augsburg, Bochum coal-owners and the employers of the Ludwigshafen chemical industry compiled extensive blacklists of 'trouble-makers.' Mass firings of strikers and trade unionists were common; whilst Krupp and Stumm agreed not to hire but also to dismiss any employee who read Social Democratic literature, attended SPD meetings, or even frequented pubs used by Social Democrats.[15]

In addition to the formal proscription of union and party membership German employers developed increasingly sophisticated methods of combating strikes and independent unions, and sometimes establishing their own labour exchanges directly to control recruitment and keep out unionists and Social Democrats. Strikes were increasingly countered by lock-outs, which in turn enjoyed more success than did the strikes they were meant to counter.[16] The ability of Imperial industrialists to mount such successful campaigns against working-class militancy was a direct consequence of the increasing concentration of capital and the growth of employers' federations, especially in the wake of the great 1903 strike and lock-out in the Crimmitschau textile industry; and although the two national and trans-sectoral federations were arguably not very effective, the same cannot be said of the regional and single-sector organizations of German employers, which overtook the unions in both numerical strength (i.e. fewer workers were members of unions than belonged to firms in their bosses' organizations) and effectiveness in industrial disputes.[17]

Apart from outright repression two other strategies were available to capital in its struggle with labour: division and integration. There were innumerable ways in which employers consciously adopted policies to fragment the labour force: differential treatment of blue- and white-collar workers, or of company-union members and non-members; different systems of pay for skilled workers and their less skilled helpers; the physical separation of workers from different regions in different accommodation; the exploitation of conflicts between German and Pole, especially in Upper Silesia.[18] On the other hand company unions could also become a mechanism of integrating workers into the firm, of inspiring loyalty. Normally financed by the employer, yellow unions achieved some importance after the great strike wave of 1903–6. By 1914 they had some 279,000 members and were especially strong in the Ruhr, and in the mining, iron, steel, electrical, and chemical industries. In some cases these company unions achieved the support of over half the labour force, as in the case of BASF in Ludwigshafen in 1913. At the outbreak of war in the following year no fewer than 82 per cent of Siemens' Berlin workforce belonged to the company union. Such organizations were committed to industrial peace, were sustained by annual celebratory rituals, and could rely on a large range of welfare benefits to maintain loyalty to the firm.[19]

Through a mixture of welfare measures and authoritarian repression, therefore, the industrialist sought to maintain exclusive powers of control in his enterprise. But what, if anything, does this have to do with 'pre-industrial' continuities or German exceptionalism? An analysis of the chronology of 'paternalism', of its advocates, and of its sectoral distribution may suggest instead that employer attitudes were rather a modern response to the modern problems of industrial society. It is surely significant that the development of formal insurance schemes and of company unions came at precisely the time that German industry was becoming increasingly concentrated and capital-intensive, when the more intimate and genuinely 'paternal' face-to-face contacts of the small firm were disintegrating, at least in some industrial sectors, and when entrepreneurs were adopting a more systematic profit-orientated approach in their business. In some places, such as Ludwigshafen, it makes little sense to talk of 'pre-industrial' continuities, for little in the way of company welfare existed before the 1870s; and in fact it was often a *second* generation of factory owners, or even and equally often the new group of salaried *managers* who initiated welfare schemes.[20] Furthermore, as we have seen, those schemes and in particular the construction of company housing can be explained in terms of market rationality: the need to attract and retain employees in a situation of acute labour shortage, high labour turnover, and the absence of private or municipal accommodation for newly arrived workers.[21] What any of this has to do with 'feudal' or 'pre-industrial' continuities is hard to see.

In particular, the greatest extension of formal company welfare provisions and yellow unions came *after* 1904 and *simultaneously* with repressive measures: increasing resort to the lock-out, work registration schemes, etc. It thus came relatively late in the day and its timing is of the utmost importance: it came after and in direct response to the enormous threat posed by increased industrial militancy between 1903 and 1906, increased trade union power and Social Democratic electoral success. Employer 'paternalism' was thus a response to the facts of life of a modern industrial society confronted with modern labour protest in the shape of strikes and working-class participation in industrial and political organizations. Equally, the fact that the distribution of employer paternalism varied enormously from one sector to another further suggests that the behaviour of German industrialists was determined more by market rational factors than by pre-industrial prejudices.[22]

It is platitudinous to say that the large-scale welfare schemes of BASF, Siemens, and Krupp were not copied by the overwhelming majority of smaller concerns, which simply could not afford them.[23] There is also considerable evidence that the smaller firms in the German electrical industry were far more prepared to conclude deals with strikers and trade unions than were AEG and Siemens. In fact the history of industrial relations in the Second Reich reveals huge sectoral variations. Of the 1,400,000 workers covered by collective wage agreements in 1913, two-thirds were in firms employing under 20 men. Such agreements were concentrated in printing and the skilled building trades. There were fewer in metalwork and textiles and virtually none in mining.[24] The reasons for this differential behaviour on the part of employers becomes clear if we compare specific industries. Printing was the leading industry in developing processes of collective bargaining: by 1911, 90 per cent of all German printers were covered by collective wage agreements. The reason for this unusual situation resides in the structure of the industry: it was not cartellized, it was dominated by small and medium-sized concerns and it was characterized by the high level of competition for labour. That labour was in turn highly skilled and strongly unionized, with bargaining power and assets in the labour market. Under such circumstances relatively weak employers found it saner to compromise with powerful workers. That such conciliation was a function of the state of the labour market can be demonstrated by contrasting evidence within the same industry: the one area in which collective wage agreements did not hold sway was Rhineland-Westphalia, where the unions were weaker and the type of work done less skilled.[25] A similar picture applies to the building industry, 44 per cent of whose workers, most notably the skilled bricklayers, had won collective agreements by 1911. Again we are dealing with an industry of skilled and unionized workers and one whose firms were especially vulnerable to strike action on account of seasonal factors and completion-date fines. Thus, as one building employer put it in 1901, not to conclude negotiations with labour was 'impractical' and 'obsolete'.[26]

The situation in the coal-mining industry, where only eighty-two (!) individuals were covered by collective wage agreements in 1913, was quite different. Here was a sector that was highly concentrated and cartellized and in which the employers were exceptionally well organized. They were thus able to operate effective blacklists, build powerful yellow unions, and maintain a hard-necked anti-union (anti-independent-union, that is) stand. In this they were further helped by the fact that their workforce was not recruited from skilled men who brought with them the benefits of apprenticeship. A similar set of circumstances prevailed in the chemical and electrical industries, textiles, and sections of engineering, where strong employer organizations had also come into existence. In engineering, however, there were also sectors and regions dominated by smaller firms, as in some parts of Saxony; and, significantly, these firms were far more willing to compromise in their competition for highly skilled labour.[27]

Thus the readiness of industrialists to reach agreement with workers and their representatives was primarily determined by the relative strength of the two sides of industry rather than anything else. This does not mean that the smaller employers were necessarily happy about this state of affairs. There is evidence from Ludwigshafen that they were even more hostile to unions than the larger ones; whilst in the building industry wage settlements were often forced upon employers by labour militancy.[28] Yet it remains the case that the entrepreneurs of the Second Reich resisted negotiation where they could and for as long as they were able. But was there anything peculiarly 'German' about this?

III

The French *patronat* before the First World War was in general no more prepared to recognize trade unions as partners in the process of collective bargaining than its German counterpart was; and French employers also sought to preserve their control in the 1890s by the creation of company unions. Mining companies created relief and pension funds to secure loyalty, but at the same time used lower supervisory staff as a police/informer network. Foreign labour was regularly imported to break strikes; and on occasion gunmen were hired to intimidate pickets. This authoritarianism, as in the German case, was also accompanied by 'paternalism', the provision of company housing, pension schemes, works canteens, or clinics, as at Décazeville and Le Creusot. In fact the Schneider concern in the latter town provides a classic case of both company welfare provision on the one hand and the demand for absolute obedience on the part of its workers on the other, possessing an extraordinary network of surveillance over its employees and dismissing immediately anyone suspected of trade union agitation.[29] The industrial bosses of the New World, where to talk of 'feudal' or 'pre-industrial' continuities makes little sense, were no more conciliatory. In the United States after the turn of the century employers drew up blacklists, created employment exchanges, established 'counter-unions', and brought in colonies of strike-breakers. In Pittsburgh that great paternalist Andrew Carnegie even employed a private army to keep the unions out of his factories; with the result that twelve people were killed in a private war to maintain employer dominance.[30]

Even in Britain, the *only* state to possess something of a system of industrial relations before 1914, factory-owners and managers responded to the growth of industrial militancy and the 'new unionism' in the late 1880s and 1890s with lock-outs, blacklists, private employment exchanges, and strike-breaking organizations.

By 1890 engineering firms in north-east England had developed a strike insurance scheme modelled on that of the Durham coal-owners; and some employers in the building industry had established a system of worker registration some twenty years earlier. It is possible to find innumerable statements from British industrialists which repeat the 'master-in-my-own-house' ideology, which we are told was so characteristically 'German'. The National Federation of Employers was established in December 1873 precisely to resist 'the interference of Trade Unions with the details of business management'. Some years earlier engineering employers stated during the 1852 lock-out: 'ours is the responsibility of the details, ours the risk of loss, ours the capital, its perils and its engagements. We claim, and are resolved to assert the right of every British subject, to do what we will with our own . . .' Here is a bold statement of employer control, but one which owes absolutely nothing to 'feudalism'. Even later, in the 1890s, when collective wage agreements were becoming much more common in Britain, employers were often conciliatory in wage agreements but utterly intransigent on issues of managerial prerogative.[31]

It would thus appear that Geoff Eley is right when he claims that 'a stronger comparative sense would diminish the belief in German exceptionalism'.[32] This is not to say there were not significant differences between German industrialists and their British counterparts. There were; and these will be examined in more detail below. Yet before doing so it is important to remember that the relative willingness of employers in Britain to engage in collective bargaining and recognize trade unions was the exception rather than the rule in international terms. In any case the following differences between the British and the German cases can be explained in precisely the same terms as the sectoral variations in employer behaviour within the Second Reich, as we shall see. Although it is true that some British employers did adopt intransigent attitudes, many did not. Mundella established arbitration boards in the iron and steel industry of the North-East as early as the 1860s. The success of engineering firms in various lock-outs did not lead to any serious attempt to destroy the unions, which were seen by several industrialists as institutions which could discipline labour and provide a route to 'orderly collective bargaining'. Nowhere is the massive gap in behaviour between the industrial elites of Britain and Germany clearer than in the number of workers covered by collective wage agreements: 230,000 in metalwork,

460,000 in textiles, and no fewer than 900,000 in mining in Britain in 1910, as against 1,376 metalworkers, 16,000 textile workers, and a paltry 82 coal-miners in Germany three years later.[33] Under these circumstances it is scarcely surprising that a German worker who came to live in Britain should comment:

> trade unionism and politics are kept distinct in this country. It would be to the disadvantage of the working classes themselves to sever themselves in the matter of politics from the middle classes, since the attitude of the latter towards the workman has been friendly.[34]

That there were significant differences between the British and the German cases is clear. How those differences are to be explained is, of course, a different matter; but a range of explanations are available which do not require resort to theories of 'feudal' or 'pre-industrial' continuities in the case of Germany. In fact those explanations which were earlier provided to explain the differential behaviour of German industrialists can also be mobilized to explain the differences between the two countries: the relative strength of capital and labour in the labour market. Collective bargaining in the British engineering industry, for example, was partly a consequence of low levels of concentration and the consequent competition between employers for labour which was both highly skilled and strongly unionized. Similarly, the British coal industry also incorporated a relatively large number of smallish firms: in 1912 only 101 out of 1,784 firms (let alone pits) employed over 2,000 men, whereas in Germany 6 giant syndicates were responsible for around 90 per cent of all hard-coal production and over 58 per cent of the mining labour force worked in pits employing over 1,000 men in 1907.[35] The relatively low costs of extraction in British mining may also have made it easier for employers to negotiate with their workers;[36] whilst the fact that British industrial expansion in the late nineteenth and early twentieth century was more labour- than capital-intensive made employers much more vulnerable to the withdrawal of labour by skilled workers, as did the fact that many British employees had a long history of trade union organizations which *antedated* the introduction of modern technology.

Where British companies were vulnerable to overseas competition, or even high levels of domestic competition, and thus likely to lose markets and suffer disproportionately in lengthy industrial disputes, there were further incentives to negotiate and avoid trouble. In Germany, on the other hand, industrialists were excused some of these pressures as a consequence of cartellization, price-fixing agreements, and import tariffs. In chemicals and electricals, the dominance of a very small number of giant concerns, and the fact that around 90 per cent of world trade in chemical dye-stuffs was in German hands, meant that employers were sufficiently secure to sit out disputes and refuse to negotiate.[37] The explanation of national differences can thus be found in terms of industrial structure rather than anything else, a contention sustained by the fact that in areas of the British coal industry where there were no unions, as in Derbyshire and Leicestershire, or where the industry was dominated by large companies, as in Lancashire and Cheshire, collective bargaining developed much more slowly.[38]

However, differences in the structure of the labour market cannot explain *all* the differences between Edwardian Britain and Wilhelmine Germany. In particular the *scale* of the difference in number of collective wage agreements is so great as not to be explicable simply in these terms. It does seem to be the case that British employers were far less neurotic about any supposed 'threat' from the unions, drew a clear distinction between 'radical' and 'reformist' trade union leaders and valued 'orderly collective bargaining', as we have seen.[39] Their German counterparts were more worried and were far keener to destroy independent trade unions than negotiate with them. Part of the explanation for this resides in the *political* context within which industrial relations developed. Historically the recognition of trade unions by employers has been a consequence of the strength of skilled labour, the relatively moderate stance of their trade unions, and the extent to which the state actually encouraged working-class combination as a route to orderly collective bargaining. In this respect Britain was almost unique in the early legal recognition of association and the subsequent bestowal of legal privileges on unions. In Britain, as Gordon Phillips writes, 'the state gave a lead which industrial employers ultimately followed'.[40] Officials at the Board of Trade and in the Home Office encouraged trade union recognition on the part of employers and with some success. In Germany, on the other hand, those administrators who favoured such an approach to labour relations never got their way. In general, state intervention in industrial disputes, and the laws which governed the rights of association, picketing, and the like generally, although by no means invariably, favoured capital.

Often the authorities and the employers worked closely together to control both industrial militancy and political radicalism, most notably in the years of the anti-socialist law (1878–90) but by no means only then.[41] In the years immediately before the First World War, German industrialists became increasingly shrill in their demands for state intervention against pickets and unions; and this with some success.[42] This turn to reaction was clearly associated with the massive industrial unrest of the years 1910–13 and the electoral triumph of the SPD in 1912. Indeed it is here, in the presence of the largest socialist movement in the world and one ostensibly committed to revolutionary Marxism, that there resides a crucial factor for an understanding of the different behaviour of German and British employers. The wave of organization that embraced German industrialists between 1905 and 1913 and which saw the creation of the yellow unions came in the wake not only of the great Crimmitschau strike but in the wake of impressive Social Democratic gains in elections to the Reichstag. Employers were as concerned to keep Social Democrats out of the factories as they were to defeat the independent trade unions; and some of the yellow unions were founded not to combat powerful independent unions (for such did not exist in the Ruhr coal, iron, and steel industry) but on the initiative of the Imperial Association against Social Democracy (*Reichsverband zur Bekämpfung der Sozialdemokratie*). This was the case at Krupp in Essen, where the company union gave explicit support to National Liberal candidates at election time, at BASF in Ludwigshafen, and the Howald concern in Kiel.[43]

Furthermore, the close contact between German Social Democracy and the 'Free' Trade Unions, forged in the 1860s and strengthened by the repression of the anti-socialist law, made it difficult to draw sweeping distinctions between trade-union activity on the one hand and socialist agitation on the other, especially as most union functionaries were members of the SPD and as about a third of Social Democratic Reichstag deputies were themselves trade-union officials. Under these circumstances it is perhaps not surprising that there are countless examples of German workers losing jobs for political reasons and of employers seeking to influence the voting behaviour of their labour force directly, as for example, in the case of BASF chemical workers, who were expected to support National Liberal Party candidates.[44] Employer attitudes towards labour in Imperial Germany were thus shaped by a variety of factors, by the structure of industry and of the labour market, and by the apparent threat of socialism. Similar attitudes can be found in many other countries; so that it seems in the end absurd to imagine that anti-socialism reflected 'feudal' rather than 'bourgeois' values.

IV

Most of the studies of business in the Weimar Republic, though by no means all, have been preoccupied with the question of the relationship between industrialists and the rise of Nazism. It is not the intention here to delve into the details of this often heated and tortuous debate, though one can, with certain reservations, accept the findings of the American historian Henry Ashby Turner: few industrialists actually joined the party, those that gave money to the Nazi Party did so in general for instrumental reasons (a kind of political insurance) rather than as a result of ideological commitment, more business money flowed into the coffers of the traditional 'bourgeois' parties (the People's Party or DVP, and the Nationalists or DNVP), and big business did not play a major role in Hitler's becoming Chancellor in early 1933.[45] This chapter is more concerned with the relationship between industrialists and the system of industrial relations that developed in the Weimar Republic, a more specific question and one more amenable to generalization than are reflections on the political stance of employers in party terms; for in those terms big business was notably divided. A few industrialists, most famously Fritz Thyssen, did become Nazis, but others, such as Gustav Krupp von Bohlen und Halbach, Paul Silverberg, and Albert Vögler belonged to the German People's Party, whilst Klöckner supported the Catholic Centre Party, at least in 1928. Thereafter party allegiances shifted, whilst other members of that informal grouping of Ruhr industrialists, the *Ruhrlade*, remained unaffiliated. As Gerald D. Feldman has pointed out, during the abortive Kapp putsch of 1920, when reactionary *Freikorps* tried to overthrow the new republic, big business as a whole did not desert Weimar but was in the main apathetic or confused on the question of its survival.[46]

It is thus clearly improper to generalize about the *party-political* stance of industry. At the same time, however, business in general confronted a new set of circumstances in the Weimar Republic in the field of industrial relations, to which it was profoundly unsympathetic. Whereas employers were loath to recognize or deal with trade unions before 1914, the situation began to change during the First World War, though not as a result of the initiative of employers. The authorities realized that the successful prosecution of the war required the co-operation of labour, and to this end they removed restrictions that had previously been placed on the recruitment of rural labourers and state employees. They also caused to be established within larger firms works committees, on which sat – and this really was a radical departure from the past – union representatives and employers. In a sense the bosses were forced to deal with those organizations of labour which they had previously sought to ignore or repress.[47] During the revolutionary upheavals at the end of the war, the field of industrial relations was also revolutionized. A famous agreement between the leading industrialist Hugo Stinnes and the chairman of the socialist Free Trade Unions Carl Legien recognized the independent unions, agreed to the dissolution of the yellow unions, established the eight-hour day as the norm, and introduced significant wage increases. These measures were subsequently enshrined in Republican legislation, as was the creation of a system of state arbitration in industrial disputes. At least until the late 1920s this system appears to have worked to the benefit of labour, particularly its unskilled sections, not least as the arbitrators recruited from the Ministry of Labour were often Social Democrats or from the labour wing of the Catholic Centre Party.[48] Furthermore labour law required trade-union recognition and made collective wage agreements legally binding.

This apparently unprecedented co-operation between capital and labour in the early years of the Weimar Republic was further expressed in the creation of a trade-union/employer forum, the so-called *Zentralarbeitsgemeinschaft*, and has been seen as a key to the survival of the new state in its early, turbulent years.[49] David Abraham also sees the famous 1926 speech of Paul Silverberg, head of the national industrial pressure group, the *Reichsverband der deutschen Industrie*, which called for collaboration with the Social Democrats, as indicative of a new willingness to co-operate with labour on the part of employers.[50] But one needs to be extremely suspicious of such a view, for the co-operation of unions and employers in 1919 and 1920 was to a very large extent *enforced*.

Collaboration in the *Zentralarbeitsgemeinschaft* was dictated by the need to combat the retention of state economic controls after demobilization.[51] It and the Stinnes-Legien agreement were also a consequence of the fear that if concessions were not made then a full-blown revolution involving the expropriation of industrial enterprise might develop. Thus co-operation with labour on the part of employers was really intended as a short-term defensive stratagem and did not indicate any profound reorientation of attitudes. This was made clear at the time. Stinnes himself spoke of a 'breathing space'; the Director of the Association of German Iron and Steel Industrialists described the prospects as threatening and saw the central question in the revolutionary upheavals as 'How can we save industry?';[52] and as early as 1922 the *Reichsverband der deutschen Industrie* drew up a programme for the future which aimed at undoing the gains of the revolution, namely, a reduction in welfare taxation, less social security provision, lower wages, and above all the abolition of the statutory eight-hour working day.[53]

Involved in drawing up this document was that supposed advocate of collaboration Paul Silverberg, which suggests that one must take his 1926 Dresden speech with more than a pinch of salt. Silverberg was a tactical opportunist who wanted to generate some popular support for industrial policies. In 1926 this may have involved collaboration with socialists; in 1932 it was the Nazis whom he saw as potential allies. In any case the 1926 speech needs to be looked at more closely: the acceptance of the Free Trade Unions and the SPD as partners was made conditional upon the abandonment of the language of class warfare and above all agreement to leave the running of the economy to those 'who knew best', i.e. the industrialists themselves.[54] This last point is crucial for an understanding of business motives: throughout the Weimar Republic employers refused to accept the right of any other group or institution to interfere with the 'economy'.[55] Equality might be allowable in the political sphere, but not in the economic. However, the distinction between the political and economic arenas became increasingly blurred in the Weimar Republic, for the democratic polity meant that labour made claims on the state which of necessity impinged on taxation and social policy, which in turn had repercussions on profitability and the organization of industry. These consequences of genuine pluralism were never really accepted by German industry.

Even here, however, we must beware of treating industrial atti-

tudes as monolithic. Not only did the attitude of individual industrialists vary in party-political terms but also some industrial sectors found labour relations in Weimar more tolerable than others.
It is true, as Henry Turner has pointed out, that crass generaliza-
tions about differences between sectors are problematical given the
vertically integrated nature of much of German industry. The
Krupp firm, for example, owned coal mines, made steel, and
produced finished products in the shape of armaments. Yet most
commentators would agree that *in general* certain sectoral differences in the behaviour and attitudes of the industrial bourgeoisie
can be identified. In general the chemical and electrical industries,
and parts of the processing and finishing industries in engineering
were more conciliatory than coal, iron, and steel. For example,
the German Democratic Party, arguably the only 'bourgeois' party
really committed to the new Republic, initially received substantial
financial support from the giant electrical firm of Siemens; whilst
Carl Duisberg of IG Farben and Hermann Bücher of AEG adopted
a position of co-operation with the unions.[56] In 1926 Silverberg's
call for partnership with the Social Democrats met with a cool
reception from many quarters of the *Reichsverband* but found some
degree of support from leading figures in chemicals, the electrical
industry, and engineering.[57] Attempts to revive the *Zentralarbeitsgemeinschaft* of employers and unions in 1930 were also initiated by
the same interests, with Bücher, Siemens and Hans von Raumer
(electricals), Carl Bosch (chemicals), Adam Frohwein (textiles),
and Hans Kraemer (paper and printing) leading the way. These
industrialists were less critical of Chancellor Brüning's retention
of some of the system of collective wage bargaining than were
those in heavy industry; and they were far less prepared to co-
operate with agrarian interests. Textiles, engineering, chemicals
and the electro-technical industry wanted low prices for raw
materials and opposed protectionism on account of their export
interests.[58]

It is not difficult to explain the position of these more conciliatory industrialists – conciliatory internationally in terms of their
readiness to seek compromise on the vexed question of reparations,
and domestically, in so far as they were prepared to deal with the
representatives of organized labour and tolerate the system of
collective bargaining. These were the most prosperous sectors of
German industry, in the case of electricals and chemicals remaining profitable some way into the world economic crisis of 1929–33.

In a sense they could thus afford welfare taxation and higher wage settlements in a way that heavy industry, already experiencing difficulties in the mid–1920s, could not. This was especially so as wage costs were only a relatively small fraction of total costs in the highly capital-intensive and dynamic sectors such as electricals and chemicals, in the latter case in fact only 15 per cent. The dependence of these two sectors on export markets also explains their opposition to tariffs and relative reasonableness on the question of reparations.[59]

The attitudes of the leaders of coal, iron, and steel were *in general* rather different. They not only succeeded in maintaining a cartellized system of inflexible price-fixing but also advocated protection against foreign imports. They played a leading role in opposing Silverberg's 1926 call for co-operation with labour; they sabotaged attempts to revive the *Zentralarbeitsgemeinschaft* in 1930; they were influential in the collapse of parliamentary government in the same year through pressure on the German People's Party not to reach agreement with its Social Democratic coalition partner on the issue of unemployment benefits; they broke with Brüning on the grounds that mandatory arbitration, statutory wages legislation, and a fixed working day had not been abolished; and they mobilized support against the Young Plan's proposed solution to the reparations issue.[60]

Just as the attitudes of the more dynamic and export-oriented industries towards labour and the Weimar Republic can be explained by rational economic calculation, so can the intransigent stance of heavy industry. Some firms in iron, steel, and coal were experiencing considerable problems by the mid–1920s. Even in the best years of the twenties companies were working well below capacity. For example, German steelworks produced at around 50 per cent capacity in 1925, 77 per cent in the peak year of 1927 and 55 per cent in 1930. Such under-utilization, in the wake of both restricted demand and the rationalization measures of 1924–6, squeezed profits (in 1927 only 4 per cent in mining, even lower in iron and steel) and proved fatal in the Depression.[61] In these circumstances companies in this sector were less prepared and less able to buy industrial peace than Siemens or IG Farben. They were also unusually sensitive to increased costs, either as a result of taxation or wage settlements. Wage levels were crucial in an industry like mining, where wage costs constituted over a half of total costs.[62]

There thus existed a division in industrial attitudes largely dependent on the economic structure of a particular branch of industry. However, as the economic situation deteriorated, so voices began to be heard, even within the 'progressive' sectors of business, calling for an end to welfare taxation and state arbitration in industrial disputes. In January 1930 Carl Duisberg stated, 'capital is being destroyed through the unproductive use of public funds . . . Only an immediate and radical reversal of state policies can help', thus criticizing Weimar's progressive labour and welfare legislation.[63] It was no conservative 'tradition' which shaped employer hostility to republican institutions; what mattered was what those institutions meant for business profitability. As a result of Social Democratic government at national, regional, and local level, often in collaboration with the labour wing of the Catholic Centre Party, a massive expansion of welfare provision took place, which in turn had to be funded through taxation, which unlike the situation before 1914 no longer came from indirect taxes. This taxation, claimed industry, was one of the factors which was ruining profitability. So were 'political wages': the introduction of statutory collective wage bargaining, state arbitration in industrial disputes, and legal restrictions on the length of the working day, all pushed up wages and gave the trade unions a power they would not have enjoyed under free market conditions. Thus the Weimar Republic was seen by many employers as a 'trade union state' and its policies described as 'cold socialism'.[64]

Business might tolerate democratic politics where they did not impinge upon the running of the economy. But political interference in the shape of imposed wage settlements forfeited the loyalty of industrialists; and in the end some industrialists, predictably in the Ruhr iron and steel industry, determined upon a head-on collision with such interference in the massive Ruhr lock-out, involving some quarter of a million workers, in 1928. This dispute was not simply about one particular arbitrated wages settlement which the employers disliked and thought they could not afford, but, in the minds of at least some of the industrialists involved, sought to challenge the whole system of collective bargaining and state arbitration, as several leading figures openly confessed.[65] In such a situation the relationship of industry to the Weimar Republic was always going to be fraught with difficulties, and from 1928 onwards those difficulties were compounded by declining profitability. In such a situation a substantial section of the business community desired the ending of 'Marxist' influence in government, by which was meant significantly that of the SPD and the Free Trade Unions, and the destruction of Weimar labour legislation. In this situation only a few industrialists turned to Nazism; but many welcomed government by decree rather than parliamentary majority. Their reasons for doing so had little to do with 'tradition'. Rather they were a reaction to the threat that a modern welfare state posed to business interests.

NOTES

1 Knut Borchardt, 'The Industrial Revolution in Germany', in Carlo M. Cipolla (ed.), *The Fontana Economic History of Europe* (London, 1971), 4(1), 157.

2 Geoff Eley, 'Capitalism and the Wilhelmine state', *Historical Journal*, 21 (1978), 741.

3 Hans-Ulrich Wehler, 'Deutscher Sonderweg,' *Merkur* (1981), 481.

4 Quoted in G. A. Ritter and J. Kocka (eds), *Deutsche Sozialgeschichte*, 2 (Munich, 1974), 77.

5 These developments are discussed in Volker Berghahn, *Der Tirpitz-Plan* (Düsseldorf, 1971); Harmut Kaelble, *Industrielle Interessenpolitik in der Wilhelminischen Gesellschaft* (Berlin, 1967); Siegfried Mielke, *Der Hansa-Bund* (Göttingen, 1976); Hans-Jürgen Puhle, *Agrarische Interessenpolitik und preussischer Konservatismus im wilhelminischen Reich* (Hanover, 1966); Dirk Stegmann, *Die Erben Bismarcks* (Cologne, 1970); Hans-Peter Ullman, *Der Bund der Industriellen* (Göttingen, 1976); Hans-Ulrich Wehler, *Das deutsche Kaiserreich 1871–1918* (Göttingen, 1973).

6 Alan Milward and S. B. Saul, *The Development of the Economies of Continental Europe* (London, 1977), 29, 37 and 50; Ilse Fischer 'Maurer- und Textilarbeiterstreiks in Augsburg', in K. Tenfelde and H. Volkmann (eds), *Streik* (Munich, 1981), 71; David F. Crew, *Town in the Ruhr* (New York, 1979), 148 and 153–4; James Wickham, 'The working-class movement in Frankfurt am Main during the Weimar Republic' (PhD., University of Sussex, 1979), 65–6; Georg Eibert, *Unternehmerpolitik Nürnberger Maschinenbauer* (Stuttgart, 1979), 94; Willy Breunig, *Soziale Verhältnisse der Arbeiterschaft in Ludwigshafen* (Ludwigshafen, 1976), 70 and 130; Lawrence Schofer, *The Formation of a Modern Labor Force* (Berkeley, 1975), 9.

7 Jürgen Kocka *Unternehmer in der deutschen Industrialisierung* (Göttingen, 1975), 79; Schofer, *Formation*, 91.

8 Crew, *Town in the Ruhr*, 154; Jürgen Kocka, 'Vorindustrielle Faktoren in der deutschen Industrialisierung', in Michael Stürmer (ed.), *Das kaiserliche Deutschland* (Düsseldorf, 1970), 271; Jürgen Kocka, *Unternehmensverwaltung und Angestelltenschaft am Beispiel Siemens* (Stuttgart, 1969), 25, 101 f., and 107–8; Heilwig Schomerus, *Die Arbeiter der Maschinenfabrik Esslingen* (Stuttgart, 1977), 201.

9 Wickham, 'Working-class movement', 63.

10 Stephen Hickey, 'The shaping of the German labour movement', in Richard J. Evans (ed.), *Society and Politics in Wilhelmine Germany* (London, 1978), 225–6; Crew, *Town in the Ruhr*, 151; Wickham, 'Working-class movement', 65; Schofer, *Formation*, 93–4; Ilse Costas, 'Arbeitskämpfe in der Berliner Elektroindustrie', in Tenfelde and Volkmann (eds), *Streik*, 101; Horst Steffens, 'Arbeiterwohnverhältnisse', in ibid., 127–8.

11 Breunig, *Soziale Verhältnisse*, 133–4.

12 Crew, *Town in the Ruhr*, 150; Stegmann, *Erben Bismarcks*, 269; Hans Jaeger, *Unternehmer in der deutschen Politik* (Bonn, 1967), 270–1.

13 Kocka, *Unternehmer*, 85; Lothar Machtan, 'Im Vertrauen auf unsere gerechte Sache,' in Tenfelde and Volkmann (eds), *Streik*, 54. The strikes in the Ruhr mines of 1889 and 1905 and in the Hamburg docks in 1896/7 saw such refusals to accept government attempts to arbitrate.

14 Hans-Peter Ullmann, *Tarifverträge und Tarifpolitik* (Frankfurt-on-Main, 1977), 97; Klaus Schönhoven, 'Arbeitskonflikte', in Tenfelde and Volkmann (eds), *Streik*, 183.

15 Crew, *Town in the Ruhr*, 146; Fischer, 'Maurer-', 76; Breunig, *Soziale Verhältnisse*, 395: Klaus Tenfelde, *Sozialgeschichte der Bergarbeiterschaft an der Ruhr* (Bonn, 1977), 527–8: Costas, 'Arbeitskämpfe', 102; Hans Rosenberg, *Grosse Depression und Bismarckzeit* (Berlin, 1967), 206 and 226; Klaus Mattheier, *Die Gelben* (Düsseldorf, 1973), 30–1.

16 Michael Grüttner, 'Mobilität und Konfliktverhalten', in Tenfelde and Volkmann (eds), *Streik*, 155; Breunig, *Soziale Verhältnisse*, 389; Dieter Groh, 'Intensification of work and industrial conflict in Germany', *Politics and Society*, 8 (1978), 374 and 380; Schönhoven, 'Arbeitskonflikte', 184.

17 Hans-Peter Ullmann, 'Unternehmerschaft, Arbeitgeberverbände und Streikbewegung', in Tenfelde and Volkmann (eds), *Streik*, 198; Dieter Groh, *Negative Integration und Revolutionärer Attentismus* (Frankfurt-on-Main, 1973), 105; Schönhoven, 'Arbeitskonflikte', 184.

18 Mattheier, *Die Gelben*, 15; Hickey, 'Shaping', 217–18 and 230; Crew, *Town in the Ruhr*, 148; Schofer, *Formation*, 157.

19 Ullmann, 'Unternehmerschaft', 200; J. Barrington Moore, *Injustice* (New York, 1978), 260–1; Mattheier, *Die Gelben*, 132–8; Breunig, *Soziale Verhältnisse*, 450; Costas, 'Arbeitskämpfe', 101f.

20 Kocka, 'Vorindustrielle Faktoren', 277; Kocka, *Unternehmer*, 79–80 and 118; Breunig, *Soziale Verhältnisse*, 82; Eibert, *Unternehmerpolitik*, 285.

21 Crew, *Town in the Ruhr*, 148; Eibert, *Unternehmerpolitik*, 97–9; Kocka, *Unternehmer*, 130. Siemens introduced pension schemes for white-collar employees at precisely the point in time that they began to organize and agitate.

22 Mattheier, *Die Gelben*, 65–71.

23 Ullmann, 'Unternehmerschaft', 200.

24 Costas, 'Arbeitskämpfe', 97; Ullmann, *Tarifverträge*, 23, 34 and 97–8; Groh, 'Intensification', 366 and 369.

25 Ullmann, *Tarifverträge*, 49, 56 and 163f. Schönhoven, 'Arbeitskonflikte', 181.

26 Ullmann, *Tarifverträge*, 56 and 81–4.

27 Schönhoven, 'Arbeitskonflikte', 181 and 197; Frank B. Tipton, *Regional Variations in the Economic Development of Germany* (Middleton, 1976), 126.
28 Breunig, *Soziale Verhältnisse*, 425; Ullmann, *Tarifverträge*, 85 and 90.
29 Peter N. Stearns, *Lives of Labour* (London, 1975); Mattheier, *Die Gelben*, 48; Roger Magraw, 'Socialism, syndicalism and French labour', in Dick Geary (ed.), *Labour and Socialist Movements in Europe before 1914* (London, 1989), 63 and 69; Michelle Perrot, *Workers on Strike* (London, 1987), 252–6.
30 Mattheier, *Die Gelben*, 42–6.
31 ibid., 42–3; Keith Burgess, *The Origins of British Industrial Relations* (London, 1975), viii, 30, 59–60, 65, 112–13 and 187.
32 Eley, 'Capitalism', 746.
33 Frank Wilkinson, 'Collective bargaining in the steel industry', in Asa Briggs and John Savile (eds), *Essays in Labour History 1918–1939* (London, 1977), 102; Stearns, *Lives of Labour*, 165 and 180–1; H. A. Clegg, *A History of British Trade Unions*, 1 (London, 1964), 362–3; Burgess, *Origins*, vii and 310–11.
34 Quoted in David Kynaston, *King Labour* (London, 1976), 152.
35 Burgess, *Origins*, 38–9 and 155; Dick Geary, 'Socialism and the German labour movement', in Geary (ed.), *Labour*, 102.
36 Burgess, *Origins*, 306.
37 ibid., 311; Wickham, 'Working-class movement', 60–1.
38 Burgess, *Origins*, 188 and 209.
39 Clegg, *History*, 362–3; Burgess, *Origins*, vii and 310–11.
40 Gordon Phillips, 'The British labour movement before 1914', in Geary (ed.), *Labour*, 39.
41 Klaus Saul, 'Zwischen Repression und Integration', in Tenfelde and Volkmann (eds), *Streik*, 209–36; Tenfelde, *Bergarbeiterschaft*, 523–5.
42 Rosenberg, *Grosse Depression*, 226; Hedwig Wachenheim, *Geschichte der deutschen Arbeiterbewegung* (Cologne, 1967), 577; Ullmann, 'Unternehmerschaft', 203–7.
43 Mattheier, *Die Gelben*, 77–9 and 88–9.
44 Breunig, *Soziale Verhältnisse*, 134–5 and 177.
45 For a discussion of Turner's work and that of his critics, see Dick Geary, 'The industrial elite and the Nazis', in Peter D. Stachura (ed.), *The Nazi Machtergreifung* (London, 1983), 85–100. For the most comprehensive and recent statement of Turner's position see Henry Ashby Turner, *Big Business and the Rise of Nazism* (London, 1986).
46 H.A. Turner, 'Big business and the rise of Hitler', in *American Historical Review*, 75 (1969), 57; Hans H. Biegert, 'Gewerkschaftspolitik in der Phase des Kapp-Lüttwitz-Putsches', in Hans Mommsen *et al.* (eds), *Industrielles System and Politische Entwicklung in der Weimarer Republik* (Düsseldorf, 1974), 198; Gerald D. Feldman, 'Big business and the Kapp Putsch', in *Central European History*, 4 (1971), 99–130.
47 On industry during the war see Gerald D. Feldman, *Army, Industry and Labor* (Princeton, 1966).
48 The most detailed account of labour and welfare legislation appears in Ludwig Preller, *Sozialpolitik in der Weimarer Republik* (reprinted Düsseldorf, 1978). See also Hans-Hermann Hartwich, *Arbeitsmarkt, Verbände*

und Staat (Berlin, 1967) and Otto Kahn-Freund, *Labour Law and Politics in the Weimar Republic* (Oxford, 1981).

49 David Abraham, *The Collapse of the Weimar Republic*, 2nd edn, (New York, 1986), especially ch. 3.

50 ibid., 27.

51 Gerald D. Feldman, *Iron and Steel in the German Inflation* (Princeton, 1977), ch. 3.

52 Quotations from Michael Schneider, *Unternehmer und Demokratie* (Bonn, 1975), 37f and 42.

53 Feldman, *Iron and Steel*, 319–45.

54 This picture of Silverberg as opportunist is central to Reinhard Neebe, *Grossindustrie, Staat, NSDAP* (Göttingen, 1981). For scepticism about the 1926 speech see Schneider, *Unternehmer*, 55–9; and Bernd Weisbrod, *Schwerindustrie in der Krise* (Wuppertal, 1978), 246–72.

55 This is the central thesis of Schneider.

56 Schneider, *Unternehmer*, 106; David Abraham, *The Collapse of the Weimar Republic*, 1st edn (Princeton, 1981), 135–6.

57 Dirk Stegmann, 'Zum Verhältnis von Grossindustrie und National-sozialismus', *Archiv für Sozialgeschichte*, 13 (1973), 409.

58 Weisbrod, *Schwerindustrie*, 492–3; Abraham, *Collapse*, 1st edn, 86–89, 171–2, and 216–18.

59 So the following report: Reichsverband der deutschen Industrie, *Besteuerung, Ertrag und Arbeitslohn im Jahre 1927* (Berlin, 1929).

60 Weisbrod, *Schwerindustrie*, 256f.; Abraham, *Collapse*, 1st edn, 47–8.

61 See note 59. Also Weisbrod, *Schwerindustrie*, 48–50.

62 ibid., also note 59 above.

63 Quoted in Abraham, *Collapse*, 1st edn, 263.

64 Schneider, *Unternehmer*, 156–7.

65 ibid., 82–3.

6

Between estate and profession: lawyers and the development of the legal profession in nineteenth-century Germany

Michael John

I

The development of the nineteenth-century German legal profession is a curiously under-researched subject. In contrast to other professional groups such as doctors, lawyers have not as yet been the subject of a modern full-length social-historical analysis.[1] Comments on the legal profession have often been subsumed into general accounts of the educated middle classes (*Bildungsbürgertum*), in which emphasis tends to be placed on processes of professional specialization and self-definition, but there are few detailed studies. Recent work on the nineteenth-century educated middle classes reflects this general neglect, tending to consider the social functions of legal ideology without really attempting to study the legal profession as such.[2] A partial exception to this general omission from the literature is provided by Hansjoachim Henning's study of the *Bildungsbürgertum* in Prussia's western provinces after 1860, a work which emphasizes the high social status, increasing social exclusivity, and genuine commitment to their vocation of the educated professionals in the area.[3] Otherwise, apart from a few important sociological studies,[4] the overwhelming majority of relevant works have been written by lawyers.

Much of this research is extremely valuable, but its provenance has certain consequences. Of these, perhaps the most important is the tendency to consider lawyers as a distinct, self-conscious status group, detached from the broader concerns of Germany's middle classes and interested mainly in rather narrowly defined professional issues, such as the reduction in the direct role of the state in recruitment to the profession during the nineteenth century.[5] This approach has its merits: like any other professional group, lawyers did have specific interests which at times coalesced with those of other groups so that lawyers gained a powerful voice. However, a weakness of this approach lies in its implicit acceptance of the profession's perception of itself as an Estate (*Stand*) and its related tendency to downplay questions of the market, personal profit, and so on. As we shall see, *ständisch* rhetoric was a constant feature of the vocabulary of the legal profession and of its claims to social respectability and prestige. But the very unanimity of that rhetoric gives rise to feelings of disquiet about the 'real' conditions beneath the surface. Such feelings almost certainly lie behind Conze and Kocka's tantalizingly brief allusion to the way in which:

> as the number of jobs increased, the occupations which required legal training became more differentiated, going beyond service to the state – a process through which a quasi-aristocratic consciousness of *Stand* remained or developed for the first time over and above the other [university] faculties, despite the strong influx from the middle and lower middle classes.[6]

As with any profession, educational requirements and recruitment practices were of central importance to the development of a lawyer's world-view in the nineteenth century. So too was the particular structure of the legal profession, in which the overwhelming majority of German laywers were career judges from the outset, at least until the end of the nineteenth century. The German equivalents of English barristers and solicitors were recruited primarily from the ranks of state-employed judges, a situation whose consequences were of fundamental significance for the development of the lawyers' professional ideology. For this reason, the tense and often difficult relationships between different parts of the legal profession and between lawyers and the state will be a major theme of this chapter. In particular, it will be argued that lawyers found it difficult to develop into a fully-fledged modern *profession*, a term which normally connotes a high degree of independent control over the profession's internal affairs, recruitment policies, disciplinary questions, and fees. On the other hand, it seems that the lawyers' frequent grumblings about their low social status and lack of esteem concealed a relatively comfortable existence for most members of the profession and that this almost certainly blunted demands for (even) more favourable treatment. Above all, it would seem that the objective wealth and status of the legal profession were such as to weaken the demand for further measures to restrict access to the profession. Until the end of the century, the obstacles to entry into the legal profession were so considerable that the majority of lawyers seem to have accepted that ostensibly open access[7] should be maintained. For this reason, lawyers on the whole managed to secure most of the perquisites of a valued, high-status profession, without being able (or perhaps needing) to develop the assertive lobbying approach to professional questions which was often found in other sections of the bourgeoisie.

For these reasons, it will be argued, lawyers both developed many of the general characteristics of the German bourgeoisie and occupied a very special, atypical place within it. As with other sections of the educated middle class, they continued to emphasize possession of educational qualifications as a basic source of status and vigorously rejected alternative criteria for entry, such as birth or wealth. Behind this approach, however, lay the frequently observed dissolution of bourgeois unity as professional specialization became the order of the day, with lawyers participating fully in 'the inner fragmentation of the educated middle classes'.[8] The most recent work on the middle-class professions suggests, however, that specialized qualifications may have strengthened rather than weakened the bourgeoisie as a social formation[9] – an issue to which this chapter will return. On the other hand, the lawyers' position within the educated middle classes was arguably peculiar in ways which were related to the type of service provided by the legal profession and to the specific structure of the legal system in Germany.

II

These introductory reflections point to the need to consider at the outset two closely related aspects of recruitment to the legal profession – the state and the developing system of legal training in the universities. These are both subjects which have spawned a substantial literature and the main outlines, if not all the details, of the relevant nineteenth-century developments are now clear. Legal training came to be the basic feature of the educational background of civil servants, in both the judicial and the administrative branches of the bureaucracy. This was especially the case in Prussia, where the famous 'Instruction' of 23 October 1817 introduced the innovation that the aspirant civil servant, having passed the first state examination, was to undergo a period of unpaid 'practical training' with a law court. This gave a decisive advantage to technical legal training over the broader concerns of eighteenth-century cameralism, which emphasized such matters as political economy and public demesne management in a bureaucrat's education. A further regulation of 14 February 1846 consolidated this legally based entrance procedure. It was technically the case that Prussian bureaucrats continued to be required to show knowledge of all manner of subjects relevant to public administration – economics, public finance, demesne management etc. – as well as a broad range of subjects within the law. In practice, however, the training of civil servants was increasingly dominated by a narrow emphasis on civil law and neglected other desirable areas of knowledge. This was an aspect of the bureaucracy which was to cause increasing controversy towards the end of the century. In the southern states, especially Württemberg, the situation was rather different and the tradition of training civil servants in public affairs and public law lived on into the late nineteenth century. Nevertheless, it would be fair to say that law, and above all private law, was by far the most important element in the education of German civil servants until well into the twentieth century.[10]

There can be little doubt that it was the Prussian state's approach to the selection of its civil servants which produced these developments. In particular, the first state examination, which was held at a local court, dealt almost solely with Roman law despite the wide range of prescribed subjects. As was frequently pointed out, there was a contradiction between the rules governing this examination and the actual conduct of the examination, which tended to stress Roman, private law above all other parts of the official syllabus.[11] There were, of course, a number of paradoxical aspects to these developments, not least in the relationship between recruitment practices and the much-vaunted emphasis on general cultivation (*Bildung*) as the legitimation of the bureaucracy's claim to social leadership. A further interesting feature was the rapid development in universities such as Berlin of a narrow approach to the study of law associated with the philological-historical techniques of Friedrich Carl von Savigny.[12] It might be argued that precisely because of this narrowly academic approach to the teaching of law, much greater emphasis was placed on the practical training-period after university study – a direct inversion of the stated priorities of the reformers. On the other hand, there is much to be said for the view that university legal education, in Prussia at least, was effectively bureaucratized, in that its major function was to provide future state officials, who would then pass through the examination and training periods.[13]

This impression is confirmed when two further aspects of legal training are considered. The first of these is the dramatic fluctuation in the numbers of university students in Germany's law faculties. In general, it may be broadly correct to see these numbers as being determined by the perceived demand for state officials.[14] That was almost certainly true of the rapid rise in the number of law students registered in the third decade of the nineteenth century. Between 1820 and 1830, the number of law students in Prussia doubled, prompting the Ministry of Justice to warn people against studying the law in 1839. By that time, the number of trainees who had yet to pass the final state examination, was allegedly four times that required by the state and the time spent in unpaid training had risen to perhaps ten to twelve years. By 1840, there were around 2,500 unpaid, qualified jurists in the Prussian judicial bureaucracy alone, with only around 20 of these being given tenured, salaried positions each year. At only one brief point, it seems, did the supply and demand of lawyers come into some form of equilibrium in Prussia – i.e. during the 1870s, at which point the number of people studying law immediately rose. Nor did this problem show any real sign of being alleviated by the massive growth in the economy during the second half of the nineteenth century. In the early 1890s, Johannes Conrad calculated that there were almost twice as many law students as were needed in Germany as a whole.[15] The continuing (if fluctuating) over-supply of trained lawyers from the third decade of the nineteenth century makes it difficult to quarrel with Konrad Jarausch's conclusion that 'in the case of law students, expectations of opportunities consistently outstripped any calculable increases in real demand'.[16]

To calculate the exact level of over-supply of lawyers at a given point is probably impossible. But the sources agree about certain major features of the legal community. The first of these is that the overwhelming majority of trained lawyers for most of the nineteenth century were employed in state service and that, furthermore, the judiciary accounted for far and away the largest section of the legal employment market. In the mid–1830s, there were 4,300 to 5,100 posts in the Prussian judiciary compared with at most 1,650 in the senior administrative bureaucracy. In the 1860s, between 6,200 and 6,800 officials were connected with the Prussian judicial administration, with around 1,000 in the senior administrative bureaucracy.[17] Moreover, the number of judges far outstripped the number of lawyers in private practice who, in Prussia and some other states, were in certain senses employees of the state until 1878. According to one recent estimate, three-quarters of Prussia's lawyers after the 1830s were judges, a figure which is roughly confirmed by Rudolf von Gneist's contemporary statement that there were 1,235 lawyers practising in Prussian courts at the end of 1838. In 1878, there were twice as many judges as there were practising lawyers, and ten years later the ratio was still 3:2, with only 5 per cent finding employment in banks, commerce, or industry in 1888. On the basis of admittedly uncertain figures, Wilhelm Lexis' calculated in 1891 that there were 7,048 positions in the Prussian judicial and administrative bureaucracies, 3,069 places for lawyers and notaries, and perhaps 250 in banks and industry in the whole of Prussia. Despite certain doubts about some of these statistics, it is quite clear that the overwhelming majority of Prussian law students found employment within the legal system, and that most of these entered the judiciary. Before the end of the nineteenth century, lawyers entering the business world were a small if growing minority.[18]

Prussia was not, of course, the whole of Germany and was in fact somewhat unusual in a number of important respects. First among these was the notoriously restrictive approach of the Prussian state with regard to the number of educated officials it was prepared to appoint. The reasons for this included fiscal parsimony, the related desire to stem calls for the extension of parliamentary rights and, at times, the wish to control or suppress the political ambitions of its 'servants', including (perhaps especially) the practising lawyers. According to Gneist,[19] who had himself endured eight years of unpaid service in the 1840s, Berlin had a quota of 59 practising lawyers, servicing a population which grew from 548,000 to 826,000 in that decade. In 1878, by which time the population exceeded 1 million, the figure was still only 98. Moreover, there were still far fewer judges in Prussia in the 1890s than in the other states, relative to the size of its population. The combined effects of the restricted numbers of judges and practising lawyers, and the lack of alternative opportunities outside state service tended to keep large numbers of people in unpaid posts for lengthy periods of time. The Prussian state's periodic attempts to scare people away from studying the law with stories of intense competition for posts and probable indigence in the medium-term future do not suggest that the bureaucracy saw poor employment prospects for lawyers as a permanent, concerted strategy of political control. Nevertheless, it is hard to avoid the conclusion that the use of growing amounts of unpaid labour in the courts undermined the much-vaunted independence of the judiciary, for example in the 1850s. Similar criticisms of the political effects of the state's employment practices were to be heard in the 1890s.[20]

Different state policies with regard to access to the legal profession were of fundamental importance in determining the shape and aspirations of the profession in the nineteenth century. In 1857, the average ratio of lawyers to the population in Germany as a whole was 1:7,000, but this concealed enormous regional variations. In the kingdom of Saxony, the ratio was 1:1,900, rising as high as 1:350 in the city of Leipzig. Bavaria, east of the Rhine, on the other hand, had a ratio of 1:13,000, with the figure falling to 1:21,000 in the Bavarian Palatinate. Württemberg, another state with very liberal rules governing access, had a ratio in 1867 of 1:5,330, while in Prussia the ratio fell from 1:10,000 to 1:12,000 between 1850 and 1879, having fallen from 1:2,000 in the preceding fifty years.[21] In practice, Frankfurt, Mecklenburg, Saxony, Württemberg, Baden, Hanover, and the Hanseatic towns had some version of free access to the profession for qualified males throughout the nineteenth century (though differences in the local laws continued). On the other hand, the number of lawyers admitted to practise was kept tight not only in Prussia but in Bavaria as well, until the principle of freedom of access was introduced by national legislation in 1878.[22]

III

Regional variations on this scale, coupled with the ubiquitous dominance of state policy-making in determining recruitment patterns to the bureaucracy and judiciary gave the development of the legal profession in Germany a distinct pattern. As has recently been argued, models of professionalization derived from British or American experience have limited application to nineteenth-century Germany, largely because of the influence of the state there. In particular, an emphasis on the independence and strength of autonomous professional organizations is arguably inappropriate when considering the development of the German legal and other professions.[23] One major problem facing Germany's lawyers was the difficulty of forming powerful pressure groups to fight for their interests or influence governments. A partial exception to this was the German Lawyers' Congress (*Deutscher Juristentag*) founded in 1860. But this organization spanned the divisions within the community of lawyers, both regional and occupational – i.e. between academic lawyers, judges, and practising lawyers. At no point was it a professional association in the strict sense of the word and it tended to concentrate on such matters as the desired national unification of the legal system and detailed discussion of legislative proposals.[24] These were subjects which were best discussed on this sort of national basis and which generally did not open up painful divisions within the legal community. With regard to professional associations proper, which sought to advance the status and position of practising lawyers, matters were very different.

Until the 1870s, the law governing the employment of lawyers was firmly in the hands of the individual states with their radically different approaches to the legal profession. Moreover, the focus of the practising lawyer's work lay not in lofty statements about legal unity or jurisprudential questions, but in the details of court procedure and the exercise of professional discipline. These were subjects which were far more likely to divide practising lawyers from the judges, who constituted the bulk of the legal profession. The rarity with which practising lawyers were elevated into the judiciary was another factor promoting division, as well as being the subject of numerous complaints from those who looked enviously at the status of lawyers in England.[25] Finally, there was the problem of the disputed civil servant status of practising lawyers. There was a widespread (and correct) perception among lawyers that the state wished to have it both ways, defining lawyers as civil servants when it came to disciplinary matters, but not when it was a question of distributing the state welfare benefits or other advantages which accrued to 'proper' bureaucrats.[26] This was an increasing source of friction and dispute to the point that Gneist described the lawyer's official status as 'the actual root of the evil' in 1867.[27] Disciplinary powers and other controls exercised by the states' ministries of justice or the courts undoubtedly hindered the activities of lawyers, seriously weakening attempts at collective organization, whether at local, state, or national level.[28]

This is not to say that lawyers's associations did not develop. The earliest – in Hesse-Darmstadt – was founded in 1821 and the 1830s and 1840s saw numerous associations established, especially in states like Saxony which had relatively liberal rules governing access to the profession. In 1846, the first national congress of practising lawyers was held in Hamburg and finally, in 1848, a German association of practising lawyers was formed. This sank without trace, however, as the revolution subsided. In Prussia and Bavaria, matters moved much more slowly and state-wide associations of practising lawyers were not established until 1861. The results of all this organizational activity were, however, relatively disappointing, especially in the Prussian case. As early as 1863, the annual congress of the Prussian association had to be cancelled because of the small numbers willing to attend. It was noted with regret that out of the whole of Prussia, the number of lawyers willing to participate was equivalent to only three-quarters of those known to be employed as lawyers in Berlin. Most commentators on this state of affairs emphasized that the remnants of the *Polizeistaat* and bureaucratic hostility played a major role in the relative weakness and late development of lawyers' associations.[29]

Yet this was by no means the whole story. The pursuit of professional independence from the state might be seen as part of a general emancipation of 'civil society' from the shackles of the absolutist, corporatist state. But, in the case of lawyers, a number of different factors limited that drive for emancipation. These factors had a common denominator, which was the profound link between the state's activities and the validation of the status of the legal profession as an Estate or *Stand*. In the first place, this was a question of the educational requirements for entry into the profession. Here, the general trend in the nineteenth century was towards making the requirements for entry into the judiciary and the corps of practising lawyers the same – a trend, which culminated in the 1878 *Rechtsanwaltsordnung*, the Reich law governing practising lawyers. But these requirements – both in terms of examinations and practical training – meant the clear involvement of the state at every point in the recruitment process. Furthermore, even a cursory analysis of the demands of practising lawyers reveals that very few, if any, wanted complete emancipation from the state. This point was made clearly by the Darmstadt liberal and practising lawyer, Heinrich Carl Hofmann. Writing in 1844, he argued that the state had the right and duty to admit only qualified and experienced people to the legal profession and that 'an absolute independence of the lawyer from the government is by no means an essential condition of the status of his *Stand*'. What was required was rather a removal of the dependence of individual lawyers on individual officials and the preservation of 'an inner, moral independence'. This point was accepted explicitly by Gneist in his influential call for liberalization of access to the profession. Both authors also agreed in rejecting the idea that practising lawyers were state officials.[30]

A basic issue at stake here was the desire of the lawyers to retain the high social status acquired from the perceived possession of *Bildung* in the nineteenth century. This of itself necessitated multiple contacts with the state, which through the university and the examination system effectively took on the role of validating the possession of *Bildung*. A related and perhaps more important point was the relative status of lawyers *vis-à-vis* civil servants. Lawyers strongly believed that they did not share the extraordinarily high social status of academically educated officials. Other evidence, however, suggests that the public often saw officials and lawyers as sections of the same educated and privileged elite. Commenting on the 1847 elections in Hesse-Darmstadt, Heinrich von Gagern noted that in some places objections were raised to candidates who were lawyers on the grounds that they wished to become state officials.[31] Nevertheless, the literature of the period is full of references to the inadequate status of the lawyer's *Stand* and there were numerous suggestions about how to remedy the problem. The prestige enjoyed by civil servants seems to have led some lawyers, like some of their counterparts in the medical profession,[32] to conclude that it would be best if their status as officials was enhanced rather than reduced. In 1832, Karl Mittermaier – a keen academic champion of the rights of practising lawyers – warned the profession against this view and argued from an explicitly liberal position for an extension of the lawyer's right to participate in public life to the full. But as late as the 1870s, there were isolated voices from within the legal profession regretting that they had lost the prestige which went with official status.[33]

This was, however, the position of a distinct and dwindling

minority of the German legal profession. From the 1830s onwards, the number of lawyers demanding greater protection from the supervisory powers of the state and its judges grew steadily, first in southern Germany and then in Prussia. Demands for the self-administration of professional discipline and for the right of lawyers to participate fully in politics without hindrance from the state were an integral part of the politics of the 1840s. Similar motives lay behind the foundation of the Prussian lawyers' association in 1861. As one Prussian lawyer, summing up the general feeling of his profession in 1862, put it, 'the profession feels the need to be independent and no longer to be held in tutelage, it wishes to have the freedom, which every citizen, profession and *Stand* possesses'.[34] This emphasis on tutelage (*Bevormundung*) was strongly reminiscent of the political language of the 1840s, in which the restrictions imposed by reactionary bureaucracies on public life were of central concern. The battles of that decade saw lawyers playing a leading role in opposition to the state governments, a role which continued into the revolution of 1848. But what is significant here is the way in which questions of the professional status of lawyers came to be both inextricably linked with and highly symbolic of the aspirations of much broader groups within German society.[35] It was in this process that many of the distinctive features of the self-perception of the nineteenth-century German lawyer were forged.

The politics of the 1840s involved a complex, often highly localized set of issues, but two broad areas stand out. The first of these was the power of the bureaucracy to control public life through censorship of the press, intrusions in local affairs, denial of rights of self-administration, and so on. The second was the widespread demand for specific legal reforms, in particular the introduction of public, oral procedure in civil and criminal cases and the use of jury courts. These reforms were an integral part of the liberal programme, particularly in the south and west of Germany, where the demands were fuelled by the fact that the Rhineland, Baden, and certain provinces of Bavaria and Hesse-Darmstadt already had these advanced forms of legal procedure as a result of the retention of French law after 1815. These French legal institutions became the focal point of much broader political movements in the 1830s and 1840s; as one Hessian liberal put it in 1846, 'even now nobody wants the French, but their institutions are being demanded for the whole of Germany'.[36]

Dirk Blasius has rightly drawn attention to the importance of reforms of criminal procedure to middle-class emancipatory politics before 1848: for him, the struggle for jury courts was 'a process by which civil society found its identity'.[37] The principal significance of this was that it tended to cement the role of lawyers as leaders of a broader opposition movement. Their expertise was, of course, required in order to discuss politically significant reforms of legal procedure in an effective fashion. But even more important perhaps was the way in which the circumstances of the time enabled lawyers to present their professional difficulties in a way which made them appear symptomatic of those of society as a whole. The disciplinary and supervisory powers of judges became symbols of the hated bureaucratic tutelage. The demand for public, oral procedure could be linked fairly easily to broader concerns about the bureaucracy's attachment to secrecy and censorship. Mittermaier and Gagern were but two prominent proponents of the common view that the status of practising lawyers could only be raised through a general advance of liberty and a rolling-back of the censoring, absolutist state. For the Darmstadt lawyer and liberal Karl Buchner, the matter was simple: 'the higher the level of political education of a people, the more respected its legal profession is'. At this stage, there was very little doubt about the coincidence of the social and career aspirations of lawyers and the broader campaign for political emancipation and reform.[38]

As has often been noted, the conditions of the *Vormärz* spawned a type of politics in which heterogeneous groups and sets of ideas could find common ground.[39] For lawyers, as for other heavily represented groups within the pre-1848 opposition, the following years showed how difficult it was to sustain the energies of the 1840s. There are good reasons for thinking that the 1850s dissolved many of those features of the 1840s, which had made it relatively easy for lawyers to link their professional and career aspirations to the broader issue of liberal emancipation. The 1840s had seen a broad campaign for independence for the legal profession and had tended to obscure the difficulties in defining that independence precisely. After 1848, the lawyers were increasingly forced to attempt such an exercise in definition. This process revealed disheartening evidence of internal discord and, coupled with the hostility of the state bureaucracies, accounted for much of the perceived weakness of lawyers' associations which was noted above (pp. 169–70).

173

IV

The problematic aspects of the notion of professional independence lay first in the variety of separate issues which were subsumed within it, and second in the way it tended to leave unclear the relationship between lawyers' status aspirations and their economic interests. Independence involved the quite separate questions of the state's disciplinary and supervisory powers, the conditions of access to the profession and matters such as the lawyer's freedom to determine the level of fees for his services. These issues were frequently conflated in the *Vormärz* period between 1815 and 1848, but this was less and less possible afterwards. In the 1850s Hanover, Baden, and a number of other states introduced chambers of lawyers, while Prussia extended the institution of the 'council of honour' (*Ehrenrat*).[40] The fact that the courts often retained certain disciplinary controls does not alter the fact that this was a significant move away from the *Vormärz* approach to controlling lawyers. Moreover, these developments occurred quite independently of the degree to which a given state was liberal, Baden and Hanover in many respects occupying opposite ends of this particular spectrum. Prussian lawyers went on demanding more extensive rights to control their own activities, but this gradually ceased to be the main concern. After 1848, many states including Prussia came to concentrate on other means of controlling their lawyers, including restrictive and politically motivated appointment practices, refusal to grant leave from state service for political activity, intrusions into the independence of the judiciary, and so on. This change in tactics meant that the question of removing the state's right to limit access to the profession was almost inevitably raised. It was increasingly unclear how the legal profession could achieve independence while the state controlled the career prospects of individuals in this way. Moreover, the long queues of unpaid assessors in the Prussian judiciary by the end of the 1850s exerted a quite separate pressure in the same direction. Opening up the possibility of practising law was one obvious way of improving the prospects of this expanding group.[41]

These changes had to be confronted by the lawyers but they were ill-equipped to do so in a united and effective fashion. Quite apart from the effects of the territorial divisions of Germany on the profession, the self-image lawyers had inherited from the *Vormärz* inhibited a clear response to change. As has often been noted, the early nineteenth-century bureaucracy had a propensity to define itself as the intermediary between the state and the people.[42] At the same time, lawyers came to see themselves as 'organs of the administration of justice', as a *Stand* whose existence and claims to status were justified in terms of an abstract notion of public service. In this, there were many parallels with the bureaucracy's self-image as a 'universal estate'. But as oppositional tendencies spread within the legal profession, lawyers began to compete with the bureaucracy's claim to be the intermediary between state and people, a position enunciated by Mittermaier when he criticized the state's hostility to practising lawyers in the 1830s. To Mittermaier, the lawyer owed his position to his role as intermediary between the law and the people.[43] On the basis of this conviction, the idea developed that the principal responsibility of the lawyer was to justice (conceived in ethical terms) rather than to the interests of his client. In perhaps the most informative of all the autobiographies written by practising lawyers, Max Hachenburg repeatedly stressed this 'ethical duty' of the lawyer and criticized Goethe and other writers for failing to present a picture of the lawyer 'as a fighter for justice, as the adviser and friend of those in need, as the representative of truth . . .' This view of the lawyer's role was perfectly captured in Weissler's comments about the 'unpartisan' public service of the legal profession. It was, he said, an indispensable guarantee of justice that service to the parties be carried out with 'the most complete lack of partisanship'.[44] Lawyers' associations and their disciplinary councils were correspondingly highly sensitive to any charge that their profession engaged in dishonest tactics in court or otherwise contravened the rules of honourable behaviour in the interests of their clients. Even Gneist was prepared to allow the state to check on the 'honesty' of the legal profession.[45]

The problem which arose after 1848 highlighted the tension between this conception that public service was the source of status and the lawyers' economic interests. The consequence of public service was that the legal profession was not considered a trade, i.e. an activity in which the goal of professional activity was private economic gain. In this respect, the legal profession diverged sharply from the medical profession, which was controversially categorized as a trade in 1869.[46] This was a subject on which contributors to the debates of the 1860s and after showed great sensitivity. Once again, Gneist symbolized a broad consensus in stating that lawyers served the interests of justice, but he departed from that consensus in claiming that competition was needed to drive up the standards of performance within the profession. Others, however, feared that the consequence of liberalization would be the impoverishment of lawyers through the expansion of the profession in excess of the growth in the number or value of legal cases. There was much talk about the danger of a legal proletariat, an issue which figured prominently in the *Juristentag*'s debates on the question of liberalization of access in August 1863.[47]

In essence, the problem arose because of the imprecise and contradictory nature of the conception of independence. The campaign for the removal of the right of states such as Prussia to limit the number of practising lawyers admitted to courts within their jurisdiction certainly focused on the established question of lawyers' independence. In states like Prussia, lawyers had good reason to seek increased independence from the state and this could only be achieved if the state's right to determine who should be admitted to practise in its courts was removed. True independence required acceptance of the principle that any properly qualified person could practise law, the accepted criterion of qualification being the possession of the educational requirements and practical training required to enter the state judiciary. Moreover, some trained lawyers – particularly the frustrated aspirant judges, who were condemned to years of unpaid service to the Prussian state – had an obvious economic interest in expanding the number of practising lawyers. But such an expansion would almost certainly threaten the livelihood of at least some lawyers, a point which Gneist was forced to admit though he argued that the *Stand* as a whole would benefit.[48] Hardly surprisingly, this prospect was unattractive to many lawyers, especially as fees for legal cases were laid down by law and charging above the legal norm was a disciplinary offence. This last point showed very clearly the restrictions placed on the ability of lawyers to fight for their interests by their image of public service to the cause of justice. Even the most fervent admirers of the cause of liberalization of access and independence, such as Gneist, insisted that controls on lawyers' fees were necessary and denied that such controls were in any way inconsistent with 'the honour and flourishing status of the *Stand*'.[49]

This problem – the reconciliation of lawyers' desire for enhanced professional autonomy and their economic interests – became central to debates about professionalization in the mid nineteenth century. Much of the debate concerned the effects on the legal profession of liberal rules concerning access in states like Saxony and Württemberg and opinions diverged sharply even among those with direct knowledge of conditions in those states.[50] Predictably, it was in the states where the legal profession was most restricted that opposition to liberalized access was greatest. The Bavarian practising lawyers' association only gave up its opposition in 1876. Its Prussian counterpart had with some difficulty accepted the idea in 1864, but had almost certainly forfeited the support of many Prussian lawyers in the process.[51]

The central issue thrown up by these deliberations was the problematic nature of the interests of lawyers as an Estate. Both sides in the debate about freedom of access argued that their proposals alone would protect and enhance the interests of the legal Estate. The Münster association of practising lawyers over-whelmingly opposed freedom of access on the grounds that it was likely to endanger 'a respectable existence'. That was at least an argument which made the major point, i.e. lawyers' incomes, albeit in a language which emphasized the status aspects of respect-ability. On the other hand, the lawyers' association in Hamm attempted to argue that freedom of access would damage the public interest by removing the guarantee that impoverished lawyers would not unnecessarily involve people in court cases.

> For these reasons, it seems sensible to restrict the number of practising lawyers in each court to the level which experience suggests is sufficient to meet the needs of the public, in order that the lawyer can be of use in the creation of true justice alone and be completely uninfluenced by the cares of life.[52]

This convenient argument converted the lawyer's comfortable existence into the public interest, a view which probably expressed the feelings of most Prussian lawyers in the early 1860s quite accurately. In late 1865, a strong supporter of liberalization esti-mated that, notwithstanding the Prussian lawyers' association's acceptance of the principle the year before, perhaps only a quarter of Prussia's lawyers were in favour of its immediate implemen-tation.[53]

Despite this opposition, the drive towards liberalization was overwhelming. In part, this was because of the evidently self-interested nature of the lawyers' opposition and the sheer intellec-tual difficulty in justifying restraints on trade in an era in which such restraints were being rapidly dismantled in other sectors of the economy. As Gneist pointedly put it: 'no honourable guild of artisans has ever so completely thought of itself as a possessor class as these lawyers do in opposing the claims of their colleagues outside the system'.[54] Opinions in the states' chambers of deputies began to change, with the Bavarian chamber moving into line with the *Juristentag* in 1868. The foundation of the German association of practising lawyers (*Deutscher Anwaltsverein*) in 1871 decisively weakened the Prussian and Bavarian associations, which dissolved in 1872 and 1883 respectively.[55] Moreover, Prussia was actually experiencing a shortage of practising lawyers in the 1870s, with allegedly 200 posts remaining unfilled for lack of applicants.[56] Most importantly of all, it was inconceivable that the Reich would actually introduce restrictions on Prussian and Bavarian lines in states where they did not already exist. Once the decision was taken that unified legislation on the legal profession was required as a corollary to the codes of court procedure and organization in the mid-1870s, it was inevitable that some form of liberalization would be introduced.

V

The outcome of these discussions was Reich legislation in the form of the *Rechtsanwaltsordnung* of 1878, which decreed that anybody who had undergone the practical training period and passed the examinations required to enter the state judiciary might practise law. A further Reich law (the *Gebührenordnung* of 1879) fixed lawyers' fees at a level which raised rates in Prussia, but lowered them in most other areas of the Reich. The government's approach to both measures was motivated by an apparent desire to mediate between sharply divergent views concerning the legal profession. The secretary of the Reich Justice Office, Heinrich von Friedberg, explained to the Reichstag that the *Rechtsanwaltsordnung* sought to find a compromise between the notions that the legal profession was a 'free academic profession' and that it was 'almost like a public office'. Policy on fees was dictated by the desire to avoid the twin dangers of making legal costs too expensive and holding them down so far 'that the legal profession's economic position would be endangered and thus would become a threat to the administration of justice and perhaps for the life of the state as a whole'. Friedberg exploited the lawyers' own rhetoric by praising

those who were willing to place the general interests of the administration of justice above their pecuniary interests. However, such
praise was small comfort to those whose livelihood was
threatened.[57] The immediate consequence of liberalization was as
the opponents of the measure had feared, especially in the larger
towns. The total number of lawyers in Prussia grew by 40 per
cent between 1880 and 1895, an increase which was heavily concentrated in towns such as Berlin, where the decade after liberalization saw the number of practising lawyers grow nearly fourfold.
On the other hand, 44 per cent of local courts (overwhelmingly
in remote rural areas in the east) had no lawyer resident in their
area as late as 1895, a situation which liberalization of access had
partly been designed to remedy.[58]. A similar development took
place in the Reich as a whole, where the number of appointed
lawyers grew from 4,091 in 1880 to 12,297 in 1913. Whereas in
1880 there had been 1 lawyer for every 11,000 inhabitants of
Germany, that ratio had fallen to 1:5,280 on the eve of the First
World War, with the most rapid changes taking place after the
turn of the century.[59]

In the current state of research, it is difficult to gain an accurate
picture of the effects that this expansion had on the economic
fortunes of the legal profession. One author estimates average
earnings in 1907 at just under 5,000 Marks. Four years later,
lawyers' earnings from civil cases varied from 3,300 to 6,600
Marks, according to the level of court at which they practised.[60]
In terms of crude averages, this placed lawyers securely within
the range of salaries earned by the groups to which they most
liked to compare themselves. In 1894, the starting salary of judges
in an *Amtsgericht* in Prussia was 2,850 Marks, that of a *Regierungsrat*
in the administrative civil service 4,800 Marks. Twenty years after
the final state examination, the administrative civil servant could
expect to earn 6,000 Marks, the judge 4,800 Marks.[61] The available
research leaves no doubt that there were considerable income
differences between individual lawyers, as was the case with the
other educated professions. But there are serious grounds for scepticism about the frequent claims that a substantial proletariat of
lawyers developed in the larger towns, especially where liberal
conditions of access had prevailed before 1878. Recent research on
Frankfurt and Saxony suggests that lawyers were in general better
off than doctors. In Saxony, for example, over three-quarters of
the legal profession had a taxable income of over 4,800 Marks in

1901 and only one-fourteenth had an income of less than 3,100 Marks; the comparable figures for doctors were just under three-fifths and one-fifth respectively. It is therefore probable that the threat of proletarianization became a reality for only a minority of lawyers in Germany as a whole.[62] It is likely, however, that greater problems were perceived by lawyers in towns like Berlin and Munich, where the sudden liberalization of access after 1878 produced dramatic and rapid changes in the size of the profession.

By the early 1890s, the problem had become serious enough to provoke renewed discussion within the legal profession about the desirability of limiting numbers by reintroducing the quotas which had been abolished in 1878. This suggestion was given considerable impetus in 1894, when the Prussian Minister of Justice recommended the reintroduction of quotas, a move whose origins lay in the growing perception of a crisis in the supply and quality of judges in the 1890s.[63] The question was debated at the congress of practising lawyers in Stuttgart that year and again at Hanover in 1905. Both congresses rejected the reintroduction of quotas but the debate would not die down. In 1911, the Würzburg congress of practising lawyers considered the question in a major debate, which was preceded by a questionnaire on the subject which had elicited responses from over one-third of the total number of practising lawyers in Germany. Of these responses, 60 per cent had favoured the reintroduction of quotas, the same proportion favoured the lengthening of the period of practical training in the administration or the judiciary required of all aspirant lawyers, and one-third wanted both measures. Only a quarter of those who responded favoured the retention of the status quo. Yet, the congress decisively rejected the results of the questionnaire and a sizeable majority followed the views of lawyers' associations in Frankfurt and Saxony, which continued to favour freedom of access despite allegations of overcrowding of the profession in those areas. In the end, 619 delegates voted to retain free access and 244 voted against.[64]

The continuing debates about freedom of access showed how difficult it was in the German context to reconcile the different aspects of professional status and independence in the late nineteenth century. Questions of material security, market power, and autonomy from the control of the state were all intertwined in the profession's debates about its place in society. The responses to the questionnaire which preceded the Würzburg congress showed very clearly that a substantial number of German lawyers were tempted by unfavourable developments in the profession to contemplate a return to more restrictive practices in order to defend themselves. In this context, the support for lengthening the period of practical training is perhaps as interesting as that for the reintroduction of quotas. As that training period was unpaid, the proposal was in effect an expression of the desire to extend the already very considerable social exclusiveness of the legal profession. Until 1911, Prussia only admitted as trainees those who could put down 7,500 Marks in cash and could show an annual income of 1,500 Marks, a part of its cheap government policy which relied on the unpaid labour of implicitly wealthy assessors.[65] Although this was beginning to change in the Wilhelmine period, the social profile of law students clearly shows this bias towards the sons of the wealthy and educated classes. In 1911–12, over half of Prussia's law students came from this group, around a quarter from the 'old *Mittelstand*' and around a fifth from the 'new *Mittelstand*'. At most, this meant that the law offered slightly wider opportunities for sons of the lower middle classes compared with a generation earlier, when Conrad's investigations had revealed a strong link between property and education, and legal study. As he put it in the early 1880s: 'the legal faculty offers the best prospects to the ambitious and to the higher classes of society; the less-moneyed classes are repelled from it by barriers which comparatively few are, without special favouring circumstances, able to surmount'. Of these barriers, the necessity of a classical education at a *Gymnasium* and the required period of unpaid service to the state were easily the most significant.[66]

This privileged status undoubtedly helps to explain why proponents of further measures of social closure could not win. As was suggested above (p. 179), it is difficult to believe that a large proletariat of lawyers was in fact the consequence of liberalization of access. Furthermore, it was lawyers from precisely those areas which had held liberal entry conditions to the profession longest, who opposed the reintroduction of quotas, while their Prussian and Bavarian colleagues were always more likely to look back favourably to the restrictive conditions of the pre-1878 period. This spirit of apparent self-sacrifice on the part of lawyers from Saxony, Württemberg, and elsewhere was undoubtedly important in giving them the moral high ground in these debates.[67] Even more important though was the effect of the system of recruitment on proposals for reform. Practising lawyers in Germany could never aspire to any real measure of control over the two key stages in the making of a lawyer: entry into a university law department; and success in the two state examinations. The level of entry to university was determined partly by the perceived demand for trained lawyers, in which freedom to practise was only one of a number of factors. The pass rate in state examinations also fluctuated, but for the all-important second examination it seems to have varied in relation to the state's views of its own needs.[68] Writing in 1894, a Prussian judge argued that the fond hopes of the 1860s about the self-regulating nature of supply and demand for places in the legal profession were necessarily illusory. The constant development of new branches of administration and the anticipated effect of major pieces of legislation such as the imminent civil code, he argued, meant that misjudgements about career chances for lawyers were inevitable. The only solution was, he said, to restrict access to trainee positions in the state service and he argued that the Prussian state required at most 400 of the 1,759 unpaid assessors currently working in its courts. Such a reform would have beneficial consequences for the legal profession in which, he said, there were many with bleak prospects. Others agreed that making the notoriously simple first public examination more difficult was urgently required, but nothing significant resulted.[69]

This lack of control over recruitment and training denied the legal profession any real possibility of attaining the level of professional independence of their English counterparts. Ultimately, it meant that, while certain recognizable features of modern professionalization were introduced, for example, the self-administration of professional discipline through local courts of honour, important spheres of decision-making lay outside the scope of professional bodies. There was no serious attempt to overturn the states' control over lawyers' fees before the end of the nineteenth century and accusations that some lawyers were demanding more than the legal norm, for example in Hamburg, were vigorously denied.[70] The German association of practising lawyers remained an ineffective lobby group, deeply divided on major questions facing the profession, while the exercise of professional autonomy remained unequivocally at the local level. At no point did an equivalent to the English Law Society develop in Germany.[71]

The crucial sources of power, both over and within the legal profession, thus remained essentially local throughout the nineteenth century, reaching up at most to the level of the individual state. In this sense, the reconstruction of the profession through the 1878–9 reforms was an aberration. The central questions – education and state employment – were still overwhelmingly the preserve of the individual states, which also continued to control the administration of justice. It is highly significant that the one (admittedly important) exception to this – the supreme court in Leipzig – should have been exempted from the general rule that all those qualified as judges were permitted to work as practising lawyers. Lawyers attached to that court, which was a conscious symbol of national unity,[72] were a race apart, at the head of their profession. The sphere within which their less successful colleagues operated was above all local and regional. Moreover, this localism was deliberately enhanced by the 1878 legislation, which intruded into the profession's autonomy in an important way by insisting that lawyers reside in the area of jurisdiction of the court at which they practised. This contentious provision was justified by the government in terms of the need to provide adequate legal services in all areas and hinder a flight from remote rural areas. It found the support of liberal spokesmen in the Reichstag and the campaign by the Centre Party leader, Ludwig Windthorst, to remove it, giving lawyers the same free professional status as doctors, was rejected.[73] Here, once again, the requirements of the state took precedence over the extension of professional autonomy.

Windthorst's comparison with the medical profession touched on an important element in the lawyers' self-image in the 1860s and 1870s. Of all the other 'free professions', doctors were widely seen as being the most similar to lawyers.[74] In both cases, professional status was connected to the possession of formal educational qualifications. Both professions linked those qualifications to an ideal of the superiority of public service over private interests. Lawyers would have no more to do with the hated 'pettyfogging lawyers' (*Winkeladvokaten*)[75] than doctors would with improperly trained medical practitioners. And, in both cases, state compulsion to use the services provided by the profession could be justified in terms of the public rather than the private interest. As Max Hachenburg put it when discussing the legal compulsion to engage the services of a qualified lawyer in court cases, 'it was no more introduced for the benefit of lawyers than compulsory education was for teachers or compulsory inoculation for doctors'.[76]

But there were difficulties here for the legal profession as well.

The public services provided by the likes of doctors and teachers were intrinsically different from those provided by lawyers, in that the former groups did not make their living principally from property transactions. This distinction holds despite the obvious connection between wealth and the quality of service gained by the public from both the teaching and the medical professions. Lawyers' fees were, as we have seen, dependent on the value of the transaction, at least in civil cases, and this naturally made cases involving large sums of money attractive. In the 1860s, there were already complaints about the difficulty of finding lawyers willing to represent clients in small claims cases (*Bagatellsachen*) or on criminal charges. A report from Mannheim in the 1880s revealed the reluctance of lawyers to enter low-level courts, where small claims were decided, on the grounds that this was the arena for the detested *Winkeladvokaten*, in which at best members of a lawyer's office staff might appear.[77] The damage done to the lawyer's status by contacts between the poor and these *Winkeladvokaten*, especially in rural areas, had been an important element in discussions about the shape of the legal profession. Supporters of liberalization of access in the 1860s had often argued that the measure would drive the *Winkeladvokaten* out of business. But this view proved to be no more accurate than the other predictions of that decade concerning the responses of lawyers to changes in the nature of their professions. The representation of the legal interests of the poor remained a low priority for most German lawyers until the end of the century and beyond. By the late 1890s, commentators were stressing the need to provide legal services for the poor in order to improve the profession's image and status, but change in this respect was painfully slow and often opposed by the lawyers themselves.[78] The issue of *Winkeladvokaten* would not disappear simply because lawyers regarded any contact with them as demeaning to their status. These despised proletarians of the legal profession survived because they met a genuine need among the poor, not only in rural areas which held few attractions for trained lawyers, but also in the towns. Here, the question of whom the legal system served became vital. As so often in late nineteenth-century Germany, the rhetoric of universality, presented here in the form of service to the public interest, came to look increasingly threadbare.[79]

VI

This prompts some concluding reflections about the general position of the legal profession in German society. The problem of reconciling different aspects of status – public esteem, market power, control of conditions of work, and so on – is one that most modern professions have had to face. In many respects, they have sought to defend a guild-like position against social developments involving the destruction of the restraints on trade characteristic of the pre-modern *Ständestaat*. In most modern societies, the interests of the professional 'guild' have been more or less successfully welded to those of the public through formalized entry requirements based on the possession of education and successful examination results. Germany, with its characteristic belief in the possession of *Bildung* as the major source of status, was an exaggerated manifestation of a common tendency. From the early nineteenth century, the ideal of *Bildung* had a vital legitimizing function in that it concealed recruitment practices which involved a high degree of social exclusivity behind an ideology which stressed universal access. *Bildung* was something which was in principle obtainable by everybody, though the social organization of the means of its acquisition through education precluded this in practice. By the late nineteenth century, these universalist claims were under attack from a number of directions. More and more commentators were complaining of the way in which students in law faculties, more than any other group of students, frittered away their time at university, relied on crammers to pass their examinations, and in general scarcely paid lip service to the ideal of *Bildung*. Much of this discussion centred on the failings of the legally trained bureaucrats, but it applied to lawyers and judges as well.[80]

This did not, however, do anything to weaken the lawyers' commitment to a rhetoric of public service over private interest. If anything, the reverse may have been the case, as lawyers desperately tried to inject meaning into a professional self-image inherited from the early nineteenth century. Much of this was, however, pure rhetoric and it is probable that lawyers on the whole shared the rising standards of living enjoyed by the other free professions around the turn of the century.[81] As elsewhere, lawyers were extremely sensitive to suggestions that they were exploiting the public for private gain. Such hallmarks of capitalist business practice as the advertising of services, the selling of legal practices, and the involvement of lawyers in secondary occupations all attracted the attentions of professional disciplinary bodies. The perception that lawyers were the servants of 'objective law' precluded such evidently profit-orientated activities.[82] So, more broadly, did the vision that the legal profession was an Estate. Early nineteenth-century conservatives were convinced that the main goal of an Estate was the pursuit of honour, rather than property or personal gain.[83] In principle at least, the *Stand* of lawyers accepted this view throughout the period. In their ambivalence to the introduction of market forces, the lawyers came face to face with one of the great problems of nineteenth-century German society – the relationship between honour and wealth in the definition of a person's social position. To put it another way, lawyers found it exceedingly difficult to come to agreement about how they could openly pursue the wealth which they felt was the due reflection of the honour earned by their contribution to the public good.

In one important respect – the vigour with which associational life was pursued – the legal profession parted company from the accepted picture of the nineteenth-century German middle classes. Commentators have frequently singled out lawyers for criticism with regard to their commitment to collective activity, arguing that lawyers' associations were characterized by indecision, lack of imagination, and conservatism. These features have been held responsible for the relatively low levels of interest in such professional bodies among lawyers.[84] On the other hand, we have already seen the impact of the regional and socioeconomic differences between different parts of the legal profession, subject as they were to widely varying local arrangements. There can be little doubt that the most favourable conditions for activism on the part of lawyers, both before and after 1848, existed in those states in which the profession was least stringently controlled by the public authorities. But excluded from the list were Prussia and Bavaria, the two largest states in the German empire after 1871.[85]

Nevertheless, it would be foolish to ignore the influence of the ideology of *Stand* and the related discussion about the civil service status of lawyers. This ideology, as we have repeatedly seen, left lawyers uncomfortably torn between contradictory public and private definitions of their role. Civil service status was increasingly irksome in practice, but offered some comfort in principle. Its final removal in 1878 completed a process by which lawyers redefined the public side of their image. A fundamental distinction was implicitly made between service to the state, which meant all sorts of unpleasant controls, and service to the law, which did not. But in practice this distinction was of little consequence. In the first place, this period saw the dominance of legal positivism, an approach which divorced the law from broader questions of social and economic policy and which has often been seen as marking a distinct turn to the right in legal philosophy. In constitutional terms, legal positivism had the effect of undermining any distinction between the state and the law as an ethical system.[86] Moreover, it is almost certain that the continued emphasis of lawyers on the essentially public nature of their duties weakened their commitment to the basically private, sectional orientation of associational activity. This is what Adolf Weissler meant, when he noted that enthusiastic participation in associational life was contrary to the pride and honour of Prussian lawyers.[87] Such participation threatened to create an unbearable contradiction between the 'objective' demands of the law and the 'subjective' demands of its practitioners. Perhaps more than any other educated profession, lawyers shared what Hans-Ulrich Wehler has recently called the Janus-faced aspects of that part of the *Bildungsbürgertum* which was linked to the state – its 'stereotypically *ständisch* lifestyle' and its development into 'occupational classes conditioned by the market'.[88]

This chapter has concentrated on practising lawyers and has not considered the other major arm of the legal profession, the judiciary, in detail. Judges were of course much more unequivocally officials, sharing the educational attributes and the conception of non-partisan public service, but not the aspirations to professional autonomy of the practising lawyers. Their independence, however vulnerable in practice to government intrusions, was enshrined in the doctrine of the *Rechtsstaat* and they too laid claim to being the embodiment of 'objective' law.[89] This was only one of a number of areas in which the structure of the law produced tensions and conflicts between those involved in the profession. Others included the court itself, where relations between judges and lawyers were often very bad, and the fact that state recruitment policies for the judiciary had obvious consequences for the legal employment market. Until the end of the nineteenth century, aspirant lawyers had intimate contacts with the world of the judiciary. As we have seen, all practising lawyers had to possess the same qualifications as career judges and the over-whelming majority had had some practical experience as judges in the lower courts. The state's employment policies meant that the two branches of the profession could neither be separated nor effectively brought together; judges and practising lawyers were thus like two sides of the same coin, intimately connected but facing different ways. There can be little doubt that this weakened the integrative power of a legal education and promoted pro-fessional divisions. By the end of the nineteenth century, there was in fact no single legal profession as such. Just as the educated middle classes had dissolved into specialized professional groups, so too the legal profession had lost any meaningful unity. The difference here lay in the fact that until the end of the nineteenth century a lawyer would often pass through different sub-groups within the legal profession at various stages in his career.

For these reasons among others German lawyers shared wider assumptions, for example concerning the formulation of the material aspects of the law. There was, for example, widespread agreement among practising lawyers and judges about the desir-ability of creating formal certainty in legal transactions through national law codes. As Gneist told the secretary of the Reich justice office in 1890, the overwhelming majority of practising lawyers and judges supported the recently published draft civil code – a work which had aroused bitter opposition among other sections of the population.[90] But such areas of agreement, though significant, had only a tenuous relationship to the issues which framed the professional aspirations of Germany's lawyers. On those issues, they could no longer create any semblance of unity, let alone plausibly claim to embody the aspirations of the *Volk*. Neither the lawyers nor the state could arrest developments, which were transforming the *Stand* of lawyers into a number of competing, more or less high-status groups. At no point could they develop the type of collective will to organization which characterized the doctors' defence of their position.[91] Lawyers lacked both the will to respond to changes and a professional ideology suited to the task of redefining their relationship to the public and the market. The all-important state, emphasizing its autonomy as a provider of public legal services, had no interest in aiding moves towards a modern market-orientated conception of the legal profession.

If the profession's self-image was uncomfortably suspended between older and more modern forms, what of its relationship to other parts of the bourgeoisie? In other words, how bourgeois were Germany's lawyers? This is a notoriously difficult question, involving a definition of 'bourgeois-ness' (*Bürgerlichkeit*), which centres on imprecise but important factors of cultural norms and values, and life-styles.[92] Nevertheless, certain comments seem possible in the light of existing knowledge. The emphasis on *ständisch* rhetoric, for example, was common to many sections of the bourgeoisie into the first decade of the twentieth century and should certainly not be automatically considered as evidence that lawyers were in any sense 'unmodern'. Moreover, a notable feature of recent discussions concerning the alleged German *Sonderweg* is the apparent unanimity concerning the dominance of bourgeois norms and values in the legal system, i.e. in precisely that area of society most directly shaped by the legal profession.[93] Above all, the legal profession clearly demonstrates the limited usefulness of Eckart Kehr's concept of a 'feudalized' bourgeoisie. Quite apart from well-founded theoretical doubts about the notion of feudalization, Henning has shown the low propensity of the educated middle classes in Prussia's western provinces to seek ennoblement or to enter the reserve officer corps, both of which have often been seen as symbols of an acceptance of 'pre-modern' attitudes.[94]

As we have seen, Germany's lawyers were not a good example of the passionate devotion to interest-group activity and associational life which constituted the *locus classicus* of bourgeois public action during the nineteenth century. Nevertheless, the reluctance or inability to organize effectively related to narrow professional matters rather than to participation in broader middle-class activities. Two important related arenas of bourgeois activity – municipal policies and sociable clubs – have not been considered in detail in this chapter, but lawyers clearly played an important, in some cases dominant, role in both. The urban history of nineteenth-century Germany provides frequent examples of the high profile of lawyers in civic affairs, with many instances of lawyers directly exercising local power. In many of Germany's towns, a period of high political excitement such as 1848–49 saw lawyers taking up antagonistic positions at the head of both the liberal and the radical, democratic movements. Even after the defeat of the radicals, the legal profession's central role in the notable politics which dominated urban life for most of the century seems clear.[95] Hannes Siegrist's suggestions of a 'trade-off' between broader forms of associational life and narrow professional organization and of the

MICHAEL JOHN

multiplicity of strategies for securing *Bürgerlichkeit* may be highly appropriate for the German legal profession. It certainly seems highly unlikely that the apparent weakness of lawyers' organizations accurately reflected the real status and social power enjoyed by the profession.[96]

The overall picture that emerges from these considerations is thus one of ambiguity. The evidently high status enjoyed by a legal education was in some ways counterbalanced by the lawyers' frequently expressed anxieties about the continuation of that status. They were never really in a position to act effectively to defend and enhance their material interests, but a major reason for this was that on the whole the state defended those interests reasonably well. In all probability, the ideology of public service, buttressed by the educational similarities of administrative bureaucrats, career judges, and lawyers in private practice, survived because not enough lawyers were seriously damaged in economic terms by its survival. Those educational similarities provided a framework within which the frustrations of the legal profession found expression, but it also limited the extent to which such frustrations developed into open hostility. To this must be added the slow development of a more diversified labour market for lawyers during the nineteenth century: the rapid increase of opportunities in finance and industry was very much a feature of the period after 1900. Before then, most German lawyers occupied a position in the upper reaches of the German bourgeoisie, never fully in control of the future of their profession, but also never fundamentally challenged in terms of their status. If the lawyers failed to achieve the much-envied organizational successes of their counterparts in England or France, the state at least allowed the continuation of a typically German blend of *ständisch* and professional aspirations. In short, it allowed the co-existence of an ideology of universal access to the profession and a very restrictive approach to the practice of professional recruitment.

NOTES

1 There is no study of the legal profession equivalent to Claudia Huerkamp's *Der Aufstieg der Ärzte im 19. Jahrhundert. Vom gelehrten Stand zum professionellen Experten: das Beispiel Preussens* (Göttingen, 1985).
2 See G. Dilcher, 'Das Gesellschaftsbild der Rechtswissenschaft und die soziale Frage', in K. Vondung (ed.), *Das wilhelminische Bildungsbürgertum. Zur Sozialgeschichte seiner Ideen* (Göttingen, 1976), 53–66; W. Conze

190

and J. Kocka (eds), *Bildungsbürgertum im 19. Jahrhundert*, 1 (Stuttgart, 1985). In the latter volume a projected chapter on lawyers by Gerhard Dilcher was withheld for future publication, but there is a certain amount of material relating to German lawyers in H. Siegrist, 'Gebremste Professionalisierung – Das Beispiel der Schweizer Rechtsanwaltschaft im Vergleich zu Frankreich und Deutschland im 19. und frühen 20. Jahrhundert', 301–1, especially 308–13. See also D. Grimm, 'Bürgerlichkeit im Recht', in J. Kocka (ed.), *Bürger und Bürgerlichkeit im 19. Jahrhundert* (Göttingen, 1987), 149–88.

3 H. Henning, *Das westdeutsche Bildungsbürgertum in der Epoche der Hochindustrialisierung 1860–1914. Soziales Verhalten und soziale Strukturen, Pt. 1, Das Bildungsbürgertum in den preussischen Westprovinzen* (Wiesbaden, 1972), pt. 2, ch. 2.

4 D. Rueschemeyer, *Lawyers and Their Society. A Comparative Study of the Legal Professions in Germany and the United States* (Cambridge, Mass, 1973); W. Kaupen, *Die Hüter von Recht und Ordnung. Die soziale Herkunft, Erziehung and Ausbildung der deutschen Juristen* (Neuwied/Berlin, 1969).

5 Major works of this sort include A. Weissler's indispensable *Geschichte der Rechtsanwaltschaft* (Leipzig, 1905); E. Döhring, *Geschichte der deutschen Rechtspflege seit 1500* (Berlin, 1953); H. Huffmann, *Kampf um die freie Advokatur* (Essen, 1967); F. Ostler, *Die deutschen Rechtsanwälte 1871–1971* (Essen, 1971); L. Müller, *Die Freiheit der Advokatur. Ihre geschichtliche Entwicklung in Deutschland während der Neuzeit und ihre rechtliche Bedeutung in der Bundesrepublik* (Diss. Würzburg, 1972); T. Kolbeck, *Juristenschwemmen. Untersuchungen über den juristischen Arbeitsmarkt im 19. und 20. Jahrhundert* (Frankfurt-on-Main, 1978).

6 Conze and Kocka, 'Einleitung', in *Bildungsbürgertum*, 23.

7 I.e. for all those who had finished the training and passed the examinations required of a career judge.

8 J. Kocka, 'Bürgertum und Bürgerlichkeit als Problem der deutschen Geschichte vom späten 18. zum frühen 20. Jahrhundert', in Kocka (ed.), *Bürger und Bürgerlichkeit*, 34–7.

9 See H. Siegrist, 'Bürgerliche Berufe. Die Professionen und das Bürgertum', in Siegrist (ed.), *Bürgerliche Berufe. Zur Sozialgeschichte der freien und akademischen Berufe im internationalen Vergleich* (Göttingen, 1988), 11–48. This collection contains a short study of judges by Hubert Rottleuthner, 'Die gebrochene Bürgerlichkeit einer Scheinprofession. Zur Situation der deutschen Richterschaft zu Beginn des 20. Jahrhunderts', 145–73, but no essay devoted to practising lawyers.

10 The essential sources for this necessarily rather compressed treatment of an important subject are C. von Delbrück, *Die Ausbildung für den höheren Verwaltungsdienst in Preussen* (Jena, 1917), esp. 6–17; C.J. Friedrich, 'The continental tradition of training administrators in law and jurisprudence', *Journal of Modern History*, 11 (1939), 129–48; W. Bleek, *Von der Kameralausbildung zum Juristenprivileg: Studium, Prüfung und Ausbildung der höheren Beamten des allgemeinen Verwaltungsdienstes im 18. und 19. Jahrhundert* (Berlin, 1972).

11 See Silberschlag, 'Die Ministerial-Verfügung vom 5. Dezember 1864 über das erste juristische Examen', *Preussische Anwalts-Zeitung*, 22 June

1865, 385–91; Delbrück, *Ausbildung*, 14; R. von Gneist, *Freie Advocatur. Die erste Forderung aller Justizreform in Preussen* (Berlin, 1867), 32.

12 For a good account of the content of law courses in different universities, see W. Siemann, *Die Frankfurter Nationalversammlung 1848/49 zwischen demokratischem Liberalismus und konservativer Reform* (Frankfurt-on-Main, 1976), 38–54.

13 See Bleek, *Kameralausbildung*, 52–4; J.R. Gillis, *The Prussian Bureaucracy in Crisis 1840–1860. Origins of an Administrative Ethos* (Stanford, 1971), 50–3; and the interesting remarks in U.K. Preuss, 'Bildung and Bürokratie. Sozialhistorische Bedingungen in der ersten Hälfte des 19. Jahrhunderts', *Der Staat*, 14 (1975), 371–96, esp. 381–6.

14 As is argued by Preuss, 'Bildung and Bürokratie', 383–4.

15 See Kolbeck, *Juristenschwemmen*, 37–42, 74–5; Gillis, *Prussian Bureaucracy*, 39–43, 233–4; R. Koselleck, *Preussen zwischen Reform und Revolution* (Stuttgart, 1967), 438–9; J. Conrad, *The German Universities for the last Fifty Years* (Glasgow, 1885), 138–40; Conrad, 'Allgemeine Statistik der deutschen Universitäten', in W. Lexis (ed.), *Die Deutschen Universitäten*, 1 (Berlin, 1893), 120–2.

16 K. Jarausch, *Students, Society and Politics in Imperial Germany* (Princeton, 1982), 46.

17 See the contrasting estimates of Koselleck, *Preussen*, 438; Kolbeck, *Juristenschwemmen*, 33; Conrad, *German Universities*, 138. An overview of the estimated numbers is provided in Wehler, *Deutsche Gesellschaftsgeschichte*, 2 (Munich, 1987), 305–6.

18 Kolbeck, *Juristenschwemmen*, 34–6; Gneist, *Freie Advocatur*, 18; for Lexis's calculations, see Jarausch, *Students*, 55–6. The number of practising lawyers overtook the number of judges for the first time at the end of the first decade of the twentieth century; see Rottleuthner, 'Die gebrochene Bürgerlichkeit einer Scheinprofession', 154.

19 Gillis, *Prussian Bureaucracy*, 63.

20 Kolbeck, *Juristenschwemmen*, 52–3, 68–73, 87–8; Gneist, *Freie Advocatur*, 66; Döhring, *Rechtspflege*, 154; C. Kade, 'Der preussische Juristenstand', *Preussische Jahrbücher*, 75 (1894), 234.

21 K. Brater, 'Advokatur', in J.C. Bluntschli and K. Brater (eds), *Deutsches Staats-Wörterbuch*, 1 (Stuttgart/Leipzig, 1857), 76; Döhring, *Rechtspflege*, 154; Ostler, *Rechtsanwälte*, 60; Kolbeck, *Juristenschwemmen*, 34–5.

22 Details of regional variations in the law are contained in Weissler, *Rechtsanwaltschaft*, 424–39, 522–41 and in Siegrist, 'Gebremste Professionalisierung', 308. In 1879, Bavaria with a population of just over 5 million had 372 practising lawyers; Munich, with a population of 230,0000, had 30: Ostler, *Rechtsanwälte*, 60. On average, the Prussian state appointed 39 practising lawyers annually between 1836 and the 1840s, see Gillis, *Prussian Bureaucracy*, 41, 234.

23 C.E. McClelland, 'Zur Professionalisierung der akademischen Berufe in Deutschland', in Conze and Kocka (eds), *Bildungsbürgertum*, 235–9; Kocka, 'Bürgertum und Bürgerlichkeit als Problem der deutschen Geschichte vom späten 18. zum frühen 20. Jahrhundert', 36.

24 On this, see M. John, *Politics and the Law in Late Nineteenth-Century Germany* (Oxford, 1989), 36–8 and the sources cited there.

25 E.g. P. Hinschius, 'Advokatur und Anwaltschaft', in F. Holtzendorff (ed.), *Encyclopädie der Rechtswissenschaft in systematischer und alphabetischer Bearbeitung. Zweiter Theil. Rechtslexicon*, 1 (Leipzig, 1870), 27; H.C. Hofmann, 'Ueber die nächsten Bedürfnisse des deutschen Advocatenstandes', *Archiv für die civilistische Praxis*, 27 (1844), 249; and the sources cited in L. O'Boyle, 'The democratic left in Germany, 1848', *Journal of Modern History*, 33 (1961), 378.

26 See Weissler, *Rechtsanwaltschaft*, 430.

27 Gneist, *Freie Advocatur*, 55.

28 See, for example, the effect of the Prussian and Bavarian ministries' ban on their lawyers' participation in the projected Mainz congress of practising lawyers in 1844: Weissler, *Rechtsanwaltschaft*, 509–14; *Preussische Gerichts-Zeitung*, 10 Feb. 1861, 77–8. Local associations of practising lawyers were banned in Waldeck in 1839 and Rostock in 1844; Weissler, *Rechtsanwaltschaft*, 503.

29 See [anon.] 'Advocatencorporationen', F.A. Brockhaus, *Allgemeine deutsche Real-Encyclopädie für die gebildeten Stände. Conversations-Lexikon*, 10th edn (Leipzig, 1851), 1:155; Weissler, *Rechtsanwaltschaft*, 518–21, 547–61; *Preussische Anwalts-Zeitung*, 5 Nov. 1863, 353; [anon.] 'Die Advocatur in Preussen', *Preussische Jahrbücher*, 14 (1864), 426; see also the important general comments in McClelland, 'Professionalisierung', 242–3.

30 Hofmann, 'Ueber die nächsten Bedürfnisse', 243–4, 249, 250–1; Gneist, *Freie Advocatur*, 55–60.

31 See the humorous account of these perceived differences in status in K. Buchner, *Ein deutscher Advokat. Schilderungen aus der Zeit und aus dem Leben* (Darmstadt, 1844), 4–11; cf. L.E. Lee, *The Politics of Harmony, Civil Service, Liberalism, and Social Reform in Baden, 1800–1850* (Cranbury, NJ, 1980), 207; Gagern to H. von Gagern, 27 Sept. 1847, in P. Wentzcke and W. Klötzer (eds), *Deutscher Liberalismus im Vormärz. Heinrich von Gagern. Briefe und Reden 1815–1848* (Göttingen/Berlin/Frankfurt-on-Main, 1959), 400.

32 Huerkamp, *Aufstieg der Ärzte*, 244.

33 K.J.A. Mittermaier, 'Die künftige Stellung des Advokatenstandes', *Archiv für die civilistische Praxis*, 15 (1832), 148; cf. the comments of the Silesian *Anwaltskammer* in relation to the loss of official status after the 1878 *Rechtsanwaltsordnung*, quoted in Ostler, *Rechtsanwälte*, 18.

34 Weissler, *Rechtsanwaltschaft*, 548; Wilmowski, 'Rechts-Anwalt. Beamten-Qualität. Disciplinar-Gewalt', *Preussische Anwalts-Zeitung*, 6 Feb. 1862, 47.

35 This was clear in the famous Soest meeting of Rhenish and Westphalian jurists in 1843; see Gillis, *Prussian Bureaucracy*, 69–70.

36 J. Brunk to H. von Gagern, quoted in W. Schubert, 'Der Code Civil und die Personenrechtsentwürfe des Grossherzogtums Hessen-Darmstadt von 1842 bis 1847', *Zeitschrift der Savigny-Stiftung für Rechtsgeschichte. Germanistische Abteilung*, 88 (1971), 171.

37 D. Blasius, 'Der Kampf um die Geschworenengerichte im Vormärz', in H.-U. Wehler (ed.), *Sozialgeschichte Heute. Festschrift für Hans Rosenberg zum 70. Geburtstag* (Göttingen, 1974), 150.

38 See Mittermaier, 'Die künftige Stellung des Advokatenstandes', 148;

for Gagern, see his important draft letter to H. C. Hofmann, written in the autumn of 1845, in Wentzcke and Klötzer (eds), *Deutscher Liberalismus*, 294–304; Buchner, *Ein deutscher Advokat*, 90. See also the comments in Lee, *Politics of Harmony*, 206 and O'Boyle, 'The democratic left in Germany', 378–9.

39 See, for example, L. Krieger, *The German Idea of Freedom. History of a Political Tradition* (Chicago, 1957), 300–1.

40 In fact, the *Ehrenrat* was conceived in the 1840s as preferable to granting more extensive disciplinary powers to lawyers. Nevertheless, it was introduced in 1847 in more liberal a form than the lawyers had demanded: Weissler, *Rechtsanwaltschaft*, 371–7.

41 Weissler, *Rechtsanwaltschaft*, 543–7, 573; Hinschius, 'Advokatur und Anwaltschaft', 28; Brater, 'Advokatur', 57; Gneist, *Freie Advocatur*, 26–7, 44–54.

42 See Bleek, *Kameralausbildung*, 26–9; R. M. Berdahl, *The Politics of the Prussian Nobility. The Development of a Conservative Ideology, 1770–1848* (Princeton, 1988), 230.

43 Mittermaier, 'Die künftige Stellung des Advokatenstandes', 138.

44 M. Hachenburg, *Lebenserinnerungen eines Rechtsanwalts und Briefe aus der Emigration*, J. Schadt (ed.) (Stuttgart/Berlin/Cologne/Mainz, 1978: 1st edn, 1927), 57, 60–2; Weissler, *Rechtsanwaltschaft*, 612–13.

45 Gneist, *Freie Advocatur*, 58.

46 Huerkamp, *Aufstieg der Ärzte*, 254–61.

47 Gneist, *Freie Advocatur*, 61–2; *Verhandlungen des Vierten Deutschen Juristentages*, 2 (Berlin, 1864), 285–94, 297–9.

48 Gneist, *Freie Advocatur*, 98–100.

49 ibid., 60.

50 See, for example, the contrasting attitudes of Lebrecht (a lawyer from Ulm) and Schwarze (a Saxon lawyer) in *Verhandlungen des Vierten Deutschen Juristentages*, 2: 307–9 and Weissler, *Rechtsanwaltschaft*, 580.

51 Ostler, 17; *Preussische Anwalts-Zeitung*, 27 Dec. 1866, 817.

52 *Preussische Anwalts-Zeitung*, 30 Apr. 1863 and 6 Aug. 1863, 143–4, 255.

53 Lewald, 'Vorschlag zur Ausdehnung der Anwalts-Thätigkeit auf den ganzen Bezirk des Appellationsgerichts', *Preussische Anwalts-Zeitung*, 2 Nov. 1865, 689–90.

54 Gneist, *Freie Advocatur*, 29.

55 Weissler, *Rechtsanwaltschaft*, 558–66.

56 This claim was made by Adolf Hoffmann in the first reading of the *Rechtsanwaltsordnung* in the Reichstag: *Stenographische Berichte über die Verhandlungen des Reichstages (SBRT)*, 12 Feb. 1878, 16.

57 For Friedberg's comments, see *SBRT*, 12 Feb. 1878, 12 and 18 Feb. 1879, 17–18.

58 These figures are taken from Kolbeck, *Juristenschwemmen*, 89; Ostler, *Rechtsanwälte*, 60; Döhring, *Rechtspflege*, 154. Cf. Kurlbaum's comments on shortages of lawyers in rural areas in East Elbia in 1876, *SBRT*, 13 May 1878, 1290.

59 These figures exclude those lawyers employed at the *Reichsgericht* in Leipzig, a category which was excluded from the general liberalization of 1878. The statistics are presented in Ostler, *Rechtsanwälte*, 60.

60 Döhring, *Rechtspflege*, 155. To this figure must be added earnings from criminal cases.
61 For these figures, see A. Wagner, *Der Richter. Geschichte – Aktuelle Fragen – Reformprobleme* (Karlsruhe, 1959), 72; Sellow, 'Rang und Gehalt im Justiz und Verwaltung', *Preussische Jahrbücher*, 78 (1894), 121–2; for more detailed figures for different categories of Prussian judges in 1910, see Rottleuthner, 'Die gebrochene Bürgerlichkeit einer Scheinprofession', 172–3.
62 Details are to be found in Huerkamp, *Aufstieg der Ärzte*, 212–13; cf. in general Henning, *Das westdeutsche Bildungsbürgertum*, 436–8, 460–1.
63 These questions were obviously related in that practising lawyers had to have the same qualifications as judges. Openings for one group thus had clear consequences for the supply of candidates for the other, especially given the relative unattractiveness of a judicial career, compared to one in the administrative civil service. For negative perceptions of the quality of the judiciary in the 1890s, see Wagner, *Richter*, 72–3; Weissler, *Rechtsanwaltschaft*, 601–2 and the material cited in K.G.A. Jeserich *et al.* (eds), *Deutsche Verwaltungsgeschichte*, 3 (Stuttgart, 1984), 465. Eckart Kehr argued that the opening of the legal profession in 1878 enticed the most capable (and liberal) younger judges to leave the judiciary with negative political consequences; see his 'Das soziale System der Reaktion in Preussen', in E. Kehr, *Der Primat der Innenpolitik*, ed. H.-U. Wehler (Frankfurt-on-Main, 1965), 75–6.
64 Ostler, *Rechtsanwälte*, 62–7.
65 Jeserich *et al.* (eds), *Deutsche Verwaltungsgeschichte*, 3; 458; Kolbeck, *Juristenschwemmen*, 83–6.
66 Conrad, *German Universities*, 68–9; cf. Conrad, 'Allgemeine Statistik, 140–2. The Prussian figures for 1911–12 are taken from P. Lundgreen, 'Zur Konstituierung des "Bildungsbürgertums": Berufs- und Bildungsauslese der Akademiker in Preussen', in Conze and Kocka, (eds), *Bildungsbürgertum*, 105. For law professors' resistance to reforms of entry requirements to university which might lower the social status of lawyers, see Jarausch, *Students*, 104–8.
67 As we have seen, analysis of the conditions of the profession in Saxony and Frankfurt suggests that behind the rhetoric of selflessness lay a high standard of living. It would seem that existing entry conditions for lawyers posed considerably greater hindrances to overcrowding than did those for doctors. In 1901, there were 1,568 doctors in Saxony and 576 lawyers. In Frankfurt in 1893, there were 217 doctors and 72 lawyers. See Huerkamp, *Aufstieg der Ärzte*, 212–13.
68 Conrad, *German Universities*, 130–7; Kolbeck, *Juristenschwemmen*, 12–19, 22.
69 C. Kade, 'Der preussische Juristenstand', 231–41; cf. [anon] *Gegenwart und Zukunft des deutschen Juristenstandes, Ein Wort aus der Praxis* (Berlin, 1887), 4, 36. For an example of the belief in the 1860s that supply and demand would regulate themselves in the legal profession, see the comments of Carl Georg von Wächter in *Verhandlungen des Vierten Deutschen Juristentages*, 2: 293–4.

70 [anon.] 'Das Extrahonorar der Rechtsanwälte' and the reply by the Hamburg lawyer Isaac Wolffson in *Preussische Jahrbücher*, 74 (1893), 285–96, 554–6.

71 The English Law Society was founded in 1823 as the representative body of English solicitors. It laid down rules concerning fees and professional discipline, came to determine recruitment through its control of the system of professional examinations and generally succeeded in defending the economic interests of its members, for example by blocking reforms of the system of land registration and conveyancing. On this last point, see A.W.B. Simpson, *A History of the Land Law*, 2nd edn (Oxford, 1986), 273–88.

72 See, for example, the Kaiser's rhetoric of 'ein Volk, ein Recht, ein Richter', in a speech when laying the foundation stone of the supreme court building in October 1888, reported in *Danziger Zeitung*, 22 Nov. 1888.

73 *SBRT*, 11 May 1878, 1244–52.

74 See, for example, Gneist, *Freie Advocatur*, 62–3.

75 *Winkeladvokaten* were generally men who had some legal training without having acquired the necessary experience and qualifications to enter the judiciary or become fully qualified lawyers. Very little is at present known about this group in terms of its size or composition, but there were almost certainly many more of them than there were fully qualified lawyers. Gneist estimated that there were 300–400 *Winkeladvokaten* in Berlin alone in the 1860s and that their principal function lay in the provision of relatively cheap legal advice on questions which did not involve appearances in court; *Freie Advocatur*, 66.

76 Hachenburg, *Lebenserinnerungen*, 57.

77 [anon.] 'Die Advocatur in Preussen', 432–3; T. Frantz, 'Ist der Rechtsanwalt ein Zwischenhändler?', *Preussische Jahrbücher*, 75 (1894), 105.

78 On the relationship between restricted access and *Winkeladvokaten* in the 1860s, see Gneist, *Freie Advocatur*, 66 and the debate between Lewald and Elbers in *Preussische Anwalts-Zeitung*, 4 Jan. and 15 Feb. 1866, 1–3, 102–4. For the 1890s, see A. v. Weinrich, 'Advokatur und Rechtsanwaltschaft', *Preussische Jahrbücher*, 99 (1900), 121–2.

79 On this, see more generally D. Blackbourn and G. Eley, *The Peculiarities of German History* (Oxford, 1984), 221–8.

80 Examples of these complaints are to be found in Jarausch, *Students*, 140–3 and Conrad, *German Universities*, 133.

81 Henning, *Das westdeutsche Bildungsbürgertum*, 438, 460–1; Huerkamp, *Aufstieg der Ärzte*, 213–15.

82 Döhring, *Rechtspflege*, 165; Siegrist, 'Gebremste Professionalisierung', 312–3.

83 See Berdahl, *Politics of the Prussian Nobility*, 74–6, 226.

84 See the views of Döhring, *Rechtspflege*, 116–17.

85 See the comments of Weissler on regional differences in the level of activism among lawyers, *Rechtsanwaltschaft*, ch. 49.

86 This is an extremely important subject in its own right. The two key works are G. Dilcher, 'Der rechtswissenschaftliche Positivismus. Wissenschaftliche Methode, Sozialphilosophie, Gesellschaftspolitik',

Archiv für Rechts- und Sozialphilosophie, 61 (1975), 497–528; and P. von Oertzen, *Die soziale Funktion des staatsrechtlichen Positivismus* (Frankfurt-on-Main, 1974).

87 Weissler, *Rechtsanwaltschaft*, 540.
88 H.-U. Wehler, 'Wie "bürgerlich" war das Deutsche Kaiserreich?', in Kocka (ed.), *Bürger und Bürgerlichkeit*, 247.
89 See Rottleuthner, 'Die gebrochene Bürgerlichkeit einer Scheinprofession', 145–73 on this.
90 Gneist to Oehlschläger, 23 Feb. 1890, Zentrales Staatsarchiv Postdam, RJM 3812, f. 84.
91 Huerkamp, *Aufstieg der Ärzte*, 285–96.
92 See the comments of Kocka and Wehler in their respective contributions to Kocka (ed.), *Bürger und Bürgerlichkeit*, 43–4, 260–1.
93 On this, see Blackbourn and Eley, *Peculiarities of German History*, 190–4, 221–3; J. Kocka, 'German history before Hitler: the debate about the German *Sonderweg*', *Journal of Contemporary History*, 23 (1986), 12; Wehler, 'Wie "bürgerlich" war das Kaiserreich?', 261–2. I have considered this argument at length in 'The pecularities of the German state: bourgeois law and society in the Imperial era', *Past and Present*, 119 (1988), 105–31.
94 Henning, *Das westdeutsche Bildungsbürgertum*, 491.
95 For some examples, see R. Koch, *Grundlagen bürgerlicher Herrschaft. Verfassungs- und sozialgeschichtliche Studien zur bürgerlichen Gesellscaft in Frankfurt am Main (1612–1866)* (Wiesbaden, 1983), 209, 250, 323–6, 340–2; R.J. Evans, *Death in Hamburg. Society and Politics in the Cholera Years 1830–1910* (Oxford, 1987), 18–22; F. W. Schaer, *Die Stadt Aurich und ihre Beamtenschaft im 19. Jahrhundert unter besonderer Berücksichtigung der hannoverschen Zeit (1815–1866)* (Göttingen, 1963), esp. 51–2.
96 Siegrist, 'Bürgerliche Berufe', 17.

7

Bourgeois values, doctors and the state: the professionalization of medicine in Germany 1848–1933

Paul Weindling

I

In analysing how pressure groups contributed to the emergence of distinctive German economic and political structures, historians have concentrated on industrialists and organized labour rather than on organizations representing the interests of the academically educated middle class.[1] Discussion of patriotic associations such as the Navy League and the Pan-German League has centred on whether these imperialist organizations represented a coalition between heavy industry and the 'traditional' ruling elite of the Junker landowners, or whether groupings within such organizations showed a populist and self-organizing capacity.[2] There has been a good deal of analysis of the social composition of these imperialist associations, but little attention has been paid to distinctive occupational groupings within them.[3] Doctors, for example, were prominent among the founders and local leadership of the Pan-German League, but their motives have usually been subsumed into a more general bourgeois fervour for nationalist culture.[4] Thus the motives for the medical profession's involvement in the nationalist movement have often been overlooked. So too has the nationalist complexion of organizations such as those which were founded in Imperial Germany for the combating of tuberculosis and sexually transmitted diseases. These campaigns too can be interpreted in terms of social imperialism.[5] The health of the nation was a major concern of the patriotic associations, and this preoccupation allowed the medical profession to claim a leading role in imposing bourgeois values of cleanliness, fitness, and sobriety onto the rest of the nation. The German medical profession, moreover, went further, and claimed world leadership both in the application of experimental natural science to medical research, and in the organization of medical education. So the influence of the medical profession and its pressure groups in shaping political attitudes in late nineteenth- and early twentieth-century Germany deserves greater attention than it has so far received.

Leading advocates of public health reforms such as Rudolf Virchow, who was both a prominent left-liberal politician and a pioneer of cellular pathology in the nineteenth century, and Alfred Grotjahn, a well-known theoretician of social hygiene in the early twentieth century, used medical arguments in their campaigns for social reforms designed to relieve the miseries of urban and industrial society. Demands by German doctors for a 'free profession' in the mid-nineteenth century gave way to corporatist models of organization and ideology during the twentieth. This transition makes it necessary to assess a range of factors more complex than just the activities of doctors in party politics. Professional groupings in party politics as well as in associations for social reform cemented the class cohesion of the bourgeoisie as well as improving public health and relieving poverty. Yet historians have tended to accept medical evidence as the objective and accurate reporting of social conditions, rather than viewing medical data as a social construct used for the imposition of professional norms. Although there is an extensive literature on doctors and their responses to the 'social question' and to the growth of socialism, the political complexion of the majority of the medical profession has generally been overlooked.[6] The medical profession not only took a major role in the shaping of the German welfare state but also played a part in defining the middle-class values which were associated with health and family welfare. This raises in turn the question of the social power of academically educated elites and the extent to which a concern with the nation and the state informed medical ideas.[7] Professionalization strengthened the authority of the educated middle class while at the same time satisfying many of their social and economic ambitions. The medical profession offered the state a range of services and underpinned bourgeois values, promising prosperity, order, and social integration.[8]

Historical accounts of the rise of the medical profession concentrate largely on the development of its internal organizations, on the doctor–patient relationship, and on the growth of demand for medical care as a result of the development of sickness insurance

199

organizations. Yet the forces generating this transformation, and the social impact of the monopolistic demands of power-hungry professionals, are poorly understood, although it is precisely at these points that the history of the medical profession contributes most clearly to mainstream German history. In the British and American sociology of the professions, a functionalist analysis of the professions, which views them as based on services applying a special body of knowledge and techniques, has been superseded by an analysis based on power and professional sovereignty. It has been argued that professions strive for autonomy and prestige, and have strong group loyalties and distinctive codes of ethics. This shift of emphasis has also altered interpretations of the German medical profession. Claudia Huerkamp, in her recent study of the subject, has argued that the state assumed a crucial role in Germany, while Reinhard Spree has applied the concept of the growth of a market for medical care in order to explain the rise of the profession in terms of state support for sickness insurance and of an expanding economy.[9] Yet there remains the crucial question of whether the interaction with the state meant that the medical profession should be seen as an agent of social control by the ruling elite, or whether the doctors manipulated the state in order to secure a monopoly of power in medical care and substantial rights over medical auxiliaries, as for example over the training and admission of nurses and midwives. Alfons Labisch has stressed the importance of informal processes, of doctors who had the power to persuade the population into adopting a healthy style of life.[10] In the nineteenth century, certain liberal principles restricted the role of the state in spheres such as welfare, which were defined by financial and judicial officials as private in character. The social problems and upheavals of industrialization thus made it necessary to define new spheres of intervention by the ruling elite in alliance with the medical profession. From the 1890s tuberculosis prevention and infant welfare were two areas in which there was close co-operation between such prominent figures as the Empress Auguste-Viktoria and leaders of the medical profession. Moreover, not only were the overall aims and organization of the profession highly responsive to change, but there were also regional and internal differences of status and income. It is necessary, therefore, to ask how far professional allegiances motivated behaviour, and how far other factors such as class and nationalism overrode professional identity. If the nineteenth century saw

Germany develop from a society based on social rank to one based primarily on class, then it becomes important to establish precisely what place the professions occupied in this process of transition.[11]

II

The German Absolutist states of the period leading up to the 1848 revolution constructed elaborate medical hierarchies in which different orders of healers each received their own particular assigned status or position. The academically educated doctors (*Ärzte*) came above surgeons (*Wundärzte*) who were in turn subdivided into various grades. Public health services were a part of the Enlightenment heritage of a so-called medical police (*medizinische Polizei*), which gave doctors a range of legal powers to detain and segregate the sick, and to remove public nuisances.[12] How much the hierarchy of practitioners actually conformed to the realities of highly diverse types of healers in differing regional contexts is an open question, but such arrangements do at least convey a sense of the official view of how medical care was provided on an authoritarian and paternalistic basis. Resentment of the hierarchy as oppressive prompted the emergence of a medical reform movement in the mid nineteenth century to demand freedom from state control. In putting forward this demand, the movement found in experimental biology an autonomous basis for a new science of hygiene which, it argued, should replace the state medical policing system.

Scientifically based professions such as medicine and engineering offered career opportunities for the commercial and academically educated bourgeoisie in the nineteenth century. Medicine had a lower status than other traditional professions such as law or administration, but ranked higher than engineering or journalism, which absorbed graduates from philosophical faculties. The results of an overcrowded medical profession were internal divisions and a growing pressure to develop specializations. The traditional elite of the medical profession – the select number of university professors at prestige universities like Berlin – was recruited from the higher echelons of the bourgeoisie from the 1890s onwards, indicating an increasing exclusiveness among the elite of the profession.[13] This was countered by the emergence of new organizations among the mass of economically struggling medical practitioners. Most prominent among these was the League to Defend the Economic

Interests of the Medical Profession (*Hartmann-Bund*), established at the turn of the century. It can be regarded as a populist type of medical protest movement which campaigned against the incipient 'state socialism' of the sickness insurance funds. The explicitly economic concerns of such organizations took on a crucial role in bringing together the traditionally divided commercial sectors of the medical profession with the academically educated elite, thus creating the basis for a unified professional identity.

The connections between politics and professionalism were made most spectacularly evident through the political activities of the noted pathologist Rudolf Virchow. In the course of the 1848 revolution, as German liberals were attempting to unify the nation around a set of common political institutions, doctors raised the demand for a national ministry of health headed by a properly qualified medical man. This scheme – advocated by Rudolf Virchow among others – represented among other things a characteristic liberal idea for reforming the late Absolutist state.[14] Although at no time in German history has the plan for a national ministry of health come to fruition, it was nevertheless symptomatic of the contemporary bourgeois aspirations to national unification. The science of hygiene provided a rationale for the substitution of policing authorities by scientific professionalism. This was not just an example of liberal politics in action, it was also the plan of a new breed of power-hungry professional men, seeking a share in the running of the state.

Virchow and the medical reformers have conventionally been portrayed as opponents of an interventionist state and as champions of liberal freedoms. In fact, however, Virchow represented very much the professionally elitist wing of the medical reform movement. Radicals such as the Polish–Jewish doctor Robert Remak demanded an alternative form of organization, that of medical co-operatives in which the doctor was accountable to worker-members. Virchow's opposition to this scheme indicated how the liberal medical reform movement remained fixated on a unified state while rejecting democratic notions of public accountability.[15] Its journal, *Die medicinische Reform* (Medical Reform), which was co-edited by Virchow and the psychiatrist Rudolf Leubuscher, was addressed to reforming doctors rather than to a broader public. Its opening article drew a distinction between 'socialist' and 'social' medicine, and it only supported the latter. The idea was that 'doctors' were the natural representatives of the poor and that the 'social question' should mainly lie within the jurisdiction of the medical profession. Thus the radicalism of the journal was circumscribed by its opposition to mass democracy and socialism. The journal outlined schemes for the reform of poor law medical practice as well as demands for increasing the influence of scientifically educated experts in state affairs. In this view, scientific and medical qualifications were to render public health administration immune to political meddling by government ministers. Later generations of medical reformers went on to demand that the minister responsible for health matters should himself be a doctor.[16]

Medical and health affairs in Prussia were in fact controlled by the so-called *Kultusministerium*, the government ministry also responsible for education and religion. This grouping together of three rather different areas of competence was officially justified in terms of combating materialism and scientific empiricism by linking medicine to Christian charity and faith, which were also central elements in the educational curriculum. Thus the demands for 'free and objective science' became a rallying cry for the radicals during the 1848 revolutions against the excessive interventionism of church and state. New sciences such as Virchow's cellular pathology had dual secularizing and political functions. Virchow demanded the abolition of advisory and consultative bodies, such as the provincial medical colleges or the Prussian Scientific Advisory Committee for Medical Affairs, which consisted largely of university professors. Instead he advocated a Health Council (*Gesundheitsrat*) as both a technical-advisory and administrative authority in the medical field. This was to consist of members elected by the medical profession. Not only was the profession to establish representative chambers (*Kammer*), doctors also, in Virchow's scheme, had to take a leading role in civic associations of a more general kind. Virchow's activities in municipal public health reform and in the left-liberal Progressive Party from 1856 onwards indicated the ability of scientific qualifications to provide political status and authority. Virchow was an active force in the Berlin municipal assembly, campaigning for municipal hospitals, disinfection facilities, and improved sewers and water supply. The premises of his civic activism were, in turn, scientific: Virchow viewed the state as a co-operative social organism, and he compared the individual citizen to an individual cell. Social life should, therefore, be constructed according to natural laws and the scientist should become a legislator. Whatever else their effects may have been, one thing such ideas certainly did was to legitimate the increasing penetration of government by expert elites such as the medical profession.

Although German professionalization was marked by a special relationship with the state, which had a monopoly on professional qualifications, Virchow's strategy was to argue against state control, and for a free market in medical practice. Only the state-sanctioned title of *Arzt* – the university-trained and qualified medical practitioner – was to be legally protected. The historian Claudia Huerkamp has, to be sure, noted the 'democratic character' of the medical reform movement, but its demand for larger numbers of poor law doctors and for the state funding of scientific facilities indicated how the state was none the less expected to step in to boost the medical profession.[17] Virchow believed that the superiority of scientific qualifications guaranteed the status of the profession. The importance of academic titles in medicine – *Doktor, Privatdozent,* and *Professor* – conferred both status and profit by attracting large numbers of patients. In addition came the titles of *Sanitätsrat* and *Geheimer Medizinalrat* which satisfied the appetite of the educated middle class for official status and prestige. This contrasts with the training and professional career patterns in Britain and the United States, where it has been forcefully argued that scientific superiority was not necessary for professional success.[18]

The unification of Germany left public health administration divided between the administrations of the federated states and the municipalities. The central Imperial state in Berlin also intervened, however, through the Bismarckian introduction of sickness and accident insurance and pension schemes. The state laid down legislative guidelines for those groups of workers who were to be compulsorily insured, and dictated the minimum contributions and benefits. There was also a system of supervisory provincial and state insurance offices. But it is important to recognize that the sickness insurance funds (*Krankenkassen*) were – within the framework of legislation and state supervision – autonomous organizations financed by and responsible to employers and workers rather than to the state as such. Partly for this reason, doctors' representative organizations (*Ärztekammer*) were officially recognized by the Prussian state in 1887. Although there had been such representative bodies in other states since their introduction in Baden in 1864, medical demands were now becoming more intense as the doctors responded to the power of the sickness funds, which soon became able to dictate the fees and conditions of medical service. There was a bitter sequence of conflicts, involving vitriolic propaganda, strikes, and boycotts in the period until the Nazi 'co-ordination' (*Gleichschaltung*) of sickness insurance funds after the establishment of the Third Reich in 1933.[19]

The relative weakness of the state is also evident when the role of the Reich in public health is scrutinized. In 1869 medical associations had petitioned the North German Confederation for the establishment of a Reich Health Office, *Reichsgesundheitsamt*, which could represent professional interests and administer public health. Owing to Bismarck's opposition and to the continuing power of liberal administrative structures in the early years of the Empire, it was not founded until 1876, and it was only provided with limited powers, being charged mainly with collating information on legislative provisions and statistics on health conditions in the different federated states. The office generally maintained a passive monitoring role rather than actively intervening in public health administration. This continued to be the case with the founding of laboratories for chemistry and bacteriology. A network of state institutions was established for monitoring the human, animal, and natural environment. It meant that medical officials had to have qualifications in biologically based medical sciences (such as bacteriology) rather than in the law (as they did in forensic medicine). This was part of a broader shift away from law and policing systems as the basis of health, towards scientific and medical training instead, a development which might be interpreted as establishing autonomous authorities on the basis of expertise and objectivity rather than representing any particular growth in the role of the state.

The emergence of the full-time state medical officer was a protracted process which only gathered momentum after 1899. 'Medical reform' had initially meant the establishment of a profession free from state controls. There had been moves since the 1860s to transform the post of local medical officer from having primarily legal responsibilities in forensic medicine (the identification of corpses, provision of evidence in murder cases, and so on) onto a much broader basis. In 1833 the Prussian Association of Medical Officials was founded in order to represent these local medical officials, of whom there were now some 900 altogether.[20] The association campaigned vigorously for full official status for the district medical officer. By the 1890s, therefore, in this respect at least, 'medical reform' had acquired meanings primarily oriented towards the state.[21] In 1899 the post of district medical officer was restricted, with some becoming full-time positions, and others part-time, allowing additional private practice. There were initially only fifteen full-time posts, but the number rapidly increased. The district medical officer in the towns and cities had the status of a technical adviser to the police, and in the countryside to the district commissioner (*Landrat*). However, in matters pertaining to infectious disease there were instructions that general adminis-trators had to pay heed to the recommendations of the district medical officer, who was also supposed to consult the newly estab-lished Health Commissions in the cities. The position was further complicated as the Prussian state founded a specialised research institute for the celebrated bacteriologist Robert Koch, discoverer of the causes of cholera and tuberculosis, and set up a network of provincial hygiene institutes during the 1890s. Some of these were under civil and others under military jurisdiction. Routine analysis of specimens and matters such as the outbreaks of infections and epidemics were also referred to specially trained experts.[22] State responsibilities could now be devolved on to the growing numbers of city medical officers. Such arrangements meant that hitherto clear-cut demarcations between municipal autonomy and the state were becoming blurred. Medical reformers pressed for an increas-ing number of salaried posts, a demand which was partially satis-fied in 1899 with the Prussian Medical Officers' Law. There was also to be a role for the profession within the state, resulting in some reorganization of the relevant administrative bodies.[23] The leading Prussian official in this area, Friedrich Althoff, sought municipal involvement in such state-sponsored ventures, as with the Institute for Serum Testing and Experimental Medicine in Frankfurt-on-Main.

In all this a changing balance of power between the profession and the Prussian state could be observed, reflected in the social composition of the relevant administrative elites. The directors of the medical department in the Prussian *Kultusministerium*, for exam-ple were legally trained officials, rather than doctors.[24] During the expansive period in medical education of the 1880s the department was headed by officials with family ties to medicine. Hermann Lucanus came from a family of pharmacists, while the Nasse family constituted a major medical dynasty of professors, hospital directors, and administrators, but this trend was not main-

Table *7.1* Directors of the medical department in the Prussian *Kultusministerium*:

Name	Dates	Period of office	Father's social origins
Düsberg	1793–1872	1841–9	
Lehnert	1808–71	1849–71	Government financial official
Sydow		1873–9	Master cabinet-maker
Gossler	1838–1902	1879–81	Official
Lucanus	1831–1908	1881–8	Pharmacist
Nasse	1831–1905	1888–90	University Professor of Medicine
Bartsch	1833–	1890–9	Local legal official
Förster	1847–	1899–1911	Estate owner

tained. Neither Bartsch nor Förster had any personal connection with medicine. Under the general administrators there were, indeed, medically qualified administrators (*Vortragende Räte*) in the ministry – twenty-nine such appointments were made between 1817 and 1906 – but their position continued to be strictly subordinate.

The position of the medical scientific advisory committee to the Ministry (*Wissenschaftliche Deputation für das Medizinalwesen*) was similarly subordinate to legally trained administrators. A parallel authority was the Imperial Health Council (*Reichsgesundheitsrat*), which since 1887 had enjoyed the status of the senior expert advisory authority in this field. These advisory bodies drew on the expertise of leading professors of medicine and clinicians.[25] Topics dealt with by the medical scientific advisory committee to the Prussian *Kultusministerium* included the pollution of rivers (1888), school doctors (1888 and 1913), midwifery (1890 and 1902), the relationship of tuberculosis and housing conditions (1895), sanatoria (1899), drinking water (1900), children's work (1902), epilepsy (1903), relations between specialists and general practice (1907), infant nutrition (1907), prostitution and sexually transmitted diseases (1907 and 1915), quackery (1908), medical officers' examinations (1909), smoke pollution (1910), tattoos (1911), the declining birth rate (1912), food adulteration (1912), school doctors (1913), poliomyelitis (1913), and abortion (1915).[26] These topics indicate how the profession was seeking authority over competing groups of healers, as well as extending its competence over environmental issues. In 1900 the committee was extended to include representatives of the Chambers of Doctors; from this point until 1907 the Prussian committee was under Friedrich Althoff as director of the Department of Higher Education.[27]

Althoff's reputation was that of a high-handed administrator, who undermined academic privileges. Yet he had also been a Professor of Law and enjoyed an ability to build up close personal ties to often unconventional academics, such as (for example) Paul Ehrlich (a medical researcher and the pioneer of immunology and of the salvarsan treatment for syphilis), who came from a Jewish commercial family. This suggests that Althoff's policies might be seen as an example of the way in which the Prussian state was creating opportunities for an expanding bourgeois intelligentsia. Althoff favoured the introduction of socially relevant medical specialisms such as hygiene, paediatrics, and dermatology, in keeping with a trend towards the appointment of specialized officials with qualifications in medicine, economics, and the natural sciences in government instead of the traditional legal qualifications. In all these ways, therefore, medical influence on the state administration was gradually increasing.

It was not until April 1911, however, that the medical department was transferred to the Prussian Ministry of the Interior. The rationale was to bring medicine into closer contact with policing authorities, allowing medical officials to acquire policing powers over such issues as containing sexually transmitted diseases and to extend their remit into the general sphere of population policy. The department was now headed by a series of medically qualified administrators (see Table 7.2).

The social backgrounds of these administrators, drawn from a variety of middle-class groups, is in marked contrast to that of the ministerial directors who were legally trained officials, and who

Table 7.2 Medically qualified directors of the Prussian Medical Department

Name	Birth/death	Years in office	Father's occupation
Kirchner	(1854–1925)	1911–19	Teacher/Pastor
Gottstein	(1857–1941)	1919–24	Merchant
Dietrich	(1860–1947)	1924–6	Pastor
Krohne	(1868–1928)	1926–8	Manufacturer
Schopohl	(1877–1963)	1929–33	Teacher
Frey	(1871–1952)	1933–7	Pastor

mostly came from families of legal officials.[28] It suggests that professional qualifications in public health provided opportunities for outsiders to rise in state service. They headed an expanding phalanx of medical officers who soon formed a highly vocal lobby.[29] The department dispensed state funds to the voluntary sector, while co-ordinating the work of voluntary agencies; and here it is relevant to note that doctors were also a powerful force in welfare organizations, such as in the societies for the prevention of alcoholism, tuberculosis, and sexually transmitted diseases.

III

In the course of the First World War, pressures grew for increased medical representation on the Prussian scientific advisory committee. The pharmaceutical industry was also represented from 1918. Further committees were established under the Weimar Republic, including one for population policy and racial hygiene that was set up in 1919. In 1921 these various groups of medical advisers were reorganized with the founding of the Prussian Health Committee, which can be seen as a step towards Virchow's old idea of a national health committee. This now amounted virtually to a parliament of professionals, able to initiate and advise on legislation and administrative procedures. Policy formulation and implementation involved, but did not depend on, parliamentary representatives, and the role of elected doctors in the Prussian Assembly in the shaping of medical legislation was also considerable.

Under the Weimar Republic, specialized officials enjoyed greater stability in office than other politically appointed civil servants did.[30] Attempts by experts in social hygiene, such as Grotjahn, to establish a unified ministry for public health, population policy, and social security were thwarted by decentralizing and democratizing tendencies. Administrators took leading roles in eugenic societies, and the state contributed substantially to welfare organizations, which provided career outlets for economically hard-pressed middle-class professionals.[31] The Prussian medical official Otto Krohne presided over the Prussian and German Racial Hygiene Societies, for example. Despite the enhanced role of the state in medical education and welfare, the majority of the medical profession resisted calls for the socialization of medicine. While there was a fear of Soviet-style 'polyclinics' and hospitals, the profession staunchly defended its private contractor status in the sickness insurance system. At the same time there was a expansion of state and local authority medical services, justified by theories of social hygiene. For the most part, social hygienists were content with clinics and propaganda measures targeted at mothers and infants, or those with 'racial poisons' such as venereal disease or mental illnesses. Although social hygiene, in its role as a form of state medicine, was generally limited to fragmentary institutional initiatives, there had been a marked growth of interaction between the medical profession and the state over the period from the 1880s to the 1920s.

This development could also be seen in relation to the efforts of the medical profession to acquire a monopoly in its field. Throughout the medical reform movement, control of so-called 'quacks' or *Kurpfuscher* had been a major concern.[32] Initially it had been hoped that scientific credentials would guarantee the superior position of the university-trained doctor in the competition for patients. This had been the rationale for Virchow's support for the designation of medicine as an occupation open to all under the Labour Statutes (*Gewerbeordnungen*) of 1869 and 1871. But, by the 1890s, monopolistic sentiments had increased, and the state was being urged to curb the right of all to practise medicine while upholding a competitive market within the profession based on the right of patients to the free choice of a doctor. Crusaders for the suppression of quackery argued that freedom of practice would cause the downfall of the medical profession as a solid middle-class group. The *Kultusministerium* pressurized the Ministry of Justice for a more effective use of the laws of criminal assault and financial deception, which constituted the most effective forms of redress against unqualified practitioners.[33] The Chambers of Doctors also became increasingly active in this area. In 1899, for example, the Chamber of Doctors for Brandenburg-Berlin offered a prize on the topic of the control of quacks by public education. It was won by Carl Alexander, who proceeded to organize a major medical association against quackery.

The Prussian medical department was highly responsive to professionalizing demands. Its grants to the Society for the Suppression of Quackery, founded by Alexander in 1904, were of the order of 500 marks a year.[34] By 1906 Chancellor von Bülow had become convinced of the need to pass a special law requiring the police registration of alternative practitioners and the banning of treatment for sexually transmitted diseases by hypnosis or telepathy. Bülow's successor Bethmann Hollweg was particularly supportive of the medical profession and its demands for the regulation of practice and of the availability of medicaments. But despite the support of professional organizations and of the Scientific Advisory Committee, a ban on quackery was regarded as non-feasible by the Prussian Ministry of Justice. It would infringe the constitutional principles of free trade and freedom of choice. Controls on the treatment of venereal diseases – particularly after the introduction of Ehrlich's salvarsan as a remedy for syphilis – also formed a major professional demand on the part of the doctors. In 1910 further demands for the suppression of birth control methods and abortions fuelled the anti-quackery agitation when a law on this matter was tabled in the Reichstag.[35] The Society for the Suppression of Quackery managed to survive the ravages of war and inflation and during the 1920s it was taken over by experts in social hygiene, and continued to flourish – a mark, perhaps, of its continuing lack of success in achieving its principal aim.[36]

Set against the rising tide of professional demands was the problem that state medical provision was administered by the federated states rather than the Reich, and that ministries within any one federated state differed in their policies. Thus, the Prussian Ministry of Justice opposed demands for a monopoly status of the medical profession, and the Finance Ministry insisted that the Medical Department should not engage in philanthropic or welfare measures. This laid obstacles in the way of the emergence of a professionalized welfare state in Imperial Germany, which was only partly overcome by the fact that the medical profession connived with state public health administrators to circumvent restrictions of professional power. Here the key role of Althoff should be noted, as he encouraged the movements against tuberculosis, venereal disease, and infant deaths from the 1890s. Ostensibly voluntary organizations were in fact acting in collusion with state officials, pressing for the extension of medical services. The aims of professionals and of a reforming group of state officials coincided.[37]

IV

In the years from 1870 to 1914, the number of doctors (including both physicians and surgeons) increased even more rapidly than the expanding population: in 1876 there were 13,728 doctors in

Germany, and by 1909 there were 30,558. In Britain, by comparison, there were 15,061 physicians and surgeons in 1876, and some 24,553 in 1911, which constituted a much lower percentage increase.[38] In German towns with a population of over 100,000, there was one doctor for 968 inhabitants.[39] The market for medical care, which grew particularly fast with the introduction of sickness insurance in 1883, provided new opportunities in the larger cities, where doctors tended to concentrate. But there was still an over-production of medical graduates during the 1880s. This resulted in acute conflicts with the sickness insurance funds, which the doctors argued were monopolizing the job market and forcing down their income. The medical profession grew more belligerent, and appropriated the socialist rhetoric of resistance to oppression, as well as the classic working-class tactic of the strike, for middle-class ends. Doctors demanded that the public should have the right of free choice of a doctor, rather than choosing from restricted lists of practitioners selected by the insurance organizations. They wished to maintain their freedom to treat without their professional competence being scrutinized by outside bodies. Thus one might see the medical profession as undergoing a type of bourgeois radicalization, creating a radical middle-class pressure group analogous to the German Navy League. Indeed, a number of doctors and medical scientists supported schemes for a national coalition of parties on the basis of science, such as was suggested in 1900 in the advertising of a 'Krupp Prize' for an essay on social evolution, or in the founding of the German Racial Hygiene Society in 1905. Doctors were also active in the Pan-German League and in the agitation for colonies.[40]

The growing militancy of the medical profession reflected a sense of financial insecurity which some historians have suggested was somewhat exaggerated. Claudia Huerkamp, for example, has evaluated doctors' protests of impoverishment by scrutinizing official income statistics, including those available for Hamburg in 1886 and Frankfurt-on-Main in 1893. She suggests that the complaints of a 'proletarianization' of the profession were absurd, given that only a small proportion earned less than the average earnings of the total population.[41] Huerkamp's approach remains constricted by the limitations of official or professional sources; no comprehensive micro-study has been made using the private papers of an individual doctor in order to assess personal income, nor has there been any more general assessments of income levels using insurance fees or advertisements for the sale of medical practices.[42] At the top end of the profession, professors of medicine not only enjoyed a substantial state income, but also earned student fees and income from private practice. University professors could also earn money by endorsing the value of patent cures, medical equipment, and nutritional products. Indeed, many medical practitioners tended to have a great variety of ancillary occupations, some conferring status, others providing additional income. Thus doctors accumulated posts as poor law physicians, police surgeons, and school medical officers. They earned money providing certificates for insurance and other purposes. Doctors participated in a great range of normal bourgeois economic activities such as speculative investments. Such varied sources of income mean that it is indeed difficult to accept the profession's complaints that it was economically hard-pressed. Just as there was no monolithic state authority in Germany, there was an immense diversity among the medical profession in its sources of income and areas of interest; but there can be little doubt that the vast majority of doctors were able to enjoy a thoroughly bourgeois lifestyle by the late nineteenth century.

Philanthropic activities also offered enhanced social status by allowing doctors – and their wives – to mix with the wealthy and the aristocratic. The medical profession in turn benefited from philanthropy through the creation of professional posts, for example, in privately funded children's hospitals and sanatoria. The concentration of population growth in major cities at the turn of the century prompted an increase in charitable activities aimed at the destitute, and money was raised for such urban amenities as public baths and children's holiday colonies. Large-scale national welfare organizations targeted not just the poor but the totality of the population. This can be seen in the organizations set up to combat alcoholism, tuberculosis, and sexually transmitted diseases. The middle class itself became an object of increasing medical concern. Medical campaigns were waged against alcohol consumption (much to the annoyance of commercial interests), and in favour of earlier marriage as a way of preventing the spread of infection and raising the birth rate of the educated elite.[43] It was pointed out that students had the highest rates of syphilis and gonorrhoea. Putting one's name to the subscription lists of philanthropic and social purity organizations was a means of converting wealth into respectability and status.

Spending and investment patterns among the medical profession revealed its essentially bourgeois character. Some doctors denounced as unhealthy the new tenements into which the working class was crowded while others invested in property and building enterprises. Indeed, some doctors' organizations recognized that their members drew their income not only from medical practice but also from personal investments.[44] Their economic interests thus ensured that doctors and medical scientists would generally share many of the opinions current among the bourgeoisie. The varying proportion of doctors to patients from place to place also shows that physicians tended to concentrate in the wealthier areas of large towns and cities. The country doctor had to serve a much larger and more widely spread population and thus earned less money. There were few incentives in opening up a practice in the countryside, although there were some subsidies for practitioners such as Robert Koch during the 1870s to settle in mixed German and Polish districts of Prussia.[45] Rural welfare came to attract a variety of campaigners by the turn of the century ranging from Heinrich Sohnrey, a disciple of the evangelical 'social liberal' Friedrich Naumann, to the ultra-conservative Agrarian League.[46] In the larger cities increased medical specialization also meant a larger number of doctors could be supported.

The suggestion that the medical care dispensed to the bourgeois and working class differed is based primarily on advice literature to doctors.[47] The literature on sexually transmitted diseases is of interest here. A shift emerges from patients being treated as virtual criminals (thus provoking a boycott of the main hospital in Berlin, the Charité, in 1893) towards the growing use of education as a means of preventive medicine, as well as the development of a scientific means of diagnosis for syphilis with the Wassermann test, and of a treatment (salvarsan therapy) around 1910. The Imperial Insurance Regulations of 1911 confirmed that sickness insurance funds would be responsible for payment of the costs of treating syphilis and gonorrhea. The Society for the Combating of Venereal Disease, founded in 1902, was dominated by doctors, while drawing support from both state medical authorities and police officials, as well as from radically controlled sickness insurance funds.[48] Medical opinion was capable of influencing official and public morality in urging the use of condoms as a barrier to infection.[49] The transition to more humane attitudes towards patients is exemplified by Alfred Blaschko, the leading expert on social methods of prevention, who advocated a relationship between, for example, military doctors and soldiers which was based on comradely sympathy.[50] Abortion shows a wide range of attitudes among doctors, some of whom were willing on commercial or humanitarian grounds to undertake abortions, while others sounded off with high-minded moral condemnations. The situation was further complicated by the fact that abortions were legal when there was a professional consensus that 'a severe threat to the health or life of the mother' existed. It is thus possible that doctors who publicly expressed a sense of outrage against abortions privately complied with patients' wishes. While some took an authoritarian line, adopting a concept of 'social medicine' based on heredity and eugenics, others were libertarian in outlook, emphasizing the importance of the personal choice of practitioner and therapy, and of health education, and stressing the economic benefits of healthy living.[51] But these were generally in a minority.

Thus doctors used the authority of science to segregate the unfit and socially deviant, and occasionally intruded into aristocratic and royal salons, prescribing diets and diagnosing insanity. Whether it acted in an authoritarian or a liberal way, the medical profession set new standards of behaviour, which pervaded many spheres of social life, including relations between members of the family, diet, housing, clothing, leisure, and sexuality. Health became a positive ideology moulding the behaviour of vast sectors of the population. It was for this reason that the profession came to assume a prominent role in broader processes of social change. Doctors were in an advantageous position when it came to interpreting the impact of mass urban and industrial society on the population, and, during the Weimar Republic, in translating political majorities into social policies. The medical profession began to play a role in state and party political organizations, with the growing professionalization of state administration and philanthropy. In the 1920s, as private sources of funding evaporated in the inflation, the Weimar welfare state sponsored increased professional opportunities in their stead. The expansion of hospitals, clinics, and other types of medical institution provided improved possibilities for the exercising of medical power.[52] Such developments prompt the question as to whether scientifically based medicine was intrinsically authoritarian, or whether Nazism with its eugenic and racial policies merely brought the authoritarian characteristics of medicine to the fore. The problem of whether Nazism allowed professional power to develop to extreme degrees, without public accountability or legal checks, raises the further issue of whether there was a special German path to professional modernity, differing from that taken in other western European countries.

Among the distinctive characteristics of professionalization in German medicine was the reliance on scientific qualifications (in marked contrast to the attitude towards science adopted by the Anglo-American medical profession). Scientific education was costly for the German state, which had to fund the building of teaching and research facilities. It was also expensive for those families whose offspring decided to embark upon a medical career. University studies lasted for several years and were not subsidized. They could provide an initiation into the rituals of academic elitism and foster the absorption of patriotic values.[53] Professors of medicine, an increasingly elitist group of men, exercised immense influence over generations of students and, through the societies and journals they founded or led, over the whole profession. Historians have largely failed, however, to probe the ideological content of the medical curriculum and the social significance of scientific innovations. There has been a generally uncritical acceptance of the positivistic literature written by historians of medicine, who have been keen to extol the genius of their academic colleagues.[54] The broad interests of provincial state authorities keen for reasons of prestige to boost the reputations of their own universities, and the narrower interests of individual researchers in competition for jobs and research funds, provided further reasons for the profession's reliance on the authority of academic credentials.

In Imperial Germany the bourgeoisie took much pride in the immense international prestige of German medical science. The German model of a scientifically educated medical profession was emulated throughout the world, from Meiji Japan to the United States of America. The Bismarckian system of sickness insurance and a variety of medical innovations such as public sanatoria for tuberculosis made a deep impression on foreign commentators in the late nineteenth and early twentieth century. At a time when Germany' was claiming a place in international power politics, German medical scientists such as Robert Koch and Rudolf Virchow – however critical some of them might have been of German militarism – supported Germany's attempt to assume world leadership in the spheres of science and medicine. Just as historians of

German imperialism have sought causes within the social tensions of a rapidly modernizing society, so too studies of medical innovations are now revealing the way in which these reflected the nationalist sentiments of the German bourgeoisie.

There was a great deal of patriotic enthusiasm in Germany for scientific discoveries made by German medical men. Underpinning the popular interest in biology, anthropology, and natural history were popular materialist currents which swayed liberal (and socialist) opinion. Scientific materialism was seen as challenging archaic clerical authority by medical men such as Rudolf Virchow and the Darwinian biologist Ernst Haeckel. The state itself attempted to encourage popular reverence for medical discoveries through journals and societies such as the Society for Popular Hygiene (*Gesellschaft für Volkshygiene*) founded with the support of Friedrich Althoff in 1900. More influential still than officially sponsored initiatives were cultural and political journals such as Maximilian Harden's famous magazine *Die Zukunft*, which gave extensive coverage to Social Darwinism and carried numerous accounts of medical and biological innovations. Here, for example, Virchow's liberal programme of sanitary reform, which saw education and civic reforms as the primary prophylactic against disease, was criticized by the bacteriologist and student of Robert Koch, Emil von Behring, who demanded centralized state medical research and centrally directed therapeutic institutions. Informed by opinion-makers such as these, a wide variety of bourgeois intellectuals looked to such disciplines as biology for naturalistic laws of development and for guidance on psychological and sexual questions.[55]

The enthusiasm for particular discoveries could be interrupted, however, by bouts of public disillusionment, as when Koch's announcement that tuberculin could cure consumption turned out to be premature. Campaigns against vivisection and human experiments, indeed, reached a high point during the 1890s.[56] There were currents of popular sentiment for alternative lifestyles (*Lebensreform*) and for nature therapy.[57] The concern with diet and with the benefits to health of a natural environment influenced the anti-tuberculosis campaign and the founding of sanatoria during the 1890s. Massive public health campaigns inculcated the virtues of clean and sober personal behaviour as a national duty. Here too, however, doctors took a prominent role in sanctifying the bourgeois values of hard work and cleanliness as positively healthy and a prophylactic against disease. In all these ways, therefore, however ambivalent popular attitudes to scientific discovery may have been, medical science underpinned medical authority, which was in turn frequently used to reinforce a wide range of characteristic bourgeois assumptions and beliefs, from patriotism and nationalism to orderliness and self-control.

V

Ute Frevert, in her study of illness as a political problem in nineteenth-century Germany, has recently reconstructed a public discourse on health which had its beginnings in the enlightened reforms of the late eighteenth century.[58] This public discourse reached a new pitch of intensity in Imperial Germany, which saw an intense effort to popularize medical discoveries, and went some way towards creating a scientifically literate bourgeoisie. There was public adulation for scientifically based medical achievements, such as Koch's discovery of the cause of cholera in 1884 or Behring's serum therapy against diphtheria during the 1890s.[59] Even the radical sexual reformers of the Weimar Republic such as Magnus Hirschfeld and Max Hodann based their demands for the liberalization of restrictions on homosexuality, contraception, and abortion on the tenets of evolutionary biology.[60]

Middle-class movements for the reform of alcohol abuse and prostitution, for the propagation of infant and child welfare, and for the prevention of tuberculosis, had ideas of positive health as their principal rationale. Welfare organizations put increasing weight on the argument that improved health was a precondition of a fit army and an expanding nation. Such organizations as the Reich League for the Prevention of Tuberculosis (founded in 1895), the German League for Combating Venereal Disease (founded in 1902) and the Empress Victoria House for the Combating of Infant Mortality (founded in 1909) explicitly included imperialism as a rationale for their activities.[61] The public support given by figures such as the liberal imperialist Friedrich Naumann to these institutions was based on the principle that social reform was a means of achieving a militarily strong and healthy nation. Naumann's support for child allowances, for the bourgeois feminist movement, and for improved housing such as that advocated by the German disciples of William Morris, indicate how positive health shaped a new type of bourgeois lifestyle. Garden cities, hygienic housing design and interior decoration, a new freedom in dress styles and fabrics, leisure activities such as cycling and walking, and the recognition of a more active economic and social participation in society on the part of women, all provide examples of this. Some aspects of this development were of course contentious. The politics of birth control were divided between radical ideas of self-help and eugenic rationales for medical supervision. Controversies over health were also at the heart of German feminism, as indicated by the demand for the removing of police controls on prostitution, and the heated discussions within the movement on abortion.[62] Whatever the precise nature of their demands, however, many political parties set themselves the goal of supporting a healthy family life. It was at this fundamental level of lifestyle that German medical reformers achieved a really lasting influence.

During the period between 1848 and 1933, therefore, professional and state power became interdependent. An increasingly vocal medical lobby was able to influence both public attitudes and state policies. There was an inherent conflict in German liberalism between the idea of a self-regulating medical profession, striving for monopoly status, and demands for the democratization of social institutions and the right of each citizen to quality and choice in health care. In Imperial Germany there was a change in public attitudes to hospitals, which had previously been regarded primarily as institutions for the poor: sanatoria, for example, became respectable as they took on the character of hotels. Sickness insurance and public health services became more comprehensive, offering services for a range of social strata. The Weimar Republic saw plans for comprehensive medical services, and hospitals and insurance schemes attracted a clientele from most social groups. The medical profession saw the Nazi takeover in the main as removing democratic checks to medical power. The exclusion of Jewish doctors from sickness insurance lists – and ultimately from all practice on those deemed non-Jews – improved the economic opportunities for the rest of the profession.[63] Eugenicists advocating sterilization opportunistically collaborated with Nazi leaders, and doctors' organizations perceived the economic advantages of dismissing Jewish colleagues. Yet, as the process of *Gleichschaltung* and the racializing of medicine were carried through, many doctors were to be disappointed by the interventionist character of the Nazi system.

Over the whole period, there can be no doubt that there was a rise in the status and a growth in the responsibilities of the medical profession. The penetration of government by an expert elite broke down traditions of administrative self-government. Under the Empire, there was a tendency for medicine to be administered by officials recruited from the ranks of the academically educated bourgeoisie. In Weimar Germany increased numbers of medically qualified officials meant that the profession increasingly arrogated such spheres of power to itself. In contrast to the ebb and flow of political parties and leaders, the institutional controls achieved by the doctors were the results of the long-term emergence of a cohesive profession which sought to influence both government and the population. The dynamics of this long-term process were complex, but it is clear that over the period in question, a silent revolution occurred, as medicine became the special province of the medical profession seeking to impose a uniformly hygienic bourgeois lifestyle onto the whole population.

NOTES

1 See, for example, H.J. Varain (ed.) *Interessenverbände in Deutschland* (Cologne, 1973).

2 See the classic study of G. Eley, *Reshaping the German Right. Radical Nationalism and Political Change after Bismarck* (New Haven and London, 1980).

3 Eley, *Reshaping*, 122–3.

4 R. Chickering, *We Men Who Feel Most German. A Cultural Study of the Pan-German League 1886–1914* (London, 1984), 102–21.

5 But, see S. Parlow, 'Über einige kolonialistische und annexionistische Aspekte bei deutschen Ärzten von 1884 bis zum Ende des 1. Weltkrieges', *Wissenschaftliche Zeitschrift der Universität Rostock*, mathematisch-naturwissenschaftliche Reihe, 15 (1964), 537–49.

6 Of the many works by F. Tennstedt, for example, *Vom Proleten zum Industriearbeiter* (Cologne, 1985).

7 For the political implications of professional ethics see E. Seidler, 'Der politische Standort des Arztes im Zweiten Kaiserreich', in G. Mann and R. Winau (eds), *Medizin, Naturwissenschaft, Technik und das Zweite Kaiserreich* (Göttingen, 1977), 87–101.

8 For the public discourse on health, see G. Göckenjan, *Kurieren und Staat machen. Gesundheit und Medizin in der bürgerlichen Welt* (Frankfurt-on-Main, 1985); A Labisch and R. Spree (eds), *Medizinische Deutungsmacht im sozialen Wandel* (Bonn, 1989). For medical societies, see E. Graf, *Das ärztliche Vereinswesen in Deutschland und der deutsche Ärztebund* (Leipzig, 1890). For medicine and liberal politics, see M. Hubenstorff, 'Sozialhygiene und industrielle Pathologie im späten Kaiserreich', in R. Müller *et al.* (eds), *Industrielle Pathologie in historischer Sicht* (Bremen,

1985), 22–107. Among the political parties only the health policies of the SPD and KPD have received detailed attention: A. Labisch, 'Die gesundheitspolitischen Vorstellungen der deutschen Sozialdemokratie von ihrer Gründung bis zur Parteispaltung (1863–1917)', *Archiv für Sozialgeschichte*, 16 (1976), 325–70; I. Winter, 'Geschichte der Gesundheitspolitik der KPD in der Weimarer Republik', *Zeitschrift für ärztliche Fortbildung*, 67 (1973), 455–72, 498–526.

 9 C. Huerkamp, 'Die preussisch-deutsche Ärzteschaft als Teil des Bildungsbürgertums', W. Conze and J. Kocka (eds), *Bildungsbürgertum im 19. Jahrhundert. Bildungssystem und Professionalisierung in internationalen Vergleichen* (Stuttgart, 1985), 358–87. C. Huerkamp and R. Spree, 'Arbeitsmarktstrategien der deutschen Ärzteschaft im späten 19. und frühen 20. Jahrhundert', in T. Pierenkemper and R. Tilly (eds), *Historische Arbeitsmarktforschung* (Göttingen, 1982).

10 A. Labisch, 'Doctors, workers and the scientific cosmology of the industrial world. The social construction of health and of the "Homo Hygienicus" ', *Journal of Contemporary History*, 20 (1985), 599–615.

11 P.J. Weindling, 'Hygienepolitik als sozialintegrative Strategie im späten Deutschen Kaiserreich', in A. Labisch and R. Spree (eds), *Medizinische Deutungsmacht im Sozialen Wandel des 19. und frühen 20. Jahrhunderts* (Bonn, 1989), 37–55.

12 G. Rosen, 'The fate of the concept of medical police 1780–1890', in Rosen (ed.), *From Medical Police to Social Medicine* (New York, 1974), 142–58.

13 P.J. Weindling, 'Theories of the cell state in Imperial Germany', in C. Webster (ed.), *Biology, Medicine and Society 1840–1900* (Cambridge, 1981), 99–155.

14 R. Virchow, 'Das Medicinal-Ministerium', *Die medicinische Reform*, 3 (21 July 1848) and 4 (28 July 1848); E. Ackerknecht, *Rudolf Virchow. Doctor, Statesman and Anthropologist* (Madison, 1953).

15 P.J. Weindling, 'Was social medicine revolutionary? Virchow on famine and typhus in 1848', *Bulletin of the Society of the Social History of Medicine*, 34 (1984), 13–18.

16 *Die medicinische Reform. Eine Wochenschrift, erschienen vom 10. Juli 1848 bis zum 29. Juni 1849* (Berlin, 1983).

17 Huerkamp, *Aufstieg*, 243.

18 M.S. Larson, *The Rise of Professionalism. A Sociological Analysis* (Berkeley, 1977), 20–1.

19 For local dimensions, see F. Tennstedt, 'Die Errichtung von Krankenkassen in deutschen Städten nach dem Gesetz betr. der Krankenversicherung der Arbeiter vom 15. Juni 1883', *Zeitschrift für Sozialreform*, 29 (1983), 297–338.

20 A. Labisch and F. Tennstedt, *Der Weg zum Gesetz über die Vereinheitlichung des Gesundheitswesens* (Düsseldorf, 1985), 44.

21 ZStA Merseburg, Rep. 92 Nachlass Althoff, Nr. 314, Bd 2: Abtrennung der Medizinalverwaltung.

22 Labisch and Tennstedt, *Der Weg*, 48.

23 *25 Jahre preussische Medizinalverwaltung seit Erlass des Kreisarztgesetzes, 1901 bis 1926* (Berlin 1927).

24 The source for Tables 7.1 and 7.2 is: R. Lüdicke, *Die Preussischen Kultusminister und ihre Beamten im ersten Jahrhundert des Ministeriums, 1817–1917* (Stuttgart and Berlin, 1918).
25 ZStA Merseburg, Rep. 76, VIII B, Nr. 30.
26 ZStA Merseburg, Rep. 76, VIII B, Nr. 38.
27 ZStA Merseburg, Rep. 92, Althoff AI, Nr. 263 Wissenschaftliche Deputation.
28 H. Kaelble, *Historical Research on Social Mobility* (London, 1981), 67 for the education sector.
29 ZStA Merseburg, Rep. 76, VIII B, Nr. 338 Medizinalbeamte.
30 W. Runge, *Politik und Beamte im Parteienstaat* (Stuttgart, 1968).
31 P.J. Weindling, 'Die Preussiche Medizinalverwaltung und die "Rassenhygiene" ', *Zeitschrift für Sozialreform*, 30 (1984), 675–87.
32 R. Spree, 'Kurpfuscherei-Bekämpfung und ihre sozialen Funktionen während des 19. und zu Beginn des 20. Jahrhunderts', in Labisch und Spree, *Medizinische Deutungsmacht*, 103–21.
33 GStA Dahlem Rep. 84a, Nr. 1240 Kurpfuscherei B1 20–22.
34 ZStA Merseburg, Rep. 76, VIII B, Nr. 1342. ZStA Potsdam, 15.01, Nr. 26248.
35 GStA Dahlem Rep. 84a Nr. 1241 Kurpfuscherei 1910–33.
36 ZStA Merseburg, Rep. 76, VIII B, Nr. 48 B1 362.
37 P.J. Weindling, *Health, Race and German Politics between National Unification and Nazism* (Cambridge, 1989).
38 H. Perkin, *The Rise of Professional Society in England since 1880* (London, 1984), 80.
39 Huerkamp, *Aufstieg*, 151.
40 For further documentation, see Weindling, *Health, Race and German Politics*.
41 Huerkamp, *Aufstieg*, 210–11.
42 P. J. Weindling, 'Medical practice in Imperial Germany. The case book of Alfred Grotjahn', *Bulletin of the History of Medicine*, 61 (1987), 391–410.
43 A. Blaschko, *20 Ratschläge für junge Männer* (Berlin n.d.).
44 Huerkamp, *Aufstieg*, 215.
45 B. Möller, *Robert Koch* (Hanover, 1950), 53–92.
46 H. Sohnrey, *Wegweiser für ländliche Wohlfahrts- und Heimatpflege* (Berlin, 1900).
47 C. Huerkamp, 'Ärzte und Patienten. Zum strukturellen Wandel der Arzt-Patient Beziehung vom ausgehenden 18. bis zum frühen 20. Jahrhundert', in Labisch and Spree (eds), *Medizinische Deutungsmacht*, 57–73.
48 For the activities of this society, see *Mitteilungen der Deutschen Gesellschaft zur Bekämpfung der Geschlechtskrankheiten*, 1 (1902) and following volumes.
49 A. Blaschko, *20 Ratschläge für junge Männer* (Berlin n.d.).
50 U. Linse, 'Über den Prozess der Syphilisation – Körper und Sexualität um 1900 aus ärztlicher Sicht', in A. Schuller and N. Heim (eds), *Vermessene Sexualität* (Berlin, Heidelberg, 1987), 163–85.
51 For abortion and contraceptive techniques, see J. Woycke, *Birth Control in Germany 1871–1933* (London, 1988).

52 Innovative hospital histories include: C. Pross and R. Winau *Nicht Misshandeln. Das Krankenhaus Moabit* (Berlin, 1984); *Totgeschwiegen 1933–1945. Die Geschichte der Karl Bonhoeffer-Nervenklinik* (Berlin, 1988).
53 K. Jarausch, *Students, Society and Politics in Imperial Germany* (Princeton, 1982).
54 Huerkamp, *Aufstieg*, 87–97.
55 A. Bebel, *Die Frau und der Sozialismus*, reprint of 1929 edn (Bonn-Bad Godesberg, 1977).
56 U. Tröhler and A.-H. Maehle, 'Anti-vivisection in nineteenth-century Germany and Switzerland', in N. Rupke (ed.), *Vivisection in Historical Perspective* (London, 1987) 149–87.
57 W.R. Krabbe, *Gesellschaftsveränderung durch Lebensreform* (Göttingen, 1974).
58 U. Frevert, *Krankheit als politisches Problem* (Göttingen, 1984).
59 R.J. Evans, *Death in Hamburg* (Oxford, 1987), 264–71.
60 M. Hodann, *A History of Modern Morals* (London, 1937).
61 See, for example, G. Lilienthal, 'Paediatrics and nationalism in Imperial Germany', *Bulletin of the Society for the Social History of Medicine*, 39 (1986), 64–70.
62 R.J. Evans, *The Feminist Movement in Germany 1894–1933* (Beverly Hills and London, 1976).
63 S. Leibfried and F. Tennstedt, *Berufsverbote und Sozialpolitik 1933* (Bremen, 1981); W.F. Kümmel, 'Die Ausschaltung rassisch und politisch missliebiger Ärzte', in F. Kudlien (ed.), *Ärzte im Nationalsozialismus* (Cologne, 1985), 56–81.

8

Localism and the German bourgeoisie: the 'Heimat' movement in the Rhenish Palatinate before 1914

Celia Applegate

I

The success of Edgar Reitz's film *Heimat* (1984), an eighteen-hour long evocation of insularity and change in a German village in this century, drew attention to a 'keyword' in the German language.[1] 'Heimat' takes its principal meaning from the idea of home and of one's own place, but its uses over the past 200 years reveal the extent to which a word – even so ordinary a one as 'home' – is accessible to political influences, to social and economic forces, to subtle shifts in cultural practices.[2] This puts it in the company of more famous 'historic' words like *Volk, Nation* and *Staat*, but unlike those terms, which identify the agents of historical movement, the term 'Heimat' seems to describe something unchanging.[3] Its historical flexibility thus has the appearance of a paradox. While preserving a feel of authenticity and time-honoured tradition – something of what the cultural critic Walter Benjamin called an aura – this German idea of home has participated in the movement of modern society away from the small communities it would seem to evoke.[4] This chapter will explore the aura of 'Heimat', in the hope of thereby illuminating one of the persistent features of middle-class German identity.

Words are not historical actors in the conventional sense, and only under extraordinary circumstances – one thinks immediately of the French Revolution – do they seem to take on a life of their own. The word 'Heimat' was never shouted from a revolutionary podium, but its quiet ubiquity in German everyday life by the end of the nineteenth century gives it a major claim on our attention.

The following pages do not present a catalogue of possible meanings of the word, nor do they do justice to literary treatments of the 'Heimat' theme. Rather they attempt an interpretation of what came to be called the *Heimatbewegung* – the 'Heimat' movement. In the context of this social phenomenon, this chapter examines a series of connections which, it argues, helped to define what it meant by 1914 to be bourgeois and German. The term 'Heimat' will illuminate two crucial elements in a historical identity: a sense of community (a *Zusammengehörigkeitsgefühl*, or 'feeling of belonging-togetherness') and a sense of place. The two joined in the celebration of locality within the German nation.

II

The 'Heimat' movement is usually taken to refer to a number of nostalgic cultural organizations founded in the 1890s.[5] The 'Heimat' art (*Heimatkunst*) movement of Adolf Bartels and Friedrich Lienhard purveyed a softened image of German rural life through the medium of popular literature. More than tinged with anti-Semitism, Bartels's 'Heimat' was a purely imaginary place, essentially a Germany purged of Berlin and the urban culture it represented.[6] Similarly, the League of 'Heimat' Protection (*Bund Heimatschutz*), founded by the eccentric racist Ernst Rudorff, sought to combat the corrupting influences of urban life on the German people. Heinrich Sohnrey's German Association for Rural Welfare and Cultivation of the 'Heimat' (*Deutscher Verein für ländliche Wohlfahrts- und Heimatpflege*) was ostensibly more rooted in real social problems. But Sohnrey, like Bartels and Rudorff, was a reactionary. The most he had to offer Germans under the rubric of 'Heimat' care was a return to paternalist structures of social and economic organization.

Given such a collection of romantics, reactionaries and anti-Semites, it is small wonder that historians have lumped all manifestations of enthusiasm for 'Heimat' among the cultural roots of National Socialism.[7] But beyond these particular organizations, there was a different 'Heimat' movement with much less obvious links to the eclectic ideology of Nazism. This other movement was not a national phenomenon at all, but a regional, even a local one. Its organizations rarely reached out beyond the borders of a particular province, except to draw in natives (*Landsmänner*) who had left their homeland. Its publications addressed a local audience, and its festivities drew together a local crowd. Each of these many movements aimed to shore up regional feelings of 'belonging-togetherness' against the encroaching sameness of mass society. Their enemy was not the modern city as such but the modern tendency to homogenize life, to rob it of its diversity. Their ideal was not rusticity but distinctiveness, or *Eigenart*.[8]

In common with its counterparts in other regions of Germany, the 'Heimat' movement of the Rhenish Palatinate reached its height in the decade and a half before the outbreak of the First World War.[9] The Palatinate seemed in many ways an unlikely region to inspire such outpourings of local patriotism. Its borders were of recent origin: before 1816, when they were fixed in a treaty between Austria and Bavaria, the land had been under French revolutionary and Napoleonic rule, and before that, it had consisted of no fewer than forty-four different political units. The most coherent sovereign ancestry it could claim was that of the Electors Palatine, but the nineteenth-century fragment called the Rhenish Palatinate did not include the great cultural and political centres of the Electors, Mannheim and Heidelberg, which after 1816 belonged to Baden. What the Palatinate had become by the nineteenth century was a small and marginal district within the Bavarian state, separated from it by Baden and the Rhine river, as well as by divergent political and cultural traditions.[10]

If history provided a shaky basis for regional identity, religion was not a much firmer one. In contrast to Catholic Bavaria, the Palatinate split almost evenly on confessional lines with the balance favouring the Protestants, a numerical advantage heightened by their greater wealth and superior social standing.[11] The Protestants of the Palatinate could look back on a tradition of fiercely defended independence, and the Catholics could derive satisfaction from their ties to Bavaria.[12] But the two together hardly added up to a strong regional identity. Indeed the seemingly haphazard distribution of Catholics and Protestants across the region itself reflected the chaotic political arrangements of the old regime, which provided such an ambiguous legacy to the nineteenth century. In addition to this crucial confessional split, folklorists of the late nineteenth century detected cultural splits between the descendants of the Alemannic tribes and those of the Franks, between the dwellers of the Rhine valley and those of the western hills, between – in one partly humorous account – the 'alluvial

Palatines', the 'rock-bed Palatines', the 'sandstone Palatines', and the 'coal Palatines'.[13]

A Palatine 'consciousness of community', of which the turn-of-the-century 'Heimat' movement was the mature expression, nevertheless grew steadily in the years following the establishment of the political unit.[14] In the most straightforward sense, it derived from the experience of political union and economic co-operation; it depended further on such lines of social communication as regional newspapers, educational and religious institutions, military cohorts, and bourgeois associations. But conflicts with the mother-state of Bavaria also conditioned the emergence of a distinctive Palatine identity. The twenty-year French passage through the region had left behind a revolutionized society in no mood for restoration. Legal equality, aristocratic and clerical eclipse, and occupational freedom had settled deeply into the political consciousness of the majority of the region's inhabitants. Not only was the Bavarian state far less enlightened, but perhaps more important, it stood for a small-state particularism that increasingly clashed with the romantic nationalism so widespread in the Palatinate. The Palatines felt, moreover, economically neglected and politically oppressed by Bavaria. Hence, the provincial middle class also espoused nationalist opinion in the expectation of improving their own situation. As in its northern neighbour, the Prussian Rhineland, regional grievances came together with nationalist aspirations in opposition to the rule of intermediate states like Prussia and Bavaria.[15]

What this meant, then, was that in the first half of the nineteenth century, the 'consciousness of community' in the Palatinate had radical political overtones. These were first expressed openly in 1832. The so-called Hambach Festival, the first large political demonstration of the liberal German bourgeoisie, brought together a miscellaneous collection of over 20,000 students, liberal activists, and local farmers and townspeople for two days of speeches in a ruined castle outside the Palatine wine centre of Neustadt-an-der-Haardt (since 1938, Neustadt-an-der-Weinstrasse). Amidst the calls for German unity, the denunciations of the French, and the proclamations of support for Polish nationalists there could also be heard specifically Palatine complaints against the Bavarian state. In 1832, local consciousness had emerged as political in form, radical in style, and national in objectives.[16] Widespread uprisings in the revolutionary years of 1848 and 1849 further demonstrated the extent to which bourgeois, local, and national interests could coalesce in a democratic politics of anti-Bavarianism.

The 1850s, however, saw the decline of localist radicalism, hurried along by repression and emigration. Politically, the Palatinate emerged by the end of the 1860s as one of the strongholds of a new kind of German liberalism, the National Liberalism that looked to Bismarck and Berlin for guidance and sought to fulfil bourgeois ambitions within the 'small Germany' of Prussia and its satellites. In the last decades of the nineteenth century, this variety of liberalism provided a touchstone for Palatine identity, particularly among the bourgeoisie. Taking their lead from the local notables (*Honoratioren*), who were National Liberal almost to a man, the Palatine middle classes ignored their radical, French-influenced heritage and found a source of local pride in the region's participation in a Prusso-German history.[17]

The ascendancy of National Liberalism also made possible the emergence after 1870 of an independent, if somewhat timid, local culture. The notables provided both patronage and purpose to groups that set about uncovering a specifically Palatine history, a Palatine folk-life, even a Palatine nature. What came by 1910 to be called a 'Heimat' movement had its origins, then, not in the region's once notorious radicalism but rather in an effort to defeat that radicalism and to reconstruct local distinctiveness along wholly different lines. The notables were aided in this effort, moreover, by the Bavarian state itself, which had long pursued a policy of cultural assimilation in the Palatinate. The celebration of the Bavarian royal house of Wittelsbach was the centrepiece of a mildly inventive cultivation of tradition. So too was the encouragement of a preservationist movement that depoliticized both local monuments (like the Hambach castle ruins) and local character traits (such as the tradition of radical discontent, which a new travel literature tended to identify as native feistiness or liveliness).[18]

Thus Bavarians and local notables joined together to make local identity compatible with Bavarian rule and to nudge it away from a politically grounded exceptionalism towards a culturally grounded integrationism. Moreover, the version of Palatine history, geography, and character that spread after 1870 emphasized the region's claim to full inclusion in German culture. The bourgeoisie, whose sense of local solidarity had always been closely tied to its nationalism, came to acknowledge a definition of its character which excluded even the possibility of French influences. Local identity, once a depository of political frustrations and ambitions, became instead the common (and German) ground of compromise and accommodation.

The social location of this reorientation of local 'consciousness of community' was the bourgeois voluntary association (*Verein*), particularly of the kind known as 'Heimat' associations. On the simplest level, a 'Heimat' association was any collection of people dedicated to the study and promotion of the things of the locality, but that such a social form – the voluntary association – with such a title – a 'Heimat' association – should have been the setting for the celebration of locality in the age of nationalism requires some further explanation. 'Heimat' was in fact a word with a noteworthy place in the development of a national German consciousness in the nineteenth century. A modern historical lexicon of the German language points to the revival of it, then neglected and impover-ished, in the late eighteenth century by writers influenced by the historicism of Herder. They valued the term's evocation of tranquillity, and they were attracted to the ancient sound of it.[19] It came to take on more significance than the simple translation of 'home' would indicate. To talk of one's 'Heimat' implied a belief in the influence of place on personality, of climate on custom, and of nature on national character. It was, moreover, a highly flexible term, capable of referring to places as specific as the village and as general as the nation. In the latter capacity, the term infused the abstraction of the nation with an aura of familiarity that immediately suggested its claim to one's deepest loyalty. The entry of 'Heimat' into the discourse of German nationalism also enabled early propagandists of the German nation to overcome the difficulty of identifying Germanness in a society whose mem-bers were divided between cosmopolitanism and provincialism. Certainly one could try to turn cosmopolitans into nationalists, but one also had to turn provincials into German patriots. The term 'Heimat' took part in a gradual re-imagining of the German locality that freed it from its isolation and made it part of the larger nation: in literary depictions of a provincial world that was at the same time quintessentially German, in new laws of domicile (*Heimatrecht*) that modernized the rights of citizenship in the old hometowns, in a new pedagogical method (*Heimatkunde*) that sought to teach universal truths through local places and familiar objects.[20]

Before 1870, the uses of the term 'Heimat' were nevertheless haphazard; only after the legal unification of Germany did 'Heimat' seem to become a 'keyword' in the vocabulary of the German bourgeoisie. The spread of a self-conscious 'love of Heimat' (*Heimatliebe*) after unification took place within the context of associational life, which, like the concept of 'Heimat', was an inheritance from the period of the German Enlightenment. In the years around the turn of the eighteenth century, associations had held together the potentially contradictory impulses of the German bourgeoisie towards individualism and fellowship, towards the public life and fraternal secrecy, towards the pursuit of equality, and the pursuit of cultivation or cultural excellence. Three-quarters of a century later, they preserved the outward structure of open fellowship and administrative rationality, but the society in which they functioned no longer made them, by contrast, into oases of free expression. Instead they had developed into a sphere of social activity complementary to that of the state – a sphere that was neither public nor private but something the historian Thomas Nipperdey has described as a 'private public sphere' (*private Öffentlichkeit*).[21]

However paradoxical the sound of it, this sphere was bursting with activity. Associations, which had certainly flourished in the 1840s, proliferated in the 1880s and 1890s, organizing people at every social level and for most conceivable purposes.[22] In the context of the late nineteenth-century big city, they provided small communities of common interest and mutual identification. Their larger social functions were thus both integrative and expressive: they made possible a reconciliation between social communion and individual liberation. This was particularly true of the 'Heimat' associations. For while the term 'Heimat' signalled the concern for community, the social forum of the association implied a voluntaristic, individual choice of community – a self-selected identity. The 'Heimat' associations were trying to make the enclosed solidarity of the old hometown compatible with the freedom of movement, vocation, and opinion that characterized their age. To put it another way, they tried to link the intimate ties of the locality with the abstract solidarity of a modern nation. They thus set about reviving local historical consciousness, local folk life, and local pride in a confident assertion of the diverse nature of German-ness.

In the Rhenish Palatinate, the first and most prestigious of the 'Heimat' associations was the Historical Association of the Palatin-ate (*Historischer Verein der Pfalz*), which was founded by Bavarian bureaucrats in 1827, dwindled into nothing in the 1850s, and was refounded in 1869, with great hopes, on the eve of unification.[23] Its chairman in 1869 was Sigmund von Pfeufer, the highest-ranking Bavarian official in the region and a Bismarckian liberal sympath-etic to local political opinion. Its first secretary was the folklorist Ludwig Schandein, a pupil and associate of W. H. Riehl, whose 1854 study *Die Pfälzer* (The Palatines) was a crucial document in the depoliticization of Palatine distinctiveness.[24] Its members were drawn from the economic and political elite of Palatine society, and its mission was to instil in the population at large an appreci-ation of the region's historical integrity and an understanding of its participation in the grander histories of Bavaria and Germany.[25] Taken together, leadership, membership, and mission reflected the intricacies of the synthesis that made up the German Empire of 1871. On the neutral ground of local patriotism, the new Historical Association sought to reconcile Bavarian particularism with German nationalism, Protestantism and Catholicism, and the inclusivity of the cultural nation with the exclusivity of a social elite, the local notables.

Not for long, however, was the Historical Association the only group devoted to the Palatine 'Heimat'. Between 1869 and 1914, well over 200 such associations were founded in the Palatinate: their collective presence was what contemporaries began to refer to as a 'Heimat' movement.[26] About half of these were local chap-ters of the premier 'Heimat' association, the Palatine Forest Associ-ation (*Pfälzerwald Verein*), which was founded in 1902 to promote outdoor recreation and to 'cultivate Heimat sensibilities'.[27] By the end of 1903 it had 2,000 members, well over half of whom were from the cities of Ludwigshafen and Mannheim, the latter of which lay across the Rhine in Baden but contained large numbers of Palatine 'emigrants', evidently eager to maintain their ties to their homeland. By 1914, the club claimed 17,000 members in over 130 chapters in the Palatinate, in Germany, and even in Paris, New York, and San Francisco.[28] The Forest Association was remarkable not only for its size but for the social diversity of its membership in an era in which social classes tended to separate off into their own associations. For although the majority of the club's members were petty-bourgeois – minor bureaucrats and office workers, small businessmen, primary schoolteachers – it also drew some of its leadership from the high-ranking bureaucrats, the local professoriate, and wealthy patrons of local culture, and some of its rank-and-file membership from the urban working class.[29]

Another category of 'Heimat' association included moderately large ones, organized at the regional level and composed of the more exalted representatives of the local educated middle class (*Bildungsbürgertum*); these included not only the Historical Association but its counterpart among naturalists (both amateur and professional), and a literary association with primarily localist interests. Of a similar sort, the Museum Association of the Palatinate, founded in 1899 to raise funds for a grand new building to house the regional artefacts, claimed a socially exclusive and highly educated membership, similar to that of its sister organization the Historical Association. In contrast to the 17,000 so-called 'Foresters' (*Wäldlern*, members of the Forest Association), the Museum Association even at its peak in 1903 never had many more than 1,500.[30]

The balance of the localist associations consisted of small groups with a single focus – a town's history, a ruined castle, a recently-revived folk festival, a local mountain. The beautification societies, of which there were by 1900 fifty-two in the region, were of this type.[31] Their members tended to be of modest middle-class backgrounds, tradesmen and unpretentious professional men, together with their wives and daughters. Unlike the members of the Forest Association, who came from the region's growing cities, these beautifiers were from small towns, often in economic decline and losing population to urban centres like Kaiserslautern and Ludwigshafen. The beautifiers were the classic 'small-town big men'; those of them who enjoyed the pleasures of social standing did so only in the modest circles of their own town or village.

One would also have to include as part of the 'Heimat' movement an outpouring of printed matter on the importance of being Palatine and a succession of festive occasions on which to demonstrate one's local pride. And although the 'Heimat' associations were responsible for much of the writing and celebrating, they neither held nor claimed exclusive rights to local identity. At the outset, they were responsible for filling the category of 'Palatine' with a rich cultural and geographic significance: they built its museums, they wrote its history, they constructed paths and monuments in its landscape, they extolled its beauty, they made jokes and wrote stories about its people, they revived its old customs and styles, they composed anthems in its honour. But as a mark of their success, the political, confessional, and cultural ambiguity of the Palatinate was by 1914 not an issue. Everyone talked at least as though local identity – local distinctiveness – was something not only real but obvious and important. They talked, in other words, as though the Palatinate was and always had been a 'Heimat'. To make local identity important to Germans in general was the chief accomplishment of the 'Heimat' enthusiasts; how they expressed its importance is what we shall next consider.

III

The 'Heimat' activities of the Palatine bourgeoisie represented an interpretation of German culture in at least three of its fundamental aspects. First, the 'Heimat' associations embodied a vision of national unity as the gathering together of diversity, especially local diversity. German national identity, which was the implicit subject of much contemplation on the Heimat, thus became an act of faith, an assertion of active belonging, rather than a collection of particular traits. No less intrinsic to the individual, the national identity of 'Heimat' imagining relied on certain emotional orientations – love of the land, endurance, piety, hard work. Second, the 'Heimat' associations performed a drama of reconciliation between the old and the new, tradition and modernity, countryside and city. They erased the conflicts between these things; they promoted a compromise that was more than rhetorical. Third, the 'Heimat' associations preached a message of social harmony among classes, confessions, political factions, and sectional interests.

The national mission of 'Heimat' associations was in many ways their first mission, out of which grew their efforts to counteract the destructive, divisive consequences of modernity. The founders of the Historical Association, for instance, understood their activities as essentially patriotic: the Association's work was a contribution to the building of national consciousness. Its goal would be to awaken a 'historical sensibility' in the Palatines through knowledge of the 'narrow Heimat': 'the love of the Fatherland', concluded one of its founders, 'is rooted in the love of Heimat'.[32]

'Heimat' history helped to shape the national myth by asserting the existence of a community of common fate (*Schicksalsgemeinschaft*), which gave the events of the Palatine past a larger German significance. The iniquities of the French were one key to such a historiography. According to it, the Palatinate carried the collective German memory of suffering and injustice in the ruins of its castles and the traces of lost villages. A recurrent figure in the literature of the past was Liselotte von der Pfalz, the unfortunate German princess whose life became a personification of the regional fate. Married off to the brother of Louis XIV of France in the seventeenth century, she lived all her adult years in what the local historians depicted as foreign exile, unable to return to the land she loved, unable to save it from French destruction in 1685, unwilling to relinquish her German ways and German identity for a more comfortable assimilation into the French court. Especially in the retrospection of late nineteenth-century local historians, Liselotte's exile seemed to prefigure the Palatinate's exile from Germany during the most recent French occupation of the Rhineland; Liselotte's resistance to French ways was also the Palatines', and her stubborn Germanness theirs too.

To serve as the passive vessel of suffering was, however, not the only role the Palatine historians claimed for their region in the 'community of fate'. The Palatinate had enjoyed glorious times under such medieval emperors as Frederick Barbarossa, as well as at various moments in the following centuries. The transformation of ruined castles into historically resonant tourist attractions, for instance, depended more on the self-congratulation than the self-pity of local cultivators of the past. Castles were a crucial element in the construction of a national historiography out of the scattered remnants of a fragmented past. Rather than allowing them to testify to the inglorious historical reality of petty principalities and feuding knights, local historians insisted on their patriotic import as monuments to (at their most extravagant) early German nationalists or (in a more subdued mood) brave and noble Germans. Castle preservation thus became a way to assert both local and national pride; moreover, as a feature of local activism it persisted well into the twentieth century. In the more troubled context of the 1920s, one local politician wrote that castle restoration would 'strengthen our Palatine population in their patriotism for Bavaria and for the German Reich'. A Bavarian bureaucrat agreed, noting that castles were 'intimately tied to [the Palatines'] feelings of Heimat'.[33] Even as late as the 1950s, local 'Heimat' enthusiasts linked castle preservation to the promotion of a usable and inspirational past: in 1951, a new 'Heimat' association was founded to maintain the old seat of the sixteenth-century knight Franz von Sickingen, who had stood for a 'tradition' of 'freedom and justice and living faith', which was 'particularly necessary and consoling to the distresses, dangers, and fears' of postwar Germans.[34]

But perhaps 'Heimat' history's most important contribution to bourgeois nationalism was not its recovery of particular historical figures and places but simply its naming and claiming of a past that was otherwise unremembered and hence without contemporary significance. The historical museums of which the culturally active bourgeoisie were so fond epitomized this contribution. At the Historical Museum of the Palatinate, constructed between 1898 and 1907 under the auspices of a Museum Commission dominated by local notables, members of the local bourgeoisie could experience with their own senses the reality of their region. The museum displayed what was in fact a random collection of objects left by the many peoples who had happened to pass through a patch of land now called the Palatinate. But the museum itself conveyed no sense of the accidental quality of that past. Instead it confidently named even a stray meteor as a 'Palatine' meteor. In so doing, it bestowed on the people of the present the dignity of a coherent historical tradition. Walking through the rooms of the museum, a local notable could feel his position of influence vindicated by the ancient stones, his modest accomplishments enhanced by the captured glories of his predecessors. Moreover, the making whole of a fragmented past must also have resonated for contemporaries with the politically parallel creation of national unity. Unity out of diversity, and diversity within the greater unity were the underlying messages of museum and nation alike.

In general, however, the 'Heimat' associations found a more profound connection to the German essence in folklife than in princely politics. Liselotte, princess though she had been, was celebrated not for her nobility but for her typically Palatine Germanness. The Historical Association, under the influence of such figures as W. H. Riehl, practised a broadly conceived cultural history that emphasized the development of local building and dress, local festivities and religious practices, and local folk customs.[35] 'Each object, even the smallest', wrote the Riehlian historian Christian Mehlis in 1877 in defence of the acquisition policies of the Historical Association, 'is a stone in a great building that mankind has alternately constructed and destroyed for thousands of years'.[36] Riehl and his followers believed that the land shaped and limited character, and hence those who lived closest to the land, in the 'pure natural life', were the clearest representatives of the Palatine type. Germanness, moreover, lay at this level of cultural experience: to discover the Palatine under the obscuring layers of modern life was also to discover Germany. For the middle-class men and women who flocked to the 'Heimat' associations after 1870, the study of folklore promised the recovery of a submerged national identity.

But local folklife proved elusive. Folklorists, amateur or professional, brought assumptions about peasant life to their study of the people that guaranteed disappointing results. In his 1854 study, Riehl had acknowledged the dearth of genuine folk survivals in the politically precocious Palatinate and had accused the French of driving out the ghosts and spirits of folk belief.[37] Certainly secularization and urbanization infinitely complicated the fieldwork of the kind of folklorists who felt at home only in the classic peasant village. But for those who cared less about accuracy than atmosphere, a little well-intentioned invention compensated for the shortcomings of the local peasantry. The Palatine Forest Association established a committee for the 'cultivation of the Heimat' (*Heimatpflege*) in 1907, which did its best to 'awaken the interests of the general public for Palatine beliefs, customs, and speech'.[38] A typical product of the committee's efforts was a manufactured midsummer festival, complete with pagan bonfires and brass bands, folk songs and the national anthem.[39] A similar venture into living folklore resulted in the creation of a 'traditional' Palatine dress, which was then vigorously promoted at all public Heimat occasions and made available to the consuming middle class through mail order catalogues.[40] It made sartorial sense only in opposition to contemporary fashions, but struck at least one observer as eminently 'patriotic' and 'most genteel', hence suitable even for the upper levels of society.[41] In its sanitized form it neatly distinguished its middle-class wearers from the truly labouring peasant while at the same time allowing them to express the folk identity that modern life had so attenuated.[42] Folk costume was the *Volk* without the dirt, and as such it enjoyed enduring popularity amongst the local bourgeoisie.

The self-conscious use of dialect accomplished similar ends for bourgeois 'Heimat' enthusiasts. Through poetry, stories, aphorisms, and even jokes, *Mundart* became the leading medium for the celebration of folk identity. To speak it, read it, or write it was to signal one's local or regional consciousness. In the words of one of its proponents, it was the 'most original expression of a people's character'.[43] It was also a fundamentally German form of expressiveness. The same spokesman suggested that the unification of Germany in 1871 ought to give Germans the self-confidence to 'abandon [their] naive prejudice in favour of foreign things', and, referring to the upper-class custom of speaking French, or at least of using French phrases, introduced by the Prussian King Frederick the Great, 'forever throw off the Frederician yoke of foreign words'.[44] In the context of a defence of dialect, this argument sounds distinctly anti-Prussian as well as anti-cosmopolitan. The solution to the German problem would be neither internationalism nor centralism but provincialism. The language of German identity was local and diverse.

Finally, the 'Heimat' associations recovered the region's mountains and forests for the cause of local patriotism and national identity. Under the sponsorship of the Forest Association, hiking became a spiritual as well as physical exercise. A love of nature was closely allied to the solemn joy of patriotism; the understanding of nature a key to the understanding of local and national character. Appreciative outdoorsmen dotted the landscape with monuments and plaques that made plain the infusion of nature with national feeling. One member of the Association even suggested that the region as a whole 'deserve[d] to be and must become Germany's National Park'.[45]

What this all amounted to – history, folklore, and nature appreciation alike – was the construction of a national identity with distinctly Palatine components. The 'Heimat' associations promoted a German nationalism of which the most important determinants were domestic: a nationalism defined by its constituent parts, not its opposing counterparts, by the regions within Germany, not the nations outside it. This domestic vision of German identity strikes us at first as odd, even anomalous, used as we are to the radical and aggressive nationalism of groups like the Pan-German League or the Navy League, with their emphasis on military strength, conquest, and colonization.[46] The two languages of German nationalism do not seem compatible, even though there were certainly individuals who subscribed to both.[47] External nationalism, with its fixation on national predominance, tended to endorse a highly centralized and powerful state, at odds with the decentralist, diversified, even potentially particularist nation-state of the domestic nationalists. From this perspective, the advocates of a Navy or a colonial empire were the radicals, determined to break down the provincialism of Germans. The 'Heimat' associations, in their belief in the distinctive nature of 'Heimat' as the key to both local and national identity were articulating, in new contexts, a more traditional conception of Germanness. They were people who felt not only 'most German', as the members of the Pan-German League claimed, but most Palatine as well.[48]

But the concern of localists for the preservation of local identity reveals more than their vision of national identity; it underlay their efforts to come to terms with modernity. The connecting thread in this discussion remains the concept of identity, for in their insistence on the importance of the Palatinate in the grand scheme of things, localists were asserting a sense of self against the forces that tended to its disintegration. Their celebration of the diversity of German culture and language responded directly to the infectious sameness of modern life, its lack of contour and contrast, its tendency towards conformity. The 'Heimat' movement adopted a familiar, even clichéd, set of contrasts by which to understand the world and changes in it – country against city, tradition against modernity, morality against corruption. But those simple oppositions worked through the 'Heimat' movement in far from simple ways. Localists drew upon a sometimes fanciful understanding of tradition and nature to counter the alienating, homogenizing tendencies of modern life. The outcome, or so one advocate hoped, would be 'a new deepening of life . . . an ennobling of our pleasures . . . a return to nature, without having to give up the sources and forms of our education'.[49]

The 'Heimat' movement's relations with nature were the clearest illustration of its slightly cock-eyed orientation to the times. The Forest Association, which became the 'Heimat' association *par excellence* in the region, organized itself around regular hikes in the countryside; from a purely instrumental perspective, its main accomplishment was to move literally thousands of people out of doors.[50] And yet it would be misleading to describe these orderly expeditions in terms of flight from the city. The trips were framed by a prompt and even enthusiastic arrival at the train station (and the purchase of a day return ticket, which obliged the nature-lover to come back to the city). The hikers' progress through nature was characterized by the greatest adherence to path markings and to posted prohibitions against littering, flower-plundering, and tree-carving. The day's schedule may have set aside time for a solitary day-dream or two, but for the most part, one hiked in formation, dined in company, and returned after it all to the isolation not of the romantic imagination but of the modern city-dweller. In a speech to the assembled members of the Forest Association, one of its founders attributed its success to a 'healthy reaction of the spirit against the victorious drive of intellect and technology' and, without noticing the irony, to its 'systematic and well-planned hikes' and 'goal-oriented organization'.[51] However much they may have perceived a contradiction between nature and technology, spirit and intellect, countryside and city, the *Verein* members did not live it. Instead they filled their leisure hours with pleasant diversions from their working concerns but managed not to let either undermine their pleasure in both.

It would nevertheless be perverse to deny the destructive tendencies of technology and industry in regard to the 'nature' that the Palatines so treasured. Wolfgang Schivelbusch has described how the spread of the railways threatened to destroy local particularity by annihilating what he calls 'in-between' space – the once-natural separation of places from one another which was an essential condition of diversity of condition and culture.[52] Those who joined the turn-of-the-century 'Heimat' associations certainly must have felt that pressure, and their efforts to combine the way of the railway with the way of the mountain path sought in part to make virtue out of what must have seemed inexorable necessity. But the success of their counteractions against the destructive side of technology remains an open question. The 'Heimat' movement did preserve the particularity of the Palatinate and did insist that appreciation of the land was an essential part of regional identity, but the cost of this victory was tourism.[53] So sensitive to the confrontation between tradition and modernity, the middle-class members of the associations were often oblivious to the confrontation between authenticity and consumability. In an era increasingly dominated by the ideal of consumption, they enthusiastically endorsed a version of local identity that could be sold in the marketplace, as the case of the invented folk costume illustrated.

It is perhaps the most telling irony of the 'Heimat' movement that it undertook an invention of tradition and a denaturing of nature in the name of a quest for the deepest wellsprings of identity.

Fearing the loss of identity and place symbolized by the modern city yet longing for a new harmony between their nature and their working lives, the participants in the 'Heimat' movement showed at least a tendency to succumb to consumer society's more subtle attacks on local authenticity. By 1960, say, the common currency of local culture had been almost irredeemably debased by the sometimes sentimental, sometimes sinister marketing of folksiness in the Nazi and postwar years. Yet, at its height in the late nineteenth and early twentieth century, the 'Heimat' movement still expressed a genuinely felt sense of identity with the land, its people, and its history, the sincerity of which cannot be doubted by anyone who has spent time with the writings of local activists. The 'Heimat' associations, through their cultivation of local and national belonging, tried to nourish the consciousness of a community that would transcend differences of class and confession. The other side, then, of the effort to preserve distinctiveness was an effort to sustain commonality. In the 'Heimat' movement, the local bourgeoisie staked its increasingly tenuous claim to represent the general interests if not of mankind then at least of the Palatinate.

History as the common heritage, folklore as the common life, and the natural world as the common good all contributed to the construction of a collective identity. The 'Heimat' movement appropriated nature, for example, as an essentially public environment that would be shared by all local people. The forest, wrote a leader of the Forest Association, was a commonly held treasure of the people.[54] Its preservation was everyone's duty; its enjoyment was everyone's right. Similarly, the search for folksiness – and the invention of it where it did not actually exist – was at a less literal level the search for a common culture available to all. Palatine folklore became the repository of a widespread longing, not for the by-gone past as such, nor for the life of the farmer, peasant, or medieval artisan, but for the unalienated, undivided life. In 1909, one local activist hoped that a new collection of Palatine folksongs might bring 'social reconciliation' among classes, 'for within [the songbook] lies something that is or should be common to us all, the emotional life (*Gemütsleben*) of a people'.[55]

The Forest Association came closest of all to realizing this rhetorical stance. Membership in it required neither education, social position, nor wealth, but simply the desire to do one's walking in the company of others. The great majority of its members were petty-bourgeois, often from the new class of urban white-collar workers, but the Association also made some effort to form chapters among workers in large industries like the chemical giant BASF.[56] Confessional differences were not reproduced in the Association; its founders had included a Catholic priest, a Protestant railway man, and a Jewish businessman. Within its social space, moreover, status distinctions received no explicit expression. A studied informality marked its forms of address, from the *Wald-Heil!* in salutation to the frequent nicknames which its members used for each other. To be sure, the leadership of the Association included a fair sprinkling of local notables, but in group photos one sees them in the same hiking gear as everyone else, in a more than symbolic accommodation to the common purpose of the organization.

More important, perhaps, than these internal measures of inclusivity, the Forest Association engaged in a deliberate popularization of the forms of local identity. Its hiking expeditions, far from reinforcing the 'clubbiness' of members, became occasions for recruitment and general proselytizing on the virtues of outdoor exercise. By 1906, it was holding, each time in a different town, an annual General Excursion. More like folk festivals than club conventions, these drew whole communities into the celebration of local and regional identity. They also provided the settings for the dissemination of revived folk culture, from poetry and song to dress and dance, and even to food and drink. In addition, the Association sponsored countless 'evenings' at which dialect poetry would be read or regional customs discussed. Representativeness, not excellence, was the watchword on these occasions: one poet would be praised for her 'generous love for the beautiful Palatine homeland, its land, people, and soul'; another for possessing the 'ready mother wit' of the Palatines; and yet another, most extravagantly, for being 'the embodied soul of our landscape'.[57]

Not to neglect any source of the regional spirit, the Association promoted a popular version of Palatine history too. In 1914, it sponsored a massive re-enactment of the Hambach Festival of 1832. Democratic politics were left out of this history; national sentiment received top billing, along with local sentiment, which had allegedly been a motivating force for the original participants as well.[58] Historical parades, with their fanciful costuming and their carnivalesque props and floats, were another favourite extravaganza. The historical parade was, according to the cultural historian Hermann Glaser, the 'most characteristic and popular product of the new historical consciousness of the nineteenth century'. It was, he argues, a dramatization of the bourgeoisie's claim to participation in the historical tradition of the German state.[59] These parades strung together the most colourful and, again, representative figures from previous centuries in an affirmation of the unity of the region's past and present alike. Kings appeared with their queens, huntsmen with huntresses, and guildsmen with village maidens, all as one big happy Palatine family, colourful and various, but also as respectable and essentially bourgeois as the people underneath the costumes.[60]

The popularization of 'Palatineness' went beyond the activities of the Forest Association. Small historical societies and journals, proliferating folk song societies and folk costume associations, popular history textbooks, novels and poetry collections all attested to the diffusion of representations of the locality among the provincial middle class. The effort to make local culture into an essentially popular good was not entirely unproblematic, of course. Disputes between the elitist Historical Association and inventors of purportedly local traditions arose over more than one issue in the pre-war decades. The construction of a new regional museum under the aegis of the local notables and the Bavarian government also reflected a decidedly high interpretation of culture at odds with the populism of the Forest Association.[61] But the newer members of the 'Heimat' movement, with their emphasis on the social inclusivity of local identity, were more in line with the political temper of the day than their critics among the notables. Public life underwent considerable democratization at the turn of the century. In light of such changes in the society that surrounded it, what the popular movement accomplished was to rescue German localism from the collapsing edifice of the localist political culture of the notables. Instead of sinking into insignificance along with political particularism and notable politics, local 'consciousness of community' flourished as never before in the form of a domestic nationalism, a folkloric consumerism, and a regionalist populism.

IV

Finally, we must ask ourselves why the German bourgeoisie displayed such passionate concern for locality. To see this concern as simply a form of nostalgic longing for times that are past and places that are changed would be to reduce the phenomenon to its most clichéd aspect. The vitality of the 'Heimat' idea among the nineteenth-century bourgeoisie suggests that it must have been connected to something more fundamental in bourgeois life than indulgent retrospection, something more akin to identity or self-consciousness.[62] In *The Fall of Public Man*, Richard Sennett proposed a definition of identity as the 'meeting point between who a person wants to be and what the world allows him to be', the 'place in a landscape formed by the intersection of circumstance and desire'.[63] In the case of many bourgeois Germans, the 'Heimat' was this 'place'. The degree of invention that one finds in celebrations of the past, the customs and the natural beauty of 'Heimat' makes sense only from such a perspective. Invention was the way one brought about the 'intersection of circumstance and desire'; invention made one's place of residence into an embodiment of one's identity.

That localism, however refurbished, could have formed the substance of bourgeois identity raises the familiar question of whether the German bourgeoisie was fit to take a leading role in the making of a modern nation. The historian Immanuel Wallerstein has recently pointed out that no bourgeoisie (not even the English) lived up to its reputation as a ruthlessly individualistic, profit-maximizing, modernizing, centralizing class.[64] Modernization itself, historians now recognize, was at the very least uneven in its transformation of society. We ought also then to adjust our expectations of the bourgeoisie as the 'modernizing' class. Persistent local attachments, which represented at least a partial resistance to the powerful modern state, may be more characteristic of bourgeois people everywhere than we have been used to allow.

The German bourgeoisie's preoccupation with the idea of home was also far from a non-starter in the modernizing race. What made their 'Heimat' so good a reflection of bourgeois identity was the inclusion of more than the locality in its meaning, as we have seen. It expressed a sense of place that could be made as general as the nation or as specific as the neighbourhood and a sense of belonging that was equally flexible. As a result, it illuminates a crucial stage in the development of modern societies, that of bourgeois identification with the nation. Ever since the celebrated observation of the Abbé Sieyès during the French Revolution, the affinity between the middle ranks of society and the forward-marching nation-state has been axiomatic.[65] The consolidation of the nation-state and the domination of the bourgeoisie are generally depicted as the twin pillars of nineteenth-century modernization. Nor is their historical closeness a question of mere coincidence in time. The bourgeoisie was the class that saw itself as a General Estate of modern men, and the nation – in which citizenship supposedly transcended divisions of class, place, and religion – was the political grouping appropriate to such presumed universality. Moreover, for a class like the bourgeoisie, which seems to have drawn so much of its identity from essentially negative sources – envy of those above, fear of those below, and suspicion of all forms of 'otherness' – the nation represented something positive, a source of commonality and inclusion that was as crucial to identity as difference and exclusion.

But if the nation provided a kind of myth-identity for the bourgeoisie, that identity had clearly to take forms in a nation-less Germany other than those taken in England or France, where the middle classes and the nation rose to prominence together by the end of the eighteenth century. In Germany, the bourgeoisie could not with any confidence claim to represent the nation as a whole, particularly after the failure of the liberal bourgeoisie to create a German nation during the revolutionary upheavals of 1848–9. In even more basic terms, the German bourgeoisie – residents of regional capitals, readers of regional journals, participants in regional political and economic circles – were ill-suited to represent the existence of a single German nation. But the collective identity summed up in the term 'Heimat' was a solution to the dilemma of nationlessness. This particular sort of 'home' accommodated the hope for a German nation, and later, the reality of that nation. It belonged, moreover, to a German patriotic tradition that saw the nation as a collection of diverse regional cultures, and consequently was pledged to the preservation of that diversity.

The quintessential citizen of this nation as 'Heimat' was the German burgher, attentive to his hometown interests but enthusiastic about Germany, nationalist if not national. Through 'Heimat', the middle class turned inward for its identity and discovered the imaginary national community not in opposition to other nations but in an expansive sense of self. The nation became a larger, more inclusive version of communities that were known from actual experience – the family, the town, the province. The ideology of 'Heimat' in the nineteenth century made that great chain of linked loyalties and affections explicit. It accommodated geographical and social mobility yet still provided a basis for familiarity and identity.

In this sense the cultivation of 'Heimat' loyalties worked for the bourgeoisie. Within its capacious borders there was room for both the actual locality and the abstract nation. It is, moreover, no anomaly that a full-blown 'Heimat' movement should have emerged only after the unification of Germany. As the historian Miroslav Hroch has persuasively argued, the nation was not 'derivative of nationalism'; rather, nationalism, the particular forms of which Hroch does not investigate, derived from the 'social reality of historical origin' that constituted the nation.[66] The conception of the nation that 'Heimat' represented – its 'nationalism' – can, for instance, be partially explained by the abruptness and the high-handedness of Bismarck's unifying work. The 'Heimat' movement allowed the provincial middle classes mentally to catch up with the nation-state.[67] Through it the idea of national belonging settled into the civic rites of the locality. Moreover, devotion to the 'Heimat', although encouraged in the schools, never became a matter for state intervention in the years before the First World War. It was a genuine product of middle-class culture, at a level of cultural production and reproduction – the association – where voluntarism characterized both form and content.

The nature of the 'Heimat' movement does not then sustain the image of an emasculated German bourgeoisie, thoughtlessly accepting its values and aspirations from above.[68] Nor does it suggest that the bourgeoisie was motivated in cultural undertakings as in political ones by fear and loathing of the classes below. Certainly the 'Heimat' movement made few inroads among the working classes before the war, but the reasons for this are many, not least among them being the limited appeal of provincialism for the Social Democratic movement. For while the 'Heimat' enthusiasts may not have done as much as they could have to include the working classes, they were more negligent and ignorant than hostile. They did not need to exclude the working classes in order to make sense of their enterprise in the way that, for instance, they clearly needed to exclude the French.

CELIA APPLEGATE

What this all implies, then, is that the localism of 'Heimat,' as a source of identity for the German bourgeoisie, was remarkably self-contained. It developed within the bourgeoisie in the matrix of associational life, and it drew its emotional strength, as well as its subject matter, from the circumstances of bourgeois life. The 'Heimat' phenomenon thus shows the limitations of thinking about bourgeois identity as a kind of perpetual uncertainty, pulled this way and that by powerful external forces and fears. Neither an overarching state nor a threatening 'other' had much to do with shaping turn-of-the-century localism. To be sure, its proponents opposed it to the alienness of the modern city, to the foreignness of the French, to the rootlessness of modern class society, to anonymity of any sort. Nevertheless, they asserted something positive against all this – the community, even if imagined, of a culturally infused and meaningful landscape. Such a confident sense of place rendered familiar and friendly even the hostile environments that industrial society had 'unbuilt'.[69] Thus even the industrial city of Ludwigshafen with its workers and its factories became in the idiom of 'Heimat' a worthy participant in the collective life of the Palatinate.

To emphasize the essentially positive contribution of the 'Heimat' movement to the construction of a collective identity brings us back to the question, raised in passing at the beginning of this chapter, of the origins of National Socialism. Even if we dismiss the blatantly anti-Semitic and reactionary organizations of Bartels, Sohnrey, and their like as being unrepresentative of provincial 'Heimat' movements, there still seems to be only a fine line separating the localists' love of place from the xenophobia, illiberalism, and outright racism of the Nazi movement. For the historian Mack Walker, Wilhelmine Germans puzzled over a communal 'conundrum': how to reconcile their locality with their nationality; how to preserve community and yet have a nation. After 1870, he suggested in *German Home Towns*, the hometown itself, the real tissue of community relations, disappeared. Only the idea of the hometown lingered on, romantically in the minds of intellectuals, and vulgarly – as an aversion to 'modern' politics – in the minds of a mass of middle-class Germans. Intellectuals and disgruntled former hometownsmen dwelt, however, in politically non-intersecting worlds, and managed to make common cause only under the banner of National Socialism. By then, the force of their embittering and immobilizing nostalgia was enough,

Walker concludes, to make the false national community, or *Volksgemeinschaft*, of National Socialism the only solution to the hometown conundrum for many Germans.[70]

Although this analysis of the problem is a powerful one, we still need to know how hometown values were transmitted across the intervening decades as well as how they spoke to the economic and political grievances that contributed to the eventual triumph of the Nazi party. These are issues beyond the scope of the present chapter.[71] But there is another perspective on 'Heimat' values that deserves a final mention. In our understandable attention to the patterns of culture that supported political negativism of the Nazi variety, we have overlooked the affinities between localist culture and a politics of democratic potential. The 'Heimat' movement shared a set of assumptions about communal life with theorists of self-government like Otto von Gierke, who emphasized the import-ance of intermediate collectivities between an otherwise identity-less individual and the state. The organic liberalism of Gierke located the principle of freedom in diversity and associationalism, not in unity and statism.[72]

Moreover, Gierke's student, Hugo Preuss, pursued the demo-cratic and decentralist implications of his work that Gierke himself ignored. His original draft of the Weimar constitution (which did not survive even the first round of constitutional consultations with the German states) sought to solve the communal conundrum by establishing a balance of medium-sized states within a unitary German state, with important administrative and self-governing powers devolving on local authorities, like municipalities, com-munes, and districts.[73] The territorial issues, which quickly became tedious to outside observers of constitution-making in Germany, were important to someone like Preuss because they contained the key to the troubled question of German citizenship.[74] For Preuss, the answer to the question of how and where to produce good democratic citizens of a new Germany was simple: in the locality, at home.[75] The citizen of the Weimar constitution's articles on 'the fundamental rights and duties of Germans' was the embedded, determined, limited social being of the old hometown. Participation in the local community remained essential to the maintenance of Weimar's national community, and the pursuit of a common good, not individual happiness, was the citizen's primary assignment. Preuss's German state would be built upwards, from the self-regulating communes. Such an order would provide a 'political education for an unpoliticized people'; it would bring about the 'awakening of the common spirit through the participation of the people in public life, the ruled in the ruling'; it would serve as 'a universal national-pedagogical system of education, bringing the participating citizens out of the narrow circle of their communal experience, step by step into the great matter of national politics'.[76]

It should thus come as no surprise to find the local culture of 'Heimat' revived in the Weimar Republic to service the building of citizens. New adult education associations, 'Heimat courses' and the pre-war collection of 'Heimat' associations pursued the study of local history and even folk life and nature, claiming that this would stimulate public life in general by encouraging a local consciousness of community. That the 'Heimat' associations failed so signally to nourish a republican consensus should not necessarily lead us to conclude that they were part of the opposition. Their failure reflected a more general collapse of public life; their inability to sustain the local community reflected an economic victimization and political marginalization of local life that went far beyond their powers to heal. The communal conundrum, which had found no resolution in the blocked politics of Wilhelmine or Weimar Germany, simply disappeared in Nazi Germany, not solved but denied or forgotten.

The sense of place that the 'Heimat' movement had set out to preserve proved in the end tragically indifferent to issues of political rule. But if the deliberate provincialism of the movement never fulfilled its democratic promise, neither did it participate easily in the radical reaction against democracy, liberalism, and modern social life. Its tone was always conservative, not radical; it was interested in going to the roots of things only in order to secure them, not tear them up. The bourgeois men and women who espoused 'Heimat thinking' at the turn of the century, and later, believed that its evocation of an increasingly intangible community expressed what they imagined themselves to be. We may rebuke them for having failed 'to identify with their own form of existence' – for having failed, in other words, to be fully bourgeois – only if we assume a fully bourgeois existence to have been rootless, brutal, and alone.[77] They themselves saw it as constituted in a tradition, in a community and in a local place.

NOTES

1 The concept of 'keywords' originated with Raymond Williams, *Culture and Society, 1780–1950* (New York, 1966), and *Keywords*, rev. edn (Oxford, 1983).

2 A popular account of the 'idea' of home is Witold Rybczynski's *Home: A Short History of an Idea* (New York, 1986).

3 Whether for this reason or not, 'Heimat' does not appear in the *Geschichtliche Grundbegriffe: historischs Lexikon zur politisch-sozialen Sprache in Deutschland*, Otto Brunner, Werner Conze, and Reinhart Koselleck (eds) (Stuttgart, 1972); it has, however, been the subject of some literary-critical attention, including the recent collection, edited by H.W. Seliger, *Der Begriff 'Heimat' in der deutschen Gegenwartsliteratur* (Munich, 1987).

4 Wolfgang Schivelbusch discusses the loss of Benjamin's aura in places in *The Railway Journey: The Industrialization of Time and Space in the 19th Century* (Berkeley, 1986), 38–42.

5 See, for instance, Klaus Bergmann, *Agrarromantik und Grossstadtfeindschaft* (Meisenheim am Glan, 1970); Leonore Dieck, 'Die Literargeschichtliche Stellung der Heimatkunst', phil. diss. (Munich, 1938); Martin Greiner, 'Heimatkunst', *Reallexicon der deutschen Literaturgeschichte*, 1 (Berlin, 1958); Ina-Maria Greverus, *Der Territoriale Mensch: Ein literaturanthropologische Versuch zum Heimat-Phänomen* (Frankfurt-on-Main, 1972); and Erika Jenny, 'Die Heimatkunstbewegung', phil. diss. (Basel, 1934).

6 Greiner, 'Heimatkunst', 629–31.

7 See Bergmann, *Agrarromantik;* and Hermann Glaser, *The Cultural Roots of National Socialism* [*Spiesser-Ideologie*] (London, 1978). A more recent interpretation of the nineteenth-century 'Heimat' movement as essentially reactionary is Anton Kaes, *From Hitler to Heimat: The Return of History as Film* (Cambridge, Mass., 1989), 163–6.

8 According to the charter of the *Bund Heimatschutz*, which was actually little more than a loose association of many independent local clubs, its goal was to preserve 'the German "Heimat" in its naturally and historically developed diversity'. Cited in 'Der Deutsche Bund Heimatschutz und seine Landesvereine', *Der Deutsche Heimatschutz* (Munich, 1930), 187.

9 For a more detailed account of this 'Heimat' movement, in the context of a century of localist activism, see my forthcoming study *A Nation of Provincials: The German Idea of Heimat* (Berkeley, 1990); the 'Heimat' writers of Schleswig-Holstein are the subject of Jörn Christiansen, *'Die Heimat': Analyse einer regionalen Zeitschrift und ihres Umfeldes* (Neumünster, 1980).

10 An excellent summary of the Palatinate's relations with Bavaria is Kurt Baumann, 'Probleme der pfälzischen Geschichte im 19. Jahrhundert', *Mitteilungen des Historischen Vereins der Pfalz*, 51 (1953); see also Heiner Haan, *Hauptstaat-Nebenstaat* (Koblenz, 1977).

11 The exact figures in 1825 were 56.9 per cent Protestants, 39.8 per cent Catholics, and 3.4 per cent Mennonites, Anabaptists, and Jews;

by 1961, the percentages had shifted only slightly, with 2 per cent more Catholics. See Willi Alter, 'Die Bevölkerung der Pfalz', *Pfalzatlas*, Textband (Speyer, 1963–81), 180, 190. The scattered distribution of the confessions is shown in Wolfgang Eger, 'Die Konfessionsverteilung im Jahre 1825', *Pfalzatlas*, 245–51.

12 On the militant Protestant tradition, see Claus-Peter Clasen, *The Palatinate in European History, 1559–1660* (Oxford, 1963).

13 W.H. Riehl, *Die Pfälzer: Ein Rheinisches Volksbild*, reprint edn (Neustadt/Weinstrasse, 1973), 50.

14 See especially Rudolf Schreiber, 'Grundlagen der Entstehung eines Gemeinschaftsbewusstseins der Pfälzer im 19. Jahrhundert', in *Die Raumbeziehungen der Pfalz in Geschichte und Gegenwart* (Bonn, 1954), 35–8.

15 On French influences in the region, see Karl-Georg Faber, 'Die Rheinischen Institutionen', *Hambacher Gespräche 1962* (Wiesbaden, 1964), pp. 20–40; and Elizabeth Fehrenbach, 'Die Einführung des französischen Rechts in der Pfalz und in Baden', in F. L. Wagner (ed.), *Strukturwandel im pfälzischen Raum vom Ancien Regime bis zum Vormärz* (Speyer, 1982). See also Max Spindler, 'Die Pfalz in ihrem Verhältnis zum bayerischen Staat in der ersten Hälfte des 19. Jahrhunderts', *Festgabe für seine königliche Hoheit Kronprinz Rupprecht von Bayern* (Munich, 1953).

16 On Palatine radicalism, see Wolfgang Schieder, 'Der rheinpfälzische Liberalismus von 1832 als politische Protestbewegung', in *Vom Staat des Ancien Regime zum Modernen Parteienstaat: Festschrift für Theodor Schieder* (Munich, 1978), 169–95; and Veit Valentin, *Das Hambacher Nationalfest* (Berlin, 1932).

17 On National Liberalism in the region, see Ernst Otto Bräunche, *Parteien und Reichstagswahlen in der Rheinpfalz* (Speyer, 1982); and Theodor Schieder, *Die kleindeutsche Partei in Bayern in den Kämpfen um die nationale Einheit, 1863–1871* (Munich, 1936).

18 A seemingly innocuous example of this effort to reorient local consciousness was the renaming of the district in 1837 from 'Rheinkreis' to 'Pfalz', the latter having a less rationalist and bureaucratic sound to it, as well as evoking the prestige of the Electors Palatine. The romantic and anti-revolutionary imaginings of Friedrich Blaul in *Träume und Schäume vom Rhein*, first published in 1838, were also typical of this trend. On the broader subject of Bavarian state-building, see Werner K. Blessing, *Staat und Kirche in der Gesellschaft* (Göttingen, 1982).

19 Friedrich Mauer and Friedrich Stroh, *Deutsche Wortgeschichte*, II (Berlin 1959), 294; on its ancient roots, Jacob and Wilhelm Grimm, *Deutsches Wörterbuch*, 4; 2 (Leipzig, 1877), 864–6.

20 This notion of local 're-imagining' owes much to Benedict Anderson's *Imagined Communities: Reflections on the Origin and Spread of Nationalism* (New York, 1983); on 'Heimat' literature, see Norbert Mecklenburg, *Erzählte Provinz* (Königstein/Ts, 1986), Dieck, 'Heimatkunst', and Jenny, 'Die Heimatkunstbewegung'; on 'Heimat' law, Mack Walker, *German Home Towns* (Ithaca, N.Y., 1971), 296, and Carl von Rotteck and Carl Welcker, *Staatslexikon*, 7 (Altona, 1839), 665; on 'Heimat'

pedagogy, Kurt Reh, 'Christian Grünewald', in Carl Heuper (ed.), *Die Pfalz auf der Suche nach sich selbst* (Landau/Pfalz, 1983), 41.

21 Thomas Nipperdey, 'Verein als soziale Struktur in Deutschland im späten 18. und frühen 19. Jahrhundert', in *Gesellschaft, Kultur, Theorie* (Göttingen, 1976), 195 and *passim.*; Otto Dann, 'Die Anfänge politischer Vereinsbildung in Deutschland', in U. Engelhardt, V. Sellin, and H. Stuke (eds), *Soziale Bewegung und politische Verfassung* (Stuttgart, 1976); Werner Conze, 'Der Verein als Lebensform des 19. Jahrhunderts', *Die Innere Mission*, 50 (1960), 226–34.

22 On the 'Verein frenzy' of the 1840s, see Nipperdey, 'Verein', 174; on the later period, Herbert Freudenthal, *Vereine im Hamburg: Ein Beitrag zur Geschichte und Volkskunde der Gesellligkeit* (Hamburg, 1968); and H.-Jorg Siewert, 'Der Verein: Zur lokalpolitischen und sozialen Funktion des Vereins in der Gemeinde', in Hans-George Wehling (ed.), *Dorfpolitik* (Opladen, 1978), 68–9.

23 Albert Becker, *Hundert Jahre Pfälzer Geschichtsforschung, 1827–1927* (Speyer, 1927).

24 He made clear the political significance of the study in his 'Gutachten über die Pfälzer', a memorandum internal to the Bavarian government; reprinted in Antonie Hornig, 'Wilhelm Heinrich Riehl und König Max II von Bayern', phil. diss. (Munich, 1938), 115–21.

25 In its first year the membership of the Association broke down roughly as follows: out of 586, high government officials and mayors accounted for 89 members or 15 per cent; minor bureaucrats, 115 or 19 per cent; teachers of all levels, 80 or 14 per cent; businessmen, including bankers, factory-owners and estate-owners, 105 or 18 per cent; clerics, both Catholic and Protestant, 95 or 16 per cent; and professionals, including doctors, lawyers, and engineers, 77 or 13 per cent. In addition, the Association included 16 men of independent means and 9 military officers. Only 1 woman belonged to it – a landowner. From the 'Verzeichnis der Mitglieder', *Mitglieder des Historischen Vereins der Pfalz*, 1 (1870), 27–41. On the objectives of the Association, 'Einladung zur Betheiligung an einem historischen Vereine der Pfalz', January 1869, Pfälzische Landesbibliothek Speyer.

26 See, for instance, 'Der Pfälzer Abend zu Frankenthal am 14. März 1908', *Pfälzisches Museum*, 25 (1908), 84; Hermann Schreibmüller, *Bayern und Pfalz* (Kaiserslautern, 1916), 62; and Albert Becker's brief memoir, 'Erinnerungen aus der Geschichte der Heimatbewegung', *Der Pfälzer in Berlin* (1940/1), 18–19.

27 Heinrich Grass, '25 Jahre Pfälzerwald Verein: Gründungsgeschichte', *Wanderbuch des Pfälzerwald Vereins* (1928), 40.

28 'Zusammenschluss der auswärtigen Pfälzer', *Des Pfälzers Heimat in Wort und Bild*, 1 (1910), 33.

29 See the lists of new members and committee reports in the association's organ *Pfälzerwald*, 1902–14; and Heinrich Grass, '25 Jahre Pfälzerwaldverein', *Wanderbuch* (1928); also '25 Jahre Pfälzerwaldverein', *Pfälzisches Museum – Pfälzische Heimatkunde*, 45/24 (1928), 49.

30 Yearly reports, *Mitteilungen des Historischen Vereins der Pfalz*, 26 (1903), 112.

31 Christian Mehlis, *Touristische Erfahrungen im Rheinlande* (Mannheim, 1900), 23.

32 Ludwig Schandein, 'Zur Einführung von Ortschroniken', *Mitteilungen des Historischen Vereins der Pfalz*, 1 (1870), 44–5.

33 Korn (Bavarian Ministry of Education and Culture) to Trendelenburg (Prussian Ministry of Education and Culture), 13 Apr. 1921, Bayerische Hauptstaatsarchiv, Munich, MK 15557; Oberforstrat Keiper to Landesamt für Denkmalpflege, 14 Feb. 1920, Pfälzisches Landesarchiv, Speyer, T1, no. 11.

34 Walter Plümacher, 'Die Ebernburg, Geschichte und Bedeutung', *Pfälzer Heimat*, 2 (1951), 111–14.

35 Typical of this tendency was Ludwig Schandein's ongoing investigation of Pfälzer *Weistümer;* see, for instance, his reports in the Verein's *Mitteilungen* in 1874 and 1878.

36 C. Mehlis, 'Die praehistorische Funde der Pfalz', *Mitteilungen des Historischen Vereins der Pfalz*, 6 (1877), x.

37 Riehl, *Die Pfälzer*, 51.

38 Report of the steering committee meeting of 10 June 1906, *Pfälzerwald*, 7 (15 June 1906), 126.

39 Account in *Pfälzerwald*, 10 (15 July 1909), 109.

40 F. Gundelwein, 'Pfälzer Volkstrachten', *Pfälzerwald*, 11 (15 Jan. 1910), 6–7.

41 Georg Berthold, 'Zur Einweihung des historischen Museums der Pfalz', *Pfälzerwald*, 11, Special edn II (Spring 1910), p. 70.

42 Compare the arguments about a revived traditional dress in Palle Ove Christiansen, 'Peasant adaptation to bourgeois culture? Class formation and cultural redefinition in the Danish countryside', *Ethnologia Scandinavica* (1978), 128; and Theo Gantner, 'Brauchtumsvorführungen in Festumzügen des 19. Jahrhunderts', in Günter Wiegelmann (ed.), *Kultureller Wandel im 19. Jahrhundert* (Göttingen, 1973), 35.

43 Emil Haas, 'Die Pflege der Mundart und die Mundartabende in der Pfalz', Part 3 in a series of articles by that name, *Pfälzisches Museum*, 22 (1905), 97.

44 Haas, 'Mundart', part 1, *Pfälzisches Museum*, 22 (1905), 5.

45 *Pfälzerwald*, 7 (15 May 1906), 94.

46 It seems also plausible, though tangential to the subject at hand, that an internalist nationalism was far more typical of the patriotic German working classes than the nationalism of a Pan-German. Such at least would seem to be the implications of Vernon Lidtke's depiction of socialist sociability in *The Alternative Culture* (New York, 1986), especially p. 92. On radical nationalism see Geoff Eley, 'Nationalist pressure groups in Germany', in Paul Kennedy and Anthony Nicholls (eds), *Nationalist and Racialist Movements in Britain and Germany Before 1914* (London, 1981).

47 For instance, Georg Berthold, a leader of the Museum Association and a participant in 'Heimat' activities, was also a leader of the local branch of the Colonial Society, and was instrumental in bringing a national meeting of the group to Speyer.

48 On the Pan-German League, see Roger Chickering, *We Men Who Feel*

Most German (Boston, 1984). An intriguing aspect of this issue, which might repay further investigation and theorizing, is the much greater participation of women in Heimat associations than in radical nationalist groups.

49 Albert Becker, *Ziele und Aufgaben eines Heimatmuseums* (Kaiserslautern, 1914), 21.

50 The Ludwigshafen chapter alone sent 1,800 people to the Pfälzerwald in 1906, and 2,000 in 1907; in other large chapters, the average number of participants *per month* was about 150; in the smaller chapters, about 50. See periodic reports on *Wanderungen* in the Verein organ *Pfälzerwald*.

51 Report of the *Hauptversammlung, Pfälzerwald*, 8 (15 Feb. 1907), 10.

52 Schivelbusch, *The Railway Journey*, 38–42.

53 In 1911, for instance, the Pfälzerwald Verein represented the region at a giant International Travel and Tourism Exhibition in Berlin; the Verein also co-operated with commercial travel agents in establishing a tourist bureau for the entire Pfalz. An extensive historical analysis of one region's deliberate decision to promote tourism rather than industrial growth is contained in the collection edited by Gert Zang, *Provinzialisierung einer Region: Regionale Unterentwicklung und liberale Politik in der Stadt und im Kreis Konstanz im 19. Jahrhundert* (Frankfurt-on-Main, 1978).

54 *Wanderbuch des Pfälzerwald Vereins* (1928), 125.

55 Review of Georg Heeger's *Pfälzische Volkslieder, Pfälzisches Museum*, 26 (1909), 28–9.

56 On the membership of the Association, including evidence of working-class participation, see note 29 above. Vernon Lidtke has pointed out that Social Democratic workers tended to have their own Social Democratic hiking organizations (*The Alternative Culture*, 64–5).

57 Paul Münch on Lina Sommer's 'E Pfälzer Blumenstraissel', *Pfälzisches Museum*, 30 (1913), appendix 3; obituary of Paul Gelbert, *Pfälzishes Museum – Pfälzische Heimatkunde*, 47/26 (1930), 98; Peter Luginsland, 'Im Memoriam Paul Münch', *Pfalz und Pfälzer*, 2 (1951), 1.

58 See Kurt Baumann, 'Hambacher Erinnerungsfeiern: Das Hambacher Fest und die politische Tradition der Pfalz', *Pfälzer Heimat*, 2 (1951), 54.

59 Hermann Glaser, *Die Kultur der Wilhelminischen Zeit* (Frankfurt-on-Main, 1984), 215–16.

60 A full account, complete with photographs, of a historical parade in Kaiserslautern is found in *Pfälzerwald*, 11 (1 July 1910), 109–12.

61 'Our collections are somewhat aristocratic', wrote one local notable, 'and require therefore an administration that will not be reduced to vulgarity through slap-dash measures and secret votes'. See Georg Berthold, 'Auszug aus der Denkschrift betreffend Historisches Museum der Pfalz, 1912', 14 Mar. 1912, Pfälzisches Landesarchiv, Speyer, T1, Nr. 4.

62 Norbert Mecklenburg, in his study of regionalism in the German novel, uses the term *Innerlichkeitskultur* to similar purpose when he argues that the nineteenth-century 'antithesis between province and

metropolis' should not be seen as a 'reflex' of the social structure but as an expression of a 'German-bourgeois *Innerlichkeitskultur*'. See his *Erzählte Provinz*, 74.

63 Richard Sennett, *The Fall of Public Man* (New York, 1976), 107.

64 Wallerstein, 'The Bourgeois(ie) as concept and reality', *New Left Review*, 167 (Jan/Feb 1988), 91.

65 He made that identification in his pamphlet *What is the Third Estate?*, published in January of 1789.

66 Miroslav Hroch, *Social Preconditions of National Revival in Europe*, trans. Ben Fowkes (Cambridge, 1985), 3.

67 Theodor Schieder once suggested that the German nation of 1871 posed problems not just of power and constitution but of 'consciousness' as well. See *Das deutsche Kaiserreich von 1871 als Nationalstaat* (Cologne, 1961), 9.

68 For more extensive reflections on the thesis of bourgeois feudalization, see David Blackbourn and Geoff Eley, *The Peculiarities of German History* (Oxford, 1984), 223–37.

69 On *Abbau* or 'unbuilding', see Lewis Mumford, *The City in History* (New York, 1961), 450–2.

70 Walker, *German Home Towns*, 425–9.

71 Rudy Koshar's careful study of associational life and the rise of Nazism, *Social Life, Local Politics, and Nazism* (Chapel Hill, 1986), fills in the gap to some extent. His understanding of the 'apoliticism' of local Germans has certain affinities with Walker's more pithy analysis. For Koshar, suspicion of national party politics accompanied the cultivation of a local, associational politics, hostile to Social Democracy and to Weimar republicanism and eventually welcoming to National Socialism. He shows, moreover, how the economic abandonment of localities by the Weimar government conditioned the localist turn to Nazism, with its promises of economic empowerment and its easy set of scapegoats.

72 On Gierke, see Ernst-Wolfgang Böckenförde, *Die deutsche Verfassungsgeschichtliche Forschung im 19. Jahrhundert* (Berlin, 1961), 147–76; Heinrich Heffter, *Die deutsche Selbstverwaltung im 19. Jahrhundert: Geschichte der Ideen und Institutionen* (Stuttgart, 1950), 731–59; and Antony Black, *Guilds and Civil Society* in *European Political Thought* (London,1984), 210–16.

73 Heffter, *Selbstverwaltung*, 769–73; Gerhard Schulz, *Zwischen Demokratie und Diktatur: Verfassungspolitik und Reichsreform in der Weimarer Republik* (Berlin, 1963), 9–17; and Arnold Brecht, *Federalism and Regionalism in Germany: The Division of Prussia* (Oxford, 1945).

74 René Brunet, in *The New German Constitution*, trans. Joseph Gollomb (New York, 1921), wrote that the territorial issue 'has not progressed one step in three generations; one studies it but does nothing about it, for there is no reality to it' (p. 71).

75 Schulz, *Zwischen Demokratie und Diktatur*, 12; Heffter, *Selbstverwaltung*, 766–7.

76 Cited in Schulz, *Zwischen Demokratie und Diktatur*, 128.

77 Bergmann, *Agrarromantik*, 82.

9

Bourgeois honour: middle-class duellists in Germany from the late eighteenth to the early twentieth century

Ute Frevert

I

'Honour', wrote a middle-class commentator in 1889, 'is a finely-meshed web, fitting closely round the individual human being.' It was, he went on, a 'covering' which no-one could 'shake off'. It was invisible and insubstantial, yet highly sensitive and vulnerable. It attached itself to a man, but not so much to his physical body as to his 'self-imagined personality'. It was this aspect of the individual which was susceptible to 'so-called insults to his honour'.[1] Some two decades later, the sociologist Max Weber also attempted a definition of 'honour'. In contrast to the strong emphasis on the individual evident in the definition of 1889, Weber's concept emphasized 'honour' as a collective phenomenon. Each social rank or status group had its own particular notion of honour, which found its expression in a 'specifically structured way of life', which it was assumed would be followed by all those who belonged to the group. In Weber's view, 'the collective honour of a status group' made 'demands of every individual member' but also 'unified all the members of the group and bound them together in spirit'.[2]

At about the same time, Weber's colleague Georg Simmel was also concerning himself with the concept of honour. He succeeded in building a bridge between these two contradictory definitions. Simmel agreed with Weber in defining honour initially as a means of socializing people into a status group or social rank, as a means by which those special collectivities which were situated in the area between large classes of people and the individual could sustain their own existence. Honour, he said, served to maintain the inner cohesion of such collectivities or status groups, and to mark them off against other groups of differing social rank. But Simmel went on to argue that the particular function of honour lay in its capacity to infuse the individual with the maintenance of his honour as his own, most heartfelt, deepest and totally personal self-interest. The individual who cultivated the maintenance of his own honour may have regarded this as essential to his own well-being, but it was in reality his social duty, whose disguise as a purely personal expression of honour ensured that it would be carried out with all the more zeal.[3]

Reflections such as these, by well-known figures in Wilhelmine society, were far more than mere academic exercises in sociological categorization. They were rooted in the life of the German middle class of the period. From the perspective of the late twentieth century it is almost impossible to realize the prominence of the role played by notions of honour in the consciousness and behaviour of middle-class men in late nineteenth and early twentieth-century Germany. The 'external functions' of honour may be clear enough to the sociologically informed observer of the 1990s, but what Simmel described as the 'internal means' by which these functions were realized appears strange and obscure. It is only possible to uncover it if we turn to the particular circumstances in which the honour of the individual directly determined social experience and action. Such was the case with the duel, the classic form of conflict in which the honour of the participants was the sole issue at stake. Two 'honourable men' stood opposite each other armed with sabres, rapiers, or pistols and fought to vindicate their 'honour'. At stake was invariably a 'point of honour', a verbal or physical insult which had caused the recipient to challenge the person who had offended him in this way.

Duelling and its cultural preliminaries thus lend themselves particularly well to a closer investigation of social honour, its contents, forms, and functions. For they constituted the classic means by which honour was expressed, the ultimate proof of an honourable character and way of life. At the same time, duelling allows us to observe in detail the peculiar ambivalence of honour in its oscillation between what Simmel called 'social duty' and what he termed 'individual well-being'. This double character of the duel offers us the rare chance to place under the historical microscope both the collective behaviour of bourgeois duellists (the 'function' of duelling) and their personal understanding of the institution and their individual grounds for participating in it (the 'meaning' of duelling). Thus a perspective 'from outside', directed towards the institutional pressures operating in favour of a duel, can cast a new and perhaps more sharply focused light on the social formation of the bourgeoisie, through the observation of internal structures and external boundaries under the aspect of a collectively binding value system. A perspective 'from inside', directed towards subjective interpretations, by contrast, can render the self-image of middle-class men more transparent and reveal their behavioural horizons more clearly, and thus illuminate an important area of the bourgeois mentality.

II

At first sight, of course, it may appear that the honour of the bourgeoisie had nothing to do with the honour of the duellist. Indeed, the duel has generally been regarded as an aristocratic phenomenon, as the expression of a specifically noble concept of honour, which reached its apogee in the eighteenth century. In the bourgeois nineteenth century, by contrast, it is usually argued that duelling experienced what was little more than an artificially stimulated Indian summer. The fact that middle-class men also fought duels has been interpreted as a sign of their susceptibility to 'atavistic "neo-feudalism" ' and as a 'deviation from the natural bent of bourgeois thinking and behaviour'.[4]

But this interpretation rests on a picture of the bourgeoisie that is both idealized and one-dimensional. It does justice neither to the image which they presented to society nor to the cultural understanding they had of themselves. When historians contrast the 'aristocratic' notion of honour, expressed in the duel, with 'bourgeois' notions of honour, they usually present the latter as generalized, democratic, and opposed to the maintenance of status barriers, as a form of citizen's honour which released the individual from all ties of social hierarchy. Civil honour, it is usually argued, only involved the obligations of the individual citizen at one extreme and the collectivity of all citizens at the other, without any intermediate groups in between. Such an interpretation can call upon contemporary witnesses who defined bourgeois honour unequivocally as the general honour of the citizens and denied 'specialized concepts of honour' any right to exist at all. Middle-class parliamentarians argued in this way in the 1840s, for example, distancing themselves from 'old notions of honour, such as have existed in society up to now', and, in view of the 'aspirations of the day', strongly contesting the validity of a 'particular, exclusive idea of honour'.[5] In March 1849 a committee of the Saxon Diet charged with revising the Articles of War produced a report which sharply criticized 'the aristocratic, status-bound understanding of honour held by the officers' and rejected it as a social anachronism: 'This pernicious caste spirit may well have been a melancholy necessity for the feudal state', declared the report, but '. . . it is completely inappropriate for the civil state, for the state in which education and political consciousness hold sway.' In civil society, it concluded, there was instead 'only one single, general human or citizens' honour, and the propagation of any exceptional or status-bound honour is an offence against morality'.[6]

Two years previously, even before the 1848 revolution, which formed the background to the Saxon deputies' plea for a general, egalitarian concept of honour encompassing the whole of the citizenry, the Rhenish merchant and parliamentarian Gustav Mevissen raised a similar protest in the Prussian Diet against attempts 'to substitute a special, status-oriented idea of honour for a general, civil idea of honour'. The latter, he argued, attached to all men, in the form of public respect, as long as they did not contravene the moral or legal precepts of society. Only if a criminal court had certified an offence against generally accepted standards of law-abiding behaviour could someone be regarded as dishonourable, as having lost his good standing or reputation. Although Mevissen refused to accept the validity of other criteria, he was obliged to admit, however, that 'a sharp distinction exists even in the present century between the concept of status-bound honour and the concept of the general honour of the citizen'. And he concluded resignedly that it was 'absolutely impossible to solve the conflict between caste honour and civil honour in our state'.[7]

'Citizen's honour' in the understanding of these liberal deputies corresponded to the political meaning of the idea of the 'citizen' as it had developed in the late eighteenth century.[8] According to this view, every law-abiding man was a 'citizen' and as such possessed the honour, and the rights emanating from it, which entitled him to active participation in the business of politics. Such a concept naturally cut across the existing status-linked division of society, according to which rights and duties were distributed unevenly among the various ranks or 'Estates', and with them honour too, in variable degrees. Prussian legislation of the period clearly reflected this principle. Thus the General Legal Code of 1794, in punishing insults to the honour of noblemen more harshly than insults offered to the 'people of common status', ascribed more importance to the honour of the aristocracy than to that of peasants and artisans. In this model, 'persons of the middle class' were located between noblemen, officers, and high state officials on the one hand, and 'common townspeople' or peasants on the other. Their honour had, as it were, an intermediate value. If insults were exchanged between people of differing status, the Law Code provided for differing degrees and forms of punishment. Insults offered 'downwards' usually attracted a fine, insults directed 'upwards' always resulted in a term of imprisonment.[9]

It was not until December 1848 that these status differences in the 'punishment of insults' were abolished, by royal decree.[10] Justifiable doubt remained, however, as to whether this meant that Mevissen's idea of the general honour of the citizen had come any nearer to being realized. The law may not have recognized such status differences any longer, but their disappearance from social reality was another matter. Indeed it quickly became apparent that the bourgeoisie enjoyed its own special status honour and was not prepared to abandon it in the interests of equal honour for all men. For, in his dual role as 'citizen' and 'bourgeois', the middle-class man not only represented the universal principles of an anti-feudal society composed of individuals but also conceived of himself as belonging to a social class which distinguished itself sharply from others further down the social scale in terms of property and lifestyle. Even if the *legal* barriers and definitions of the old hierarchical system had been removed, therefore, the *material* and *symbolic* demarcation lines did not disappear, but continued to evolve in the process of class formation that was taking place in this period.

These symbolic elements of social differentiation included in the first place the consciousness of honour and the behavioural expectations associated with it. All nineteenth-century commentators agreed that honour was essentially immaterial and therefore not quantifiable in terms of people having 'more' or 'less'. This made it particularly useful as a distinguishing label. It was an indissoluble part of the individual, like a natural, distinguishing feature. As Weber observed, it stood in this sense 'in sharp contrast to the pretensions of mere property-ownership'.[11] Thus it appeared as a completely immaterial quality, 'an immanence which could not be derived from possessions, a *nature*'.[12] Nevertheless, of course, it still required economic and social foundations. For the rules of the honour game were not comprehensible to everyone; still less could they simply be learned. They presupposed leisure, education, and a certain social *cachet*, and so were tied to a definite class situation, to a minimum of economic security. Apart from this, they could in addition only emerge and be experienced in situations where such distinctions could actually be made, or in other words, when there were a number of players in the game who understood the rules and kept an eye on one another as they played.

Among the characteristic attractions (or prerequisites) of bourgeois honour was the requirement that its social determinants had to be denied and removed from all the forms in which honour was expressed, in order to avoid giving the impression that it was a merely superficial and hence contingent constraint. It was for this reason, indeed, that the attempt on the part of some middle-class spokesmen to link honour exclusively to a number of trades and professions met with scant approval. In 1849, deputy Köchly argued in the Saxon Diet that since 'we no longer have any Estates now, we just have professions', it was time to replace the notion of status-bound honour with that of 'professional ability'.[13] He was of course prepared to uphold the principle of a general 'citizens' honour'. But by proposing the attachment of a specific form of honour beyond this only to particular trades and professions – merchants' honour, scholars' honour, entrepreneurs' honour, workers' honour, lawyers' honour, and so on – he failed to conceive of a wider social honour which would integrate the bourgeoisie across all its fragmented groups into a single whole and at the same time allow each individual member of this social class the feeling that he was an autonomous person and could take himself seriously as such.

It was quite clear that Köchly's idea of a form of honour orientated towards economic functions or professions was not going to gain very widespread support among the bourgeoisie. To be sure, it is undeniable that the bourgeois professions of medicine and the law developed a veritable craze for honour in the last third of the nineteenth century. In the course of their professionalization, they established special 'courts of honour' and promulgated 'rules of honour' which they saw as securing their profession's reputation and motivating its members to ensure that standards were maintained. But by insisting that these courts of honour were empowered to deal with the behaviour of lawyers or doctors outside the exercise of their own profession, it was clear that they were thereby going far beyond a merely functional, exclusively professional definition of honour.[14]

Beyond this, too, the records of the cases that came before the two courts of honour make it clear that matters falling under the heading of 'professional honour' were dealt with differently from insults which affected individuals as such. Thus if a physician tried to drive a competitor from the field by exaggerated self-advertisement or some other underhand means, it was normal for this uncollegial behaviour to land him before the court of honour. But if two doctors engaged in mutual personal insults, then a challenge to a duel was the more likely outcome. Difficult though it might have been to draw a clear dividing line between a man's professional role and his personality, there was still an unmistakable tendency to respond to defamatory attacks in one way or the other according to the context in which they had been made. Julius Fischer, a lawyer in Karlsruhe, confirmed in 1903 that, in his experience, 'persons who are quite resolute in their adherence to the principle of duelling, declare a challenge to be unnecessary when they are attacked and slandered in their profession'.[15] In other words, if a middle-class man felt offended in his business or professional activity, he took the offender to court. But if the offence was personal, he challenged the offender to a duel.

III

Nevertheless, civil honour could not, either as the general honour of the citizen or as professional honour, be precisely equated with the honour of the middle class. Many middle-class men reserved for particular occasions a special form of duelling honour which involved radical claims for the individual and at the same time was structured in an extremely status-bound and exclusive way. The kinds of points of honour at issue can perhaps best be illustrated by a brief examination of some concrete incidents.[16] On 27 May 1861 a duel with pistols was fought between a senior legal official in the city of Berlin, Karl Twesten, and the Chief of the Prussian Military Cabinet, Major-General Edwin Baron von

Manteuffel. Manteuffel had sent Twesten his card because he felt personally insulted by a reference to himself in one of Twesten's publications as a 'sinister man'. Since Twesten had refused to retract the allegation, Manteuffel had felt obliged to salvage his honour by challenging him to a duel. Twesten too, although a liberal, considered it a point of honour to take up his pistols and thereby document the fact that he stood by his opinion.[17] As an anonymous commentator noted, a refusal to accept the challenge would have condemned him as cowardly and untrustworthy in the eyes of 'society'. It was his duty to underline his criticisms of Manteuffel and the state of affairs in the Prussian Army 'with all his manliness' and to set aside those 'sentiments of a higher, citizens' honour' which conflicted with the necessity for a duel. Manteuffel, for his part, as the same author noted, was obliged to issue the challenge by virtue of the claim he himself laid to the possession of a sense of honour appropriate to his aristocratic and military status. This claim, continued the writer, was based on 'the preparedness to sacrifice one's person completely, and on the manly courage to fight to the death for life's most noble causes, including one's own honour'. Such courage, he continued, was 'the *sole*, and therefore the *universally valid yardstick of manliness*'. It followed, in conclusion, therefore, that 'any attack upon one's personage can only be requited by a trial and test of one's courage, of personal bravery'.[18]

Thus both Manteuffel and Twesten submitted themselves to the test, even though they gave repeated mutual assurances that they believed each other to be honourable men. After the duel, they parted in reconciliation with a firm handshake. Twesten, indeed, had consistently maintained that he had neither intended a slander upon Manteuffel nor a slur upon his honourable character. However, Manteuffel had felt himself insulted not only in his official capacity but also in person. For his part, Twesten had been convinced that to have refused the challenge would have been to have 'destroyed' himself 'morally'. When both parties were brought before the courts, Twesten declared that he had acted in his capacity as a citizen who was not prepared to surrender his right of political criticism because of being threatened with a duel. He believed duelling to be anachronistic, but he had accepted the challenge not least in order to disprove the suspicion that political authors were nothing but loud-mouths.[19]

It was precisely such a charge that another German writer, the poet Heinrich Heine, levelled in 1837 at a colleague, the Stuttgart editor Wolfgang Menzel. Menzel had criticized the members of the 'young Germany' group of writers, to whom Heine at that time was still closely connected, as un-German, unpatriotic, and un-Christian. But when Karl Gutzkow, who felt personally insulted by this Philippic, proceeded to challenge him to a duel, Menzel refused and referred him back to the battlefield of journalism, where men fought with pens rather than with swords. It was at this point that Heine entered the quarrel, with an article 'On Informers', published in 1837, in which he accused Menzel of personal cowardice. 'If you will constantly bluster about German nationality', he wrote, 'if you will regard yourself as a Germanic hero, then you have to be courageous, you have to take up your pistols when an honourable man whom you have slandered asks for satisfaction, you have to put your life on the line for the things you have said.' But instead of 'defending himself like a man on the field of honour', Menzel, Heine said, had preferred to 'scold his opponents in his scandalmongering rag like an old woman'.[20]

By publicly accusing Menzel of cowardice, it was of course Heine's intention to provoke him into issuing a challenge. 'I hope to drive him to take up his sword . . . This time I will wield my own with the greatest pleasure, for the point is to chastise a traitor, at the very least by making him afraid.' Heine's publisher, Julius Campe, although by this time a man of advanced age, offered to back him up. 'Should I do the fellow the honour? I'm a good shot! And the thing doesn't worry me', he wrote. Campe agreed that it was Menzel's duty to challenge. 'He *must send his card*, or he will be regarded as infamous . . . The reply he gave to Gutzkow *he cannot*, in my opinion, *give to you*: he would be branded as a coward wherever he mingled with men.'[21] However, although Heine himself, as he admitted, did not shirk at employing under-hand methods to force an opponent to issue a challenge, Menzel remained adamant. He preferred to submit to publicly stated and repeated accusations of personal cowardice rather than to partici-pate in a passage of arms that – as Heine had declared – would certainly not have taken place without blood being spilt ('I am not', Heine had written, 'going to shoot at the blue sky').[22]

The quarrelsome poet himself displayed no lack of 'manliness' in such situations. In 1841, the Frankfurt banker Salomon Strauss confronted him on a Paris street about an insult which he believed Heine had offered to his wife, and subsequently put it about that he had slapped the poet in the face. Heine immediately sent his card. Despite the fact that he denied having been slapped in public by Strauss, Heine none the less considered himself obliged to issue a challenge because of the public attention which the affair was attracting, above all in Germany. As he wrote to Strauss: 'I am less concerned to receive satisfaction from you than to demonstrate to my compatriots by my action that the offensive calumnies which you are causing to appear in German newspapers are wholly without foundation.' But the situation became even more delicate when Strauss named three witnesses who, he said, had been present at the incident. Heine's honour, as he reported to Campe, got 'into serious difficulties . . . I have to admit that I was never so depressed as on the day when I read that infamous claim.'[23]

Campe for his part gave full backing to his author's determination to counter such rumours as strongly as he could. 'You *cannot* allow this kind of slander to go unanswered, not for any reason! Better dead than dishonoured, the object of the world's mockery!' Heine's friends and acquaintances were united in their view that the injured party could only remove the stain of the (real or imaginary) physical assault from his character through fighting a duel. Were he to fail to demand satisfaction in this way, he would brand himself definitively on the public mind as a coward. This would be tantamount to pronouncing a sentence of social death upon himself, for he would then become a kind of social outlaw whom 'every lousy youth' could insult with impunity.[24] Moreover, when the lawyer Gabriel Riesser wrote in a newspaper article that Heine had deserved his slap in the face from Strauss, the writer Jakob Venedey, who was a friend of both men (and later became a leading democrat in the revolutionary Frankfurt Parliament in 1848) considered that a duel was unavoidable in this case as well. Riesser, he wrote, was 'a man of courage and honour'. His attacks on Heine were thus more than a mere attempt to make a name for himself. So Heine, argued Venedey, was obliged to take up the gauntlet and 'make an end of the affair by doing the honourable thing'. This time, however, Heine declined, declaring that 'if you have dealt with the comet itself, you don't need to bother with its tail'. Venedey was piqued and disappointed. 'You may', he wrote to Heine, '. . . reconcile yourself to this action; but I would just like to advise you as a friend, and as a man who believes his sensibilities in matters of honour to be as delicate as anybody's, not to make any more fuss about this matter'. For, Venedey opined, Heine might have vindicated himself through his duel with Strauss, thereby not only putting into effect Campe's advice to stop 'people's mouths' in the affair, but also clearing himself of the charge of cowardice; but his refusal to call out Riesser was bound 'to have a completely different effect on the outcome' and cast renewed doubt upon his honour.[25]

Despite being beset on all sides, Heine stuck by his view that *one* duel was sufficient to deal with the matter. After he had agreed the choice of weapon with Strauss, the two men, accompanied by the usual escort of seconds, neutrals, and physicians, met outside Paris on the early morning of 7 September 1841. Strauss's pistol shot hit Heine in the hip, and although not seriously wounded, the poet was obliged to take to his bed for a week until he recovered. But this did not upset him unduly. For he had now been morally rehabilitated. In fact he had been seriously concerned beforehand about the outcome of the duel, so much so that a few days before the fateful morning he had married his mistress Mathilde, invoking the 'authority of the church and the law' in order to restore her honour, which had been seriously damaged by the fact that they had been living together unmarried for six years. So he had not quite shared the youthful insouciance of his elderly publisher Campe, who had declared in one of his letters to Heine: 'What does it matter if one fights a duel? A wound is nothing: it will heal. I myself have gunshot wounds and I'm as fit as a fiddle!' The poet, for his part, might have been as cool as a cucumber in his letters and his literary works, but he showed himself in this instance to be more tender-hearted: he did not rule out the possibility of receiving a fatal wound, and took steps 'to secure Mathilde's position in the world' in advance of the event.[26]

In Heine's case it was not clear whether or not Strauss had really assaulted him in public, thereby offering an insult which could only be made good by a duel. But in the case of a duel fought over half a century later between Assistant Judge Ernst Borchert and First Lieutenant Seidensticker there was no doubt at all. The two men had both taken part in a masked ball held at the Königsberg Exchange on 2 February 1896. After a night of heavy drinking and vigorous dancing, Borchert, who was wearing a sailor's costume, was pinched in the behind by the visibly inebriated Seidensticker, who was also in costume, and ordered to fetch a glass of beer. There was no question of Borchert's having been mistaken for a serving-wench. So he considered himself seriously insulted. He told Seidensticker he was behaving like a 'pimp' and said he would like to box him on the ears. Enraged by the failure of these words to arouse in the lieutenant more than the faintest of smiles, Borchert put his wish into action knowing full well that a public assault such as this, upon an officer, was bound to provoke a duel. By doing all he could to bring about this outcome, Borchert was demonstrating his view that this was the only way he could erase the shame the lieutenant had brought upon him.

Sure enough, the officer sent his card to the judge the very next morning. The duel took place three days later in a copse outside Königsberg. After three rounds had been exchanged on each side with no ill-effect on either party, Borchert made an offer of reconciliation to his opponent. But Seidensticker rejected the offer. He paid for it with his life. In the next exchange of fire, Seidensticker was hit. He died shortly afterwards from internal bleeding. Brought before the courts, Borchert was sentenced to two years' confinement in a castle. The conditions were not too arduous. Before long, however, Borchert sent in an appeal for clemency to the Prussian Minister of Justice. It was rejected, on the grounds that Borchert had 'handled the affair of this duel with an uncommon degree of thoughtlessness, bordering on frivolity'. He had, charged the minister, been determined from the outset to fight a duel, and had failed to explore any other means of obtaining satisfaction.[27]

While the zeal with which the judge had sought a duel stood in no relationship to the seriousness of the insult he had received, and was duly regarded by the authorities as a legitimate reason for punishment, the challenge which Adolf von Bennigsen, a District President in the Prussian province of Hanover, sent to Oswald Falkenhagen, the lessee of a landed estate in the area, was generally regarded as fully justified. For eighteen months Falkenhagen had been enjoying sexual relations with Bennigsen's wife while remaining on friendly social terms with the cuckolded husband. The lovers' secret meetings did not go unnoticed, however, and eventually Bennigsen came to hear of them. He challenged his rival to a duel 'to the finish'. The challenge was accepted without hesitation. The two men met on 16 January, 1902, in the Saupark, near the town of Springe. Both parties' seconds, together with the neutral witnesses, attempted to have the exchange of fire limited to ten rounds on each side, but Bennigsen refused. After the first two rounds had been fired without loss of blood, Falkenhagen's third shot wounded the District President in the abdomen. Attempting there and then to beg his victim's forgiveness, Falkenhagen was rebuffed by Bennigsen's brother, who had accompanied him to the meeting. Bennigsen died of his wound the next day.

Shortly afterwards, Falkenhagen was condemned to six years confinement in a castle. He served his sentence in Weichselmünde, near Danzig. This relatively severe sentence was upheld despite several appeals for clemency from Falkenhagen. The court justified it on the ground 'that through the occasion for the duel, Falkenhagen offered his opponent, whom he subsequently killed, the greatest affront that can be given to a husband, namely the adulterous relationship which he carried on for a lengthy period of time with the deceased's wife'. It was accepted as self-evident in the circles to which Bennigsen belonged that this 'affront' could only be met with a challenge. Falkenhagen's offence was aggravated in the eyes of the court by the fact that 'he continued to pay social visits to his opponent in his own house despite his culpable relationship with his wife'. This offered an additional insult. Even when the whole world was talking about the scandal, Falkenhagen was still playing the reliable family friend to his mistress's husband, thereby making him as complete a cuckold as it was possible to be.[28]

There was only one way of answering such an insult: a duel. Had Bennigsen failed to issue a challenge he would certainly have called upon himself the disapproval and incomprehension of the circles in which he moved. Even the opponents of duelling took it for granted that a challenge was the inevitable result of an offence to 'family honour'. Although some contemporaries at least took the view that it was better and more appropriate to shoot the adulterer straight away, instead of putting one's own life at risk in a formal duel with him, such spontaneous acts of vengeance were normally left to men from the lower classes to carry out. 'Honourable men' possessed after all a method of dealing with such matters that was more appropriate to their elevated status. A duel gave the injured party the chance of 'wiping away' the 'stain' on his honour by throwing down the gauntlet at the offender's feet. Revenge was not the issue: the point was to provide a positive proof of one's own honourable nature by demonstrating that one regarded honour as more important even than death itself. To be sure, it was not always possible to rule out revenge as a motive in individual cases. It was clear, for instance, that by

insisting upon a fight to the finish with his opponent, Bennigsen
was making it clear that the world was too small for both of them
and that he wanted to see the man who had disrupted his marriage
die. In theory, however, duels 'to the death' were against the rules,
and seconds were under an obligation to reject rules of combat
that were excessively severe, such as a very high number of rounds,
or an extremely short distance between the two opponents. For,
in the final instance, what was decisive in vindicating the honour
of the participants was not the result of the duel but their preparedness to risk their lives. Killing one's opponent was neither a subjective aim nor an objective duty.

It would in any case have been absurd for society to have laid
down such a duty because the chances of being killed were the
same on both sides. Murderous and vengeful emotions were hardly
likely to find their fulfilment in the duel, as indeed the Bennigsen–
Falkenhagen case so clearly illustrated. As the challenger, it was
Bennigsen who set the terms, and he did so as severely as he
could. But although he clearly had no intention of sparing his
opponent's life, his shots all went wide of the mark. Falkenhagen,
on the other hand, submitted evidence before the court that he
had deliberately tried to avoid hitting his opponent, and yet his
third shot still succeeded in killing him! In view of the unreliable
quality of the duelling pistols of the day, the final outcome indeed
could never be accurately predicted, and death or survival was
largely a matter of chance.

Duels such as these, which ended in death, of course attracted
widespread public attention. Again and again they sparked heated
debates about the pros and contras of the duel as an institution.
Indeed, it is only because of such debates, and because of the
investigations subsequently carried out by the police and the
courts, that documentation exists which allows the historian to
reconstruct the course of actual duels in the past, including the
occasion for the original challenge. And yet, even though it is
possible on the basis of this material to document hundreds of
duels that took place in nineteenth- and early twentieth-century
Germany, this is only the tip of the iceberg. The true dimensions
of the practice begin to be hinted at if we turn to the biographies
and autobiographies of bourgeois men of the period. In these
works, duelling is a constantly recurring theme, and their authors
frequently discuss cases either involving themselves or their friends
and acquaintances. It is, for example, only from the memoirs of

his daughter Katia that we know that Professor Pringsheim, a Professor of Mathematics in Munich, and an impassioned partisan of the music of Richard Wagner, fought a (bloodless) duel with a complete stranger whom Pringsheim had hit on the head with a beer glass in a restaurant because he had overheard him making derogatory remarks about the composer.[29] The great majority of duels, indeed, went unreported either in autobiographies or in police and court records or in the press.

For this reason it is not easy to determine whether the duels described in this chapter were typical or not. Certainly it was far from usual for duels to end in the death of one of the parties involved. And the prominence of the participants in these cases – Manteuffel and Twesten were well-known politicians, Heine a famous poet, and Bennigsen a senior official with widely ramified and politically influential family connections – was also untypical. Characteristic, on the other hand, were the reasons why these duels were fought: personal insults, slaps in the face, adultery. In all these cases someone felt dishonoured and demanded satisfaction. Honour was intimately bound up with a person's claim to self-regard and public reputation. As soon as a 'man of honour' was subjected to something that challenged this claim, he was obliged to do everything in his power to vindicate it. Honour was a quality, the contents of which eluded positive definition: it was discernible solely through the perceptions of others, and material-ized itself through continuing processes of social communication. It may have been characterized as a completely subjective emotion, but it only remained in existence as long as others, people who were generally regarded in this context as important, continued to recognize that a man was deserving of his claim to possess it. The individual saw himself, for his part, reflected in his social milieu, and even if he may have purported to have experienced emotions as individually determined, his behaviour was none the less stam-ped by anticipation of his expectations in which 'honour' occupied a firm place as a concept and as a social fact.

It seems clear that honour in this sense had a great deal to do with the need to disprove even the smallest suspicion of cowardice. In the eyes of that part of society which regarded itself as capable of giving satisfaction, the only appropriate response to attacks that touched upon a man's honour was to issue a challenge to a duel. By entering into a duel, a man certified that honour was for him the highest of all human, 'manly' possessions. It signified that he was setting aside all material considerations and anxieties. Thus to avoid a duel was to display a deficiency of courage and thus a lack of honour. To put it in a nutshell: a man who failed to put honour above life and was not prepared to prove it in a duel, was a man without honour. Or, as the historian Hans Delbrück expressed it: 'The basic psychological feeling is in all events that an essential part of the complete manly personality is the courage to commit oneself in one's own cause. The possession of this courage is a man's honour.'[30] Max Liepmann, Professor of Criminal Law at Kiel University, put it even more pointedly in 1909: 'A man's honour does not consist in a kind heart or good deeds, but in personal courage and dependability. A man's honour consists in the fact that his word, his energy and he himself can be relied upon.'[31]

The honour which a man fought to defend in a duel revealed itself, behind the veils of language which concealed its real meaning, to be no more than a derivative of the current definition of the masculine character. It was a symbolic representation of courage, bravery, self-discipline, and coolness. The many and varied issues over which duels were fought, from insults to adultery, were only of secondary importance. What really mattered was what Heine called, in a conscious departure from the concept of 'satisfaction', 'manifestation': the public attestation of personal bravery, as a pledge of masculine honour. Few people put this more clearly than the judge Adolph von Kleist, President of the Berlin Supreme Court, in a brief, obscure, and anonymously published newspaper article he wrote in 1864. By far the most important, indeed, the only purpose, he declared, for which a duel could be rationally justified, was the verification of manly dignity: 'Manly dignity', he contended, 'requires above all manliness, that is, the consciousness of personal courage. *The demonstration of this characteristic seems to us to be the principal aim of the duel.*'[32]

The fear that one's masculinity would be called to question, that one would be regarded by the men and women of one's acquaintance as pusillanimous, unmanly, and dishonourable, was thus the central driving force behind the institution of the duel in nineteenth-century Germany. Only by accepting this argument is it possible to explain why an initially harmless conflict could escalate into a deadly showdown, why even the mere rumour of a slap in the face could provoke a challenge, and why a challenge which one might well have considered unnecessary none the less had to be accepted. Such fears had stamped themselves so deeply on the masculine self-image that even a severe critic of the 'duelling mania' like the Viennese doctor and writer Arthur Schnitzler was affected by them. Ignoring the advice of his closest friends, Schnitzler refused to call a colleague out in 1889 for a derogatory remark which he had made about him; but despite his firm conviction 'that it would have been the most incredible folly to have risked life, health, or even the smallest of my fingernails for such a trifle', he was unable 'for some time to rid myself of the feeling that I was actually under an obligation . . . to behave in a much more dashing way'.[33]

Pluck – or nerve – was the demand made of all those who wished to cut a figure as 'men of honour' in 'society'. But such pluck was a refined sort of quality. It had nothing in common with aggressiveness or braggadocio. It was more conservative, more protective in character. A man who trod the field of honour with courage did not thereby gain any honour that he did not already possess: he merely kept the honour he had intact and strengthened his claim to continue being regarded as a 'man of honour'. The rules of the game as practised by 'society' laid down that honour could only be lost, it could not be gained. Such rules revealed once more its genuinely status-bound quality. By belonging to a distinct social group, one possessed honour as an ascribed characteristic: if one was not already part of 'society' by virtue of property, socialization, and way of life, it was not possible to acquire honour of this sort through personal actions, however outstanding they might be.

But if this concept of honour was indeed so status-bound, then how was it assimilated to the bourgeois lifestyle of the nineteenth century? Did it not, after all, contradict all the leading programmatic ideas of the bourgeoisie, whose self-perception rested on achievement, competition, profit, mobility, and education? Did it not in fact belong to a world that had long since passed into irrevocable oblivion, a world the empty brilliance of which now shone only fitfully, reflected here and there to the fascination of no more than a mere handful of degenerates? Even if this had been the case, however, it still leaves open the question of why so many bourgeois men of the period fell victim to the allure of this brilliance and why, in the end, it gradually faded and disappeared.

IV

There can be no doubt that duelling in the Early Modern period was an almost exclusively aristocratic phenomenon. Equally clear was the determination of the Absolutist (and Late Absolutist) state to perpetuate its restriction to the exclusive confines of the military and service nobility. Carl Gottlieb Svarez, the author of the Prussian General Legal Code of 1794, spoke in his lectures before the Crown Prince in 1791–2 only of 'officers and noblemen' when he came to discuss the place of duelling in the law.[34] The code itself reserved the offence of duelling explicitly for these two groups and laid down that 'when persons who belong neither to the nobility nor to the officer corps issue or accept a challenge to a duel, such action shall be deemed to be attempted murder and be punishable as such'.[35] Thus, middle-class men were unable by definition to fight duels. Should they none the less attempt to do so, they were treated as potential murderers. Such a stipulation was intended as a deterrent. For although at the time of the Code's first drafting, in 1784, by and large only aristocrats engaged in the practice of duelling, and the 'citizenry' were regarded in any case as 'less sensitive to insults', the legislator still thought it necessary to guard against a possible growth of the practice in the latter by laying down high penalties for them.[36] When it came to the Code's application to concrete cases, the Berlin Supreme Court took the line that bourgeois duellists were not to be judged under the paragraphs relating to duelling but were to be punished differently from noblemen or officers who were found guilty of the same offence. Even in the late 1830s the most senior judges in Prussia were still adhering to this principle, even if they found themselves obliged to admit that 'opinions have changed on the matters of honour and the capacity to give satisfaction'.[37]

A decade earlier the Bavarian judicial authorities had already registered the fact that substantial sections of the middle class had effectively acquired the 'honour' necessary to take part in duels. In 1826, King Ludwig I had promulgated a draft Law on Duelling on the assumption that 'the belief that honour can only be upheld by gaining satisfaction for oneself, that is, by an illegal act, is current almost exclusively among the nobility, officers, higher civil servants and those of a similar rank, and university students'. But the legislative commission called upon to consider the draft felt it necessary to caution against the adoption of such a narrow view. It remarked:

> Affronts to people's honour occur in all ranks of society, and duels can take place in other social groups as well. One need only think of bankers, of middle-ranking civil servants, of propertied men who, without being titled, live from the revenues of their property, of capitalists . . . One may take into consideration indeed all those who belong to the so-called educated classes.

The commission then proceeded to draw up a list of those categories of men whom it regarded as possessing the status necessary to fight a duel or appear before a court of honour. These included not only circuit judges, assistant judges, and middle-ranking state officials but also doctors, surgeons, lawyers, merchants, and artists.[38]

Such mainly bourgeois professional groups were indeed beginning to appear more frequently in the files of the criminal justice authorities. Affairs of honour were increasingly fought out between middle-class men in the course of the nineteenth century. The proportion of noblemen among those involved underwent a clear decline. Apart from officers, it was mainly academics, professionals, and university-educated state officials who now vindicated their honour in the dawn hours. Businessmen and merchants were relatively seldom to be found. Generally speaking, they lacked the necessary knowledge of the rules according to which challenges could be delivered and accepted, and which distinguished duels from brawls. Nevertheless, time and again, cases occurred which demonstrated that there were indeed businessmen who had mastered the duelling code. One such was, for example, that of the duel fought by Moritz von Haber in Oggersheim, in the Bavarian Palatinate, in 1843. Son of a Jewish court banker who had received the title of nobility in 1829, Haber described himself as 'a man of private means' and acted as financial broker for numerous European princely houses. He knew the rules of honour as well as did his second, a 27-year-old merchant from Stuttgart, Peter Julius Thouret. Still, Thouret had mugged up the rules only during the lengthy prehistory of the duel in which he was now involved. Initially, indeed, he had confessed that he 'understood nothing of the regulations' and had wanted to ask an army officer for advice about them.[39]

Officers indeed were generally regarded as the highest authority in matters of honour. They belonged to a profession which was expected to behave in all respects according to the dictates of honour: the king's honour, namely, for which the officer went to war and laid down his life. In exchange for this, the shadow of the monarchical honour fell upon the officer, visible to all in the form of the 'king's uniform', which was the officer's 'cloak of honour'. Already as a cadet he was made aware of what an officer was in honour bound to do. As he served in his regiment, the colonel would issue regular instructions to ensure that the junior officers remained aware of the paramount importance placed upon the dictates of honour. From time to time, in addition, the Commander-in-Chief would promulgate special orders on the matter, which were drummed into the officers by repeatedly being read out to them. An order of this kind issued by Wilhelm I in 1874, began, for example, with the words:

> I expect of the entire officer corps of my army that they will regard honour, henceforth as hitherto, as their greatest treasure; to keep it pure and unstained must be the holiest duty of the whole corps, as of the individual officer.

The monarch then defined honour as consisting more precisely of 'faithfulness unto death', 'unshakeable courage, firm resolve, self-denying obedience, transparent honesty, strict confidentiality' and 'self-sacrificing' devotion to duty. An officer had to behave in a manner appropriate to his rank, avoid 'debauchery, drink, and gambling' and 'never pledge his word of honour casually'. He had to cherish his honour as highly as he did that of his fellow officers, otherwise he would damage the reputation of the entire corps. The royal and imperial prolegomena concluded with a warning: 'I will therefore no more tolerate in my army an officer who is inclined wantonly to insult his comrades' honour than I will an officer who does not know how to defend his own.'[40]

This statement could be variously interpreted. It could mean, for instance, that an officer who refused to respond to an insult by issuing a challenge to a duel was not wanted in the Prussian Army. Such a principle, indeed, had been applied before 1874, and was constantly giving rise to violent public controversy. After all, it meant that the officer corps was compelling its members to behave in a way that was officially outlawed and punished both by civil and by military law. On the other hand, many contemporaries who were sceptical about the general principle of duelling none the less allowed it a certain justification when it was applied among army officers. Hans Delbrück admitted in 1896, for example, that officers had a particular duty to uphold their honour, and referred to 'the proud and delicate sense of honour which the officer corps of the German Army can boast of and which constitutes the strength of our military'.[41] The special honour of the army officer went together with a special obligation, demanded by his calling, to avoid even the slightest appearance of cowardice. Officers were well known for reacting with extreme vigour to personal insults. Should they fail to do this, and allow an affront to go unanswered, they could be certain of an investigation by a military court of honour which could perhaps even end by cashiering them.

As long as the officer corps had recruited itself exclusively from the aristocracy, its honour had been in principle identical with theirs. But this changed as more and more middle-class groups were recruited. By 1861, nearly 20 per cent of higher-ranking German army officers were bourgeois; although some regiments (notably the cavalry) had managed to maintain their exclusively aristocratic composition, others (such as the engineers, artillery, or supplies) had a higher than average number of middle-class officers.[42] By the eve of the First World War, the proportions had shifted much further in favour of the bourgeoisie. By then, as many as 48 per cent of Prussian generals and colonels were middle class, while three-quarters of the majors and first and second lieutenants were of bourgeois origin.[43] Middle-class representation was particularly high in the naval officer corps, which had only been created under the Empire and had no aristocratic tradition to look back on.[44]

Even here, however, in these mainly bourgeois parts of the armed forces, a distinctive code of honour began to emerge. Naval and artillery officers not only fought duels, but did so with particular zeal. Precisely because they were engaged in the less fashionable branches of the profession of arms, they felt more than usually obliged to demonstrate that their regard for their own honour was no less exalted than that of their fellow officers in the cavalry or in respected regiments of the line. Apart from this, the Kaiser left them in no doubt that the strict code of honour current in the traditional areas of the armed forces was valid for the more modern parts too. When, for example, in 1900, First Lieutenant Walther

Strauss was slapped in the face during a voyage by his shipmate Purser Rönnebeck, and delayed challenging him until they reached home port, Wilhelm II issued an order sharply condemning the long delay. Strauss, he complained, had 'sought satisfaction in a manner totally lacking in energy'; his superiors on board ship, declared the Kaiser, were also guilty of a grave dereliction of duty. The Kaiser went on to underline 'a man's right to obtain immediate satisfaction for serious insults over which no settlement can be made'. He ordered all his commanding officers 'to ensure that the views which your officer corps adopts of the duties appertaining to its rank are clear and are to be expressed in flesh and blood, and that these views become the guiding light for all the officers' professional and private activities'.[45]

The sooner in his career an officer internalized these views, the greater was the assurance that they would fit him, as it were, with the closeness of an extra layer of skin. Thus great stress was laid on the honourable settlement of conflicts even among naval cadets. In 1902, for example, two midshipmen were reported to have fought a duel with sabres in the Kiel Naval Academy gym, in the presence of officers. The liberal press was outraged. But the Chief Inspector of Naval Training merely reported that it had been a normal students' duel with sabres, with all possible precautionary measures. It thus needed no special justification.[46] A similar zeal for duelling also characterized the Military Engineers' and Artillery School in Berlin, as Werner von Siemens later remembered. He himself had already fought a duel with the head of his dorm in his freshman year in 1835, and had served as a second in two other duels.[47]

Middle-class officers seem to have behaved in matters of honour in the same way as their aristocratic fellow officers did; indeed, they were possibly even more dashing in this respect, as a way of laying claim to their status as full and equal members of the corps. This impression is strengthened if we turn from serving officers to officers of the reserve. At the beginning of the 1860s, with the dissolution of the 'middle-class' militia and the institutionalization of the reserve officer corps, an increasing number of sons of the bourgeoisie applied for a commission in the reserve at the end of their one-year voluntary enlistment. They adapted to the behaviour of their fellow officers on active service with the faithfulness of true mimics, and continued to behave in the same way when they went back into mufti. Such behaviour included the duty of upholding a strict code of honour. Special military courts of honour ensured that the reserve officer did not go unpunished if he neglected to demand the honour due to his rank even in the course of his everyday life in the non-military world. The high degree of social prestige which the armed forces enjoyed, especially under the German Empire, cast a powerful spell over a great part of the middle class.[48] As a parliamentary deputy noted in the Reichstag in 1896, the custom was growing in bourgeois professional circles 'to lay more stress on one's military rank in the militia and the reserve than on one's professional position'.[49] In this way the officer corps' concept of honour won wide acceptance in the bourgeoisie. Contemporaries observed, indeed, that duels among reserve officers seemed to take place more frequently than among officers on active commission.[50] Everyday civilian life, of course, provided opportunity enough for conflict; and reserve officers, as parvenu 'social climbers' in the military world, were often unsure precisely how to behave, and so were likely to be over-zealous in the defence of their honour.

V

Many reserve officers had already made their acquaintance with the rules of duelling even before enlisting as one-year volunteers, particularly if they had been to university and belonged to a student fraternity. Here too there existed throughout the nineteenth century and well into the twentieth a detailed code of honour, modelled closely on its military counterpart. It differed only in the fact that student duelling involved rapiers or, in more serious cases, sabres, whereas in the armed forces the normal choice of weapons, almost without exception, was pistols. All the same, pistols were also used with increasing frequency among students in the last third of the nineteenth century, not least in order to assert the equal status of affairs of honour in these circles with those fought out among the military.

Like the officer corps, whose members served together day by day, messed together, and enjoyed a common social life largely cut off from the rest of society, students too formed a social group that was sharply demarcated from the outside world and bound closely together by manifold social ties, by common age and social status, and by a shared consciousness which distanced them clearly from the 'philistine' environment outside the university. Most

German university towns in the nineteenth century were relatively small, and students here created for themselves a world apart, 'a state, which stood above all doubt, beyond all questioning: a privileged state', as the writer Heinrich Laube (born 1806) wrote, recollecting his student years in Halle. In similar vein, the physician Adolf Kussmaul also recalled that 'German students had created for themselves, within the everyday philistine world, a particular student world with its own peculiar manners and customs, festivals and weapons, songs and melodies, even with its own language.'[51] The student world was subject to special rules which it created for itself, to particular forms of discipline, and to a particular kind of academic freedom: the freedom to be one's own master after years of dependency and subordination at home and at school. Students were eager to grasp this new freedom, but subjected themselves at the same time to new ties. At the end of the nineteenth century nearly every second student belonged to a fraternity of some kind.[52] The young men who did so may have experienced their student days as a time of sowing wild oats, but they were also subject at least to some form of regulation in the process. In drinking evenings and in duels, this phase of their life gained an important place in forming their identity. Fraternities laced their members into a tight corset of behavioural rules and disciplinary sanctions, which governed their intercourse with one another, with non-fraternity students, and with non-university 'philistines'. The backbone of this code of behaviour was formed by the duel (or *Mensur*, as it was increasingly termed in student circles, to distinguish it from the civil-military form of duelling practised among their seniors, the *Duell* or *Zweikampf*). The student code of honour was directed exclusively towards removing any possibility of doubt over how to behave in the case of an insult. As the Jena University Code of Honour of 1809 succinctly put it: 'The Code of Honour is the norm according to which the student must behave in matters of honour.'[53]

Matters of honour were attended to in student circles with the greatest punctiliousness. A misdirected glance, a hasty word, a thoughtless gesture – any one of these could without further ado be regarded as an insult to someone's honour. The honour of German students was a scaled-down version of aristocratic and military practices, and was a conspicuously tender bloom, sensitive to the slightest change in climate, and therefore requiring to be nurtured with the utmost care and attention. Such care was provided by the student fraternities and by duelling (which was indeed frequently regarded as their *raison d'être*). The fraternities preserved and organized the rites of student honour. It was, as university professor Friedrich Paulsen argued in 1902, the necessary concomitant of academic freedom. Academic freedom meant that students were not subjected to any form of overt compulsion in the course of their university career. So, Paulsen asserted, it imposed upon them 'all the more ineluctably the duty of self-control and self-discipline'. Such a duty, he went on, could not be fulfilled 'in solitude' by the individual student, but required a 'community life' which was formed most appropriately in the fraternities. Here the student learned subordination and self-assertion, on the one hand through conforming to the community and on the other through 'drawing up the lines of defence of his own existence against everyone' who belonged to it.[54] Thus honour possessed a characteristic double face, combining the urge to individuality with the acceptance of compulsions imposed by a collectivity. It thereby served a purpose whose importance could scarcely be over-estimated. It strengthened the determination of the young man to take himself seriously and to render visible the boundaries of his person so that no other individual could trespass upon them with impunity. At the same time it bound him to a community of like-minded people which provided a forum for the acknowledgement and control of the honour of each of its members.

In the course of the nineteenth century, however, it became clear that the individual conception of student honour was declining in importance compared with the collective and status-bound aspects. Affairs of honour among students took on an increasingly ritualized form. More and more, it became the custom, not to fight a duel because one considered oneself to have been insulted, but to issue an insult because one wanted to fight a duel. The fraternities celebrated a cult of aggressive and quarrelsome masculinity, which involved a way of behaving that was characterized by a touchiness so extreme that it became provocative in itself. This mode of behaviour was imposed not only on fraternity members but also on all those non-fraternity students who did not want to be publicly ostracized as cowards. Indeed, the member of a fraternity was constantly in danger of overlooking a word, gesture, or action that might be taken as insulting, but was not immediately recognizable as such. If this happened, he could then be regarded as having 'flunked' the challenge, as a 'wet' who did not know how to defend his honour with the requisite vigour. On the other hand, an intentional insult, once offered, could not be withdrawn, and for much the same reason, withdrawal would also amount to a dereliction of the duty to prove one's courage in public. Thus the only students admired in the fraternities were those who had shown themselves to be men by fighting a series of duels. Since it takes two to fight a duel, it was increasingly the practice for students to arrange in advance a formal, instrumental exchange of insults in order to gain this highly desirable status. This in turn ran counter to the original real meaning of the duel – obtaining satisfaction for a genuine insult to one's honour – and thus discredited the institution itself.

From the 1860s onwards, therefore, in order to prevent the institution of the duel from losing its reputation altogether, the fraternities began to arrange 'fixed duels' for their members. These no longer possessed the character of 'affairs of honour' but fell under the category of 'passages of arms'. Here courage had emancipated itself completely from honour. As an active fraternity member wrote in 1887, the point was now 'to train the student in the strength of his own manliness through toughening and increasing his personal courage'.[55] Bravery, as experienced student duellists reported, was measured principally in blood. If 'warm blood was flowing down his body' and the student still awaited the next blow with equanimity, 'personal courage and self-confidence were strengthened' and would not desert him in 'difficult situations' in later life. A physician in Jena who had attended nearly 500 student duels reported seeing participants continue fighting with their skin cut to ribbons and the ends of their noses chopped off. 'I have observed,' he wrote, 'student duellists who did not yet seem to have lost a great deal of blood suddenly fainting, and when they were attended to, their boots were filled inch-high with blood.'[56] The more blood that flowed, the greater was the demonstration of courage. Students' honour had become completely identified with the public staging of coolness and bravery, or, in the language of the day, the 'superiority of manly determination over animal cowardice'.[57]

Although student duels corresponded less and less to genuine duels, they none the less continued to function in a certain sense as a training-ground for them. A man who had absorbed the combative atmosphere of the duelling fraternity in his student days did not lose it after he had sat his finals. He continued as an 'old boy' to enjoy a close relationship with his old fraternity and continued to feel himself bound by its code of honour.[58] As he grew older, he may well have lost the touchiness of youth, but he retained the same basic views of manly honour and its satisfaction. He had been and carried on being part of a society of honourable men, which, as one of its members testified in 1936, 'revealed in me, as in every other fraternity student, just as it did in every officer in the armed forces, what the educated classes at that time held to be the personification of German honour', acquired through 'shared education in the same rank and the same fraternity' and 'shared German notions of honour'.[59]

These notions were shared, it might be added, not only by officers (and reserve officers) in the armed forces, not only by fraternity members, but also by the members of many other student associations and organizations; and the 'educated classes' included not only higher state officials, doctors, lawyers, university professors, and schoolmasters, but also, with increasing frequency, bankers, financiers, merchants, and industrialists as well. For as businessmen became more liable to complete their education by taking a degree, so they too were drawn in to the specific culture of honour that existed among university students. Beyond this, military service, and the opportunity it offered to obtain a commission in the reserve, contributed further to the spread of this culture among the male industrial bourgeoisie.

The concept of honour and its satisfaction may thus have lost its aristocratic exclusivity in the course of the nineteenth century, and gained a footing in the bourgeoisie, but the middle class was none the less very concerned to stop it spreading any further down the social scale. The fact that the institutions which transmitted it were not open to men from a petty-bourgeois or working-class background placed an almost insuperable barrier to its downward diffusion. Should it come despite this to a duel between two men who were not in possession of the invisible certificates of honour necessary to engage in this practice, then the judges before whom such cases were generally brought, themselves fully paid-up members of the honourable classes from their university days onwards, would see to it that those concerned were treated differently from two fully honourable duellists. In 1870, for example, when two waiters fought a pistol duel in Berlin, the court did not sentence them to the customary period of honourable detention in a castle, but sent them to prison instead, a 'dishonourable' institution.

281

Prussian Minister of Justice Eulenburg concurred with Wilhelm I in rejecting the waiters' appeal for clemency. Eulenburg pointed out

> that the condemned belongs to a class of society in which it is not customary to settle one's affairs in a duel. As far as we can see, the defence of his honour and reputation does not demand that he engage in a duel and thus contravene the law of the land, as often happens in such cases, and does not weigh in favour of the condemned.[60]

VI

Duelling and the honour it defended were thus the exclusive preserve of a small group of men qualified by property and education and the military and academic socialization that went with them. In this 'honourable society' aristocracy and bourgeoisie were fused together by shared values on points of honour. That this fusion was achieved by a unilateral assimilation of the bourgeoisie to aristocratic values, as critics of the 'feudalization' process, both among contemporaries and historians, have maintained, must be doubted in view of the way in which bourgeois writers on the subject presented it. Middle-class men did not merely ape alien models of behaviour, nor were they compelled to do so through institutions like the fraternities and the officer corps. Instead they derived their own meanings from these models, meanings which directly corresponded to the bourgeois cult of individuality rather than being opposed to it.

For the construction of honour of a kind and degree that could be satisfied in a duel offered the possibility of an appropriate appreciation and defence of the autonomous, individual personality in itself, beyond the influence of any pressures exerted by the collectivity. There is abundant documentation of the demand to be master of one's own honour and to tolerate no other judge of the matter.[61] This reflected the need to give absolute priority to a man's individuality and to defend it against all attempts to render it captive to others. On the terrain of honour was reserved a 'last refuge for the freedom of the individual';[62] here the regulatory interests of the 'omnipotent state', which had already reached much too far into the social existence of its citizens and imposed painful limitations on their freedom of action, could be successfully defied.[63] By touching upon the 'innermost, ideal person', duelling escaped the clutches of the state and constituted an 'individual authority' which acknowledged a man's personality as 'an object in itself' rather than alienating it as a 'building block' in a larger whole.[64]

The concept of an autonomous personality that took itself seriously necessarily involved the urge to present it as a complete and perfected whole. Thus the supporters of duelling were tireless in their insistence that words had to be followed by deeds, and that a man's physical existence had to be placed in the balance in the interests of his honour. By taking up their pistols, men whose professional weapon was the pen could prove that they possessed other virtues besides eloquence, such as death-defying courage and active resolution. They thereby made light of what a professor of philosophy called in 1858 the fashionable 'separation of heart and head', which in his view 'has gone so far that it no longer regards the human being as a single individual entity but as a whole army of separate beings'.[65] In contrast, duellists let the world know that they were prepared to stand up for their personality as a whole, without reserve, in defiance of the differentiating spirit of the age. Instead of dividing themselves up into various roles and bringing them into play as they were needed, they continued to insist on the unitary nature of their person and their honour. Irrespective of family, professional, social, or political obligations, they reserved the right 'to be first of all a complete *human being*'[66] rather than be divided into 'a thousand different souls'.[67]

This represented a radical claim to the autonomy of the individual, and to the integration in a single whole of a number of different aspects of the human personality. Such a claim gave duelling a considerable degree of credit among the bourgeoisie. Socialized into a culture which accorded high importance to independent individuality, they were particularly open to the appeal of these components of honour and its satisfaction. But they also found the status-bound, socially exclusive character of duelling attractive, since it promised them the clear delineation of the boundaries that separated them from other groups lower down the social scale, above all the lower middle class. They placed high value on securing this particular social frontier. Their constant references to duelling honour, as something which only men of a distinguished family and educational background could naturally possess, sounded a warning signal to social climbers that they lacked, in the end, the cultural capital necessary for acceptance into honourable society. These 'bourgeois' qualifications were also reflected in the forms taken by duelling itself, which were clearly separated from the brawling of the uneducated by their controlled and regularized nature. There was no place in the duel for 'primitive' motives and passions. Duelling was detached from the 'lower' emotions such as anger and vengefulness by the temporal and spatial distance which separated the occasion for the challenge from the duel itself, a distance which simultaneously helped to prevent the conflict from escalating any further. Following a challenge and its acceptance, it was forbidden for the two opponents to meet again until the moment of the duel arrived. Here they were obliged by the rules of encounter to display steadiness and coolness, to avoid any sign of aggression, to act as fairly as possible, and to exercise careful control over their emotions. 'The educated man', an unnamed author wrote in 1858, 'has found a means of protecting himself against the excess of his own passion, and that means is the duel'.[68]

But duelling did more than merely assert the validity of such external distinctions. It also served the function of securing the cultural hegemony of the university-trained group within the extremely heterogeneous social formation of the bourgeoisie as a whole. Honour and its satisfaction were regarded as idealistic, in explicit opposition to the 'ignominious domination of materialism'.[69] This lent considerable emphasis to the neo-humanist values adopted by the educated within the bourgeoisie. In order to be accepted into the charmed circle of 'men of honour', merchants, financiers, and businessmen had to assimilate the language of a kind of honour alien to that of commerce. Highly formalized, regulated down to the last detail, unbending and inflexible in its grammar, this language could never be learned or understood by more than a small group of the elect. It exerted some fascination over others, but it could not be transmitted to the public at large, and remained the cryptic code of a closed society living in regulated and closely defined circumstances. As soon as these circumstances became more fluid, as soon as social relationships changed and social signs lost their former, fixed meaning, this language began to lose its communicative power. It became antiquated, old-fashioned, and ridiculous, and in the end it disappeared altogether.

Just such a process took place in the case of duelling in Germany after the First World War. Revolutionary social transformations, latent for some time, now erupted to shatter the cultural order of the bourgeois world. The end of the bourgeois age was heralded on all sides. With its passing, the end came too for one of its legitimating icons, the 'autonomous personality', whose obituary the historian Friedrich Meinecke penned in elegiac terms in his memoirs. In its stead, wrote Meinecke, there had appeared the personality of the 'instrumental human being', who had sunk to the level of carrying out 'a mere function, without value of its own', and had been taken over by 'impersonal life-forces'.[70] Feelings such as these had already unsettled the *fin-de-siècle* generation and found their expression in various movements seeking to inaugurate new lifestyles and new forms of culture. Indeed, the enthusiasm with which men of the educated middle class greeted the outbreak of the First World War in 1914 owed not a little to their longing for 'manly deeds' that would restore the individual to his old rights and replace the anonymity and alienation of everyday life by 'the great, the strong, the festive'.[71] And not a few such men saw the war as a kind of duel writ large, in which honour could once again be put to the test.

Such hopes were quickly dashed. Students who, inspired by 'blazing manly ardour', had volunteered for the front and were still comparing the battle with their duels in the first days of the war – 'strict self-discipline is part of it, the ability to stand there in the duel and take it without batting an eyelid' – soon had to confess the error of their perception. 'The whole way of fighting is what repels one. To seek to fight and not to be able to defend oneself! The attack, which I had thought would be so beautiful', wrote one, 'what is it, except a rush across to the next cover from this hail of vicious bullets!? And not to see the enemy who fires them!'[72] Such a situation indeed had nothing in common with the classic form of the duel. The First World War was not at all about looking the enemy straight in the eye, squaring up to him in person, or fighting him with the same weapons and at the same risk, for honour and the assertion of manly courage rather than victory or defeat. The experience of 1914–18 did not strengthen men in their individuality. Instead, it caused them to experience their final subjection to the dictates of technology and industrial mass-production. Military defeat in 1918 and the subsequent emasculation of the German armed forces in the Weimar Republic further undermined the legitimacy of duelling honour and helped brand it as atavistic.

Beyond this, it was above all changes in the relations of the sexes from the end of the nineteenth century that began to rob the duel of its function as a means of demonstrating manly honour. The strict separation of spheres between men's lives and women's became increasingly redundant as more and more people crossed the boundary between them. Men were forced to give up an increasing number of privileges and monopolies. As this happened, the duel correspondingly lost its social contours and its power to create identity through providing a symbol of manliness. Women began to enter areas such as the universities, the professions, politics, and sport, which had previously been exclusively male preserves. Thus the old lines of demarcation between the sexes lost their function and had to be replaced by new, more flexible boundaries. The opinion of a Berlin professor such as the philosopher Paulsen, who rigorously denied that women had any 'independent honour', whether of a political or a social nature, belonged to the nineteenth century. Paulsen's wish had been merely to allow 'the woman' a limited share in the honour of 'the man', and his conclusion had been that 'her desire for honour can therefore only be indirectly requited: the appointed way for her to every goal under all circumstances is to be attractive to the man'.[73] But whether this message found a ready hearing among the women who were struggling to improve their own chances of education and professional advancement around the turn of the century may be doubted.

For women students in the lecture theatre, the library, or the laboratory, preparing themselves for an academically qualified professional career, were hardly likely to be content with such a simple and passively constructed notion of the 'honour of their sex' while their male fellow students were acquiring a far more ambitious social, political, and personal honour of their own. Feminists such as Helene Lange angrily rejected the 'patriarchalism' of such a divided concept of honour. She wrote

it is a peculiar way of putting it, when someone says that 'a man's wife or daughter is seduced away from him'. It is an expression which every self-assertive woman must find disturbing. It is as if one were saying that 'a man's cat is stolen from him' . . . She is completely excluded from the settlement of such an affair: men simply deal with it themselves, as owners of the property in question. And this concept of 'family honour' is nothing other than an enlarged version of men's honour. It may be varied by a woman, but it cannot be asserted by her.[74]

Few women, to be sure, went so far as to demonstrate their claim to equality on the field of honour. And if women occasionally really did dare to fight duels, they could be sure of attracting the irritated scorn of the male sex. Names such as 'duelling Furies' or 'viragos' were applied to them. 'Female deeds of derring-do' of this kind were usually, at most, to be found in the pages of novels or comedies on the stage. Women who fought duels in reality not only made themselves look ridiculous, however; they also ridiculed, by implication, the conventions of the duel itself. For by demonstrating that women too could display the courage, coolness, and discipline necessary for fighting on the field of honour, they also destroyed the masculine aura which surrounded the practice, and undermined the clear distinction conventionally drawn between men's honour and women's.[75]

But there was in the end no need for a campaign against the duel as a masculine symbol, no need to attack it directly in order to rob it of its character as a signifier of the relations between the sexes. The increasingly obvious presence of women in the male domain, their public and visible emancipation – however incomplete – from restricting role prescriptions in the economic, social, and cultural spheres, were enough to raise relations between the sexes onto a different level and to deprive the former insignia of masculinity and femininity of their unquestioned validity. The 'female character' had hitherto been socially accepted as 'natural' and meaningful. Now it was gradually dismantled. With it came a new self-definition on the part of men. The rigid, formal and correct type of man, who found fulfilment in honour and in death-defying decisiveness, did not go well together with the type of 'new woman' who trained for employment, formed political opinions, went to the cinema, learned to respond with as much flexibility as possible to changing role demands, and, in the Weimar Republic, cast her vote at the polls.

This reorientation of relations between the sexes combined with the demilitarization of social life and the changing position of the bourgeoisie in politics, society, and culture after the fall of the German Empire in 1918 to make it possible for people 'to regard the principle of duelling to a certain extent as breached' in the

Weimar Republic.[76] Cases in which men regarded a duel as 'the means by which the integrity of the person is maintained'[77] became increasingly rare. It became increasingly common for libels, slanders, and insults to be settled before the courts or, indeed, simply to be ignored. Nevertheless, there still remained men, especially in academic circles, who stuck to the old elitist concepts of honour and firmly resisted the 'egalitarian' spirit of the age. In a society characterized by modernity in the form of economic rationality, social democratization, and standardized mass culture, duelling acquired an honourably dysfunctional character, whose oppositional nature retained its charm for many years. Even Arthur Schnitzler, who had made a name for himself as an unbending critic of hollow social convention, was not wholly immune to this charm. In one of his last stories, written between 1927 and 1931, he portrayed a former duelling second engaging in a melancholy monologue:

> I know that it has become customary in our day and age to laugh at such affairs. But I don't think this is right. I can assure you that life was nicer then, or at least it had a nobler appearance, among other things undoubtedly because you sometimes had to lay it on the line in the cause of something that in a higher or at least a different sense possibly wasn't there at all, or at least, measured by today's standards, wasn't worth it, for your honour, for example, or for the virtue of a woman you loved, or the good name of your sister, and other futile things like that. Still, you've got to remember, people have been forced to sacrifice their life in the course of the last few decades for much less, for completely useless things, and at other people's command or at their whim. At least your own inclinations had something to say in the matter when it came to a duel, even in cases where it looked as if you were being made to fight under duress, or by some convention, or for mere snobbery.[78]

NOTES

This chapter was translated by Richard J. Evans. A German version has recently been published in the *Historische Zeitschrift*.

1 J. Eckstein, *Die Ehre in Philosophie und Recht* (Leipzig, 1889), 38, 73, 76.

2 M. Weber, *Wirtschaft und Gesellschaft* (Tübingen, 1972), 635, 722.

3 G. Simmel, *Soziologie*, 5th edn (Berlin, 1968), 403–6.

4 V.G. Kiernan, *The Duel in European History. Honour and the Reign of Aristocracy* (Oxford, 1988), 271, 274; similarly, H.-U. Wehler, *Das Deutsche Kaiserreich 1871–1918* (Göttingen, 1973), 163; A.J. Mayer, *Adelsmacht und Bürgertum. Die Krise der europäischen Gesellschaft 1848–1914* (Munich, 1984), 109–10. For the counter-argument, based on a comparison between Britain and Germany, see U. Frevert, 'Bürgerlichkeit und Ehre. Zur Geschichte des Duells in England und Deutschland', in J. Kocka (ed.), *Bürgertum im 19. Jahrhundert*, 3 (Munich, 1988), 101–40.

5 *Mittheilungen über die Verhandlungen des ordentlichen Landtags im Königreiche Sachsen während des Jahres 1849. Zweite Kammer* (Dresden, n.d.), 851, 864.

6 ibid., 880.

7 E. Bleich (ed.), *Der Erste Vereinigte Landtag in Berlin 1847*, part 2 (Berlin, 1847), 202–3.

8 M. Riedel, 'Bürger, Staatsbürger, Bürgertum', in O. Brunner *et al.* (eds.), *Geschichtliche Grundbegriffe* 1 (Stuttgart, 1972), 672–725, esp 683–5.

9 *Allgemeines Landrecht für die Preussischen Staaten von 1794. Textausgabe* (Frankfurt-on-Main, 1970), 690–1.

10 Quoted in R. Koselleck, *Preussen zwischen Reform und Revolution*, 2nd edn (Stuttgart, 1975), 103.

11 Weber, *Wirtschaft und Gesellschaft*, 635.

12 P. Bourdieu, 'Klassenstellung und Klassenlage', in Bourdieu, *Zur Soziologie der symbolischen Formen* (Frankfurt-on-Main, 1974), 42–74, here 60.

13 *Mittheilungen über die Verhandlungen*, 876.

14 On lawyers, see M. Rumpf, *Anwalt und Anwaltstand* (Leipzig, 1926), and *Die Entscheidungen des Ehrengerichtshofes für deutsche Rechtsanwälte*, several vols (Berlin, 1885 and later); on doctors: M. Gärtner, *Staatliche Ehrengerichte für die Ärzte* (Breslau, 1896); *Entscheidungen des Preussischen Ehrengerichtshofes für Ärzte*, 2 vols (Berlin, 1908/11); C. Huerkamp, *Der Aufstieg der Ärzte im 19. Jahrhundert* (Göttingen, 1985), 265–7.

15 J. Fischer, *Zur Duellfrage* (Karlsruhe, 1903), 21.

16 For a systematic and chronological study of the social and cultural history of duelling in Germany since the late eighteenth century, see the author's book *Ehrenmänner. Das Duell in der bürgerlichen Gesellschaft* (Munich, 1991).

17 *Neue Preussische Zeitung*, no. 123, 30 May 1861; ibid., no. 126, 2 June 1861.

18 *Duell von Manteuffel-Twesten* (Berlin, 1861), 14, 12, 10.

19 *Neue Preussische Zeitung*, no. 126, 2 June 1861; A. Kohut, *Das Buch berühmter Duelle* (Berlin, 1888), 104.

20 H. Heine, *Prosa 1836–1840*, Säkularausgabe, 9 (Berlin, 1979), 263–4.

21 *Briefe an Heine 1837–1841*, Säkularausgabe, 25 (Berlin, 1974), 27.

22 H. Heine, *Briefe 1831–1841*, Säkularausgabe, 21 (Berlin, 1970), 176, 199, also 226, 230, 236, 238; Heine, *Prosa 1836–1840*, 275.

23 Heine, *Briefe 1831–1841*, 410, 422.

UTE FREVERT

24 *Briefe an Heine 1837–1841*, 327–8.
25 ibid., 335, 336, 339; Heine, *Briefe 1831–1841*, 414.
26 Heine, *Briefe 1831–1841*, 423, 422, 427; *Briefe an Heine 1837–1841*, 327.
27 ZStA Merseburg, Hist. Abt. II, 2.2.1., Nr. 17838.
28 ibid., Nr. 17839.
29 K. Mann, *Meine ungeschriebenen Memoiren* (Frankfurt, 1983), 12.
30 H. Delbrück (ed.,), *Preussische Jahrbücher* 84 (Berlin, 1896), 376.
31 M. Liepmann, *Die Beleidigung* (Berlin, 1909), 13.
32 *Militärische Blätter*, no. 34 (1864), 62. Kleist's authorship is attested by his correspondence with Ludwig von Gerlach: H. Diwald (ed.), *Von der Revolution zum Norddeutschen Bund. Politik und Ideengut der preussischen Hochkonservativen 1848–1866. Aus dem Nachlass von Ernst Ludwig Gerlach*, 2 (Göttingen, 1970), 1228.
33 A. Schnitzler, *Jugend in Wien. Eine Autobiographie*, 2nd edn (Vienna, 1968), 315.
34 C.G. Svarez, *Vorträge über Recht und Staat* (Cologne, 1960), 411–18, esp. 415–16.
35 *Allgemeines Landrecht*, 694.
36 'Duell zwischen zwei Bürgerlichen, bei welchem ein Theil getödtet worden und der überlebende wahrscheinlich die Absicht zu tödten nicht gehabt', in *Zeitschrift für die Criminal-Rechts-Pflege in den Preussischen Staaten*, 17:33 (1831), 150–93, esp. 180–2.
37 H. Gräff *et al.*, *Ergänzungen und Erläuterungen des Preussischen Criminal-Rechts durch Gesetzgebung und Wissenschaft*, part 1, (Breslau, 1842), 514.
38 HStA Munich, Staatsrat Nr. 2450: Gesetzentwurf v. 14.3.1826; Vortrag des Ministers v. Zentner v. 21.8.1826; Staatsrat Nr. 597: Bemerkungen der Gesetzeskommission zu Ziffer II des Gesetzes über Ehrenbeleidigungen und Zweikämpfe.
39 *Die reine Wahrheit über die Streitsache zwischen Moritz von Haber und Freiherrn Julius Göler von Ravensburg* (Strasburg, 1843), 67.
40 Printed in W. L. Solms, *Verordnung über die Ehrengerichte der Offiziere im Preussischen Heere* (Berlin, 1883), 1–6.
41 H. Delbrück (ed.), *Preussische Jahrbücher* 86 (Berlin, 1896), 445; similarly P. Stauff, *Das Duell* (Leipzig, 1908), 6.
42 F.C. Endres, 'Soziologische Struktur und ihr entsprechende Ideologien des deutschen Offizierkorps vor dem Weltkriege', *Archiv für Sozialwissenschaft und Sozialpolitik*, 58 (1927), 282–319, here 290–1.
43 K. Demeter, *Das deutsche Offizierkorps in Gesellschaft und Staat 1650–1945*, 4th edn (Frankfurt, 1965), 29.
44 J. Steinberg, 'The Kaiser's navy and German society', *Past and Present*, 28 (1964), 102–10.
45 Bundesarchiv-Militärarchiv Freiburg, RM 5/v 643: Ordre v. 26.11.1900.
46 ibid., RM 3/v 4937: Schreiben v. 3.10.1902.
47 W. v. Siemens, *Lebenserinnerungen* 17th edn (Munich, 1966), 24.
48 E. Kehr, 'Zur Genesis des Königlich Preussischen Reserveoffiziers', in Kehr, *Der Primat der Innenpolitik*, (Frankfurt-on-Main, 1976), 53–63; H. John, *Das Reserveoffizierkorps im Deutschen Kaiserreich 1890–1914* (Frankfurt-on-Main, 1981).

49 *Stenographische Berichte über die Verhandlungen des Reichstags. IX. Legislatur-periode. IV. Session. 1895/97*, 2 (Berlin, 1896), 998.
50 *Vossische Zeitung*, 24 April 1896.
51 H. Laube, *Erinnerungen 1810–1840* (Leipzig, 1909), 71; A. Kussmaul, *Jugenderinnerungen eines alten Arztes*, 3rd edn (Stuttgart, 1899), 117.
52 K.H. Jarausch, *Deutsche Studenten 1800–1970* (Frankfurt, 1984), 69.
53 'Vierzehn der ältesten SC-Komments vor 1820', *Einst und Jetzt. Sonderheft 1967 des Jahrbuches des Vereins für corps-studentische Geschichtsforschung*, 106.
54 F. Paulsen, *Die deutsche Universität und das Universitäts-studium* (Berlin, 1902), 341, 473.
55 G. Pusch, *Über Couleur und Mensur* (Berlin, 1887), 11.
56 H. Karus, *Schläger, Säbel und Pistole* (Halle, 1888), 13; F. Eichholz, *Der Paukarzt* (Jena, 1886), 11
57 Pusch, 24; similarly Paulsen, *Universität*, 485, celebrating the 'control of the physical system by the will' in the duel.
58 Cf. the autobiography of the former fraternity student Willy Ritter Liebermann von Wahlendorf, whose father had been ennobled in 1873. In 1935 Willy was expelled from the fraternity because he was a Jew. He confessed that 'the corps was the most important group of people in my life apart from my close family up to October 1935', *Erinnerungen eines deutschen Juden 1863–1936* (Munich, 1988), 42.
59 ibid., 216.
60 ZStA Merseburg, Hist. Abt. II, 2.2.1., Nr. 17834: Schreiben v. 18.8.1871.
61 A. Frhr. v. Eberstein, *Über Ehre* (Leipzig, 1899), 38, 57.
62 O.H.A. v. Oppen, *Beiträge zur Revision der Gesetze* (Cologne, 1833), 44.
63 H. Wagener (ed.), *Staats- und Gesellschafts-Lexikon*, 23 (Berlin 1867), 200.
64 H. v. Gauvain, *Das Duell und seine Rechtfertigung* (Berlin, 1866), 13, 21, 29, 57.
65 J.E. Erdmann, *Vorlesungen über Akademisches Leben und Studium* (Leipzig, 1858), 217–8.
66 B. Meyer, *Was nun? Ein Beitrag zur Duell-Frage* (Berlin, 1896), 17.
67 R. Scheu, 'Duell und kein Ende', *Die Fackel*, 7:196 (1906), 7.
68 [anon.] *Kirche, Duell, Freimaurerei nebst einem Anhange: über Wohlthätigkeit. Ein wahres Wort auf die Angriffe gegen Duell und Freimaurerei*, 3rd edn (Berlin, 1858), 16.
69 C. Welcker, 'Infamie, Ehre, Ehrenstrafen', in C. von Rotteck and C. Welcker (eds), *Das Staats-Lexikon*, 7 (Altona, 1847), 390.
70 F. Meinecke, *Erlebtes 1862–1919* (Stuttgart, 1964), 244.
71 E. Jünger, *In Stahlgewittern*, 30th edn (Stuttgart, 1986), 7.
72 P. Witkop (ed.), *Kriegsbriefe gefallener Studenten* (Munich, 1928), 16, 11, 15, similarly 58, 100.
73 F. Paulsen, *System der Ethik mit einem Umriss der Staats- und Gesellschafts-lehre* (Berlin, 1889), 451.
74 H. Lange, 'Die Duelldebatten im Reichstag (1912)', in Lange, *Kampfzeiten*, 2 (Berlin, 1928), 99.
75 F. Mayer, *Der Zweikampf. Ein sittengeschichtlicher Beitrag* (Erlangen,

1843), 29; Kohut, 45. For a literary example, designed to provide amusement for the public, see A. Schloenbach, 'Sie will sich duellieren', *Die Gartenlaube*, 32–3 (1865), 497–500, 513–16. The story ends with the frustrated would-be duellist sighing: 'I really would rather be a woman than an amazon' (p. 516).

76 R. Pantenburg, 'Über die Zusammenhänge von Duell und staatlichem Ehrenschutz' (Ph.D., Cologne, 1928), 25.

77 A. Lasson, *System der Rechtsphilosophie* (Berlin, 1882), 548.

78 A. Schnitzler, 'Der Sekundant', in Schnitzler, *Erzählungen* (selected by W. Jens, Stuttgart, n.d.), 523.

10

Liberalism, Europe, and the bourgeoisie 1860–1914

Geoff Eley

I

It is hardly necessary to rehearse the conventional wisdom about German liberalism. It was formed, most historians would agree, by a series of political defeats – in 1848, in the 1860s, in 1878–9, in countless smaller compromises, and in the disastrous *dénouement* of the Weimar Republic. Because of the dramatic circumstances of 'revolution from above' in which Bismarck seized the initiative from an impressively resurgent liberalism under novel circumstances of party-political mobilization, with the united German Empire as its result, the 1860s, it is generally accepted, occupy a pivotal place in this approach. This was a major political watershed, in which certain possibilities of constitutional development were foreclosed and others entrenched. In the 'Constitutional Conflict' the Prussian liberals first pushed the monarchy against the wall, but were then breathtakingly outmanoeuvred, as Bismarck stole much of their programme and proceeded to unify Germany in his own way. A majority of Prussian liberals made their peace with Bismarck's four years of unconstitutional government by passing the 1866 Indemnity Bill, and then reached an accommodation within the framework of the small-German, semi-constitutional Reich.

The poor political staying-power of the liberals in the 1860s is thought to have had long-range consequences. The absence of a combative liberalism on the British model meant – on this reading – that Germany failed to develop a parliamentary-democratic and participatory political culture based on positive ideals of citizenship, and in this sense the decisions of the 1860s set the points for the long-term future. These longer-range implications are accurately reflected in Leonard Krieger's decision to end his 500-page book, *The German Idea of Freedom*, with a ten-page 'Epilogue', which takes the story all the way up to the Federal Republic in the 1950s. As Krieger says: 'the pattern of liberal politics for the half-century of the Empire's duration scarcely changed at all from its structure and posture in 1870'. And:

> Political liberalism, which had fought frontally in the main arena over the forms of the state and had been defeated, was calcified into an institutionalized party existence. It became compatible with the recently constitutionalized Germany and pressed only for certain policies from it.[1]

Moreover, in compromising with Bismarck the liberals cleared the ground for the *Sonderweg*, which was paved from the wreckage of their good intentions. In other words, this was the point at which Germany departed from the norms of western political development. As Heinrich August Winkler says of the liberal dilemma in the 1860s: 'there can no longer be any doubt that Germany's deviation from the secular and normative process of democratization laid the foundations for the catastrophes of the twentieth century'.[2] Or, in the words of Hans-Ulrich Wehler (although here the argument already slides from liberalism to the bourgeoisie): 'The outcome of this conflict was to seal the political impotence of the bourgeoisie up until 1918.'[3]

Much could be said about the historiographical syndrome such statements reflect. The experience of Nazism casts a long shadow over the previous century of German history, obscuring the rich indeterminacy and internal complexities of earlier times, leaving visible only such logics and potentials that seemingly point to a right-wing and authoritarian terminus. But the belief that German liberalism was already fixed in a fifty-year posture of impotence by the decisions of the 1860s, and that the resulting authoritarianism of the Empire's essential political culture was the decisive factor in Germany's future susceptibility to Nazism, is an extraordinarily determinist one. German history under the *Kaiserreich* becomes a plot whose basic scenario is already inscribed in the circumstances of the Empire's foundation, once the liberals stopped short of a full parliamentary constitution. There have been, of course, major historical works that have shown how liberalism subsequently failed to recharge itself for further progressive development. These works include Theodor Schieder's essays on the concept of party in the liberal tradition, Thomas Nipperdey's account of party organization, Lothar Gall's book on governmental liberalism in Baden and his arguments regarding liberalism's 'pre-industrial' parameters, Hans Rosenberg's work on the context of the 'Great Depression', and the research of Dirk Stegmann and others on the economic bases of liberal fragmentation. Wolfgang Mommsen's study of Max Weber (which is really about the thresholds of liberal creativity in the era of high imperialism after 1895–6), also comes to mind.[4] But because the starting questions are so firmly in place, research on the period between the 1860s and 1914 becomes very much an empirical exercise rather than the conceptual construction of new interpretations. It is striking how little innovation there has been since the early 1970s in the overall analysis of the *Kaiserreich*, as opposed to the opening of new empirical fronts.[5]

The accepted view of liberal weakness reflects a larger argument about the social forces dominant in the German Empire's political system and about the governing bloc that consistently corresponded to them between the 1870s and 1918. The weakness of liberalism is thought to have reflected the continuing primacy of 'pre-industrial traditions' in the political culture, which in turn bespoke the domination of the traditional power elites, that is, 'the aristocratic forces of the military and the landowners'.[6] In other words, the accepted view makes a strong correlation between the possibility of a successful liberalism and the kind of social base that would have been necessary to sustain it. The failings of German liberals (for instance, their growing inability to transcend the organized sectionalism of economic interests) are linked to a still larger deficit, namely, the failure to unify the interests and aspirations of the bourgeoisie as a class. A vital consequence of the liberals' cumulative capitulation between 1866 and 1878–9, according to Wehler, was that 'there was now no united liberal party to represent the bourgeoisie in internal politics'. Or, as Winkler puts it:

What distinguishes the German from the West European bourgeoisie seems to me to be above all the lack of a common consciousness for the bourgeoisie as a whole (*gesamtbürgerlichen Bewusstseins*) – a consciousness which grew out of the conflict with the bearers of the ancient regime, as in France, and

which under certain circumstances overlaid the social differentiation within the Third Estate.[7]

It has been argued many times that the German bourgeoisie was
somehow lacking in political ambitions, and that its 'weakness and
lack of political maturity' provide the crucial explanation for the
liberals' failings.[8] Germany's missing liberalism – its 'mis-development' – was at root the 'mis-development of the German bourgeoisie', its persistent 'inability to develop an independent class
consciousness' of its own.[9]

There is a lot of conceptual slippage in making this equation.
Two categorical non-equivalents – the one political (liberalism),
the other social or economic (bourgeoisie) – come to be used
interchangeably, and the weakness of the one (liberal capitulation)
becomes causally attributed to deficiencies in the other (certain
peculiarities of class formation, or the bourgeoisie's willingness to
compromise with the forces of the old social order). In the process,
the chances of a successful liberalism become linked to the class
interests of a strong bourgeoisie in a directly instrumental or
expressive way: no (strong, class conscious) bourgeoisie, no (successful) liberalism. The formation of liberal traditions from other
kinds of influences is comparatively neglected. I have in mind here
the positive contributions of subordinate groups other than the
bourgeoisie, such as the peasantry, petty bourgeoisie, and working
class, or the role of organized religion in the form of popular
Protestantism, or varieties of anti-clericalism. That liberalism was
a complex political growth, with a richly varied sociology, is often
fudged in the German discussion. Imperceptibly, liberalism
becomes elided with the class consciousness of the bourgeoisie.
According to Winkler: 'Political liberalism emerged as the political
outlook of the rising bourgeoisie.'[10]

Finally, this negative judgement on German liberalism has to
imply some notion of what a successful or more authentic liberalism would have been. In this sense, most writers proceed from a
particular reading of the British and American pasts. Liberalism
tends to be equated with parliamentary democracy and civil rights,
a conciliatory system of industrial relations (including the legal
recognition of trade union rights and collective bargaining), and at
least the potential for a welfare state, so that German inadequacies
become teleologically conceived by reference to an exterior and
idealized model. The post-1945 'welfare-state mass democracies'

become the measure of maturity for a liberal-democratic form of development, abstracted into an indictment of German omissions, the course of development German history failed to take. In fact, German history becomes the ideal-typification of the opposite route, that of the 'authoritarian regimes'.[11] This tends to obscure the specificity of Germany's own historical development, using more successful liberalisms as a normative measure of where Germany went 'wrong', until the rationality and coherence of the German experience is gradually undermined. In extreme versions – as in Dahrendorf, where the appeal to an idealized western liberalism is both open and partisan – this easily reduces to the question: 'Why was Germany not England?'[12]

Of course, there is much more to the standard views of the weakness of German liberalism. Most authors, for instance, see it as the casualty of capitalist development in the last quarter of the nineteenth century, whose scale and unevenness unleashed social forces and social contradictions it could not contain. In another sense, it was also disabled before the processes of organized interest-representation became a defining feature of the Imperial governing system. But in the most fundamental of conceptual terms, the argument hinges on the two major assumptions already noted. These are, first, that the weaknesses of German liberalism reflected deeper weaknesses of the German bourgeoisie as a class; and secondly, that the appropriate measure of German liberalism's inadequacies is the experience of liberalism in Britain and the United States which is thereby elevated to superior normative significance.

However, in the meantime there has been some willingness to admit that older notions of bourgeois self-abnegation – the oft-asserted 'lack of bourgeois virtues' (*Defizit an Bürgerlichkeit*), which cleared a path for Germany's 'special development' (the *Sonderweg*) – were misleading. They obscure the extent to which bourgeois values were in the ascendant after the 1860s – in taste, fashion, and the everyday transactions of polite society; in the ethos of local administration; in the prevailing conceptions of law, social order, and morality; in notions of private property and social obligation; and in the general conduct of public affairs. In effect, the key foundation of the old-established interpretation – the direct correlation between the failure of the liberals and the failure of the bourgeoisie, in which one determines the other – has been removed. Simultaneously, a key assumption about the social bases of liberalism's more general European success – its class properties as an expressive ideology of bourgeois self-emancipation – is necessarily brought into question.

This uncoupling of bourgeois societal hegemony from a necessary degree of constitutional liberalism is an important gain of recent discussion. It makes possible a fresh look at the character of German liberalism as a distinct political tradition, unencumbered by the class-reductionist assumptions that have previously stereotyped its character. Moreover, it is also worth re-examining the second major pillar of existing interpretations, namely, the normative critique of German liberalism by the standards of liberalism in Britain and the United States. If instead we take a genuinely European view of liberalism's emergence and ascendancy as a political creed, focused in particular on the continental transformations of the 1860s, when German unification featured as one of the major progressive changes concerned, there is a greater chance of generating some new perspectives. For, arguably, the conventional bases of comparison tell us as little about the 'actually existing' liberalism of Britain in the period between the 1860s and the First World War, as they do about liberalism in Germany itself. And it is to the more sensible basis for such a German-British comparison that we must now turn.

II

The contemporary meanings of 'liberalism' for an educated and propertied European observer of the 1860s are difficult to recover, given the disjunctions and transformations of the intervening hundred or more years. There can be little doubt that the main referent was British rather than French; the abstraction of clear liberal principles from the French experiences was made more difficult by the variegated radicalism of the revolutionary republican tradition, which extended from classical liberalism to Jacobinism and related forms of popular democracy. What was taken from the French experience, of course, was a general notion of constitutionalism, but by the 1830s even this was being mediated by the British example of parliamentary reform and representative government. But the basic principle of constitutional government could be realized in a variety of ways, with stronger or weaker forms of executive responsibility to parliament, and a greater or lesser degree of popular access to the franchise, not to speak of the form of protection for civil liberties under the law. Otherwise, liberalism was defined as much by a type of social morality and philosophical outlook as by a political programme with a highly specific content. In this sense, liberalism involved a theory of the sovereign individual, a particular tradition of thinking about human nature as the constitutive basis for social relations and the moral life, with its dual foundations in a specific philosophical tradition (the thought of Bacon, Hobbes, Locke, sometimes referred to as 'the political theory of possessive individualism') and in the larger public discourse of rights and responsibilities (in the upheavals of sixteenth- and seventeenth-century England and Holland, eighteenth-century Whiggery, the Scottish and French Enlightenments, the American and French Revolutions, and liberal political economy). As Anthony Arblaster says, 'individualism' is liberalism's 'metaphysical and ontological core'.[13]

Classical liberalism reached a climax of intellectual sophistication in the thought of John Stuart Mill and his famous tract *On Liberty* (1859). The interesting thing about Mill is that he took this classical tradition furthest towards democracy – and then stopped. The philosophical basis for representative government in his thinking was the rational ideal of humans realizing their potential through active citizenship, with the enhancement of liberty linked to the cultivation of reason, and the possibility of excellence linked to the maintenance of individuality and social difference. This easily lent itself to democratic forms of political address, and Mill was unusually consistent in following this through, declaring his support for integrating the working class into the political system, strengthening popular participation in decision-making, and extending the franchise to all women as well as men.[14] But at the same time, he showed an elitist suspicion of the masses that was far from just residual. He advocated plural voting that gave extra weight to those with intelligence and talent, whose demographic distribution was deemed implicity to follow class lines. In practice, he thought, the best and wisest came from property and privilege.[15] By comparison, the working class was a 'mass of brutish ignorance', whose untrammelled instincts could be not trusted. Mill's statements are littered with references to 'the common herd' or 'the uncultivated herd'. As he said: 'We dreaded the ignorance and especially the selfishness and brutality of the mass.'[16]

It is vital to grasp this limited quality of the liberal concept of citizenship. Most nineteenth-century liberals bitterly resisted democratic notions of political organization. Citizenship – meaning in the first instance the vote – was not a natural or universal right so much as a faculty to be learned and a privilege to be earned. It was heavily qualified by possession of property, education, and a less tangible quality of moral standing – what Gladstone called 'self-command, self-control, respect for order, patience under suffering, confidence in the law, and regard for superiors'.[17] In fact, most liberals were a lot less restrained in their disparagement of the masses' civic capabilities than Mill, whose thinking about democracy stands out by comparison as an example of radical and courageous consistency. From Burke to de Tocqueville through to the ideologues and practitioners of liberalism in its 1860s heyday, a powerful motif was the fear of the mass, reaching a crescendo in the 1848 revolutions and a subsequent climax in the first general European upsurge of popular enfranchisement in 1867–71. In liberal discourse 'the democracy' was virtually synonymous with tyranny and rule of the mob, and only with the turn of the century did liberals begin seriously rethinking their attitudes on this score. As Guido de Ruggiero put it, in liberal democracy 'the adjective Liberal has the force of a qualification'.[18]

This necessarily has a bearing on how we evaluate the particular limitations of German liberalism in the same period. The allegedly most 'progressive' exponents of the most 'advanced' liberalism in later nineteenth-century Europe – Mill and his co-thinkers in Britain – explicitly limited the polity against democratic participation. Moreover, the actual extent of the franchise in Victorian and Edwardian Britain remained highly restricted: by contrast with the German Constitutions of 1867 and 1871, the 1867 Reform Act conceded the vote to only a small section of the working class, while the Third Reform Act of 1884 fell far short of democratic manhood suffrage, leaving Britain the only representative system of government in Europe apart from Hungary without manhood suffrage by 1914.[19] Of course, some classical liberals were democrats, such as many in the radical wing of the Gladstonian party after 1867 (roughly a third of the parliamentary party between 1868 and 1885), and other groups falling more ambiguously within the bounds of the latter, like the small group of English Positivists who acted as advisors and advocates of the British trade unions in the 1860s and 1870s. But such minorities of liberal democrats had the luxury of keeping the possibility of an independent labour movement politics at arm's length, given the restrictive nature of the franchise; it is unclear how they would have reacted to the circumstances facing liberals in Germany, where universal manhood suffrage opened the way for an independent socialist party at a very early stage. In other words, it was not some peculiar national failing of the German liberals that left them so cautious in their constitutional inclinations. More important were the respective configurations of popular democratic politics German and British liberals had to face. For British liberals the parliamentary constitution contained working-class political aspirations within the available liberal framework; for their German counterparts any further parliamentary reforms would only increase the likelihood of those aspirations finding independent social-democratic expression.[20]

At the most general level, it is worth remembering that the 1860s provided a moment of significant liberalization in Europe as a whole. Indeed, by contrast with the French Revolution, when European liberalization was largely imposed by the expansion of French arms, and 1848, when the popular constitutionalist movements were largely suppressed, the 1860s amounted to one of the three great constitution-making watersheds of modern European history, together with the two political settlements after the world wars, during which the territorial and institutional landscape of the continent was radically redrawn. The most dramatic changes were the unifications of Germany and Italy under broadly liberal auspices, but to these we may also add: the Second Reform Act in Britain (1867); the collapse of the Second Empire and foundation of the Third Republic in France (1871); the Austro-Hungarian constitutional compromise in the Habsburg Empire (1867); the liberal revolution in Spain (1868–9); constitutional reforms in Greece and Serbia (1864, 1869); and the emancipation of the serfs in Russia (1861), which stimulated the first independent constitutionalist movement among sections of the gentry and the attendant concession of limited local government measures in the *zemstvo* reform of 1864. (This catalogue may be further extended by adding the transatlantic upheaval of the American Civil War.) Altogether, this amounted to an impressive victory for specifically liberal principles of political order, as we encounter them on a European scale in the middle third of the nineteenth century. Given the European scale of this process of reform, it is unclear why the British experience in particular should be singled out as the absolute standard for the authenticity of the rest.

301

If liberal constitutional norms became generalized during the 1860s into the predominant – or 'hegemonic' (after Gramsci) – mode of organization of European public life, it is also important to remember that the accepted territorial framework for the latter was the nation-state. There is a tendency in the literature to present German liberalism as being somehow compromised by German nationalism, so that the acquiescence in Bismarck's resolution of the German question is taken to be the critical moment of liberal betrayal. Yet this is an unhelpful way of judging German liberalism and the context in which it operated. By contrast with the 'core' states of western Europe, nationalities east of the Rhine lacked the advantages of an early-acquired statehood, so that demands for a liberal constitution became indissolubly linked to the prior achievement of national self-determination within the territorial framework of a viable nation-state, which by the mid nineteenth century was generally regarded as a condition of 'progress' in the liberal sense. Moreover, given the survival in Central Europe of pre-national state forms – petty monarchical and aristocratic jurisdictions of one kind or another – the real work of constituting the 'nation' had to be conducted in opposition to the existing sovereign authorities by private rather than public bodies, and by civil initiative and voluntary association rather than by government – in brief, by the political action of the people organized as potential citizens. In other words, the process of proposing the category of the German nation was identical with the growth of a public sphere, with the 'nation' conceived simultaneously as a new political community of citizens. The fusion of these two terms – 'nation' and 'citizenry' – in liberal discourse was an inescapable reality of liberal politics east of the Rhine and south of the Alps in the middle third of the nineteenth century.

From this perspective, the creation of a united Germany (whatever its particular agency) may be justly regarded as the highest achievement of German liberalism in its classical phase, for all the parliamentary shortfall of the 1871 Constitution. This was so in three principal ways. First, the very creation of a centrally constituted national political arena on the ruins of the region's historic particularist jurisdictions was a decisive liberal advance. Secondly, unification created the legal and institutional conditions for a German-wide process of capitalist industrialization, involving the political consolidation of a national market and an impressive body of forward-looking economic legislation. Thirdly, unification also embodied the characteristically liberal vision of a new social order. Between 1867 and 1873, demands for a new national constitution and other national institutions, for national economic integration, and for the rule of law became the centrepiece of the new German state. Moreover, beneath this level of dramatic political innovation were deeper social processes of class formation, bringing self-conscious bourgeois notables to regional, municipal, and local pre-dominance, and precipitating their claims to moral leadership in society. In this sense, unification brought the cultural ascendancy of a distinctive set of values, stressing merit, competition, secular-ism, law and order, hostility to hereditary privilege, ideas of per-sonal dignity and independence, and generalized belief in the modern morality of progress.

This broader cultural front of activity was at least as important to liberals' sense of themselves as the formal political demand for an advanced constitution. They saw themselves as engaged in a struggle to unlock the potential for social progress, to free society's dynamism from the dead hand of archaic institutions, not the least of which in much of the continent (as liberals saw it) was the Catholic Church and its control of key institutions, from schooling to charities and the agencies of popular sociability. The attack on clericalism in these terms was a general European phenomenon, of which the *Kulturkampf* was the particular German form. More-over, the attack on the Catholic religion *per se* was perhaps less important than a positive ideal of how the future German – or French, or Italian, or British (given the salience of Nonconformity to Gladstonian liberalism) – society was to be shaped.[21]

Mid-nineteenth-century liberalisms displayed a common soci-ology. On the one hand, liberal coalitions always extended down-wards from the industrial, commercial, and professional bour-geoisie into the petty bourgeoisie, peasantry, and nascent working class. On the other hand, they were never exclusively an urban formation, but always had strong links to the countryside, not just by appealing to the rural masses, but through close relations with the landed interest. At the same time, while this heterogeneity applied to all liberalisms to a greater or lesser degree, its specific manifestations appeared differently across different societies. Both the forms of dominant class integration (e.g. among urban and landowning factions, through intermarriage, associational net-works, commercial interpenetration, corporate political alliance, etc.) and the precise relationship to different kinds of popular constituency were a powerful source of variation in national liberal-isms, and a major factor affecting their political cohesion. In this respect, there is an enormous amount of work still to be done on German liberalism between the 1840s and 1880s.

The extent of the specifically democratic change the various national liberalisms proved willing to sponsor depended very much on the character of the popular coalitions that had to be formed. Specifically democratic initiatives owed far less to the spontaneous inclinations of liberal leadership themselves than to the pressures applied by independently constituted popular forces. Such pres-sures materialized in a variety of ways: in a dramatic revolutionary crisis (the 1790s, 1848); in the course of more protracted struggles (the various reform agitations in Britain); or by being articulated into the liberal coalitions themselves (as in the primary case of Gladstonian liberalism in the 1870s and 1880s). Here again, we are very ill-informed about the German case, although there is now a good monographic base for liberalism's popular constituencies in certain regions during the 1860s and 1870s, of which the south-west is the most important.[22]

When liberalism came under attack at the end of the century, its dominance was questioned not just in ideas, but because its earlier social bases were starting to decompose. Liberal parties' former strengths derived in large part from an ability to speak convincingly for broadly based popular aspirations in the peasan-try, petty bourgeoisie, and working class. To a great extent their decline resulted from the loss of that same moral-political leader-ship, once subordinate classes began demanding a more indepen-dent voice of their own. This raises the question of the distinctive forms of political life that had sustained the liberal parties' popular credibility. To put it another way, it brings us to the question of the liberal mode of politics. This has to be tackled in terms not only of its restrictive and exclusionary definition of the public sphere through the franchise and other means, but also of the more informal participatory structures through which popular poli-tics was actually engaged. From this point of view, we know vastly more about the bases of popular liberalism in Britain as these took shape between the ebbing of Chartism in the 1840s and the emergence of the Gladstonian Liberal Party in the 1860s.[23]

Taken together these points provide a framework for comparing different national liberalisms. At all events, they suggest a better way of judging the success and authenticity of German liberalism than by simply measuring it against an ideal-typical standard of maximal liberal democracy, which is also projected backwards from the mid twentieth century, quite misleadingly, onto the mid nineteenth-century British case. To measure German liberalism in this way seems unacceptably teleological. Otherwise, it is unclear why British liberalism is being privileged analytically in that kind of way. Or, at least, that particular construction or representation of the British liberal experience has to be explicitly argued through, as opposed to being simply assumed.

III

If we are to compare German and British liberalism more sensibly, therefore, we have to change the terms in which the comparison is usually assumed, for there is surprisingly little explicit comparison in the literature.[24] This requires both dethroning British liberalism from its privileged place in perceptions of later nineteenth-century liberalism, and according greater recognition to what German liberals positively achieved. It means both relativizing the British, and normalizing or depathologizing the German case.

When dealing with the 1860s, it is easy to overlook the crucial fact that it was only in the 1860s that the British Liberal Party was actually formed. When the so-called capitulation of the German liberals is bemoaned, their failure is implicitly measured against an ideal of successfully realized liberalism that is thought already to be in existence in Britain. It is true, of course, that, between the Whig revival of the late 1820s and the repeal of the Corn Laws in 1846, certain recognizably liberal ideals came to dominate the practice of government in Britain, concerning the political economy of free trade, a definite conception of the state-society relationship, and a social morality of propertied individualism. But it is also possible to make similar claims of Germany after 1850, where, despite the failure of the 1848 revolution, governments proceeded to adopt economic and social policies that were by and large liberal.[25] Obviously, the power of the aristocratic landed interest in Germany did not disappear overnight, but the post-Peelian Conservative Party was also a powerful repository of traditional aristocratic interests in that way; and the tendency of recent British scholarship has been to stress the resilience of the landowning aristocracy more generally in British society and government during the nineteenth century. The point is that both

305

societies were in flux, gripped by a fundamental process of social transformation, with far-reaching debates about the distribution of power and social value that were extremely divisive. The difference was in the chronology, pace, and intensity of economic development, but also in the forms of political articulation and the nature of the balance struck between the forces of inertia and the 'party of movement'. Likewise, while we can also point quite properly to the conservative nature of the 1850 Prussian Constitution, the British reformed electoral system of 1832 was hardly a glowing example of functioning parliamentary democratic representation. In short, in neither the British nor the German case was the ascendancy of liberal ideology accompanied by any significant liberalization of the political system before the 1860s.

More specifically, what both Germany and Britain lacked till the 1860s was an independently constituted and politically coherent liberal party. In both cases this absence was then made good by an impressive upsurge of liberal organization, which was also accompanied, in both cases, by a broader-based mobilization of popular aspirations for political reform, partly directed through the emergent liberal parties, partly autonomously organized on a radical-democratic footing. The literature on Germany in the 1860s is now extensive, that on Britain rather less so, although we do have two great classics of the 1960s, Royden Harrison's *Before the Socialists* (London, 1965), and John Vincent's *Formation of the Liberal Party* (London, 1966). As Vincent showed, it was only in the 1860s that the loosely connected parliamentary groupings of liberals became freshly constituted as the national representation of a flourishing substructure of locally grounded political cultures, that is, the familiar Gladstonian Liberal Party. Moreover, there were really two distinct processes at work: not only 'the slow adaptations of the parliamentary party', but more importantly 'the adoption of that parliamentary party by a rank and file' in the country.[26] Vincent sees this latter process as a conjunction of three new extra-parliamentary forces – 'the new cheap Press, militant Dissent in its various forms, and organized labour' – whose emergence was then 'ratified' by Gladstone's 'placing himself in a relation to popular feeling quite new in a minister'.[27] And the practical and institutional intersection of these three forces occurred in local structures of associational activity, taking philanthropic, charitable, educational, recreational, high-mindedly cultural, social-political, and moral-crusading forms, which allowed the energies of notables and people to be joined in a common enterprise of moral-political improvement.[28]

So the 1860s were the crucial founding period for both German and British liberalisms as independently constituted political parties. In fact, sociologically and ideologically the similarities of British and German liberalism in the 1860s were very great. On the critical questions of popular politics there was the same qualified openness to certain kinds of trade union reform, the same willingness to sponsor forms of popular improvement, and there was the same associational nexus of locally grounded popular participatory forms. In the German case it is usually said that in the later 1860s this popular basis of liberal politics was decisively lost via the fundamental rupture between party-political liberalism and the labour movement, what Gustav Mayer called the 'separation of proletarian from bourgeois democracy'.[29] But despite the precocious formation of a separate socialist labour movement by comparison with Britain, we should not exaggerate the strengths of either of the two groups into which the German socialist movement was divided. It was not until the final years of the Anti-Socialist Law in the later 1880s that the SPD promised to become a genuinely mass movement on a genuinely national scale. In the meantime, German liberals managed to maintain their links to popular constituencies in town and country rather more successfully than existing accounts tend to suggest.

This is not to suggest that there were no real differences between British and German liberalisms in the 1860s. Gladstonian liberalism was clearly a far more popular formation and was far more successful at containing the labour movement within its own structures. Conversely, an independent space for socialist politics was created in Germany as a result of the 1860s. Various explanations might be cited for this, including the relatively more favourable circumstances of those skilled craftsmen who formed the bulk of the trade-unionized workers who were integrated into the Gladstonian coalition, or the constitutive importance of the Non-conformist tradition for popular liberalism in Britain, for which there was no real German equivalent.[30] John Breuilly has recently stressed the differences in the overall political context in Britain and Germany at the end of the 1860s. Whereas in Britain the novel liberal synthesis was forged in a state structure that was constitutionally modified in 1867 but was territorially unchanged, in Germany it proceeded in a territorial-constitutional context that was being totally transformed. As Breuilly says, it was the fact that the first stage of Germany's unification occurred through a North German Confederation dominated by a narrowly restricted Prussian polity that not only drove a wedge between the 'proletarian' and the 'bourgeois' democracy, but also divided North German from South German liberals. This not only reduced the incentive for North German liberals to pursue a more generous social definition of the constitutional nation, but even rendered the latter nugatory. In Britain, by contrast, the logic of the 1867 settlement pushed Gladstonian Liberals further into forms of popular accommodation.[31]

After 1867–71, in fact, the countervailing political logics of the respective national situations continued to differentiate the political effectiveness of the two liberalisms. Thus, in Germany (as elsewhere in Europe, apart from Britain) liberals faced a set of objective circumstances which structurally undermined their claim to a classless and universalist representation of society's general interest. For one thing, Germany was confessionally divided, and the aggressive anti-Catholic confrontationism of the *Kulturkampf* – which (again, no less than in Italy and France) was an essential rather than an optional or contingent aspect of the liberal outlook – ensured that a majority of German Catholics were practically ruled out as a potential liberal constituency. Moreover, under the duress of the depression of 1873–96, the structural indebtedness of small-scale agriculture in many of the old liberal heartlands, the transformation of the world market in agricultural produce, and the accelerating transition into a mainly urban and industrial form of society, it became harder and harder to hold small farmers, handicraftsmen, and other categories of traditional property-owners and tradesmen to a liberal political allegiance. Stressing the virtues of economic progress, liberalism inevitably possessed a diminishing appeal for the latter's perceived casualties. To a great extent, of course, these two problems also coincided, because some of the most recalcitrant bastions of popular Catholicism (the regions of Trier, Catholic Baden, southern Württemberg, and large parts of Bavaria) were simultaneously the backward agrarian periphery of the Empire. When the crisis of liberal popular support arrived in the 1890s, it was agrarian and *Mittelstand* mobilization that did the most damage.

In Britain, by contrast, neither the Gladstonian nor the post-Gladstonian Liberal Party had to deal with those problems, for the simple reason that the peasantry and traditional petty bourgeoisie were an insignificant part of the English social structure, while Catholicism was a much smaller minority creed than in Germany. To the contrary, in a mirror image of German liberalism's metropolitan prejudices, Gladstonian liberalism made itself precisely the mouthpiece of these disadvantaged groups: not only the Nonconformist masses of the industrial North, but also the Irish and the surviving peasantries of the 'Celtic fringe'. Moreover, the key to this popular allegiance, and the constitutional foundation of the Gladstonian Liberal Party's exceptionally resilient popular coalition by European standards, was not British liberalism's democratic modernity by comparison with its German counterparts, but in a sense its very backwardness. Paradoxically, it was the absence of universal manhood suffrage in Britain until after the First World War that permitted the Liberal Party's greater popularity and political staying-power before 1914. For, while the franchise was held to the quite restrictive levels of the Second and Third Reform Acts, the kind of independent breakout of popular constituencies that proved so damaging to the German liberals in the 1890s were simply not feasible in Britain. This was most dramatically illustrated by the respective progress of the two countries' labour movements. In Germany, universal suffrage was the *sine qua non* of the SPD's independent advancement. But, in Britain, the practical disfranchisement of around half the male working class after 1884 remained a decisive impediment against launching an independent party of labour. This, and all the weight of existing tradition, remained a powerful argument for keeping labour's liberal alliance, until wartime conditions and the further Reform Act of 1918 laid the basis for the Labour Party's complete independence. In this respect, the British labour movement was quite exceptional in European terms.

Whatever set of explanations are preferred, the main point is that a conjunctural comparison is the appropriate framework for judging German liberalism in the 1860s rather than one that presumes the essential superiority of the British case from the beginning. In both cases the 1860s saw an impressive effort at liberal synthesis, in innovative party-political frameworks, on an expanded popular basis, and with a commitment to far-reaching constitutional change. The divergent forms of liberal politics thereafter arguably had more to do with the radically different overall political contexts than with the inherent qualities of the respective liberal movements themselves.

A comparison of German and British liberalism in the quarter-century before the First World War shows a comparable pattern of similarities and differences. If we turn to German liberalism in the 1890s, we are dealing with a situation in which the majority tendency, the National Liberals, were experiencing serious difficulties, which by 1900 had resulted in a permanent reduction of that party's parliamentary base, with a loss of some forty Reichstag seats to the liberal strength overall. These difficulties were partly precipitated by a crisis of popular support, as the liberals' historic post–1860s constituency began to defect, either to the SPD on the left, or to new agrarian movements on the right. Simultaneously, Germany's transition to a predominantly urban-industrial capitalist economy imposed itself more powerfully onto public consciousness, and with the end of the Depression in the mid–1890s German capitalism began to face a new expansionist challenge in the world market. In other words, liberals not only had to redesign their practice for the dictates of the new mass politics; the changing socio-economic environment also compelled the reorientation of liberal ideology.

German liberalism was partially reinvigorated before 1914 by a dynamic synthesis of imperialism and social reform, hinged on a new ideology of state intervention, social welfare, and national solidarity. In the course of their rethinking, liberals revised some shibboleths of existing liberal thought – concerning the nature of the state and its field of relations with the individual, the economy, and civil society – and registered a sharp break with the classical liberal tradition. A principal incubator of these new ideas was the *National-Sozialer Verein*, which (despite its small size) richly fertilized German politics during its brief existence (1896–1903). In the 1890s and at the turn of the century such departures were mainly confined to left-liberal discourse. But by the time of the Bülow Block in 1907–9 such ideas had also won considerable resonance in the National Liberal Party too, particularly through the Young Liberal movement. The diffusion of such perspectives in the National Liberal Party was also facilitated by a restabilizing of the National Liberals' parliamentary influence in the later 1890s, which together with the emergence of the Centre Party under Ernst Lieber from its previous confessional ghetto promised to restore the party to something resembling its former centrality to the governing system. Between the mid–1890s and 1902 a series of successful and moderately liberal parliamentary fronts took shape, organized around a National Liberal/Centre Party axis, and enabling a relatively stable parliamentary culture to emerge. Particularly important here were the passage of the Civil Code (1896), the naval legislation (1898, 1900), the consistent blockage of government attempts to pass new anti-labour legislation (1895, 1897, 1899), and the tariff legislation (1902). The relative stabilization of political life within given parliamentary and electoral forms, lasting roughly from 1897 to 1911–12, created enough space for certain sections of the National Liberals – above all, a younger generation led by Stresemann – to respond creatively to the new thinking coming from the left liberals. This facilitated a gradual convergence which by the eve of 1914 was delivering the materials for a potential liberal regrouping.

The post–1890s ideological innovations in German liberalism – the state interventionist synthesis of imperialism and social reform – were remarkably like the British departures of the same period which are usually taken to characterize the New Liberalism. Allowing for certain major differences of context – most importantly, to do with position in the world market, and the absence of an independent socialist party – the British New Liberalism was a response to economic, social, and political problems that also existed in Germany and elicited a very similar response. Furthermore, much of the impetus for the British new liberalism came from an intense intellectual engagement with specific features of the German social and political system. The British ideology of 'national efficiency' was predicated to a great extent on the German example. As Karl Rohe has said, if we view Imperial Germany:

> as many interested Britons saw it, there is much to be said for the case that behind an historically outmoded constitutional façade were concealed politico-cultural and in part politico-institutional realities which in their content and formal aspect must be described as typically modern.[32]

And, of course, if the British New Liberal intelligentsia could view the *Kaiserreich* as a model for 'modernization' in this way, there may be ground for reappraising both the usual view of German liberal 'failure' and the much-vaunted 'backwardness' of the Imperial German political system.

If that constitutes a similarity between the British and German variants of new liberalism in the same period, there is also a major difference. It concerns the relative success in composing a popular political coalition under the new liberal aegis. Controversy over the long-term viability of the British Liberal Party by 1914 has not been resolved in recent years, and the Liberal resurgence of 1906 may have rested on a very volatile and precarious base. But there was none the less an extremely interesting juncture of 'progressivist' ideology in the decade before 1914 that retained profound implications for the Labour Party traditions of the inter-war years.[33] In Germany the capacity of the new liberalism to attract the working class was far less, partly because the political space was already aggressively occupied by the SPD, partly because the liberal appeal was always positively directed much more towards the peasantry, the *Mittelstand*, and the white-collar petty bourgeoisie. The new reform liberalism was far better at devising potential legislative packages for the so-called 'new *Mittelstand*' than for the working class, and consequently proved an unstable basis for effecting a lasting juncture with moderate elements in the labour movement. In the parliamentary arena it proved feasible to imagine new levels of co-operation with the SPD, particularly for certain kinds of 'modernizing' constitutional, administrative, fiscal, and economic reform, especially during the war, and it was that surely which laid the basis for the original Weimar coalition after 1918. But the peasant and white-collar constituencies of the left liberals proved extremely difficult to hold beneath the reform banner, and (as we know) it was partly the defection of such elements in the later 1920s that subsequently fed the growth of the NSDAP. The problem of how such strata could be won lastingly for a liberal-cum-democratic politics is one of the most important, but least-investigated and least-understood questions of pre–1914 German history. It marks the single most important area of difference in the kinds of problem faced by the new liberalism in Germany and Britain.

IV

It we are to take German liberalism seriously, the liberal politics of the unification decades should not only be freed from the grid-like and anachronistic comparison with a model of British liberal democracy which is itself historically misconceived, it should also be uncoupled from the determinist and reductionist assumption that the fate of liberalism was causally dependent on the 'strength' or 'weakness' of the bourgeoisie – not because there was no empirical relationship between bourgeois interests and aspirations and the character of German liberalism, but because a (mistaken) analysis of the one has been allowed too often to substitute for a proper analysis of the other. Consequently, German liberalism should be evaluated more sensitively in its own terms, by recognizing its national authenticity and restoring the actual, as opposed to the imputed, parameters of its activity. It should be emphasized that this does not imply a rejection of comparative enquiry. On the contrary, it means searching for the right comparative context in which to mount such an analysis. The Gladstonian Liberal Party was not the only liberalism in Europe in the 1860s. The appropriate context for comparing the German liberals must be wider than the bilateral juxtaposition across the North Sea. Such a limited framework necessarily skews the terms of the discussion. It privileges certain questions and judgements which have more to do with ideal-typical (and ideological) representations of the two national histories over the nineteenth and twentieth centuries than with the actual context of the time. Instead, the comparative context should be European liberalism in the fullest sense: the European-wide conjuncture of constitutional revision, nation-forming, and state-making in the 1860s, powerfully over-determined by the global process of capitalist boom, spatial expansion, and social penetration, articulated through the pattern of uneven and combined development. In that sense, the more appropriate and illuminating comparison for Germany would be Italy.

NOTES

1 Leonard Krieger, *The German Idea of Freedom* (Boston, 1957), 458.
2 Heinrich August Winkler, 'Bürgerliche Emanzipation und nationale Einigung: Zur Entstehung des Nationalliberalismus in Preussen', in Winkler, *Liberalismus und Antiliberalismus. Studien zur politischen Sozialgeschichte des 19. und 20. Jahrhunderts* (Göttingen, 1979), 35.
3 Hans-Ulrich Wehler, *The German Empire 1871–1918* (Leamington Spa, 1985), 21.
4 Theodor Schieder, *Staat und Gesellschaft im Wandel unserer Zeit* (Munich, 1958); Thomas Nipperdey, *Die Organisation der deutschen Parteien vor 1918* (Düsseldorf, 1961); Lothar Gall, *Der Liberalismus als regierende Partei. Das Grossherzogtum Baden zwischen Restauration und Reichsgründung* (Wiesbaden, 1968), and 'Liberalismus und bürgerliche Gesellschaft. Zu Charakter und Entwicklung der bürgerlichen Bewegung in Deutschland', *Historische Zeitschrift*, 220 (1975), 324–56; Hans Rosenberg, *Grosse*

Depression und Bismarckzeit (Berlin, 1967); Dirk Stegmann, *Die Erben Bismarcks* (Cologne, 1970); Wolfgang J. Mommsen, *Max Weber und die deutsche Politik 1890–1920* (Tübingen, 1959).

5 One exception to this has been the work of Rauh, but the form and tone of his contribution have not been especially constructive, while the simple 'parliamentarization' thesis remains unpersuasive. See Manfred Rauh, *Föderalismus und Parlamentarismus im wilhelminischen Reich* (Düsseldorf, 1972), and *Die Parlamentarisierung des Deutschen Reiches* (Düsseldorf, 1977). For a more interesting contribution, see the late Stanley Suval's *Electoral Politics in Wilhelmine Germany* (Chapel Hill, 1985); and for a general discussion, David Blackbourn and Geoff Eley, *The Peculiarities of German History. Bourgeois Society and Politics in Nineteenth Century Germany* (Oxford, 1984).

6 Wehler, *German Empire*, 31.

7 ibid.' Winkler, 'Zum Dilemma des deutschen Liberalismus im 19. Jahrhundert', in *Liberalismus und Antiliberalismus*, 20.

8 Gerhard A. Ritter (ed.), *Historisches Lesebuch 1871–1914* (Frankfurt-on-Main 1967), 'Einleitung', 12.

9 Dirk Stegmann, 'Zwischen Repression und Manipulation: Konservative Machteliten und Arbeiter- und Angestelltenbewegung 1910–1918', *Archiv für Sozialgeschichte*, 12 (1972), 351. The second phrase comes from Werner Sombart, *Die deutsche Volkswirtschaft im 19. Jahrhundert* (Berlin, 1909), 508.

10 Winkler, 'Liberalismus: Zur historischen Bedeutung eines politischen Begriffs', in *Liberalismus und Antiliberalismus*, 15. Jürgen Kocka, 'Bürger und Arbeiter. Brennpunkte und Ergebnisse der Diskussion', in Kocka (ed.), *Arbeiter und Bürger im 19. Jahrhundert* (Munich, 1986), esp. 335–9.

11 See, e.g., Hans-Ulrich Wehler, *Krisenherde des Kaiserreichs* (Göttingen, 1970), 131. For the *locus classicus* of such an ideal-typification of the German experience in comparative social science, of course, see Barrington Moore Jr, *Social Origins of Dictatorship and Democracy* (Harmondsworth, 1966).

12 Blackbourn and Eley, *Peculiarities*, 164.

13 Anthony Arblaster, *The Rise and Decline of Western Liberalism* (London, 1984), 15. See also C.B. Macpherson, *The Political Theory of Possessive Individualism* (Oxford, 1962); and for a recent general discussion, Nicholas Abercrombie, Stephen Hill, Bryan S. Turner, *Sovereign Individuals of Capitalism* (London, 1986).

14 The role of government in this view was to protect the bases of individual liberty and to maintain the public sphere as a political arena for the pursuit of individual interests. See Mill's classic statement of the liberal principles of government as he saw them, in *On Liberty*, Gertrude Himmelfarb (ed.) (Harmondsworth, 1974), esp. 68f.: 'the only purpose for which power can be rightfully exercised over any member of a civilized community, against his will, is to prevent harm to others . . . Over himself, over his own body and mind, the individual is sovereign.' Here, it goes without saying, the sovereign individual is still gendered.

15 This was linked to the idea that legislation should originate in the

projects and counsels of experts and the talented few, which would
then go for approval to parliament, rather than issuing directly from
the elected assembly itself. Government by democracy, untempered
by the directive initiative of intellectuals, was a recipe (in Mill's view)
for mediocrity. The role of the democratically elected assembly was
'not to make the laws, but to see that they are made by the right
persons, and to be the organ of the nation for giving or withholding
its ratification of them'. For Mill 'rational democracy' was 'not that
the people themselves govern, but that they have *security* for good
government . . . the best government (need it be said?) must be the
government of the wisest, and these must always be a few. The people
ought to be the masters, but they are masters who must employ
servants more skilful than themselves . . .'. See J.H. Burns, 'J.S. Mill
and democracy, 1829–61', in J.B. Schneewind (ed.), *Mill* (London,
1969), 315; Geraint L. Williams (ed.), *John Stuart Mill on Politics and
Society* (London, 1976), 182.

16 Quoted from Arblaster, *Rise and Decline*, 280, 279.
17 ibid., 273.
18 Guido de Ruggiero, *The History of European Liberalism* (Boston, 1959),
   379.
19 The most authoritative estimate (Blewett) puts the enfranchised population at around 59 per cent of adult males in 1911. Moreover, Matthew, McKibbin, and Kay have shown that the franchise was disproportionately low in the boroughs as against the counties, sinking to
   lower than 57 per cent in 32.6 per cent of all borough seats (70 in
   all, of which 34 were in London, including figures as low as 20.6 per
   cent in Whitechapel and 35.7 per cent in Tower Hamlets). See Neal
   Blewett, 'The franchise in the United Kingdom, 1885–1918', *Past and
   Present*, 32 (Dec. 1965), 27–56; H.C.G. Matthew, R.I. McKibbin, J.A.
   Kay, 'The franchise factor in the rise of the Labour Party', *English
   Historical Review* 91 (1976), 723–52.
20 ibid., 737: 'the growth of the Labour Party before 1914 was limited
   not by "natural" social and political restrictions, but by an artificial
   one: a franchise and registration system that excluded the greater part
   of its likely support'.
21 By far the most illuminating recent discussion of German liberalism
   from this cultural point of view, to my mind, is the collection of papers
   edited by Gert Zang on the Konstanz region, *Provinzialisierung einer
   Region* (Frankfurt-on-Main, 1978). An excellent study from another
   perspective is Jonathan Sperber, *Popular Catholicism in Nineteenth-Century
   Germany* (Princeton, 1984). Also stimulating, though ultimately perverse (arguing that political Catholicism was the real liberalism of late
   nineteenth-century Germany), is the work of Margaret L. Anderson.
   See her *Windthorst: A Political Biography* (Oxford, 1981), and 'The
   Kulturkampf and the course of German history', *Central European History*,
   19:1 (1986), 82–115.
22 E.g. Zang (ed.), *Provinzialisierung*; Dieter Langewiesche, *Liberalismus und
   Demokratie in Württemberg zwischen Revolution und Reichsgründung* (Düsseldorf, 1974); Wolfgang Schmierer, *Von der Arbeiterbildung zur Arbeiter-*

politik. Die Anfänge der Arbeiterbewegung in Württemberg 1862/63–1878 (Hanover, 1970); David Blackbourn, *Class, Religion and Local Politics in Wilhelmine Germany. The Centre Party in Württemberg before 1914* (New Haven and London, 1980).

23 For a brilliant exploration of this question on the maturity of Gladstonian Liberalism, see Stephen Yeo, *Religion and Voluntary Organizations in Crisis* (London, 1976). There are a number of fruitful theoretical starting-points for approaching the German experience in this way, including Schieder's *Staat und Gesellschaft*, Habermas's conception of the public sphere, and Gramsci's reflections on the *Risorgimento*, on the role of intellectuals in social movements, and on the concepts of hegemony and civil society. See Jürgen Habermas, *Strukturwandel der Öffentlichkeit* (Neuwied, 1962); and Antonio Gramsci, *Selections from the Prison Notebooks* (London, 1971).

24 See the following exceptions: John Breuilly, 'Liberalismus oder Sozialdemokratie? Ein Vergleich der britischen und deutschen politischen Arbeiterbewegung zwischen 1850 und 1875', in Jürgen Kocka (ed.), *Europäische Arbeiterbewegungen im 19. Jahrhundert* (Göttingen, 1983), 129–66; Karl Rohe, 'The British imperialist intelligentsia and the Kaiserreich', in Paul Kennedy and A. J. Nicholls (eds), *Nationalist and Racialist Movements in Britain and Germany before 1914* (London, 1981), 130–42; Paul Kennedy, *The Rise of the Anglo-German Antagonism, 1860–1914* (London, 1980); Wolfgang J. Mommsen, *Britain and Germany 1800 to 1914. Two Developmental Paths Towards Industrial Society* (London, 1986). The German Historical Institute under Wolfgang Mommsen played a vital role in stimulating the beginnings of serious British-German comparison, partly via the framework of its conferences, partly via its sponsored research. A number of the monographs produced by fellows of the GHI have been implicitly comparative, including Peter Alter, *Wissenschaft, Staat, Mäzene. Anfänge moderner Wissenschaftspolitik in Grossbritannien 1850–1920* (Stuttgart, 1982); Wolfgang Mock, *Imperiale Herrschaft und nationale Interessen. 'Constructive Imperialism' oder Freihandel in Grossbritannien vor dem Ersten Weltkrieg* (Stuttgart, 1982); Ulrich Wengenroth, *Unternehmensstrategien und technischer Fortschritt. Die deutsche und britische Stahlindustrie 1865–1895* (Göttingen and Zurich, 1986).

25 This point is made especially forcefully and compellingly by Eric Hobsbawm, *The Age of Capital 1848–1875* (London, 1975).

26 Vincent, *Formation*, Penguin edn (Harmondsworth, 1972), 19.

27 ibid., 289.

28 Aside from Vincent's general and pioneering account, see the collection edited by Patricia Hollis, *Pressure from Without* (London, 1974), which provides a good introduction to the associational world of British liberalism in the mid nineteenth century, and Eileen and Stephen Yeo (eds), *Popular Culture and Class Conflict 1590–1914* (Brighton, 1981), which opens a window on its relationship to popular culture. See also the essays on 'Animals and the state', 'Religion and recreation', 'Traditions of respectability', and 'Philanthropy and the Victorians', in Brian Harrison, *Peaceable Kingdom. Stability and Change in Modern Britain* (Oxford, 1982), 82–259, which remain fundamental to this

subject. Monographs on particular associations and places may be cited indefinitely: Stephen Yeo's *Religion and Voluntary Associations in Crisis* (on Reading) is the most unruly, but also the most interesting. And for an excellent view of the whole Gladstonian show in motion, see Paul McHugh, *Prostitution and Victorian Social Reform* (London, 1980).

29 Gustav Mayer, 'Die Trennung der proletarischen von der bürgerlichen Demokratie in Deutschland, 1863–1870', in Hans-Ulrich Wehler (ed.), *Radikalismus, Sozialismus und bürgerliche Demokratie*, (Frankfurt-on-Main 1969, orig. pub. 1912), 108–78.

30 In a real sense the functional equivalent in Germany of populist religion in Britain (i.e. Non-Conformity) is political Catholicism. See esp. Blackbourn, *Class, Religion and Local Politics*, and Anderson, 'The *Kulturkampf*'. For the argument concerning artisans/craftsmen, see John Breuilly's various essays: 'Arbeiteraristokratie in Grossbritannien und Deutschland', in Ulrich Engelhardt (ed.), *Handwerker in der Industrialisierung* (Stuttgart, 1984), 497–527; 'Artisan economy, artisan politics, artisan ideology: the artisan contribution to the nineteenth-century European labour movement', in Clive Emsley and James Walvin (eds), *Artisans, Peasants and Proletarians, 1760–1860* (London, 1985), 187–225; and 'Liberalismus oder Sozialdemokratie?'. There is a helpful summary in Mommsen, *Britain and Germany 1800 to 1914*, 14ff. As always on such matters, the discussion is heavily indebted to the essays of Eric Hobsbawm. See most recently, *Worlds of Labour. Further Studies in the History of Labour* (London, 1984).

31 See Breuilly, 'Liberalismus oder Sozialdemokratie?'

32 Rohe, 'British imperialist intelligentsia', 141.

33 The main protagonists in this British discussion have been Peter F. Clarke and Kenneth O. Morgan. For the former, see his original *Lancashire and the New Liberalism* (Cambridge, 1971), and the more general 'The Progressive movement in England', in *Transactions of the Royal Historical Society*, 5th ser. 24 (1974), 159–81, together with the more recent *Liberals and Social Democrats* (Cambridge, 1978). Morgan's ideas are best approached through his many reviews in the *Times Literary Supplement* over the last fifteen years, esp. 'The Liberal regeneration', *TLS*, 22 Aug. 1975, and subsequent correspondence. For a useful introduction to the terms of the controversy, see Alun Howkins, 'Edwardian Liberalism and industrial unrest', in *History Workshop Journal*, 4 (1977), 143–62.

11

The middle classes and National Socialism

Thomas Childers

I

In spite of numerous and often extremely bitter controversies that have swirled around the National Socialist movement and regime over the years, until relatively recently a remarkable consensus existed concerning at least one important issue: the relationship between the NSDAP and the German middle class. Regardless of theoretical orientation or methodological approach, virtually every analysis of Nazi support produced between 1930 and 1980 concluded that the social bases of the NSDAP were to be located almost exclusively in elements of the German *Kleinbürgertum* or petty bourgeoisie. It was from the under-educated, economically marginal, and socially insecure lower middle class that the Nazis mobilized the overwhelming bulk of their support in the years before 1933, the traditional and still widely accepted interpretation tells us. Driven by intense economic distress, especially after the onset of the Great Depression in 1929, and desperately afraid of 'proletarianization', these small shopkeepers, independent craftsmen, white-collar workers, low-ranking civil servants, and small farmers of the lower middle class deserted the traditional parties of the bourgeois centre and right after 1928 for the radical NSDAP. The increasingly strong appeal of National Socialism was, therefore, based on 'the psychological reaction of this lower middle class' to both the economic and political traumas of the postwar era as well.[1]

For a over a decade now, this conventional wisdom has been under assault from new studies that have employed a variety of methodological approaches, especially increasingly sophisticated statistical techniques, to analyse both the membership and electoral constituency of the NSDAP. Although these studies differ in some interpretive points and considerable sniping has occurred on methodological issues, they are in basic agreement that the traditional definition of Nazi social support is far too narrow. Indeed, a new consensus in the recent literature has arisen that views National Socialism less as a distinctly middle- and especially lower-middle-class phenomenon than as a broadly based political movement that drew its support from a wide variety of social sources. According to these new researches, the NSDAP was not only able to tap the oft-described reservoirs of petty-bourgeois (*kleinbürgerlich*) resentment but also found considerable support within the well-educated, economically secure upper middle classes and even among some elements of the blue-collar working class. By the summer of 1932, at the apex of its electoral popularity, the NSDAP had most certainly become the long-sought party of bourgeois integration and could make at least a plausible claim to be a socially heterogeneous people's party (*Volkspartei*).[2]

Given the remarkable burst of scholarly work on these issues over the past decade, its seems appropriate at this juncture to take stock of this recent revisionist wave, to assess its historiographic and theoretical implications. What can we now say about the appeal of National Socialism to elements of the German middle classes, both upper and lower? Indeed, how does one now assess the role of the middle classes in the rise of Nazism? To what extent did long-term, structural factors in German political culture such as the 'failed liberal tradition', the 'feudalized bourgeoisie', and 'pre-industrial traditions' within the German bourgeoisie, factors emphasized by proponents of the *Sonderweg* interpretation, play a role in explaining the popularity of the NSDAP with the diverse segments of the middle class? What weight should be given to more immediate – especially economic – factors in the turbulent Weimar years? If, as the new sociographic literature on National Socialism emphasizes, the NSDAP had managed to attract a remarkably diverse social constituency, how stable was that support? What were the limits of Nazi popularity? If support for National Socialism was, as I have argued elsewhere, a mile wide but an inch deep at critical junctures, can one speak of a genuine *Volkspartei* or might one more legitimately describe the NSDAP as a highly volatile catch-all party of protest?

II

Although historians and many contemporary analysts were quick to label the NSDAP a lower-middle-class phenomenon, the Nazis themselves vigorously denied this interpretation. From its very inception in Munich in 1919 the NSDAP insisted that it was not a class-based party at all but a genuine people's party or *Volkspartei* that transcended the traditional lines of social, religious, and regional cleavage around which the German party system had developed during the last half of the nineteenth century. Friends and foes alike were certainly perplexed about the proper locus of the NSDAP within the Weimar party system, and if one looks at the day-to-day efforts of the party to mobilize political support at the grassroots level, it is easy to understand something of that confusion. According to the well established practices of German political culture, parties made little effort to cross social boundaries in mobilizing electoral support, seeking instead to define for themselves a clear position along the traditional lines of class, religious, and/or regional cleavage. From the conservative DNVP to the left-liberal DDP, the bourgeois parties rarely sought to recruit support from the blue-collar working class. Although each of the major Weimar parties claimed to be a *Volkspartei*, speaking for the entire nation, the traditional bourgeois parties concentrated their mobilization efforts almost exclusively on elements of the middle-class electorate. In their appeals to the middle-class voters these parties were determined above all else to establish their credentials as stalwart defenders of middle-class interests and values against the threat of the Marxist left. Similarly, the Social Democrats (SPD) and Communists (KPD) competed fiercely for the blue-collar electorate but made little effort to draw support from the politically and socially fractious bourgeoisie. Only the Catholic Centre party (*Zentrum*), whose appeal was based on religious confession, sought to straddle the great social divide of German politics, but almost exclusively within the Catholic community.[3]

From its very first appearance on the electoral landscape, however, the NSDAP refused to follow in these well-worn grooves of German political culture. Like virtually all the other Weimar parties, the NSDAP announced to a sceptical public that it was a genuine people's movement committed to the ideal of a classless people's community (*Volksgemeinschaft*). There was little that was striking about this claim or the rhetoric in which it was cloaked.

Virtually all the bourgeois parties had invoked the 'people's community' well before the NSDAP would appropriate it, and even the left-liberal DDP occasionally adopted the language of *Volksgemeinschaft*, addressing its would-be supporters as *Volksgenossen* (people's comrades).[4] Yet, in striking contrast to their bourgeois competitors, the Nazis actually adopted a political strategy that reflected this claim. Alone among the parties of the Weimar era, the NSDAP attempted to mobilize support in every sector of the economy, in every occupational group, in every region, and in both Protestant and Catholic populations. It mounted campaigns to recruit not only the small shopkeeper and artisan and farmer but the coalminer and steelworker as well, attacking in the process both Marxist socialism and large-scale corporate capitalism. Nothing could be further from the truth than Karl Dietrich Bracher's claim that the NSDAP made little sustained effort to appeal to working-class Germans. Even after 1928, when the NSDAP intensified its efforts to cultivate a middle-class constituency, the party was unwilling to concede the working-class vote to the parties of the left.[5]

The National Socialists were pioneering a radically new political course, a catch-all strategy aimed at capturing support from right across the social landscape. The NSDAP 'represents a new political synthesis of seemingly antagonistic and contradictory currents', one internal Nazi circular explained to its operatives in the field. 'On national issues it stands on the far right, on social issues on the far left.'[6] The Social Democrats and Communists vigorously disputed this claim, but the result of the NSDAP's unorthodox catch-all strategy was to produce considerable confusion concerning the true nature of National Socialism. To the conservatives, the NSDAP represented little more than 'Bolshevism in nationalist wrapping', while the liberals relentlessly sought to depict the Nazis as 'brown socialists'. The Social Democrats and Communists, on the other hand, issued repeated warnings to working-class Germans not to be taken in by 'the counterfeit socialism' of the Nazis.[7] Even within the NSDAP's own ranks, local party officials occasionally expressed confusion about the social locus of the 'movement'. 'Are we a worker's party or a middle-class party?' one perplexed member of the Stuttgart NSDAP enquired of the leadership in 1923.[8] The question might just as easily have been posed ten years later.

Were the Nazis successful in their efforts to transcend class and become a genuine *Volkspartei*? On this central question the research of the past decade, despite different methodologies and interpretative emphases, has struck a note of surprising unanimity. Whether examining the party's membership or electoral constituency, these studies have discovered and documented a National Socialist constituency of far greater demographic and social diversity than that of any other Weimar party and certainly of far greater heterogeneity than the conventional lower-middle-class thesis has suggested. Between 1928 and 1932 the NSDAP had become far more than a party of *déclassés* and petty-bourgeois misfits, drawing followers from the socially established and affluent upper middle class and from elements of the blue-collar working class.

The hard core of the NSDAP's constituency was, indeed, drawn primarily from the lower middle class, just as the traditional literature assumed. That support, however, was not uniformly developed among the various groups usually considered integral parts of the lower middle class. Support for the party among small shopkeepers and independent artisans of the so-called old middle class was both stable and strong between 1924 and 1932, though it certainly intensified and broadened after the onset of the Great Depression. Significant support for the Nazis among the peasantry, on the other hand, was slow to develop, emerging only after 1928 and becoming stronger with each passing election down to November 1932. Perhaps most surprisingly, white-collar employees – often depicted as the quintessential socially insecure 'little men' of the lower middle class – seem not to have been drawn irresistably to the NSDAP, as the traditional literature maintains, but to have scattered their electoral support all across the spectrum of Weimar politics.[9]

Nor was support for the NSDAP within the middle class confirmed to the petty bourgeoisie. Richard Hamilton's analysis of voting patterns in thirteen major cities reveals that the Nazis did quite well in affluent, upper-middle-class neighbourhoods.[10] Similarly, civil servants, though under considerable financial and social strain during the Weimar Republic, were hardly undereducated or socially marginal, and yet analysis of both the party's membership and electorate suggests that the NSDAP exerted a stronger appeal for civil servants than for white-collar employees.[11] Significantly, Michael Kater's study of the NSDAP's membership indicates that this support was by no means confined to the lower ranks of the civil service. By 1932, despite considerable pressure from several state governments, most notably in Prussia, not to join the party, civil servants from the middle and upper grades were over-represented in the NSDAP.[12]

Perhaps the most surprising finding of the past decade, however, has been the discovery of considerable support for the NSDAP within the German working class. Although the National Socialists proved unable to make significant headway with workers in the mining or industrial sectors, strongholds of the KPD and SPD, or, significantly, among the blue-collar unemployed, the party was able to attract a significant following among workers in handicrafts, small-scale manufacturing, and in agriculture. These workers were usually employed in small shops, in government enterprises, or in the countryside and were rarely integrated into either the organized working class or the entrepreneurial sectors of the bourgeoisie.[13] Despite considerable research on the social and labour history of the period, we still know relatively little about such unorganized workers, who comprised a sizeable percentage of the blue-collar population.[14] Richard Hamilton has described them as 'Tory workers', who had previously supported the conservative German-National People's Party (DNVP) or other bourgeois parties;[15] but Jürgen Falter's more recent and extensive analysis of voter cross-overs suggests that the NSDAP was surprisingly successful in winning support from former Social Democratic voters. Indeed, Falter estimates that 40 per cent of the National Socialist vote by 1932 was drawn from the working class.[16] Just who these workers were is a question requiring considerably more research and investigation, the evidence that has emerged from the studies of the past decade makes it quite clear that the NSDAP had made considerable strides toward bridging the great social divide of German electoral politics, winning support from all elements of the bourgeoisie and among the working class as well.

It was this extraordinarily heterogenous base of support that allowed the Nazis to maintain, with some degree of credibility, that they alone among the Weimar parties had indeed become a genuine *Volkspartei*. The National Socialists still continued to do much better among Protestant voters than among Catholics. Their efforts to establish a significant foothold within the industrial working class were consistently frustrated by the parties of the left. But by 1932 the NSDAP's constituency was certainly far more diverse than those of the relatively stable leftist parties or the traditional bourgeois parties, whose electoral support evaporated in the scorching heat of the Nazi ascent after 1928.[17]

III

The Nazi electoral surge between 1928 and 1930, when the party's vote jumped from 2.6 per cent to 18 per cent, is often described in the literature as stunning or sudden, a product of middle-class radicalization in response to the economic traumas of the Great Depression. But the spectacular Nazi breakthrough of the Depression era was possible only after a profound disruption of traditional bourgeois electoral loyalties first signalled during the inflation and stabilization crises of 1923-4. The political impact of these interrelated crises, in which wide sections of the middle class felt victimized, was registered not, however, in a sustained surge of radical political behaviour within the middle class but rather in an ominous transformation of middle-class electoral loyalties between 1920 and 1928. That transformation was vividly reflected in the sudden emergence and surprisingly strong showing of a swarm of single-issue, special-interest, and regional parties in the woefully mislabelled 'Golden Twenties.'[18]

Between the elections to the national assembly in 1919 and the last pre-Depression Reichstag election in 1928, middle-class political loyalties underwent a profound transformation that would seriously undermine the stability of the Weimar party system well before the onset of the Depression. During this period the major bourgeois parties, each of which had served prominently in at least one of the unpopular cabinets of these years, suffered a steady haemorrhage of electoral support to a bewildering array of middle-class special-interest or regional parties. Parties such as the Christian-National Peasants' Party, the Reich Party of the German *Mittelstand (Wirtschaftspartei)*, the Christian-Social People's Service, and the Tenants' Party, were but a few of the dozen or so bourgeois alternative parties that crowded onto the already congested terrain of middle-class political culture between 1920 and 1928. These parties appealed exclusively to specific occupational, economic, or regional groups within the middle class, and have traditionally been dismissed as symptoms of narrow, myopic 'interest politics' within a badly fractured middle class. Yet while these parties spoke to quite specific sets of interests within the middle class, they were far more than reflections of a growing interest-group politics. For when the rhetoric of their appeal is examined, it is clear that these parties shared an implicit ideological orientation that challenged the very economic, social, and political foundations on which the Weimar Republic was constructed.[19]

Although these parties were, of course, rabidly anti-Marxist, their real fury was directed against the mainstream liberal and conservative parties for their failure to protect specific sectional interests during the inflation and stabilization crises of 1923–4. The mainstream bourgeois parties, they believed, had betrayed the small shopkeeper, the peasant, the independent artisan, and other lower-middle-class interests. Their rage against the established liberal and conservative parties and the Weimar system which these parties represented grew rather than decreased during the twenties. Virtually all these groups expressed scorn for Weimar party politics, which they regarded as no more than sordid 'cattle-dealing'. They had boundless contempt for the Republic's parliamentary system, which they viewed as a veil behind which both the 'wire-pullers' of big business and the 'bosses' of big labour secured their selfish dominance of German politics and society. Most of these alternative bourgeois parties were also hostile to Weimar 'big business' and advocated some vague notion of a corporatist economic and political order, a *Ständestaat*, which would reduce the power of both organized labour and 'international finance capital'.[20] Echoing the populist themes and rhetoric of resentment that had surfaced in the 1890s,[21] these parties were expressions of a growing protest against a party system that was widely perceived to have failed the lower middle class even before the Great Depression catapulted the NSDAP into the forefront of bourgeois politics.

The inflation and stabilization crises of 1923–4 thus mark a significant turning point in the evolution of bourgeois political loyalties in the Weimar era. In the elections of January 1919, these alternative parties had captured less than 2 per cent of the national vote and only 3.7 per cent in the first Reichstag elections a year later. In 1924, however, after a year of nightmarish hyper-inflation and in the midst of a draconian economic stabilization that would ultimately destabilize Weimar politics, these middle-class interest-group parties more than doubled their share of the vote (8.3 per cent), surpassing the faltering left-liberal DDP and almost matching the vote of Gustav Stresemann's centre-right German People's Party (DVP). Equally revealing, the popularity of these alternative parties did not fade during the ensuing years of relative economic recovery and political tranquillity. Indeed, the elections of 1928, usually viewed as the high-water-mark of Weimar's illusory stability, saw these alternative bourgeois parties claim over 14 per cent of the electorate. That total exceeded the combined vote of the two liberal parties and virtually equalled the conservative showing. Since these parties recruited their support exclusively from different groups within the bourgeoisie, their strong performance suggests that on the eve of the Great Depression roughly a third of the middle-class electorate had *already* abandoned their traditional liberal and conservative choices. Two years before the NSDAP would make its dramatic breakthrough into the middle-class electorate, the traditional bourgeois parties had proved unable to contain middle-class protest. Bourgeois voters were not yet completely radicalized, not yet ready for a party such as the NSDAP, but in scornfully turning their backs on both the traditional liberal and conservative options of middle-class politics, they displayed a growing affinity for the social and political protest which the Nazis would articulate so effectively in the following period of economic crisis.[22]

As the economic situation deteriorated after 1928, the National Socialists would march from the fringes of German political consciousness to a series of spectacular electoral victories that would transform the NSDAP into Germany's largest political party and carry Hitler to the very threshold of power. During this steep ascent the NSDAP simply devoured the constituencies of the bourgeois parties. Although the Nazis would benefit *after* 1930 from a sharp increase in turnout and, as Falter's analysis has demonstrated, would win some defectors from the SPD, the parties of bourgeois centre and right watched helplessly as their middle-class supporters defected in massive numbers to the NSDAP.[23] In the Reichstag elections of July 1932, as the Nazis captured roughly 38 per cent of the national vote, the liberal parties together managed to win only 2 per cent, while the conservative figures had plummetted to 5.9 per cent. The totals of the middle-class alternative parties remained relatively high in 1930, buoyed by the fragmentation of the DNVP and the establishment of a spate of new conservative splinter parties. But by the summer of 1932 these parties could attract a mere 3 per cent of the vote. Between 1928 and 1932, the NSDAP had virtually consumed its stumbling bourgeois rivals and succeeded in mobilizing a unprecedented level of support across the socially diverse middle class.

Why, or at least how was the NSDAP so effective in mobilizing support within the German middle class? Traditionally much of the party's appeal has been explained by pointing to the sheer economic misery, social anxiety, and political desperation within the middle classes as the Depression deepened and the existing system groaned ineffectually from one crisis to another. Although their experiences were hardly uniform, the various groups within the middle class suffered bitterly during the Depression. Anger at the inability of the Weimar system either to halt the disastrous slide of the economy or to provide political security for middle-class interests saturated bourgeois political discourse between 1928 and 1932.[24] Yet, while economic and social conditions may help explain this widespread dissatisfaction with the 'system' and with the 'system parties', does it adequately explain the appeal of National Socialism to the German middle classes? In confronting this question, most analyses, whether focusing on local, regional, or national developments, have emphasized the important role of Nazi propaganda, suggesting that the strategy and techniques of the party's propaganda played a critical role in mobilizing middle-class discontent. Certainly the organization and conduct of Nazi propaganda, as numerous case studies have indicated, were remarkably sophisticated within the Weimar context and no doubt had a considerable impact on the party's success.[25]

Limitations of space preclude an analysis of the various techniques and themes of National Socialist propaganda here, but some suggestive clues concerning the success of National Socialist propaganda may be found by examining briefly the relationship of the NSDAP to certain well-established patterns of middle-class political mobilization. All parties employed a battery of political symbols, rituals, and languages to construct their own public identity and to mobilize their followers. So an examination of how the bourgeois parties defined, conceptualized, and addressed their prospective supporters is particularly revealing. From the Nazis to the left-liberal DDP, the bourgeois parties disaggregated the middle class by occupation, directing their appeals to highly defined occupational groups – to artisans, shopkeepers, peasants, white-collar employees, or civil servants. Although the parties also sought to mobilize support on the basis of gender, generation, and religion, the social vocabulary of bourgeois politics in the Weimar

Republic was dominated by *Beruf* (occupation). Appeals to occupational identity, to *Berufsstände* (occupational estates), constituted the basic operational approach of all the bourgeois parties to the middle class throughout the Weimar period. Despite significant differences in ideological orientation, all the bourgeois parties were convinced that occupation was the key ingredient in the formation of middle-class social identity. The content of their appeals differed considerably, but the bourgeois parties were in obvious agreement that the most effective way of mobilizing their constituencies was through such occupational appeals. Each party, therefore, produced a plethora of pamphlets addressed to specific occupational groups, each held special recruitment drives for each of the major bourgeois occupational groupings, and, of course, during electoral campaigns drafted and distributed millions of occupation-specific leaflets explaining the party's stance on the problems and concerns of each of the major middle-class *Berufsstände*.[26]

Some of the political parties developed form letters for different occupational groups and delivered occupationally oriented propaganda directly to the homes of prospective voters. Local affiliates of the NSDAP, for example, were ordered to analyse address books in their communities to determine the occupations present in each household and then deliver relevant occupation-specific material directly to the door. These efforts would often be followed by what the Nazis referred to as *Hauspropaganda*, a visit to the recipient's residence and an invitation to a National Socialist meeting devoted to issues of concern to the occupation in question. At such meetings most of the major political parties, including the NSDAP, offered relevant specialists from their ranks on civil servants, peasants, shopkeepers, artisans, and white-collar employees to address the audience. Typically, by 1930 over half the NSDAP's cadre of national speakers counted occupational themes as their speciality. Similarly, the other parties also endeavoured to produce broad occupational representation in composing their lists of electoral candidates. The point was to do everything possible to convince its targeted occupational audience that the DDP or DVP or DNVP alone appreciated the historical position, special economic problems and social status of the targeted *Berufsstand*.[27]

In the social language of bourgeois politics these occupational concerns were frequently expressed in the imagery of *Stand*, or estate. References to the *Bauernstand, Beamtenstand, Mittelstand,* and even, on occasion, the *Angestelltenstand* flow through the electoral appeals of all the bourgeois parties. Even those parties with little sympathy for the corporatist economic and political ideas implied by such terminology found the idiom of *Berufsstand* irresistible when addressing middle-class audiences. For the liberals, in particular, the prevalence of such corporatist imagery in bourgeois political discourse proved problematic. The conservatives, the middle-class interest-group parties, and ultimately the Nazis, too, were, to varying degrees, comfortable with this corporatist or *ständisch* idiom, calling for the establishment of a corporate state or *Ständestaat* and couching their attacks on the Weimar 'system' in such language. But its use forced the liberals to operate within a linguistic terminology that was at the very least inconsistent with the content of their social and political vision. As the DDP complained in 1930, 'We are in danger of seeing the idea of the people (*Volksgedanke*) overwhelmed by the idea of occupation (*Berufsgedanke*).' German political culture, the Democrats complained, was 'unsurpassed in the organization of the occupational estate or economic stratum (*berufsständischen oder wirtschaftlichen Schicht*) but pathetic in . . . fitting the self into a conception of the general welfare.'[28]

Appealing to specific occupational or economic groups was axiomatic in the political culture of the Weimar Republic; indeed, the various bourgeois parties considered it an operational necessity. Yet, this strategy also presented a growing dilemma for the traditional liberal *and* conservative parties seeking to mobilize support across the different occupational and regional interests of the socially heterogeneous middle class, a dilemma greatly exacerbated by the emergence of the special interest parties. By 1928 both liberals and conservatives alike were finding it increasingly difficult to formulate a credible political language that would permit them to address both the sectarian interests of shopkeepers, white-collar employees, peasants, and civil servants, and, at the same time, forge a broadly based middle-class coalition. The arrival of the Great Depression only aggravated this problem.

The Nazis, on the other hand, were ideally positioned to benefit both from the mounting anger and anxiety of wide segments of the bourgeoisie and the *berufsständisch* language of middle-class special interest. Unlike the major bourgeois parties of the centre and right, the NSDAP had never been burdened with government responsibility and had, therefore, never been forced to make hard policy decisions that might satisfy one group while disappointing others. Nor, of course, was it tainted with the failures of Weimar, as were the liberals and conservatives. Moreover, unlike the small bourgeois interest-group parties, the NSDAP was not identified with any one set of interests, either economic, occupational or regional. As a consequence, the NSDAP alone could speak the language of both transcendent class or even national solidarity *and* sectarian special interest. It alone could employ the pervasive *ständisch* idiom of middle-class politics to embrace occupation-specific interests while simultaneously condemning the petty interest politics of all its bourgeois rivals and calling for the creation of a *Ständestaat* that would at last bring an end to the class conflicts that had bedevilled German politics since unification. It was a potent political combination.

The prominence of this *ständisch* language in the discourse of middle-class politics has prompted some historians to stress the role of 'pre-industrial' mentalities in explaining the attraction of the middle class to National Socialism. Indeed, emphasis on the vestigial presence of pre-industrial social and political values occupies a central position in the German *Sonderweg* thesis, which asserts that the lingering presence of such values or traditions within the bourgeoisie distinguished the German middle classes from their counterparts in England, France, and the United States. Despite some differences of emphasis and argumentation, advocates of the *Sonderweg* thesis have contended that the persistence of such 'pre-industrial, pre-capitalist' traditions or groups fundamentally distorted bourgeois political culture in Germany in the last half of the nineteenth century, contributing directly to the failure of liberal democracy and ultimately to the rise of National Socialism. In an extreme but none the less characteristic formulation of this view, Heinrich August Winkler contends that:

> the commercial *Mittelstand* did not . . . constitute the only pre-industrial element in the National Socialist mass support. Peasants were no less a pre-industrial stratum with a pre-capitalist economic mentality. . . . This also applies even to the white-collar employees, who . . . were also oriented toward pre-industrial, *ständisch* traditions.[29]

Such blanket characterizations of complex social, occupational, or demographic groups as 'pre-industrial' have been vigorously challenged over the past decade, as social historians have repeatedly demonstrated that peasants, civil servants, white-collar employees, and even independent artisans can hardly be described so categorically as backward-looking, nostalgic captives of a 'pre-capitalist economic mentality'.[30] Moreover, recent research has also disputed the significance of 'pre-industrial' vestiges in bourgeois political culture, demonstrating the wide discrepancy between the social and political rhetoric of the middle-class interest groups and parties and more complex social realities. The German middle-class, this revisionist scholarship insists, was 'not a static, tradition-ally minded group faced with the traumas of modernization' but 'a hybrid class with fluid class boundaries'. According to this view, a *Mittelstand* did not exist in either Wilhelmine or Weimar Germany, and the entire language of *Stand*, with its implied pre-indus-trial values and norms, was, in David Blackbourn's view, 'more prescriptive than descriptive . . .'[31]

This critique is in many ways very compelling, but the problem of bourgeois political language and its prevailing *ständisch* idiom cannot be resolved quite so easily. It is true that while the terms of bourgeois sociopolitical address were firmly anchored in the language of *Berufsstand*, the content that filled those terms had undergone tremendous change since the genuinely pre-industrial era. The linguistic forms of *Stand* and *Berufsstand* had clearly sur-vived the social and economic conditions they had evolved to describe, and they were no doubt employed in a 'prescriptive' way in bourgeois political discourse as an alternative to a language of class. But the terms routinely used by middle-class interest organizations, political parties, state agencies and individuals in everyday experience also operated far beyond the bounds of con-scious manipulation or prescription. Indeed, they continued to provide middle-class political discourse with its distinctive contours and defined the terms in which politics and society were under-stood. If language and other 'representations of the social world', as Roger Chartier and others have argued, should be viewed not as reflections but as 'constituent[s] of reality',[32] then whether these *ständisch* terms provide 'objective' descriptions of bourgeois life is not the critical issue. What is critical is that this corporatist termin-ology remained at the centre of bourgeois political language throughout the Weimar era and that it played a major role in shaping middle-class political and social consciousness. Pre-indus-trial residues in bourgeois political culture were, therefore, not to be found in the existence of 'pre-industrial groups with pre-capitalist economic mentalities' or in manipulative 'pre-modern elites' but rather in the very language adopted by middle-class Germans to define themselves for political action. This was of tremendous importance in the Weimar Republic, for it meant that bourgeois political discourse was largely confined to a linguistic terrain that was far more congenial to conservative and fascist than liberal, not to mention social democratic, politics.

These observations are not meant to imply that the Nazis succeeded in mobilizing their middle-class supporters merely because of their language, nor is it a summons to replace a social interpretation with a semiotic one. Nor does it mean that the appeal of National Socialism can be reduced to an 'anti-modernist' reaction. After all, this language was used not to call for a return to some pre-industrial or pre-capitalist past but to articulate an anti-Marxist, anti-big-capitalist form of bourgeois populism that emerged in the last decade of the nineteenth century. In addition, more immediate and powerful developments – particularly the economic crises of the Weimar era – had a far greater impact on Nazi electoral performance than language. Still, as Gareth Stedman Jones has argued in another context, the success of any political movement, even in times of great social discord, is dependent on 'its capacity to persuade its constituency to interpret their distress or discontent within the terms of its political language'.[33] In the battle for middle-class support, the Nazis, in the end, had the right words at their command.

IV

In July 1932, the NSDAP, employing its revolutionary catch-all strategy, became the largest political party in Germany, constructing a constituency of extraordinary social breadth. The party seemed to stand on the brink of power. Yet, less than six months later, it suffered a serious electoral setback, when in the first week of November its share of the national vote dropped significantly for the first time in a major campaign since the party had begun its dramatic surge forward in 1929. Even more distressing for the Nazi strategists, the party's losses in the last Reichstag election of 1932 marked the beginning of a trend; in regional elections later in November and December, the NSDAP's vote continued to slide precipitously.[34]

In a top-secret analysis of the election, based on local reports from Nazi operatives from all over the country, Goebbels's propaganda staff concluded that the party had reached the limits of its potential support within the middle class in July. For a number of reasons, they declared that the middle-class constituency was now beginning to erode. The report suggested that the catch-all strategy had at last run into serious difficulties. In particular, the party's aggressive efforts to win working-class support – symbolized by its support for the Berlin transport strike – and its radical social rhetoric, attacking the Papen 'cabinet of barons', had alienated many middle-class voters. In addition, the report concluded that the party's protest appeal was also wearing thin. It conceded that many of the voters who had flocked to the party since 1928 were not committed ideologically to National Socialism and that the party's continued failure to attain power had disappointed many, particularly in the upper middle class, who had either stayed at home on 6 November or defected to the conservative right. Finally, the NSDAP was finding it increasingly difficult to reconcile the desires of the party's radicals, especially in the Brownshirt organizations, the SA, with their impatience for action and growing propensity to public violence, with the insistent demand for 'law and order' voiced by the respectable middle class. Indeed, Goebbels's staff were convinced that mounting SA terror and violence during the summer and autumn had repelled many middle-class voters in November.[35]

The National Socialist constituency, striking in its social and demographic heterogeneity, was also, party leaders understood, a highly unstable political compound. Between 1928 and 1932 the NSDAP had attracted support of unprecedented social breadth, but that support was, at critical points, remarkably shallow. Even within the middle class, where the appeal of National Socialism found its greatest resonance, the composition of the party's constituency changed significantly over time and differed from group to group in both depth and duration. What made the NSDAP's success so remarkable was its ability, in a period of severe economic distress, to reach beyond its lower-middle-class base to attract crisis-related protests voters from a wide variety of social backgrounds. During the Nazi electoral triumphs after 1928, the hard core of the party's petty bourgeois support was swamped by a surge of volatile protest voters. These people carried the NSDAP to dazzling heights. But their commitment to National Socialism, Nazi leaders conceded, was tenuous at best and secondary to their anger at the Weimar 'system' and the parties associated with it.

Even in the heady days of electoral triumph in early 1932,

Goebbels had realized that the Nazis had only a narrow window of opportunity in the context of free parliamentary elections, and by the end of the year that window seemed to be rapidly closing.[36] After years of apparently inexorable growth, the National Socialist constituency was clearly unravelling. Nazi strategists had no solution for halting that disintegration. 'On the basis of numerous contacts with our supporters', the top secret report grimly concluded, 'we are of the opinion that little can be salvaged by way of propaganda . . . New paths must be taken. Nothing more is to be done with words, placards and leaflets.' Above all, 'it must not come to another election. The results could not be imagined.'[37]

As a catch-all party of protest, the NSDAP had reached the limits of its electoral popularity. The November elections of 1932 would prove to be the final genuinely free elections of the Weimar era, and in that contest two out of every three German voters had chosen parties other than the NSDAP. These votes cannot, of course, be interpreted simply as expressions of anti-Nazi sentiment, but they do at the very least underscore just how fragile and contingent Nazi electoral success actually was. In the gloomy aftermath of those elections, Nazi propaganda leaders believed that only a Nazi assumption of power could rekindle the party's crumbling appeal, and in late 1932 that prospect seemed to be rapidly receding. It is, therefore, a particularly monstrous irony that, at just the moment when the NSDAP's electoral constituency had begun to dissolve, Adolf Hitler would be appointed chancellor on 30 January 1933. The Nazi assumption of power would, therefore, come not at the crest of rising popular appeal, but as a result of a palace intrigue of conservative forces who myopically and tragically believed that the appeal of National Socialism could be safely harnessed for their own reactionary politics.

NOTES

1 For contemporary statements of the lower-middle-class thesis see Harold D. Lasswell, 'The psychology of Hitlerism,' *Political Quarterly*, 4 (1933), 373–84, and Svend Ranulf, *Moral Indignation and Middle Class Psychology: A Sociological Study* (Copenhagen, 1938). Far more nuanced formulations of these classic views are found in Karl Dietrich Bracher, *Die Deutsche Diktatur. Entstehung, Struktur, Folgen des Nationalsozialismus* (Cologne, 1969), 166–7; and Seymour Martin Lipset, 'Fascism – Left-Right, and Centre', in Lipset, *Political Man: The Social Bases of Politics* (Garden City, 1960), 127–79.

2 On the Nazi electoral constituency see in particular, Thomas Childers, *The Nazi Voter. The Social Foundations of Fascism in Germany, 1919–1933* (Chapel Hill, 1983); and the articles collected in Childers (ed.), *The Formation of the Nazi Constituency 1919–1933* (London, 1986); Richard F. Hamilton, *Who Voted for Hitler?* (Princeton, 1982); Dirk Hänisch, *Sozialstrukturelle Bestimmungsgründe des Wahlverhaltens in der Weimarer Republik. Eine Aggregatdatenanalyse der Ergebnisse der Reichstagswahlen 1924 bis 1933* (Duisburg, 1983); Jürgen W. Falter, 'Die Wähler der NSDAP 1928–1933. Sozialstruktur und parteipolitische Herkunft', in Wolfgang Michalka (ed.), *Die nationalsozialistische Machtergreifung 1933* (Paderborn, 1984); and Falter, 'Wahlen und Wählerverhalten unter besonderer Berücksichtigung des Aufstiegs der NSDAP nach 1928', in Karl Dietrich Bracher, Manfred Funke, Hans-Adolf Jacobsen (eds), *Die Weimarer Republik 1918–1933. Politik, Wirtschaft, Gesellschaft* (Bonn, 1987), 484–504. On the Nazi membership, see Michael Kater, *The Nazi Party. A Social Profile of Members and Leaders, 1919–1945* (Cambridge, Mass, 1983); Lawrence D. Stokes, 'The social composition of the Nazi party in Eutin, 1925–1932', *International Review of Social History*, 23 (1978), 1–32.

3 See Childers, *The Nazi Voter*, 15–49.

4 See Thomas Childers, 'Languages of liberalism. Liberal political discourse in the Weimar Republic', in Konrad Jarausch and Larry E. Jones (eds.), *In Search of a Liberal Germany. Festschrift for Theodore Hamerow* (New York, 1990), 323–59.

5 See Bracher, *The German Dictatorship*, 158. On Nazi appeals to the working class see Childers, *The Nazi Voter*, 102–12, 178–88, 243–57. See also Max H. Kele, *Nazis and Workers. National Socialist Appeals to German Labor, 1919–1933* (Chapel Hill, 1972).

6 'Der völkische Block', National Socialist circular, 8 Feb. 1924, Bundesarchiv Koblenz (BAK), Zeitgeschichtliche Sammlung (ZSg) I, 45/13.

7 Quoted in Reginald Phelps, 'Dokumente aus der Kampfzeit der NSDAP – 1923', *Deutsche Rundschau*, 84 (1958), 1037.

8 The efforts of the liberal, conservative, and leftist parties to demask the National Socialists to their respective constituencies are treated in Childers, *The Nazi Voter*, 107–12, 153–5.

9 ibid., 262–9.

10 Hamilton, *Who Voted for Hitler?*, 64–219.

11 On the white-collar and civil service votes, see Thomas Childers, 'National Socialism and the new middle class', in Reinhard Mann (ed.), *Die Nationalsozialisten: Analysen faschistischer Bewegungen* (Stuttgart, 1980).

12 Michael H. Kater, 'Sozialer Wandel in der NSDAP im Zuge der nationalsozialistischen Machtergreifung', in Wolfgang Schieder (ed.), *Faschismus als soziale Bewegung: Deutschland und Italien im Vergleich* (Hamburg, 1976), 34–5.

13 See Childers, *The Nazi Voter*, 253–7; and Jürgen W. Falter and Dirk Hänisch, 'Die Anfälligkeit von Arbeitern gegenüber der NSDAP bei den Reichstagswahlen 1928–1933', *Archiv für Sozialgeschichte*, 26 (1986), 179–216; and Jürgen W. Falter, 'Warum die deutschen Arbeiter

während des "Dritten Reiches", zu Hitler standen', *Geschichte und Gesellschaft*, 2 (1987), 217–31.

14 See Timothy W. Mason, *Sozialpolitik im Dritten Reich. Arbeiterklasse und Volksgemeinschaft* (2nd edn, Opladen, 1978), 57.

15 Hamilton, *Who Voted For Hitler?*, 88–9.

16 See Falter, 'The first German *Volkspartei*: the social foundations of the NSDAP', in Karl Ruhe (ed.), *Factions, Parties and Political Traditions. Social Foundations of German Parties and Party Systems 1867–1987* (New York, 1980), 78.

17 Childers, *The Nazi Voter*, 262–7.

18 These developments are treated in Thomas Childers, 'Inflation, stabilization, and political realignment in Germany 1924–1928', in Gerald D. Feldman, Carl-Ludwig Holtfrerich, Gerhard A. Ritter, and Peter-Christian Witt (eds), *Die Deutsche Inflation. Eine Zwischenbilanz* (Berlin, 1982), 409–31. See also Larry E. Jones, 'Inflation, revaluation, and the crisis of middle-class politics: a study in the dissolution of the German party system, 1923–1928', *Central European History*, 12 (1979), 143–68.

19 See Thomas Childers, 'Interest and ideology: anti-system politics in the era of stabilization, 1924–1928', in Gerald D. Feldman (ed.), *Die Nachwirkungen der Inflation auf die deutsche Geschichte 1924–1933* (Munich, 1980), 1–20.

20 ibid.

21 On the advent and evolution of *mittelständisch* populist politics in the Kaiserreich see David Blackbourn, 'The politics of demagogy in Imperial Germany', *Past and Present*, 113 (1986), 152–84; and his 'Politics as theatre: metaphors of the stage in German history, 1848–1933', *Transactions of the Royal Historical Society*, 5, 37 (1987), 149–67; and Geoff Eley, *Reshaping the German Right: Radical Nationalism and Political Change after Bismarck* (London, 1980).

22 Childers, 'Inflation, stabilization, and political realignment'.

23 See Jürgen W. Falter, 'The National Socialist mobilization of new voters: 1920–1933', in Childers (ed.), *The Formation of the Nazi Constituency*, 202–31.

24 See Theodor Geiger, 'Panik im Mittelstand', *Die Arbeit*, 7 (1930), 637–59. The impact of the Depression on the different elements of the middle class and the Nazi efforts to exploit it are treated in Childers, *The Nazi Voter*, 142–78, 211–43.

25 Still the most effective treatments of Nazi propaganda in a local context are William S. Allen, *The Nazi Seizure of Power. The Experience of a Single German Town, 1930–1935* (Chicago, 1965, revised and expanded edition, 1985); and Jeremy Noakes, *The Nazi Party in Lower Saxony 1921–1933* (Oxford, 1971). See also Detlef Mühlberger, 'Central control versus regional autonomy: a case study of Nazi propaganda in Westphalia, 1925–1932', in Childers, *The Formation of the Nazi Constituency*, 64–103.

26 These ideas are more fully developed in Thomas Childers, 'The social language of politics in Germany. The sociology of political discourse in the Weimar Republic', *American Historical Review*, 95 (1990), 331–58.

27 ibid.

28 The quotation is from 'Zum 18. Marz 1928', *Der Demokrat*, 9, 6, 18 Mar. 1928. See Childers, 'Languages of liberalism', 346–58.

29 On the importance of 'pre-industrial' residues in the *Sonderweg* thesis, see Hans-Jürgen Puhle, *Von der Agrarkrise zum Präfaschismus* (Wiesbaden, 1972), 53; Jürgen Kocka, 'Ursachen des Nationalsozialismus', *Aus Politik und Zeitgeschichte*, 21 June 1980, 9–13; and Heinrich August Winkler, 'Die "neue Linke" und der Faschismus: Zur Kritik neomarxistischer Theorien uber den Nationalsozialismus', in Winkler, *Revolution, Staat, Faschismus* (Göttingen, 1978), 78–80.

30 See, for example, Robert G. Moeller, *German Peasants and Agrarian Politics, 1914–1924* (Chapel Hill, 1986); Jane Caplan, *Government without Administration: State and Civil Service in Weimar and Nazi Germany* (Oxford, 1988); and Adelheid von Saldern, 'The old Mittelstand 1890–1939. How "backward" were the artisans?', paper delivered at the regional conference of the German History Society (Toronto, April 1990).

31 David Blackbourn, 'The *Mittelstand* in German society and politics 1871–1914', *Social History*, 2 (1977), 409–33, esp. 432–33.

32 Roger Chartier, 'Intellectual history or sociocultural history? The French trajectories', in Dominick LaCapra and Steven L. Kaplan (eds.), *Modern European Intellectual History: Reappraisals and New Perspectives* (Ithaca, New York, 1982), 30.

33 Gareth Stedman Jones, *Languages of Class: Studies in English Working Class History 1932–1982* (Cambridge, 1983), 96.

34 Thomas Childers, 'The limits of National Socialist mobilization: the elections of 6 November 1932 and the fragmentation of the Nazi constituency', in Childers (ed.), *The Formation of the Nazi Constituency*, 232–59.

35 The report, a *Stimmungsbericht* for November 1932, is found in BAK/NS22/1, and is analysed in detail in Childers, ibid.

36 See Goebbels's entry in his diary on 23 April 1932. 'Something has to happen now', he writes following the Nazis' strong showing in the Prussian elections. 'We have to come to power in the near future or we will win ourselves to death in these elections.' Joseph Goebbels, *Vom Kaiserhof zur Reichskanzlei* (Berlin, 1934).

37 *Stimmungsbericht der Reichspropaganda-Leitung*, November 1932, BAK/NS22/1.

Index

market/marketing 3, 145, 185, 204,
239–40: employment 187–8
Martin, Rudolf 47, 54, 56, 126
Marx, Karl *xv*
Marxism 151, 157
Marxist left/socialism 320, 321
Mayer, Arno J. 88
Mayer, Gustav 307
Meckel, Wilhelm Kaspar 95
Mecklenburg 168
medical: administrators 207–11, 220;
associations 205; authority for
bourgeois values 217–18; care,
demand for 199–200; matters and the
Church 203; co-operatives scheme
202; hierarchies 201; innovations
215; institutions 215; officials 205–6;
reform 202–20; services and social
hygiene 204–5, 210, 219; influence on
the state; *see also* National Socialism
medical profession 199, 212, 214, 215,
216; and honour 260–1; income 56,
200, 212–13, 214; power of 202, 206,
207, 209, 211, 216; and social welfare
200, 210; and state 202, 206, 210, 211;
see also autonomy; insurance
schemes; quackery; training
Mehlis, Christian 236
Meinecke, Friedrich 2, 285
Mendelssohn, Franz von 58, 62
Mendelssohn, Giulietta 62
Mendelssohn, Robert 62
Mendelssohn-Bartholdy, Felix 62
mentality/mentalities 23, 68, 73, 257
Menzel, Wolfgang 262–3
merchants 3, 131
Merck family 126, 130
Merton, Wilhelm 51
Mevissen, Gustav 104, 258, 259
middle class: and business elite 47, 64,
68, 69; classification 76n; duellists
and honour 255–92; family, role of
119; honour 259; 261, 281, 282; and
lawyers 162, 186; and National
Socialism 22, 26, 27, 29–30, 318–34;
and nation–state relationship 244;
Palatine 228; professionals 208–9;
provincial 242; reform movements
218; and working classes 27; *see also*
bourgeoisie; Catholic; culture;
education; Depressions; 'Heimat';
identity 224; localism
'middle Germany' 25

military, the 90, 206, 237, 272, 277, 278,
282, 295; *see also* army
military: jurisdiction, medical 206 and
nationalism 237
Mill, John Stuart 299–300
Minden 103
Mittelstand and liberals 14, 312
Mittermaier, Karl 171, 173, 175
modernity *xv*, 19, 238–40, 246, 288, 311
Moltke, General Field Marshal
Helmuth von 61
Mommsen, Hans 30
Mommsen, Wolfgang J. 295
Mönckeberg family 122, 130
Mönchen-Gladbach 95
morality 214, 258, 262, 297, 299, 300,
305
Mosse, Rudolf 62, 64
Mosse, Werner 119
Munich 50, 54, 180, 320
municipal government/policies 22, 189
Münster 177
Muthesius, Hermann 52

Nasse family 206, 207
nation: German 3, 244–8; 'Heimat' and
community 244–8; -state 19, 244, 302
national: aspirations, Palatinate 227;
-authoritarianism 28–9;
consciousness 229, 233; solidarity 310
National Association 26
National Community 247
nationalism 19, 29, 227, 229, 237–8,
302: domestic 237–8; 242; and
medical profession 200, 217, 218
nationalist culture 198
nationality and locality 246, 247, 248
National Liberal Party 19, 103, 228,
310, 311
National Socialism/National Socialist
Party (NSDAP)/Nazi/Nazism 1,
29–30, 46, 152, 158, 219, 318, 332,
333, 334; and bourgeoisie 23, 29–30,
132, 318–37; electorate 29; and
'Heimat' 229, 240, 246–8; and
medical profession 219; policies and
scientific medicine 215–16;
propaganda 327–34
National-Sozialer Verein 310
nature 217, 237, 238–9, 240, 248
Naumann, Friedrich 107, 214, 218
Navy League 22, 189, 212, 237
Netherlands 107
Neustadt-an-der-Haardt 227